ESSAYS
IN LABOUR HISTORY
1886–1923

EDITED BY

ASA BRIGGS
Professor of History and Vice-Chancellor
University of Sussex

AND

JOHN SAVILLE
Reader in Economic History
University of Hull

D1126576

ARCHON BOOKS
1971

GARDNER WEBB COLLEGE LIBRARY

Editorial matter and selection © Asa Briggs and
John Saville 1971

Chapter 1 © Asa Briggs 1971
Chapter 2 © Fred Reid 1971
Chapter 3 © The estate of the late Henry Collins 1971
Chapter 4 © J. E. Williams 1971
Chapter 5 © P. S. Bagwell 1971
Chapter 6 © The estate of the late C. L. Mowat 1971
Chapter 7 © James Hinton 1971
Chapter 8 © Sidney Pollard 1971
Chapter 9 © Royden Harrison 1971
Chapter 10 © Margaret Cole 1971
Chapter 11 © Frank Matthews 1971

ISBN 0–208–01239–7

*First published in the United States of America
Archon Books, 1971*

Printed in Great Britain

ESSAYS IN LABOUR HISTORY
1886–1923

Also by Asa Briggs

THE AGE OF IMPROVEMENT
THE BIRTH OF BROADCASTING
CHARTIST STUDIES (*editor*)
ESSAYS IN LABOUR HISTORY, Volume 1 (*editor with John Saville*)
FRIENDS OF THE PEOPLE
THE GOLDEN AGE OF WIRELESS
HISTORY OF BIRMINGHAM (1865–1938)
PATTERNS OF PEACE-MAKING (*with D. Thomson and E. Meyer*)
A STUDY OF THE WORK OF SEEBOHM ROWNTREE
VICTORIAN CITIES
VICTORIAN PEOPLE
WILLIAM COBBETT
THE NINETEENTH CENTURY (*editor*)
THE WAR OF WORDS

Also by John Saville

ESSAYS IN LABOUR HISTORY, Volume 1 (*editor with Asa Briggs*)
DEMOCRACY AND THE LABOUR MOVEMENT (*editor*)
ERNEST JONES, CHARTIST
RURAL DEPOPULATION IN ENGLAND AND WALES, 1851–1951

HD
8390
B838
1971b

CONTENTS

Contents

FOREWORD

MORE than ten years ago we edited what became a memorial volume to G. D. H. Cole. The essays spanned the nineteenth century and this present volume takes the story forward into the twentieth century. We hope it will be followed by a further volume dealing with the years between the wars.

We have to record the melancholy fact of the deaths of two of our contributors while this book was in production. Dr Henry Collins of the University of Sussex and Professor Charles Mowat of the University College of North Wales at Bangor were our friends as well as our colleagues. Their deaths were a serious loss to historical scholarship. We mourn their passing and we offer our sympathy and understanding to their widows.

Among those who have helped with this volume we wish to thank Rex Allen and Tim Farmiloe of Macmillan, for their patience and co-operation; Dr Joyce Bellamy, Hugh and Kate Inglis, and Mr David Martin, who all assisted with proof-reading; and Mrs Ann Jones, Senior Library Assistant of the University of East Anglia, who compiled the Index.

A. B.
J. S.

1

ASA BRIGGS

INTRODUCTION

THE first volume of *Essays in Labour History* appeared in 1960. The essays had been written with a view to presenting them to G. D. H. Cole on the occasion of his seventieth birthday. Cole died before the book appeared, but since then the essays have had a life of their own. They have been read and commented upon in many countries.

Since 1960 there has been something of an international boom in the study of labour history. It was in 1960 itself that the Society for the Study of Labour History was founded in London: its regular meetings, which have been well attended, have brought together labour historians with different academic interests and with quite different points of view, and its *Bulletin* is an invaluable guide to current research and controversy. There are now parallel bodies in several other countries, and joint sessions have been held with labour historians in France and the United States. During the same period a new generation of labour historians in the universities has turned increasingly to 'history from below', sometimes collecting new kinds of historical source materials, sometimes interpreting afresh familiar themes, usually in local or national contexts, less frequently comparatively with reference to different countries. In addition several major studies in British labour history have been published, some of them by well-known authors in this field.

Much, though by no means all the research, has focused on the twentieth century, reflecting both the general tendency of historians to 'move forwards' and the special interest for historians of the labour movement of the changes which have taken place during this period. This second volume of *Essays in Labour History* fills in some of the gaps: it does not claim

1

either to be comprehensive or to do full justice to historians working in new directions. It will be followed by a third volume covering the still more recent period between 1920 and 1950, a testing time for theories, institutions and personalities.

Unlike the first volume, in which the essays dealt with a wide range of topics from the late eighteenth to the early twentieth century, this present volume focuses mainly on the relatively narrow period from the late nineteenth century to the early 1920s. Short though the time-span is, the period bustles with incident, and much of its excitement and importance stems from the fact that it encompasses not only the 'great divide' in human experience of the First World War but also the Russian Revolution of 1917 which transformed the international context of socialism.

In Britain itself this was obviously a formative period in relation to the history of organisations – societies, parties and trade unions, the scaffolding of the modern labour movement – and it is now just far enough away from our own time to be seen in rough perspective, just near enough to be illuminated by oral evidence. It is also a period which remains enshrouded in myth, mainly the myths of contrast between 'then' and 'now'. The myths bemuse as well as fascinate: sometimes, indeed, they too easily satisfy an understandable yearning for simple models of future action. These were still pioneering days when the message mattered, even when it seemed so often to be falling, not least in working-class circles, on stony ground.

By the late 1920s it was clear that this particular period was over. As Ramsay MacDonald, one of the key figures in British labour history, whose long career is examined critically in this volume, told the Labour Party Annual Conference in 1928:

up to quite recently our method was mainly a propaganda method. We laid down doctrines – right is right and wrong is wrong ... we had to familiarize you with the fundamentals upon which we stood. We have now to carry our Movement another stage. It is always unfortunate for the poor pioneer who has gone through the pioneering days and who lives into the stage after. You have got to go on, in that stage after, with whoever is with you....[1]

[1] Labour Party, *Annual Conference Report* (1928), pp. 196 ff.

2

Introduction

The concept of 'stages' in labour history may mislead the historian, particularly when it is propounded as flabbily as MacDonald propounded it in his evolutionist writings on 'socialist theory' or when, as in this revealing passage, he chose the simplest historical model of all in arguing about immediate practical politics. There are far too many constants in British labour history, too many recurring determinants of tactical decisions, economic and political, too many dubious appeals to history and too many old conflicts and compromises expressed in new guise. Yet there is real value in labour history, as in other branches of history, in thinking in terms of 'generations', trailing their own experience, not least because when we consider generations we have to get away from the kind of labour history which remains imprisoned in the chronicle of formal organisational structures. There is real value, too, in retaining the concept of 'our Movement', though it has often been dismissed in recent years: indeed, when we speak of a 'movement' we are turning from the relatively straightforward issues concerned with the defence or promotion of specific (if sometimes ill-defined) 'interests' to far more complex problems of associations, traditions, loyalties and ideologies, and to the relationships between 'leaders', 'militants' and 'rank and file'.

It is not difficult to show first that 'interests' counted during the period covered in this book, as they do in any period of labour history, and second that there were sharp divergences between different unions and different groups and factions of socialists on major as well as minor subjects. Yet it is insufficient to label talk of a 'movement' as mere rhetoric[2] or to dismiss the matter quite so simply as it was dismissed in the last three pages of one of the most useful books on labour history to appear during the last ten years, *A History of British Trade Unions since 1889* by H. A. Clegg, A. Fox and A. F. Thompson. There it was argued that

it is misleading to speak of a 'labour movement' as a constant in the history of this period [1889–1910]. The term describes an aspect revealed by the unions and their political arm from time to time. The quality showed more clearly in 1910 than

[2] See, for example, A. Beattie (ed.), *English Party Politics*, ii (1970), pp. 226–7.

3

in 1889. A sympathetic leader could sometimes call it out; an astute leader could sometimes use it for his own ends; and it might sometimes assert itself unbidden. But it was often apparent only to the discerning eye, rarely visible in day-to-day union business, and only very rarely powerful enough to over-ride the self-interest of any union.[3]

How and why did it 'assert itself unbidden'? How did it differ from the concept of 'labour movement' in other countries where there were different social structures, different styles of life, different ideological combinations, conservative, liberal and socialist? Certainly by 1914, leaving on one side socialists of various persuasions who believed in the complete transformation of society, gradual or sudden, large numbers of working men had come to the conclusion that they had to provide a countervailing power to check that of their employers. Something more than collective bargaining was at stake. Twenty years earlier T. H. Escott, the very shrewd journalist who was concerned with 'the anatomy of Britain' of his day, had written of 'union' as 'the inevitable response on the part of the labourer to a sentiment which is quite as natural and quite as sure in some way or other to assert itself on the part of the capitalist'.[4] The 'weapons' available to the working man and to the capitalist, whose own organisation and modes of operation were changing, were already different. Without the concept of a 'movement' setting out to extend its influence over working men who were frequently indifferent – this was the immediate significance of 'propaganda', thought of by those who spread it as propaganda for an 'unprepared people' – the very terms of the 'struggle' would have been different, as they were in the United States.

MacDonald himself recognised this in his *Socialism and Government* (1909), where he argued, again in evolutionary mode, that

society in modern times includes a state of political liberty and of economic bondage. The workman who has become politically free is still beset with all the economic bondage.

[3] H. A. Clegg, A. Fox and A. F. Thompson, *A History of British Trade Unions Since 1889*, i (1964), p. 488.
[4] T. H. Escott, *England, Its People, Polity and Pursuits* (1887), p. 283.

4

The workman who has become politically free is still beset with all the economic pains and disabilities of a wage-earner. Economic forces have been organised to such an extent that the economically independent individual has become a mere myth for credulous people to believe in. The individual has become a member of an economic class.... There is a steady tendency to increase the financial power in industry, as more and more people, shirking the responsibility of using their own possessions, hand them over to someone else who uses them as a hired servant. Thus, the official and impersonal use of capital has been established already.[5]

It was necessary, MacDonald believed, to mobilise a 'movement' to free men from 'economic bondage'.

The same point was made in much the same terms nine years later by Arthur Henderson when he introduced the important resolution proposing a new constitution and programme of the Labour Party in 1918, an important date in British labour history.

Unless the citizens were organised, they could not free themselves, and one of the tasks of a highly organised political Labour Party in a reconstructed society will be to remove wage slavery.... How were these people to be organised? They could only do so by saying to every man and woman who was a citizen ... 'Come along with us, our platform is broad enough and our Movement big enough to take you all.'[6]

The fact that many working men were for long suspicious of the power of the 'State', which they often identified, as Dr. Pelling has shown, with repressive forces,[7] reinforced belief in a 'movement' with economic, political, co-operative and educa-

[5] J. R. MacDonald, *Socialism and Government* (1909), pp. 30–42, quoted in Beattie, *op. cit.* pp. 296–7.
[6] Labour Party, *Annual Conference Report* (1918), p. 100.
[7] See his controversial essay 'The Working Class and the Origins of the Welfare State' in *Popular Politics and Society in Late Victorian Britain* (1968), pp. 1–18. The essay underestimates the concern of organised labour groups for specific forms of State intervention either in the form of 'palliatives' as they were thought of by the S.D.F. (see below, pp. 56–61) or of moves towards more 'equal' citizenship.

tional 'wings', even – though perhaps less comprehensively than in continental Europe – with a way of life of its own; and both before and after the Labour Party changed its constitution in 1918 there were always groups, sometimes small, at other times with a far wider appeal, who believed that the 'movement' was bigger than 'politicians' or 'party' and was or should always be concerned with something other than 'government'. Among the early converts to socialism there were some who considered it a 'gospel', convinced that only within the framework of a 'socialist society' could they achieve true 'individuality',[8] while among trade unionists there were always some, as is shown in several of the essays in this volume, who put their trust in 'direct action'.[9] Much of the local history of the labour movement is concerned with the detail of individual commitment and the density of collective effort – with the establishment of centres of socialist propaganda (different places had different chronologies) and with the intricate relationships, often still unplotted by historians, between trade unions, trades councils and different political groups. It is necessary to remember, however, that there were many working men who joined a wide variety of labour organisations and cared little about the varieties of socialism they expressed or the personal tensions between their leaders. To them the 'movement' counted for more than the men or the theories.

The 'movement' had to be 'big' to take everyone in: indeed, the concept carried with it an inherent pluralism, which distinguished the British labour movement from many other labour movements overseas, and a deep suspicion of 'narrow sectarianism' was usually apparent, not least at the grass roots level. In comparative terms this 'pluralism' was one of the most important features of the labour history of the period (as it had also been of nineteenth-century British Liberalism), and it

[8] 'Socialism itself,' wrote Oscar Wilde in *The Soul of Man under Socialism* (1891), 'will be of value simply because it will lead to Individualism.' G. B. Shaw made the same point in a lecture which influenced Wilde, and it recurs frequently throughout the multitudinous literature of the 'late Victorian revolt'. The young Tom Mann related changes in 'the industrial and social life of our country' to 'the making of true individuality. For, let it be clearly understood, we labour men are thoroughly in favour of the highest possible development of each individual.' 'Preachers and the Churches', in *Vox Clamantium* (1894) p. 303.

[9] See below, esp. Chs 5 and 7.

was related within its own specific context to what had gone
before and what was to come after.

The long experience of industrialisation in a complex and
highly localised society was the main factor in the past: there
were different layers as well as different strands. In the future
there was always to be some uneasiness, at times dramatically
expressed, about the relations between the 'party in Parliament'
or 'high politics' in the Cabinet and the 'movement' outside.
The uneasiness was anticipated in Bradford, the home of the
Independent Labour Party, in 1914, a few months before the
outbreak of the War, when F. W. Jowett, knowing that there
were then less than forty Labour Members in Parliament, remarked firmly, 'I don't want a Cabinet system under even
Labour domination. I have no wish to see Ministerial control
applied to any department of State even if the Minister be a
Socialist – because it means bureaucracy; because it means the
people are not having control.'[10] What sustained British labour
throughout the War through a difficult period of political division
and finally prepared the way for its replacing the Liberal Party as
the second party in the State was less the sense of imminent office
than the continuing sense of 'movement'. For all the differences
about the War itself there was a continuing, at times strengthened, desire to stick together.[11] After the Spen Valley by-election
in January 1920 the political complications multiplied with
success.

To follow this line of argument it is necessary to avoid the
obvious danger of ignoring or underestimating the influence
of immediate and sectionalised grievances. These were plain
enough during the War while the very first essay in this volume,
appropriately devoted to Keir Hardie, who by 1914 was already
thought of as one of the true 'pioneers' of the labour movement,
shows how absurd it is to 'refine' British labour history even
before 1914 in simple idealistic terms.

Hardie is rightly associated in British labour history with a
'moral approach to politics'. 'The pursuit of wealth,' he told the
House of Commons in 1901, 'corrupts the manhood of men.
We are called upon at the beginning of the twentieth century

---

[10] Independent Labour Party, *Conference Report* (1914), pp. 116–18.
[11] See below, pp. 211 ff.

to decide the question propounded in the Sermon on the
Mount as to whether or not we will worship God or Mammon.
The present day is a mammon worshipping age. Socialism proposes to dethrone the brute-god Mammon and to lift humanity
into its place.'[12] The 'problem' of Hardie's later career was that
of adapting such an approach to the exigencies of 'parliamentary
tactics'. Yet, as Mr. Reid shows, Hardie's nineteenth-century
conversion to socialism, a critical event in British labour history,
must also be considered, like that of MacDonald, within a
particular localised context. What later looked to be 'instinctive'
and 'inevitable' involved initial choices and a deliberate dis-
entanglement from hitherto acceptable Victorian 'Liberalism'.[13]
In dealing with labour biography – and once more MacDonald
provides an instructive, alternative example – the sensitive biographer can no more rest content with a linear arrangement of
measured time than he can with hagiography: like a modern
film maker, he must proceed through changes of pace and
rhythm, exploring 'subjective time' and exploiting throw-backs
and ambiguities.

The same to some extent is true of labour history as a whole.
Memory plays tricks with landmarks like 1889, 1918 and, above
all, 1931, the terminal point of Professor Mowat's essay. They
seem to loom ahead before they actually appear, and once past
they remain for a long time, from different vantage points, a
part of the scene. While there is usually evidence, as Professor
Pollard suggests, of 'steady and natural growth', when we turn
either to 'webs of dissatisfaction, disillusionment and distrust'[14]
or to bursts of vigour, enthusiasm and anger, we have to go
backwards and forwards in time in order to understand them
fully. 'Refinement' can best be avoided if there is a clear recognition of the interplay of what Philip Wicksteed, the economist
(and socialist), thought of in 1894 as 'material' and 'spiritual'
forces. 'If the labour movement is purely material,' he wrote,
'it nevertheless deserves our undivided sympathy in its aims
and objects, however hard we may find it to sustain our enthusiasm, and on the other hand ... if it is indeed the greatest
religious movement the world has ever seen, if it is indeed the

[12] *Hansard*, 4th ser. xcii, col. 1180.
[13] See below, pp. 40 ff.
[14] See below, p. 206.

8

summons of humanity to enter upon its heritage, it must needs speak out loud and long the language of material demands.'[15]

Throughout the period covered in this volume the trade unionists were, of course, the most pressing of all the labour groups in relation to 'material demands', the language of which they formulated for themselves; and much of the interest in the history of the period from 1900 to 1914, in particular, pivots on the relationships between socialists and non-socialist trade unionists. Mr. Collins shows in his important essay how a failure to understand the dynamics of these relationships bedevilled the history of the S.D.F.[16] There were other factors also which limited the numbers and influence of the party – not least its catechising – but it was this factor more than any other which prevented it from 'belonging' fully to a movement about which it so willingly theorised in over-rigid Marxist terms. Its leaders found it difficult to cope with the 'labourist' arguments of a forceful and experienced trade unionist like Ben Tillett who stated boldly that

> the Trade Union official who did something towards adding a shilling to the wage and to put more food upon the table of the worker was doing a greater work than sentimental men talking about theories. Trade Unionism was a class-conscious movement. Its general tendency was to become class-conscious, not only in dealing with employers, but in a wider political sense.

The last adjective to apply to the leaders of the S.D.F. at any time in the party's history is 'sentimentalist' – and doubtless when he made his remarks Tillett has his eyes mainly not on the S.D.F. but the I.L.P. – yet by ignoring changes in the composition, numbers and role of trade unionists during the critical years after 1900 the leaders of the S.D.F. were theorising in a closed, sectarian manner about the subject that mattered most.

The debate at the Labour Party Conference of 1907, where Tillett made his pronouncement, is rightly picked out by Professor Mowat as a memorable occasion at which two motions were defeated – the first (heavily) to confine the party to

---

[15] P. Wicksteed, 'The Advent of the People', in A. Reid (ed.), *The New Party* (1894), pp. 340–1.
[16] See below, pp. 52 ff.

9

socialists, the second (moved by Tillett) to confine it to trade unionists. Yet the point of this is surely not so much that 'all they could agree upon was their independence [seldom completely uncompromised in Parliament] and their Labour name' as that they were debating one of the issues in labour politics which really did matter in open fashion. Characteristically Harry Quelch of the S.D.F., representing the London Trades Council, said nothing of the trade unions at all in his speech on the first resolution; and in his reply Pete Curran of the Gasworkers, a union whose local activities are described below by Dr. Williams in his revealing case-study of a 1913 strike in Leeds, accused the S.D.F. of attempting 'to get in by the back-door' and deliberately appealed to 'the solidarity of the Movement'. 'Surely,' he argued, 'the mover and seconder realised that the carrying of this resolution would be the destruction of the Movement as it existed today. If they did not, they did not understand the Movement as he understood it.'

This was common sense, not rhetoric, and it was echoed by another trade unionist who told the Conference that if they thought to make trade unionists into socialists 'by taking them by the scruff of their neck they would be making a mistake'. In the light of later labour history he may have been more optimistic in continuing that 'by education they would come along in these matters as they had done in other things'. On the second resolution, supported by Quelch ('he could not conceive of a Labour Party objecting to all of its members being members of trade unions'), another trade unionist opposing Tillett asked specifically for 'common sense' to be brought to bear in the consideration of the issues, while a further trade unionist once more accused Quelch of not understanding 'the spirit of the Movement.... The Labour Party is wider than the Trade Union Movement, and it ought to find a place for all those who were genuinely in earnest for the advance of the cause of Labour.' Characteristically an I.L.P. speaker appealed to members of the Conference 'to make an effort to lift the subjects and the tone of the discussion on to a higher level than it had reached before'.[17]

It may be said of the participants in this debate of 1907, as Edward Thompson has said of the delegates from the London

[17] Labour Party, *Annual Conference Report* (1907), pp. 51–8.

Corresponding Society when they met Pitt in 1794, that they were each rehearsing what looked like prearranged parts, but the great difference on this second occasion was that they were arguing openly not with 'opponents' but with each other on one of the two or three great issues of the day. By failing to win either/or victories they were guaranteeing a future for a movement which, for good and/or ill, was never to be shaped by theory or pseudo-theory, Marxist or Fabian. It is important to put the proposition in this form because the tolerance and the eclecticism of the British labour movement certainly limited the possibilities of bold, purposive action, revolutionary or otherwise. The Parliamentary Labour Party before 1914, the product of a coalition of forces, lacked any clear-cut 'line'. It had no 'general staff', and there were times when, as Mrs. Webb put it, it seemed to be 'drifting into futility'.[18] The real build-up which mattered was not in Parliament but in the country, where the number of trade unionists increased by two-thirds between 1906 and 1914 (to 1,572,391), with a consequent augmentation of party funds, where the number of local Labour Parties and affiliated societies more than doubled (to 177), and where the number of Labour members of local government authorities more than trebled. In examining this expansion we have to explore adventurously the contours of working-class culture (and its relationship to the changing social situation and the changing culture of the middle classes) in the same way as J. R. Vincent explored the contours of middle-class culture (and its relationship to the world of the working classes) in his important book *The Formation of the Liberal Party* (1966).

There is very little in this volume of essays on relations between the Labour Party and the Liberal Party in the period of Liberal power between 1906 and 1914,[19] although the pattern of these relations (and more searching questions about the

[18] M. Cole (ed.), *Beatrice Webb's Diaries*, 1912–14 (1952), p. 6: entry of 11 October 1912.
[19] The way was prepared for an understanding of the prelude to this subject in the important book by F. Bealey and H. Pelling, *Labour and Politics, 1900–1906*)(1958). The most relevant book published on the subject since 1960 is R. Gregory, *The Miners and British Politics, 1906–1914* (1968), reviewed by J. E. Williams in the *Bulletin of the Society for the Study of Labour History*, No. 19 (Autumn 1969). See also H. Pelling, 'Labour and the Downfall of Liberalism' in Pelling, *Popular Politics*, pp. 101–20.

relationship in Britain between liberalism and the various versions of socialism) is the second great issue of the period. The fact that Liberal governments were in power from 1906 to 1914 is one of the most important facts of the period. There is ample evidence of suspicion and estrangement between Liberals and supporters of a Labour Party at the local level, but we still need further studies of the Liberal 'left', some representatives of which were later converts to the Labour Party, if we are to clarify the situation at the centre. In so far as 'welfare state' issues were identified during this period – thereby setting the terms for much of the subsequent history of this century – there is scope first for a closer examination of the differences between the Liberal and the Labour contributions to the making of the 'welfare state' and second for a study of the developing socialist *critique* of the concept.[20] We obviously need a full study of the Parliamentary Labour Party between 1906 and 1914, a sequel to the account of the party between 1900 and 1906 which was written by Bealey and Pelling in 1958.

One of the issues raised in several essays in this volume – that of 'syndicalism' – also requires more general treatment. The crucial influence of the Plebs League and the Central Labour College on a small group of talented miners cannot be dismissed quickly. The story of events in south Wales is fascinating in its contrasts of mood and of purpose – the passivity of the Mabon days; the lateness of the break with the economics of the sliding scale of miners' wages; the ineffectiveness of trade-union organisation before 1896; the Welsh 'revival' of 1903–4; and from 1906–7 onwards the upsurge of militancy. Much that happened can be explained in terms of 'interests' and the effects of 'economic squeeze', but by no means all. There are other episodes of equal interest in Glasgow, and the British story needs to be compared at every point with the overseas story – in France, in the United States and in Australia. What is said of 'syndicalism' in this volume of essays is, none the less, of interest in its own right. Margaret Cole's essay on Guild Socialism and the Labour Research Department is autobiographical in character, an important link with the autobiographical sections of the first

---

[20] See for a general account, A. Marwick, 'The Labour Party and the Welfare State in Britain, 1900–1948', *American Historical Review*, lxxiii (December 1967), pp. 380–403. Local trends are unexplored.

volume of essays which appeared ten years ago. It chronicles the story of 'two diminutive movements' – Guild Socialism and the Labour Research Department – explaining why the latter in its origins at least merits the title of 'movement'. It also relates what they were doing or seeking to do to broader movements in labour history, including the burst of direct industrial action between 1910 and 1914.

It is frequently the case in labour history – and not least in the history of strikes – that, as Mrs. Cole points out, 'diminutive' movements can exercise 'an influence out of all proportion to the number of their direct adherents'.[21] The sense of 'spontaneity' in local movements at several critical moments during the period covered in this volume contrasts sharply with the sense of contrivance at the centre. Locally the 'official' as well as the 'politician' was turned into a target of criticism. He remained such a target throughout the War, as the 1917 Report of the Commission of Inquiry into Industrial Unrest noted, a note taken up by that year's President of the T.U.C., who stated categorically that 'as leaders we were appointed to lay down the hammer or the trowel, and stand on the ramparts to warn our members of danger, and in their opinion we had either fallen asleep at our posts, or we have sold our birthright for a mess of pottage'.[22]

The essay by Philip Bagwell traces in detail the history of the Triple Alliance formed in 1914 between the Miners' Federation, the Transport Workers' Federation and the National Union of Railwaymen. It makes it clear that whatever the views of the rank and file, so far as the leading 'officials' were concerned there was little support for the view that 'the control of industry' was the ultimate object of the Alliance. Cramp of the N.U.R. who held this view was more than checked by his colleague from the same union, J. H. Thomas.[23] The testing time of the Alliance came not in 1914, when industrial relations were stormy, but in the period from 1919 to 1921, when the post-war boom broke and when some of the leaders of the Alliance, looking by then to a Labour electoral victory (still unthinkable in the near future in 1914), were anxious 'not to

[21] See below, p. 260.
[22] T.U.C., *Annual Report* (1917), p. 55.
[23] See below, pp. 101 ff.

queer the pitch of growing middle-class support by over-hasty industrial action'.

The events of 1921 belong unmistakably to a new period in labour history, forecasting, as they do, disillusionment first with trade-union action and then with political action. Yet the essay by Frank Matthews on the Building Guilds, which expands in detail a paragraph in Mrs. Cole's essay, catches the high note of optimism among building operatives in 1920 and explains the burst of local initiative which for a brief period recalled the early days of building trade unionism during the early 1830s. 'Utopia,' Mr. Matthews writes, 'once more reared its ambiguous head.'[24] It is interesting that at this point in the volume the syndicalist story touches the story both of the 'welfare state' and of the relations between the Liberal Party and the Labour Party, for it was the Housing Act of 1919, a landmark in social legislation (and a new departure from the prewar pattern of social policy), which gave the Building Guilds their opportunity. The controversial Liberal Minister who introduced it, Christopher Addison (a war-time Minister of Munitions), was to join the Labour Party in 1930 and to play a prominent part in the Labour government of 1945.

The failure of the Guild experiment echoes many earlier failures in labour organisation in the early nineteenth century, but it, too, was a prelude to the gloomy story of British trade unionism during the 1920s, when the unions were fighting a desperate battle to defend the interests of their threatened members and when a tolerated high rate of unemployment made the battle impossible to win. In 1922, when the National Building Guild was forced to go into liquidation, the *Daily Herald*, which had once included in its lively pages brilliant syndicalist articles, was driven to forfeit its independence and accept a subsidy from the Labour Party and the T.U.C.

One hitherto unpublished document of the Guild Socialists, the so-called 'Storrington Document', prepared in its final form early in 1915, is printed as the final item in this volume. It is interesting that it does not list 'defence' under the functions of the State. Britain was at war, but it would not be possible to gather this essential fact from anything in the document. There is little doubt, none the less, taking this volume of essays

[24] See below, p. 301.

as a whole, that the First World War was a most important experience in the history of the Labour Party, not only in political terms because of the split in the Liberal Party between Asquith and Lloyd George, which opened the way to a Labour electoral victory, but because of its psychological and social effects on the working classes.

Its immediate effect was to divide individuals not only in the Labour Party but in the various socialist and trade-union groups which made up the labour movement, but, as it continued as a war of attrition, it encouraged both sectional militancy and class solidarity and it raised the whole level of working-class aspirations in relation to the future. James Hinton, using hitherto unpublished materials, examines in his essay the dilution struggle on the Clyde, separating the facts from the myths and in the course of his examination drawing attention to the hidden role of William Beveridge, another of the architects of the twentieth-century 'welfare state', in quelling 'the rebellion on the Clyde'. He also has new things to say about the militants, their relations with each other and their attitudes towards 'workers' control'. Sidney Pollard shows how the Co-operative movement, concerned with far more than immediate war-time shortages, grievances and discontents, made a sharp leftward turn in 1917–18, perhaps for a time moving further left than other sections of the labour movement and hastening the Labour Party's plans to prepare a new constitution. Royden Harrison brings the War Emergency Workers' National Committee to life, 'at once the most, and the least, representative ever established in the British labour movement: uniquely close to the experience of the rank and file and yet extremely dependent upon established bureaucracies; formative of crucial new departures, but pathetically responsive to events over which it made no pretence of control'.[25] He reveals that the W.E.W.N.C. was a body which not only dealt with individual or group complaints but turned to general slogans, particularly 'Conscription of Riches' (on which there were from the start characteristic differences in basic interpretation as well as emphasis), which must be studied carefully if the famous clause 4 in the 1918 constitution of the Labour Party is to be placed in its proper historical setting.

[25] See below, p. 212.

Given the increasing interest in the effects of war on twentieth-century society,[26] each of these essays adds a new dimension to the discussion, though it would have been interesting to have had British experience in this connection compared more fully with that of other countries. This still remains the great *lacuna* in labour history.[27] Britain emerged from the most relentless war in its history with no experience of political or social revolution, but with a brand-new Labour Party constitution. In 1919 and 1920 it seemed that there might be a revolutionary situation in the making. Indeed, Lloyd George, the Prime Minister, was preparing for it, as he collected regular reports on 'revolutionary organisations' from his 'Directorate of Intelligence'. The newly founded Communist Party (31 July 1920) was not only expressing its 'joy at being able to march hand in hand with the great Russian and Communist parties of the world' but considering the appointment of food, fuel and house controllers to take over when the revolution came. The moment quickly passed as it had done before in British history. As in the nineteenth century, Englishmen were to be left to study revolution at a distance, and very quickly they were to disagree, not least in the labour movement, about what they saw. It was J. A. Hobson who identified what still seemed the only way ahead for most of the people who were to *vote* Labour in Britain – and there were 2,385,472 of them in 1918 and 4,438,508 in 1923, just before the Labour Party took office for the first time. 'Whatever may be the views of a capitalist State,' Hobson stated, 'there is only one remedy, viz. to convert it into a democratic State.' And it was not simply revolution that Hobson relegated into the background. 'The vision of a working-class organisation building up for itself an economic State, governed by the workers, within the political State but virtually independent of that State, for the regulation of economic life,' he added, 'is a dangerous phantasy.'[28] The direction was clear. The signposts seem already to be pointing to 1926, 1929 and 1931.

[26] See, for example, A. Marwick, *The Deluge* (1965) and *Britain in the Century of Total War* (1968), and A. Calder, *The People's War* (1969).

[27] For some of the *lacunae* in 1960, see *Bulletin of the Society for the Study of Labour History*, No. 1 (Autumn 1960), pp. 2–3.

[28] J. A. Hobson, *Democracy after the War* (1917), pp. 180–81.

2

FRED REID

KEIR HARDIE'S CONVERSION TO SOCIALISM

MUCH in the early life of James Keir Hardie is still shrouded in the mysteries of hagiography, nothing more so than the problem as to how and when he became a socialist.[1] Two of his best-known biographers, Emrys Hughes and William Stewart, are agreed upon one point concerning his conversion: the ideas and propaganda of the organised socialists in Britain in the 1880s had nothing to do with it.[2] According to Hughes, his father-in-law became a socialist at the age of 21, that is, in 1877, under the influence of Burns, Carlyle and Henry George and before the ideas of Marx could possibly have been known to him.[3] Since George's *Progress and Poverty* was not published in England until 1880, it is incredible that the American propagandist of the land tax could have had anything to do with Hardie's political development at so early a stage, though the claim for the influence of George accords well enough with Hardie's own account of conversion:

> Some years later, Henry George came to Scotland and I read *Progress and Poverty*, which unlocked many of the

---

[1] For a list of writings on Hardie, see F. Reid, 'Keir Hardie's Biographers', *Bulletin of the Society for the Study of Labour History*, No. 16 (1968), pp. 30 ff. Cf. the comment of M. Cole, *ibid*. No. 17 (1968), p. 27. Neither mentions Garth Lean, *Brave Men Choose* (1961), which contains an essay on Hardie from the standpoint of Moral Rearmament. A fuller treatment of the problems touched upon in this essay will be found in the author's doctoral thesis, 'The Early Life and Political Development of James Keir Hardie, 1856-92' (Oxford, 1969).

[2] By definition, this means the Social Democratic Federation, established in 1884, and the Socialist League, which seceded from the S.D.F. in 1885, since no one has ever claimed that the Fabian Society, also established in 1884, was responsible for Hardie's conversion.

[3] E. Hughes, *Keir Hardie* (1956), p. 24.

17

industrial and economic difficulties which beset the mind of the worker trying to take an intelligent interest in his own affairs and led me, much to George's horror in later life when we met personally, into Communism.[4]

Stewart, Hardie's official biographer, was equally sure that socialist ideas had contributed nothing to his development. Hardie's class-consciousness was 'inherent in his very nature and intensified by his own life experience'.[5] Thus a seal of authority was given to the myth that Hardie was a simple-minded, loyal son of the people. As J. Bruce Glasier, writing soon after Hardie's death, had put it: 'He derived his Socialism from his own thought and feelings, the pride of the workers and the state of the world.'[6]

Unfortunately, this version has found its way all too easily into history.[7] Of the historians of the origins of the Labour Party, only G. D. H. Cole and Henry Pelling seem to have referred to any primary sources to discover Hardies political views before he became a socialist.[8] Both refer to Hardie's enthusiasm for the Temperance cause and show that, by the end of 1886, he had at least heard of the propaganda of the Social Democratic Federation in London and that he might have read some numbers of its organ, *Justice*. Their treatment of Hardie's early development is coloured, however, by the view of the biographers that his socialism was 'instinctive'. Pelling writes, for instance:

His mind did not run on simple logical lines, above and beyond the comprehension of the people from whom he had sprung. On the contrary, he was of the same stuff as they were, with the same instinctive attitudes, with the same religious turn of mind and phraseology, the same inability to distinguish politics from morality, or logic from feeling.[9]

[4] Hardie, in *Review of Reviews* (June 1906), pp. 57 ff.
[5] W. Stewart, *James Keir Hardie* (1925), pp. 24 ff.
[6] J. Bruce Glasier, *Keir Hardie, a Memorial* (n.d. ? 1915), p. 61.
[7] H. Pelling, *Origins of the Labour Party* (2nd edn., Oxford, 1965), p. 64. Cf. A. M. MacBriar, *The Fabian Society and English Politics, 1884–1918* (Cambridge, 1962), who makes a similar judgement (p. 295).
[8] G. D. H. Cole, *James Keir Hardie* (1941), pp. 13 ff.
[9] Pelling, *op. cit.* p. 64.

The accounts so far available of Hardie's early political development seem open to three main lines of criticism. First, they are too circumstantial and so fail to explain the precise sequence of events in which Hardie developed from Radical to socialist. Second, they miss the point that Hardie's rejection of the Liberal alliance was the result of a serious debate over politics conducted with the socialists of his native coalfields. Third, with the single exception of Cole, they make the Mid-Lanark by-election of 1888 seem the starting-point of this rejection. At the same time they reduce its significance to the level of a quarrel about class representation in Parliament when, in reality, it was a test of the Liberal Party's willingness to recognise Labour, and what it stood for, as a separate political party.

This essay attempts to establish the perspective of Hardie's early political development. It will try to show that Hardie's earliest political views were characteristic of what was known in the early 1880s as 'advanced' Radicalism. It will then reveal how the crisis of 1886–7 in the Scottish coal-mining industry forced him to accept certain fundamental ideas of the socialists which previously he had resisted. Finally, it will suggest that the Mid-Lanark by-election should be seen as the test of a strategy already fully worked out in Hardie's mind by the middle of 1887, rather than as a spontaneous gesture of stubborn independence against the 'unexpected'[10] resistance of the local Liberal Association to Hardie's nomination.

I

Hardie was well endowed with one attribute which his pious biographers never stressed – restless ambition. In his youth, he was powerfully attracted by those characteristically Victorian values, respectability and success, an attraction which was intensified by the circumstances of his birth and of his upbringing. He was born on 15 August 1856, the illegitimate child of Mary Keir, a farm servant, who had been herself the illegitimate daughter, born on 22 September 1830, of James Kerr (weaver)

---

[10] J. G. Kellas, 'The Mid-Lanark By-Election (1888), and the Scottish Labour Party (1888–94)', *Parliamentary Affairs*, xviii (1965), pp. 318–29.

and Agnes Patterson.[11] Mary Keir had been baptised in her infancy into the Church of Scotland and seems to have preserved her connections with the Kirk, for she married David Hardie, a ship's carpenter, according to its rites on 22 April 1859. In the light of everything that can be discovered about her, there can be little doubt that this douce, church-going country girl formed a passionate determination to make something of the child upon whom she had conferred the stigma of illegitimacy. The fact that she herself had been illegitimate suggests that she had personal experience of what that stigma could mean. At all events, she was sufficiently aware of her son's rights, and of her own, to bring an action of paternity in the Sheriff Court, which resulted in William Aitken, miner, being declared the father of the child. Time and again, in later life, Hardie was to recall how she worked with Calvinistic endurance to preserve decent standards for herself and her family:

> ... her idea o'Heeven seemed tae be that it was a great big fairm, whaur ye could get workin' on frae year's end tae year's end withoot stoppin'.[12]

Mary's marriage, therefore, to a time-served ship's carpenter must have seemed a heaven-sent opportunity to remedy the injury she had done the boy by bringing him fatherless into the world.

She found, however, that marriage was merely a step from the relative comfort of single life, in which she could earn enough at farm work to support her child, into the second trough of the poverty cycle, as Rowntree described it, when the insecure earnings of the male breadwinner had to be used to feed, clothe and house a rapidly growing family of children. This is suggested by the fact that Hardie's one reminiscence of his infancy with his mother before her marriage is idyllic when compared with the dark tones in which he was wont to paint his childhood in the Hardie household.[13] At any rate, it is clear enough that the insecurity and poverty of these years thwarted

[11] In 1965 the present writer commissioned the Scots Ancestry Research Society to investigate the ancestry of Hardie and the evidence used in this section as to records of birth, marriage and death is taken from their MS. report which is in his possession.

[12] *Ardrossan and Saltcoats Herald*, 3 June 1882.

[13] *Ibid.* 16 May 1882.

Mary Keir's ambition to achieve decent respectability. She could not afford to keep young James at school for more than a few months, though she herself taught him to read from scraps of newspaper picked up in the streets. She put him to work in a brass-finishing shop of the Anchor Steamship Company, intending that he should serve an apprenticeship, but had to take him away when it was learnt that he must serve the first year of his time without wages.[14] Thereafter he drifted, an eight- or nine-year-old boy, at the mercy of casual employers, and soon learnt to resent, like his mother, the arbitrariness of their treatment of him. The famous story of how he was dismissed from his employment as an errand-boy by a Glasgow baker, a noted Christian, and fined a week's wages for punctuality is too well known to need repetition here.[15] By the time he was 10, his stepfather had to go to sea in search of work and James himself had to take employment as a trapper in a coal mine in Lanarkshire. Once again, his later reminiscences suggest poignantly the resentment which Mary Keir felt at this lapse into the dangerous work of a miner and life among the rough-living, hard-drinking colliers. To cheer her up, on the morning when she was sending her husband to sea and her son to the pit, David Hardie said: 'Ye hae this consolation at least, that sailors and colliers are the twa classes that meenisters pray maist for, if that does ony guid.' She could not speak, but threw her arms round the boy's neck and kissed him, turning abruptly away to make up the fire.[16]

There could be no joking about poverty with Mary Hardie. She knew that her son was fit for better things than errand-running and trap-minding, and there can be little doubt that she passed this thirst for respectability on to James. Indeed, there is some evidence that Hardie himself believed that he had been born to better things. Allan A. Durward, a veteran of the Aberdeen Socialist Society of the 1880s, wrote down about 1948 an account of researches into the early life of Keir Hardie, which he claimed to have conducted in the 1920s.[17] Durward

14 D. Lowe, *From Pit to Parliament* (1923), pp. 10 ff.

15 Hardie, in *Merthyr Pioneer*, 26 December 1914, quoted by Hughes, *op. cit.* pp. 16 ff.

16 H. Fyfe, *Keir Hardie* (1935), p. 17.

17 A. A. Durward, 'The Truth about James Kerr alias James Keir Hardie and the I.L.P.': MS. copy in the possession of Mr. H. Pelling, St. John's

recalled his surprise at discovering, from the records of the local registrar, that Hardie had been illegitimate and gave an account of an interview with a Lanarkshire miner who claimed to have worked with Hardie in the pits as a young man. According to this account, Hardie had believed that his real father was a doctor who had bribed William Aitken to abscond in order that the paternity of Mary Keir's child might be attributed to him, thus averting scandal from the doctor's name. 'Aye,' concluded Durward's informant, 'he was a damned sight prooder tae think himsel' the son o' a doctor wha disowned him than the daicent man wha gaed him and his mither a name and brocht him up.' It is impossible to vouch for the truth or otherwise of this gossip, but the fact that it could have persisted about the coalfields so long after Hardie had lived and worked there suggests that he was remembered as a young man with more than a normally good conceit of himself.

Working-class respectability in Victorian Britain was a two-edged sword. At one level of consciousness it entailed a healthy self-respect, an assertion of personal worth over external condition:

> The honest man, though e'er sae puir,
> Is king o' men, for a' that.

But these famous lines from Burns, whose poetry Hardie came to know and love as he grew up,[18] express only one of the motives for seeking after respectability. In mid-Victorian Scotland respectability entailed precisely that acquisition of external characteristics of dress, manner and even of spoken attitudes which Burns could so trenchantly scorn:

> The man o' independent mind,
> He looks and laughs at a' that.

All too often it was the fate of a working man who believed that the fustian was the equal of the broadcloth in personal dignity to become shut up in a structure of attitudes which stressed

---

College, Cambridge, to whom I am grateful for the opportunity to consult this and other MS. sources on Hardie.

[18] Hardie, in *Review of Reviews* (June 1906), pp. 57 ff.

personal responsibility for poverty and equated independence with worldly success.

This ambivalence was present in Hardie's early consciousness. He soon came to believe that self-improvement was the key to the solution of poverty, his own and that of the miners among whom he lived. Under his mother's influence, he took the Pledge and joined the Independent Order of Good Templars. Mary Hardie's experiences after her marriage seem to have destroyed her faith in Christianity and she brought young James up to be an atheist, but in 1879 he was converted and joined the Evangelical Union, an anti-Calvinist sect with a strongly working-class membership in the west of Scotland.[19] As a preacher at Bradford Labour Church in 1893, Hardie recalled his state of mind at this time:

> He was brought up without any kind of religious belief. . . . At twenty-one, he thought it time to begin to think on his own account and became extremely orthodox, even to the purchase of a frock coat. He insisted upon personal responsibility in this life, the life to come, and to a Supreme Being.[20]

Such a shining example of self-reliance was naturally valued and Hardie rose quickly in the Temperance and Evangelical armies. By 1883 he was the District Deputy, or organiser, for the Good Templars in Ayrshire and was publicly complimented by the Grand Lodge of Scotland for the success of his recruitment work.[21] When he and his family moved from Lanarkshire to Cumnock in Ayrshire in 1881 they found no church of the Evangelical Union conveniently situated and so joined its nearest equivalent, the Cumnock Congregational Church.[22] The church had a rather fashionable congregation, by the standards of a provincial Scottish town, but Hardie was soon being invited to lead the prayer meetings.[23] He was now moving in

[19] Stewart, *op. cit.* pp. 7 ff. For the Evangelical Union, see J. Escott, *History of Scottish Congregationalism* (Glasgow, 1960), pp. 163 ff., and J. Ross, *History of Congregational Independency in Scotland* (Glasgow, 1900).

[20] Quoted in *West Ham Herald*, 22 July 1893.

[21] *Paisley Daily Express*, 25 July 1883.

[22] Minute Books of Cumnock Congregational Church, 9 July 1882. I am grateful to Dr. J. Strawhorn of Mauchline, Ayrshire, for this reference.

[23] Hardie, Diary Fragment, 1884.

circles where he rubbed shoulders with active members of the Liberal Party and, in 1884, was invited to second a resolution at a public meeting to form a Junior Liberal Association in Cumnock. Later he confided to his diary:

> Have heard since that it was considered *the* speech of the evening. This seems egotism, but it is simply the opinion of those who have no interest served by flattery.[24]

A man who could hold so naïve a view of this situation might be thought to be standing very close to 'that trap for politically active working men', as Lloyd Jones once described the Liberal caucus.[25] Yet the self-improving Hardie was not free from doubts about the elements of double standard in Victorian philanthropy. While organising the Temperance movement, he was privately contemptuous of men who preached total abstinence to the working classes without living by the precept themselves. This is revealed by another diary entry of 1884:

> Went to Muirkirk to attend free breakfast given by G. T. [Good Templar] Lodge to aged people. C. H. in chair and ministers of parish on platform. Heard a lot of twaddle talked about the benefits of temperance by men who enjoy their wine every day.[26]

Until 1887, however, such doubts were not allowed to disrupt Hardie's relations with Scottish Liberalism, in which he saw the only hope of securing the reforms that would raise the social condition of the miners among whom he had lived since the age of 10, and whose trade unions he began to try to reorganise in 1878. It is essential, therefore, to turn to the problem of building organisation among the miners.

II

Trade-union organisation had been built up among the Scottish miners while Hardie was still a boy in the late 1860s and early

[24] *Ibid.* 11 March 1884.
[25] H. A. Clegg, A. Fox and A. F. Thompson, *A History of British Trade Unions Since 1889,* i (Oxford, 1964), p. 51.
[26] Hardie, Diary Fragment, 4 January 1884.

1870s. It had reached a peak during the boom of 1871–3, when the Fife miners were organised and a number of district unions established in Lanarkshire.[27] The onset of depression in the coal trade in 1874, however, put an end to high money wages and brought short-time working, so checking the development of unionism in Lanarkshire. It was not until 1878 that miners there were able to set up, with the support of Alexander Macdonald, a county union, a shaky structure of federated district unions whose governing executive was a board of 'agents' or organisers representing the various districts. The elected secretary was Hardie, now agent of the Hamilton district.[28]

The Scottish miners were now living through the 'Great Depression', a period in the history of British industry of falling prices and of downward pressure on money wages. In spite of G. D. H. Cole's assertion that Macdonald did not support the policy of getting wages regulated by sliding scales, the fact is that Macdonald advised the Scottish miners at this time to accept wage reductions as consequent upon falling coal prices and to try to get the employers to agree to sliding scales.[29] His solution to the problem that such scales slide downwards regardless of the movement of the cost of living was to advise the new union to impose a policy of restriction of output upon its members. Restriction of output, as is well known, was intended to limit the supply of coal and so raise its selling price, thereby enabling mine owners to pay higher wages. So crude an appeal to self-help on the part of the Lanarkshire miners was bound to be fruitless, for here the labour market in the coal industry was glutted by immigrant Irish farm labourers, and by the unemployed of Glasgow, who could easily reach the coalfield on cheap workmen's trains. Any collier who refused to 'fill the master's darg' – as the daily output of a hewer was called – and who tried to produce only the union's 'wee darg' was simply shown the way out of the workings, or disciplined in some other way by the company. Nor was there the least likelihood of the employers agreeing to a restricted

---

[27] R. P. Arnot, *History of the Scottish Miners from the Earliest Times* (1955), pp. 51 ff.

[28] Stewart, *op. cit.* p. 10.

[29] See report of Macdonald's speech to the Lanarkshire miners, *Glasgow Weekly Mail*, 6 September 1879. Cf. G. D. H. Cole, *A Short History of the British Working Class Movement* (1948), p. 229.

level of output or, for that matter, to sliding scales, for the Lanarkshire and Ayrshire coal producers were dominated by the big iron companies, who mined their own coal, and who had set their faces against the recognition of trade unionism in their works, being hard pressed by competition from other British producers and from the rising steel industry.[30] Moreover, as has been observed by other writers on the coal trade, the economic interest of the employer during a period of dull trade lay in producing as much coal as possible.[31]

Hardie profoundly admired Macdonald, whom he had once compared to Martin Luther as a benefactor of humanity, a remark which infuriated the Irish Roman Catholics among the miners in his audience.[32] He agreed with Macdonald's policy and was at pains to urge restriction and the need for sliding scales among the Lanarkshire men. In the autumn of 1879, however, faced with a series of wage reductions, the miners in the Hamilton and Larkhall districts of Lanarkshire rejected this cautious and futile policy and demanded strike action, resolving, some of them, against 'ever again taking the advice of Mr Macdonald, M.P.'[33] According to his own ideas on policy, Hardie should have supported Macdonald in trying to restrain the Hamilton men, and this at first he tried to do. But when it became clear that to persist in such a course would be to forfeit all influence over the men, he not only acquiesced in their defiance of the union's 'back to work' order, but aided and abetted them in the formation of a breakaway or 'Reformed' Lanarkshire County Union.[34] Not for the first time, as it was to prove, Hardie had learnt that in order to retain leadership over the miners it was necessary to follow them in certain moods, to allow them to work out their own salvation through their own

[30] On the avowed opposition of the Bairds, largest iron company in Scotland, to trade-union organisation among their miners, see evidence of A. K. McCosh, partner in the firm, before the *Royal Commission on Labour* (1892), viii, Q. 13667.

[31] J. W. F. Rowe, *Wages in the Coal Industry* (1923), pp. 137 ff. Cf. J. E. Williams, *The Derbyshire Miners* (1962), p. 271.

[32] Stewart, *op. cit.* p. 11.

[33] *Glasgow Weekly Mail*, 15 November 1879. For an account of the strike, see T. Johnston, *History of the Working Classes in Scotland* (Glasgow, 1946), pp. 336 ff.

[34] *North British Daily Mail*, 21 November 1879; *Glasgow Weekly Mail*, 20 December 1879.

hard experience, and not to restrain them in the interests of policies such as restriction and sliding-scale wage agreements, which seemed to confer no adequate improvement in return for the prolonged and disciplined sacrifices which they involved. It is true, of course, that the strike of Hamilton miners obtained only a very modest increase of wages compared to the savage cuts which had sparked off the outburst.[35] It is also true that the effort to keep 1500 men on strike for more than three months forced the 'Reformed' union to pile up large debts to local farmers by purchasing potatoes to feed the strikers and their families. The union, so encumbered, died before the end of 1880, and Hardie's opponents in Lanarkshire, the followers of Alexander Macdonald, were quick afterwards to hurl in his teeth the taunt of the disastrous 'Tattie Strike'.[36] But the real significance of the incident, obscure at the time, was that Hardie had now established a reputation as a leader who, while preaching the principles of self-help to the men, would not abandon them in their hour of danger because they refused to listen. This reputation he further enhanced when, in the autumn of 1880, he went down into the neighbouring county of Ayrshire to lead a strike for an increase in wages which had broken out there. This action was also long, and even less successful than the Tattie Strike, and the Ayrshire Miners' Association which Hardie then formed died with the strike.[37] The quarrel with Macdonald now became extremely bitter, and Hardie seems to have decided to settle down in Ayrshire at the market town of Cumnock, which remained his home until the end of his life.[38]

It is important to establish clearly the nature of Hardie's relationship with the Lanarkshire and Ayrshire miners at this time. An ambitious, respectable man, he was making his way in Temperance and Liberal circles and had already been successful in obtaining recognition in them. Undoubtedly this success depended, at least in part, upon his ability to influence the miners. Thus, the Independent Order of Good Templars had honoured him for his success in recruiting members among

[35] *Ibid.* 10 January 1880.
[36] Stewart, *op. cit.* p. 12.
[37] There is a good account of the strike in the *Ardrossan and Saltcoats Herald,* August–September 1880.
[38] Hughes, *op. cit.* p. 27.

them and it can hardly have failed to occur to the Cumnock Liberals that this eloquent and worthy member brought them valuable influence over the working-class community. In this relationship with the philanthropists and Liberal–Radicals, however, it is obvious that Hardie was not entirely a free agent. He was the leader of the miners. He thought of himself as belonging to that 'class' and as working for its elevation and improvement.[39] However, as the events of 1879 had shown, the miners were sometimes inclined to see their salvation rather differently, and to think that the slow business of self-improvement was serving the immediate interests of the coal owners rather well. On that occasion, Hardie had been forced by the action of the miners to choose between retaining his influence over the class for whose salvation he was working, by sticking to their cause through thick and thin, or opposing the men in the name of the laws of political economy and of the principles of self-improvement. In 1879–80 his instinct appears to have led him to follow the men. Thereafter his intellect, working upon that experience, led him back to self-help ideas, though with the introduction, as we shall see, of an important qualification in the form of the demand for a legal eight-hour day for miners.

Hardie's social and political views may be discovered from the largely neglected source of his weekly column of mining notes which he contributed from 1882 to 1886 to Ayrshire's Radical newspaper, the *Ardrossan and Saltcoats Herald*. Organisation among the Ayrshire miners had broken down and he took to journalism as a means of earning a living. He did not regard himself as having abandoned the miners. On the contrary, they had abandoned him. He now began to urge upon the Ayrshire miners a policy of building a union by extreme caution, avoiding strikes, strengthening a sound restriction policy and seeking all the time to win the coal masters' consent to sliding-scale agreements. He had returned, in fact, to the full policy of Alexander Macdonald and wanted to forget that he had ever been so weak as to follow the desperate colliers. He frequently lectured the men in his column for their thriftless, improvident

[39] See Hardie, in 'Black Diamonds', *Ardrossan and Saltcoats Herald*, 24 June 1882, in which he contrasts the miners, as 'the class to which he belongs', with cotton workers, another 'class' with whose grievances he can feel 'sympathy'.

28

lives, lives of toil broken by drink and gambling, of irregular work with short time in the summer and long shifts at the end of the year when the collier all but broke his back to get out the 'master's darg' for no better reason than to be sure of a big drink at the New Year.[40] Little could be done to organise such men until they had been taught the value of self-improvement. Commenting on their spending habits in 1883, Hardie wrote:

> Hungers and bursts are the rule. On a cash night, a load of provisions will be brought in. Jelly, biscuits, fancy bread, etc. are all spread out at once and everybody has a feast. Then for a day or two previous to the next cash day they are in semi-starvation. This is the history of hundreds of our miners at the present day. The remedy is plain enough, the application is not quite so easy. Better education in youth, regular family entertainment, lessons on temperance and thrift at school.[41]

This was the dominant voice of mid-Victorian trade unionism, of 'the aristocracy of labour'. The strength of organised labour was held to depend upon the manliness of the individual workman. Hardie often argued that the strong miners' unions of Northumberland and Durham, with their sliding-scale agreements and boards of conciliation, had been built up by this spirit.[42] Moreover, as soon as the working classes had proved their capacity for self-improvement they would be entitled to demand admission to their true inheritance, the partnership of Capital and Labour, when each would be rewarded in proportion to its actual contribution to production. Indeed, Hardie saw in the schemes of profit-sharing which Radicals of many kinds frequently discussed in the 1870s, an outline of the future industrial order.[43] The achievement of strong trade unionism, he

[40] *Ibid.* 8 September 1883.
[41] *Ibid.* 5 January, 1883.
[42] *Ibid.* 14 September 1883.
[43] *Ibid.* 22 July 1882. Cf. Sedley Taylor, *Profit-Sharing between Capital and Labour* (1884); H. Fawcett, *Pauperism, Its Causes and Remedies* (1871). Hardie mentioned these works in his column and followed the discussion in the Scottish Co-operative movement of profit-sharing schemes for workers employed in factories owned by the Scottish Co-operative Wholesale Society. Cf. J. A. Flanagan, *Wholesale Co-operation in Scotland* (Glasgow 1920), pp. 14 ff.

argued in the preamble to the rules which he drafted for the Ayrshire Miners' Association, would hasten the arrival of

> that good time . . . when the war hatchet will be buried forever and when Capital and Labour shall meet together under one roof-tree to smoke the pipe of peace and, as the smoke slowly ascends, it shall carry with it into oblivion all the feelings of discord that ever existed between those twin brothers, whose best interests are inseparable.[44]

Between 1882 and 1886, however, the miners of the west of Scotland ignored Hardie's eloquent cajolings. Nor is this surprising. The weakness of trade unionism in the region was due not to the relative lack of independent spirit among the miners there but to the abundant supply of labour which the coal and iron masters drew from among the Irish and Highland immigrants to the Scottish Lowlands and from the unemployed workmen of Glasgow.[45] Because there was no shortage for the employers of men with muscle enough to work at the coal face, it was impossible for the hewers to capture and maintain that essential requirement of a labour aristocracy, control of entry into their jobs.[46] Any man who refused work on the master's terms could simply be replaced. 'Restriction of output' was therefore an empty, meaningless slogan so long as it depended upon the voluntary action of the hewers. It was this basic reality of the situation which forced Hardie in 1883, long before he had heard of socialism, to put forward the idea of a legal eight-hour day for underground workers.[47] This demand had been made at the inaugural conference of the National Association of Miners in 1863, when Alexander Macdonald had suppressed it because he knew how strongly it ran counter to the *laisser-faire* prejudice which, though not unchallenged, was

[44] *Rules of the Ayrshire Miners' Association* (Kilmarnock, 1881); Scottish Record Office, FS 7/3.

[45] J. H. Handley, *The Irish in Modern Scotland* (Cork, 1948), *passim*. See also J. G. Kellas, 'Highland Migration to Glasgow', *Bulletin of the Society for the Study of Labour History*, No. 12 (1966), pp. 9 ff. I am grateful to Dr. Kellas for the opportunity to read the full text of this interesting paper.

[46] E. J. Hobsbawn, 'The Labour Aristocracy in Nineteenth-Century Britain', ch. 15 in *Labouring Men* (1968 edn.), pp. 272 ff.

[47] *Ardrossan and Saltcoats Herald*, 26 January 1883.

the dominant attitude to industrial legislation at the time.[48] Hardie was just as aware of the opposition which the proposal would encounter, but it seemed clear to him that the Ayrshire miners were almost as helpless as the boys and women whose work underground had already been brought under statutory control or prohibition. He had read Carlyle's *Sartor Resartus* at the age of 16 and had imbibed much of the author's anti-Utilitarian sentiment and, as a good Evangelical, he was accustomed to think that the State should have a moral function. If the State could pass a law to shut pubs, he saw no reason why it should not pass one to shut mines. In the last analysis, however, his case for the legal regulation of the hours of adult male underground workers rested, not upon any theory but upon what was to him an observable fact, the absence of a spirit of self-help among the Ayrshire and Lanarkshire miners:

> I admit that it would be much better were the men to carry out any eight-hour movement without the aid of Parliament, but, since this is barely possible then Parliament would be justified, even from an economical point of view, to pass such a measure.[49]

As Hardie saw the politics of the early 1880s, the demand for many forms of State intervention was growing within the Liberal Party. Besides prohibition of the liquor traffic and free education, nationalisation of the land was being canvassed by 1885 in those Scottish Liberal circles described at the time as 'advanced'. The best interest of the miners, Hardie believed, lay in co-operating closely with the advocates of such proposals to form a Radical wing that could push the Liberal Party's leadership forward along the road of State intervention.

Once again, Hardie was not altogether free from doubts about the good faith of his middle-class Radical allies. During the agitation to get the House of Lords to pass the bill for extending the suffrage to the counties in 1884, he thought them too timid because they would not include in the agitation the demand for abolition of the Lords.[50] He also thought that the Liberal lumin-

[48] S. and B. Webb, *History of Trade Unionism* (1920), p. 303.
[49] *Ardrossan and Saltcoats Herald*, 26 March 1883.
[50] *Ibid.* 25 July 1884.

aries in Cumnock were too ready to assume that the Ayrshire miners would vote Liberal as a matter of course, and that it was beneath their dignity to go out into the mining villages and canvass support.[51] In the general elections of 1885 and 1886, however, all such doubts were suppressed as Hardie worked to organise the miners' vote for the Liberal Party. He issued a fulsome manifesto in praise of the Liberals as the party of the cheap loaf, the free press, of statutory mining regulation and of 'its great and venerable head, William Ewart Gladstone'.[52] He interpreted the Gladstonian defeat of 1886 as a temporary setback which had at least left the Liberal Party in the control of its Radical section:

> The Whigs have gone from us. Thank the powers that be for that! We are left with a free hand to deal with the questions which affect ourselves.[53]

By 1886, however, he had heard of the new socialist propaganda in London and may have seen some copies of *Justice*, the organ of the Social Democratic Federation.[54] This is strongly suggested by the language in which he drew up the preamble to the rules of the new Ayrshire miners' union, formed in that year:

> All wealth is created by Labour. Capital is part of this wealth which, instead of being consumed when created, is stored up and used for assisting Labour to produce more wealth. Interest is a charge made by those who own Capital for the use of it made by those who labour.
>
> Rent is a charge made for granting the use of the land to those who are willing to use it for production of wealth. Profit is the part of wealth which remains after wages, interest and rent have been paid. If all land and capital were owned by those who produce wealth, the wages of Labour would be the same as the wealth produced by Labour, but, as land and capital is [*sic*] owned by men who are not labourers and as Labour cannot be without these, it follows that those who own land and capital are the masters of those

---

[51] *Ibid.* 12 September 1884.
[52] *Ibid.* 20 November 1885.
[53] *Ibid.* 26 March 1886.
[54] J. Neil, 'Memoirs of an Ayrshire Agitator', *Forward*, 4 July 1914.

who toil. Thus, capital, which ought to be the servant of Labour and which is created by Labour, has become the master of its creator.

The principles of trade unionism, properly understood and applied, aim at a reversal of this order of things.[55]

For all the textbook clarity of these lines, which have a strong odour of plagiarism about them, Hardie was still a Liberal and saw no reason why the proposals of the socialists should not simply be adopted into the Liberal pantheon. When, in 1886, he read a paper on 'Socialism' to the Cumnock Junior Liberal Club, he concluded that 'the legislation of the future must advance on the lines of socialism until the people are in possession of the land',[56] and his audience assented. Nor did he give up his view that the chief cause of poverty was drink. When, in 1884, Henry George had toured Scotland asserting that, in modern times, the gulf between rich and poor had been widening, Hardie accepted, not George's assertion but that of his opponent, the statistician Robert Giffen, who purported to show that the working classes had got richer during the previous half-century, while the rich had not.[57] Of Giffen's conclusions, Hardie wrote:

> If we accept these as correct, why is it that there is so much bare poverty in the land? ... To my mind, the answer is clear as the noonday sun. The people are pouring it down their throats in intoxicating drink.[58]

So much for Hardie's assertion that Henry George led him to communism. Even as late as November 1886, when he had certainly become acquainted with socialist literature, he could write that:

> but for the drink traffic, bad trade would be next to an impossibility, and most of the misery and poverty now existing would pass away.[59]

[55] *Rules of the Ayrshire Miners' Union, 1886;* Scottish Record Office FS 6/18.
[56] *Ardrossan and Saltcoats Herald,* 19 November 1886.
[57] Henry George, *Progress and Poverty* (1881 edn.), p. 7. Cf. R. Giffen, *Essays in Finance, Second Series* (1886), pp. 361 ff.
[58] *Ardrossan and Saltcoats Herald,* 12 November 1886.
[59] *Ibid.*

Up to the end of 1886, then, Hardie did not think that socialist ideas involved him in abandoning his allegiance to the Liberal Party. Socialism at this point in time seemed to him no more than a demand for increased State intervention and, since most 'advanced' Liberals had never opposed State intervention as such, he saw no incompatibility between the two positions. In reality, Hardie's position was based upon an optimistic assessment which events were shortly to dispel. In the first place, it presumed the goodwill of Radicals towards an increase in the strength of miners' trade unionism in the west of Scotland. In the second, it assumed that the Liberal Party, which had carried the Coal Mines Regulation Act of 1872, would accede readily to the miners' demand for the legal eight-hour day in return for their support at the polls. When both of these assumptions fell to the ground in the second half of 1887, Hardie was forced to consider seriously the socialist demand for an independent party of the working class, insisting upon the enactment of a programme of reforms in the interest of labour, regardless of the interests of either Liberals or Conservatives. It is important to notice that he was forced to make this choice because socialist propaganda had made so much headway among the miners of the west of Scotland that, unlike the situation in 1879, a new political leadership offering alternatives to the traditional policies of Alexander Macdonald actually existed.

III

Anti-Liberal ideas were spread among the miners of the west of Scotland by the Irish and Highland land agitations of the 1880s.[60] To these influences was added the impact of Henry George's second lecture tour in Scotland in 1884.[61] His meeting in Glasgow resulted in the inauguration of a Scottish Land Restoration League, a body pledged to 'restore' the land to the

[60] On the influence of the Irish land agitation, see T. W. Moody, 'Michael Davitt and the British Labour Movement, 1882–1906', *Transactions of the Royal Historical Society*, iii (1953), pp. 53 ff. On the Highland land question, see D. W. Crowley, 'The Crofters' Party, 1885–92', *Scottish Historical Review*, xxxv (1956), pp. 119 ff.

[61] E. P. Lawrence, *Henry George in the British Isles* (Lansing, Michigan, 1959), p. 35.

people of Scotland.[62] When, therefore, the Marxist ideas of the S.D.F. began to be accepted in Scotland, account had to be taken of the strong appeal of the land issue for industrial workers, many of whom were themselves recent recruits to industry from Ireland or the Highlands.

The first step was taken by J. L. Mahon, a young engineering apprentice who was converted to socialism by Andreas Scheu, an Austrian member of the Council of the S.D.F. In 1884 Mahon organised in Edinburgh a body called the Scottish Land and Labour League which united the demand for land nationalisation with public ownership of industrial capital.[63] The Glasgow branch of the S.D.F., formed in the same year, officially held aloof from the land agitation, which some of its members regarded as a distraction, but there was a personal link with the Land Restoration League through J. Bruce Glasier, a member of both bodies.[64] When, at the end of 1884, the S.D.F. split, the Land and Labour League and the Glasier faction within the Glasgow branch of the S.D.F. joined the Socialist League, formed by William Morris in opposition to Hyndman and the S.D.F.

The link between the west of Scotland miners and both the land and socialist agitations was a man whose contribution to their affairs has been too frequently neglected. William Small was a draper in the mining village of Cambuslang, Lanarkshire.[65] In the early eighties he became interested in the land question and read the work of Thorold Rogers, and soon came to the conclusion that there was no more justification for private ownership of mineral royalties than for private ownership of the surface of the land.[66] In 1884, he entered into correspondence on the question with, among others, Michael Davitt, leader of the Irish Land League, who wrote advising the Scottish miners to commence a campaign for the nationalisation of mineral royalties and for the application of the funds to the

[62] C. A. Barker, *Henry George* (Oxford, 1956), pp. 403 ff. Cf. D. C. Savage, 'Scottish Politics, 1885–6', *Scottish Historical Review*, xl (1951), pp. 118 ff.
[63] E. P. Thompson, *William Morris, Romantic to Revoluntionary* (1961 edn.), p. 406.
[64] J. Mavor, *My Windows on the Street of the World* (1923), p. 178.
[65] See the 'Papers of B. Small Relating to Her Father', National Library of Scotland, MS. Acc. 3359, hereafter cited as Small Papers.
[66] Cf. obituary notice in *Scottish Co-operator*, February 1903.

provision of State insurance for miners.[67] By this time, Small had begun research in the British Museum on the origins and extent of mineral royalties in Scotland in the hope of being able to show that the Crown had made the welfare of miners a condition of the original grants.

It was probably Small's growing local reputation as a scholar that attracted some of the younger leaders among the Lanarkshire miners, just as Alexander Macdonald's superior education had attracted the leaders of the previous generation. Macdonald had died in 1881, and in 1884 Small was asked by the young Robert Smillie and others to come and address a miners' meeting.[68] In September 1884 he convened a conference in Hamilton on the question of mineral royalties, which was attended by representatives of the Scottish Land Restoration League and of the Lanarkshire miners.[69] The conference decided to set up a Scottish Anti-Royalty and Labour League. This was an extremely significant decision, the first step towards the creation of a separate political party for labour with its own objectives. Already Small was proceeding to the logical consequences, the acceptance of a view of politics which emphasised the common interests of the workers as a class. He learnt his socialism from Dr. John Glasse, minister of Greyfriars Church, Edinburgh, and a member of the Scottish Land and Labour League,[70] and in November 1884 Small set up his political organisation of the Lanarkshire miners as a branch of the Land and Labour League.[71] From the middle of 1885 he was urging the Lanarkshire miners to imitate the Highland crofters and run their own candidate at the forthcoming general election, with improved mining legislation as their programme, and a miners' meeting resolved that:

[67] *Hamilton Advertiser*, 20 September 1884.

[68] R. Smillie, *My Life for Labour* (1924), pp. 40 ff. See also B. Small, 'William Small the Man', MS. in Small Papers. Cf. Small's own account in his evidence before the *Royal Commission on Labour* (1892), xviii, Q. 10271.

[69] *Hamilton Advertiser*, 9 September 1884.

[70] See note inserted by B. Small in her copy of D. Lowe, *Souvenirs of Scottish Labour* (1919): Small Papers. For Glasse, see Lowe, *op. cit.* p. 12, and R. P. Arnot, *William Morris, the Man and the Myth* (1964), pp. 77 ff.

[71] *Hamilton Advertiser*, 15 November 1884.

There is no miner in this county but will do his utmost to prevent any iron or coal master or any employer of labour from entering the Reform Parliament at the ensuing general election, at which the miners of this county will possess an enormous power.[72]

At another meeting Small attacked the sitting Member for Mid-Lanark, Stephen Mason, for allegedly advocating that the miners work longer hours.[73] At the same time he was reviving the Lanarkshire Miners' Union and openly supporting the independent candidatures of the Scottish Land Restoration League in Glasgow. He even had his name canvassed as a miners' candidate for Mid-Lanark, but did not proceed to nomination, presumably because of the weakness of his organised support.[74]

Isolated in Cumnock, Hardie took no part in these developments, though he was aware of them from the press. His attitude to Small's activities was sceptical, even hostile. He refused his co-operation when Small sought his adhesion, and that of the Ayrshire miners, to the proposed Anti-Royalty and Labour League, arguing that the question was of interest only to the employers and that it would distract the men from their first task of organising a trade union: 'Get the miners consolidated in union,' he wrote to Small, 'and then this and other matters will be righted, but out of union, there is no hope.'[75] Hardie's retort arose from an assessment of the miners' political situation fundamentally different from that of Small. He still saw them as one element in a broad radical movement. They should give general support to issues such as royalties raised by other radical groups – in this case, radical coal owners – so long as they got reciprocal support for their own demands such as the eight-hour day. In Small's opinion, radical employers constituted a political obstacle to the concession of the workmen's demands and had to be opposed. Hardie regarded these as wrecking tactics. In 1884 one of

[72] *Ibid.* 20 June 1885.
[73] *Ibid.* 8 August 1885.
[74] Kellas, in *Bulletin of the Society for the Study of Labour History*, No. 12 (1966), p. 9.
[75] *Ardrossan and Saltcoats Herald*, 26 September 1884.

the Lanarkshire miners' agents had criticised local Liberal coal masters for compelling their men to take part in a political demonstration at which a large block of coal was on display, urging that the coal was simply a portion of the overweight of which the men, unprotected by checkweighmen, were robbed at the pithead. Hardie attacked the remarks as 'injudicious' and 'not the way to encourage good feeling'.[76]

Until the end of 1886 Hardie saw no reason to abandon his faith in the goodwill of the Radicals. Then, in the winter of 1886–7, events in the west of Scotland coalfields took a sudden violent twist which drove a wedge between the Radicals and the miners and forced Hardie to choose between them.

IV

The steady fall in money wages during the depression in the coal trade of 1884 to 1886 drove the Scottish miners to new efforts at trade-union organisation. In Ayrshire the miners decided to re-form a county union and asked Hardie to become its secretary and to draft its rules.[77] In Stirlingshire the miners were being organised by a young newcomer, Robert Chisholm Robertson, who brought into existence the Forth and Clyde Valley Miners' Association.[78] Lanarkshire and Fife already had county unions in being in 1886. As luck would have it, the onset of winter saw an upward turn in coal prices and the moment seemed propitious to try to recover the loss of wages of recent years.

For this purpose the four miners' unions – Lanarkshire, Ayrshire, Fife and the Forth and Clyde Valley – brought into being the Scottish Miners' National Federation (S.M.N.F.). This step was a new departure for the Scottish miners. Whereas Alexander Macdonald had seen federal organisation as a way of uniting miners' unions for political pressure, leaving wages policy to be decided at the local level, the S.M.N.F. was an attempt to co-ordinate the wages policy of all the miners' unions in Scotland. As such it seemed to present a new challenge to the employers, while it confronted the miners' leaders with for-

[76] *Ibid.* 22 August 1884.
[77] *Ibid.* 22 July 1887.
[78] For Robertson, see sketch in *Miner*, January 1887.

midable problems in tactics. Hardie, who became secretary of the new Federation at its inauguration, clung to the old restriction policy, urging the constituent unions to adopt a common practice of working only five days a week and eight hours a day. He vehemently opposed any strike action, recalling the disasters of 1879–80.[79] As restriction had failed to get the support of Lanarkshire men in 1879, however, so it failed to get their support in 1886. One after another the Lanarkshire pits stopped work until, by the end of the year, coal production throughout the county was at a standstill.[80] Seeing that his policy of restriction was hopeless, Hardie began to urge that coal production should be limited by a series of one-week 'holidays', and the first of these was decided upon by the S.M.N.F. in January 1887.[81] Once the Lanarkshire men had thus got the bit between their teeth, however, there was no holding them. At the end of the week they refused, upon the advice of the agent for the Larkhall district, Robert Smillie, to go back to work until a wage increase had been conceded.[82]

For a short time it looked as though the miners' leaders would be torn apart by dissension. Hardie groaned: 'It was to be a week and no more, win or lose.'[83] He sent his Ayrshire men back to work, leaving the Lanarkshire miners on their own – but not quite alone or leaderless. In Glasgow the Socialist League and S.D.F. branches organised a large demonstration in support of the Lanarkshire miners and the League opened its club room as a strike headquarters.[84]

Faced with the twin menace of an emerging Federation of miners and of a socialist-led strike, the Lanarkshire iron masters decided upon a show-down with their men. Mounted police were drafted into the villages to escort blacklegs through the picket lines and to supervise strikers' meetings. The inevitable friction developed between strikers and police and burst out in a night of rioting at Blantyre from 7 to 8 February 1887, when shops were looted and prisoners released from the jail. Thereupon hussars were sent out from Glasgow and a night

[79] *Hamilton Advertiser*, 4 September 1886.
[80] *Ardrossan and Saltcoats Herald*, 22 December 1886.
[81] *Ibid.* 20 January 1887.
[82] *Miner*, February 1887.
[83] *Ardrossan and Saltcoats Herald*, 4 February 1887.
[84] *Commonweal*, 19 February 1887.

of arrests ensued, leading ultimately to a series of convictions.[85] The S.M.N.F. leaders at once closed their ranks and called out the Fife and Ayrshire miners in support of the Lanarkshire men, now seen as victims of an attack upon the right of trade-union organisation.[86] This display of solidarity came too late, however. The Lanarkshire men had been out too long and were near breaking point. When, therefore, the masters offered to meet representatives selected from among their workmen – that is, they refused to negotiate with officials of either the S.M.N.F. or of the county union – upon condition that the men returned to work first, their condition was accepted. Once back, the miners could not be made to answer a second strike call and their negotiators were as clay in the hands of the masters, who offered to introduce a sliding-scale agreement on condition that the miners gave up all claims and attempts to regulate the output of coal. Hardie and the other S.M.N.F. leaders could only stand aside helpless as the workmen threw this ultimatum back in the masters' teeth, and they must have known that so great a set-back after so prolonged a struggle marked the end, for the time being, of miners' organisation in Lanarkshire and, consequently, of the S.M.N.F. And so it proved.[87]

V

Hardie had regarded the action of the Lanarkshire men in not returning to work after the one-week holiday as foolish, but their claim for wage increases and for the right of trade-union organisation aimed at restriction of output he regarded as fully justified. 'Miners', he wrote,

> are prepared to render a fair day's work to the employers in return for which they demand a fair day's pay, with all the rights of freedom to boot.[88]

What the Lanarkshire strike revealed to him was that the two Liberal newspapers in the West of Scotland, the *North British*

[85] *North British Daily Mail*, 8–10 February 1887; *Labour Tribune*, 22 February 1887; *Commonweal*, 26 February 1887.
[86] *North British Daily Mail*, 17 February 1887.
[87] *Ibid.* 24, 25 February, 1, 9, 10, 12 March 1887.
[88] *Miner*, February 1887.

Daily Mail and the *Glasgow Weekly Mail,* owned by the prominent local Radical, Dr. Charles Cameron, were prepared to remain silent while the rights of trade unionism were crushed by the combined forces of the law, the military and the iron masters. To Hardie, this seemed on a par with condoning coercion in Ireland:

> Newspapers can devote page after page to the sufferings of the Irish tenant, whilst they are completely silent about an even greater amount of suffering which is being endured at their own door.[89]

Once again, the militancy of the Lanarkshire miners had forced him to consider whether he could really reconcile his aspirations for their social improvement with his strategy of co-operation with the Radicals. That strategy depended, as we have seen, upon an optimistic assessment of the chances of the Liberal Party becoming increasingly responsive to working-class demands. It would have been difficult for such an optimism to have survived the Blantyre incident, for the socialists were offering to a new generation of miners' leaders an alternative political programme of opposition to both Liberals and Conservatives in the interests of labour. Until the end of 1886 Hardie had been extremely reluctant to accord any support to Small's political views. After the Blantyre incident, he moved rapidly in that direction.

Indicative of a change in fundamental thinking in Hardie is his article in the *Miner* of May 1887, on 'Poverty', in which he completely inverted his old view that the chief cause of poverty was intemperance:

> Suppose the money now spent on drink to be divided equally among the working men of Great Britain ... it would not remove poverty from our midst. What we complain of is that the honest, indigent, sober toiler is kept from year's end to year's end with only one step between him and pauperism.... The remedy is a simple one, if only the Nation had sense enough to apply it. Get rid of the idea that

[89] *Ibid.*

the capitalist is an indispensible adjunct of an industrial system and the problem is solved.[90]

The change of front which Hardie here shows on the social question is remarkable. Not only has he abandoned the view that poverty is the result of personal shortcomings but he has accepted that poverty cannot be completely abolished until the means of production pass out of private hands. In other words, the system of society that he had once seen as a distant objective, to be gained when once the working class had elevated itself out of its poverty, now became itself the condition of that elevation. Two notes among the papers of William Small's daughter suggest that the ex-draper had contributed something to this acceptance of socialist ideas. These run: 'Smillie opposed Socialism taught by my father in our home, Olivia Cottage' and 'Hardie Smillie taught at my home by Papa'.[91]

At the same time Hardie showed a greater readiness than previously to extend the demand for State intervention on behalf of the miners. From February 1887, he took up vigorously the demand for State insurance for miners (to be financed partly out of nationalised mineral royalties), State arbitration of wages disputes in the coal industry (a proposal known to the miners as the 'Wages Court'), and these demands, together with the legal eight-hour day, became the main planks in the political programme of the S.M.N.F.[92]

Thus the Blantyre incident, and not the Mid-Lanark by-election, should be seen as the turning-point in Hardie's early political development. It brought him into closer agreement with the socialists than he had previously acknowledged. Not that he developed a profound understanding of socialist theory – few, if any, of even the avowed social democrats in Britain in the 1880s were gifted theorists. But the experience drove him to the conclusion that a new political strategy for the miners was necessary, a strategy which took no account of the convenience of Liberal interests and which made the alleviation of

[90] *Ibid.* May 1887.
[91] The reference to Smillie is an annotation by B. Small on p. 21 of Lowe, *op. cit.* The combined reference to Hardie and Smillie is an annotation by the same hand in *The Indepedent Labour Party, 1893–1943, Jubilee Souvenir*: Small Papers.
[92] *Miner*, May 1887; *Ardrossan and Saltcoats Herald*, 25 February 1887.

the condition of the working classes the first priority in politics. The socialist claim that labour had distinct political interests and that its task was to create a party dedicated to furthering these interests now became congruent with Hardie's long-standing desire to lead the Scottish miners out of the bondage of their poverty. It is in April 1887 that we find him writing:

> Working men should be taught to be members of a Labour Party first, and Whigs or Tories, after. The classes do not fail to make the most of the great Party names to keep the masses divided, and, while working men are quarrelling as to whether Whig or Tory should rule them, both are fleecing him and sharing the plunder between them. We want a new Party, a Labour Party pure and simple, and trades unions have the power to create this.[93]

One further event of the year 1887, following hard on the heels of the Lanarkshire strike, served to drive home the lesson. This was the passage of the Coal Mines Regulation Bill in June, which brought the Scottish miners into collision with the 'Lib-Lab' Members of Parliament over the question of the legal eight-hour day, and which was the occasion for Hardie to make contact with the two factions of London socialists around Engels and H. H. Champion, who were setting out to try to build up an independent Labour Party in Britain. Only the briefest mention of the most relevant sources can be made here. Their significance lies in showing how completely Hardie's new strategy had been developed before the Mid-Lanark by-election.

Until the end of 1886 Hardie had been a strong admirer of most of the Lib-Lab M.P.s, especially Thomas Burt, the Northumberland miners' leader, though Henry Broadhurst had always seemed to him diminished in stature through not being a total abstainer.[94] Burt's lukewarmness when speaking on a Scottish miners' amendment of the Coal Mines Regulation Bill – an amendment which would have limited the working hours of boys underground to eight – contributed largely to its defeat.[95] Likewise, a statement to the House by Broadhurst that

[93] *Miner*, April 1887.
[94] *Ardrossan and Saltcoats Herald*, 3 December 1886.
[95] *Parl. Debates*, 3rd ser. cccxvi, 632.

there was no demand among Scottish miners for the legal eight-hour day helped to defeat another of their amendments, and ignored all the decisions of the unions built up in Scotland since 1886.[96] Hardie now rounded upon them as 'dumb dogs who will not bark'.[97] In July 1887 he published in the *Miner* a programme for a new Labour Party, which included a legal eight-hour day in mines (and in other industries where, on inquiry, it might be found judicious), national insurance and State ownership of mineral royalties and mines.[98]

The lobbying of M.P.s by the S.M.N.F. leaders which the enactment of the new Coal Mines bill occasioned between February and June 1887 took Hardie for the first time to London. There he attended socialist meetings and was repelled by the boozing atmosphere of their clubs.[99] But he met Eleanor Marx, and she took him to see Engels. Engel's version of what socialist tactics should be, explained while he was in the course of criticising the S.D.F., seemed congruent with Hardie's experience of the miners' needs; and he kept in touch with Engels by correspondence.[100]

Of more immediate consequence was Hardie's meeting with Tom Mann, a fellow-teetotaller and, in Hardie's eyes, one of the 'moderate or constitutional section of the Socialists'.[101] Mann gave Hardie a copy of his pamphlet *What a Compulsory Eight Hour Working Day Means to the Workers*, with the result, as we have seen, that Hardie raised the question of the wider application of statutory regulation when he drew up his programme for labour in Scotland. Mann was at this time working closely with H. H. Champion, and the relationship between the three bore fruit in Hardie's outspoken attack on Broadhurst for his support of Sir John Brunner, the Liberal M.P. for Northwich and chemical magnate, at the Trades Union Congress in September 1887.[102]

[96] *Ibid.* cccxix, 900 ff.
[97] *Miner*, July 1887.
[98] *Ibid.*
[99] Pelling, *op. cit.* p. 64.
[100] *Labour Leader*, 24 December 1898. See also letters from Hardie to Engels, April–June 1889: Engels Papers, International Institute of Social History, Amsterdam.
[101] *Ardrossan and Saltcoats Herald*, 24 May 1887.
[102] Tom Mann worked incognito in Brunner's factory and provided the data for an exposure of the unhealthy conditions and long hours endured

One final contact arising out of the London visits needs to be noted. This was R. B. Cunninghame Graham. Graham's even-handed attacks upon both the Conservative government and the Liberal front bench for ignoring the condition of the working class attracted Hardie's admiration. Indeed, it would not be too much to say that Graham offered Hardie a model for parliamentary agitation, as the following letter from Graham to the West Bromwich paper, the *Labour Tribune*, published simultaneously by Hardie in his own column of mining notes, suggests:

> A working man in Parliament ... should go to the House of Commons in his work-a-day clothes, no matter if he has to leave his basket of tools.
>
> He should address the Speaker on Labour questions and give utterance to the same sentiments, in the same language and in the same manner that he is accustomed to utter his sentiments and address the President of the local Radical Club in. Above all, he should remember that all the Conservatives and the greater portion of the Liberals are joined together in the interest of Capital against Labour.[103]

By the middle of 1887, then, Hardie had a clear conception of what would be needed if working-class demands were to be carried through Parliament: a specific programme, uninhibited in its demands for State intervention by any assumptions concerning personal responsibility for poverty; and a political party, backed by the existing organisations of the workers and bearing their name. As early as July he had been writing of a political organisation, independent of the miners' unions, to sponsor three candidates for Parliament in Scottish mining constituencies.[104] By October 1887 J. L. Mahon, then a Socialist freebooter agitating in the north of England and in Scotland,

---

by the workers there. Champion published the account of these conditions which formed the basis of Hardie's onslaught on Broadhurst at the Trades Union Congress, September 1887. H. Pelling, 'H. H. Champion, Pioneer of Labour Representation', *Cambridge Historical Journal*, vi (1952), pp. 222 ff.

[103] *Labour Tribune*, 14 May 1887; *Ardrossan and Saltcoats Herald*, 15 July 1887.

[104] *Ibid.* 15 July 1887.

reported in *Commonweal*: 'As appearances go at present, there may soon be a Scottish Labour Party of which Mr. Cunninghame Graham will be the chief.'[105] All this amounted to a dramatic change in Hardie's political viewpoint, brought about by the Lanarkshire miners' strike and by the complex of social and political consequences arising out of it.

This perspective suggests a modification of recent assessments by historians of Hardie's intervention in the Mid-Lanark by-election. If Hardie saw the need both for a programme and for a Labour Party to oppose the Liberals in Scotland as early as July 1887, it can hardly be claimed that 'His quarrel was solely with the local caucus' and that this quarrel 'hinged on the refusal of the caucus to allow the miners their own choice of member'.[106] At Mid-Lanark Hardie and his local supporters, who had come with him through the travails of 1887, were putting to the test the issue of whether the Liberal Party could any longer be regarded as a party with any right to claim the franchises of working men. True, the issue was raised by the miners insisting upon choosing the Liberal candidate, but their choice was known among them as one who stood for a policy that constituted a far-reaching challenge to the interests represented by the Liberal caucus.

Finally, in the perspective adopted in this essay, it cannot be said that the class-consciousness behind the demand for separate labour representation in Scotland was the sudden result of unexpected opposition from the local Liberal Party workers towards Hardie's candidature for Mid-Lanark in 1888 and not a long-standing sore in Scottish society'.[107] Hardie's position has been shown to have developed before the question of his standing for Parliament arose. Far from being unexpected, his rejection by the caucus was clearly implicit in the view he had come to take of the Scottish Liberal Party in 1887, and this view had undoubtedly developed out of a long-standing sore in Scottish society: the continuous repression of trade unionism in the coal industry.

[105] *Commonweal*, 22 October 1887.
[106] Pelling, *Origins of the Labour Party*, p. 65.
[107] Kellas, in *Parliamentary Affairs*, xviii (1965), p. 320.

3

HENRY COLLINS

THE MARXISM OF THE SOCIAL DEMOCRATIC FEDERATION

THOUGH Karl Marx lived more than half his life in England he made no attempt to found a Marxist party here. To have done so would have been incompatible with his outlook, according to which 'the emancipation of the working classes must be conquered by the working classes themselves'.[1] While Marx was never what the French called 'ouvrieriste', since he believed that conscious socialists equipped with scientific theory had an indispensable contribution to make, he always saw this function as the injection of socialist ideas into working-class organisations which had formed more or less spontaneously. When 'the working classes themselves' were ready to move and had, in fact, begun to do so, then socialist organisations which would include intellectuals as well as workers could help show them the way. Until this had happened attempts to initiate working-class organisations from outside would be futile and harmful.

I

In the early 1880s, shortly before Marx's death, H. M. Hyndman helped to establish the Democratic Federation and then to transform it, by 1884, into Britain's first Marxist party, the Social Democratic Federation. It is widely known that both Marx and Engels looked askance at the experiment, and historians have emphasised, perhaps excessively, their personal antagonism towards Hyndman. But there were also fundamental political reasons why Marx and Engels were likely to think the S.D.F. misconceived. The Democratic Federation out

---

[1] *Provisional Rules* of the International Working Men's Association, drafted by Marx and adopted 1 November 1864.

of which it developed included Radical working men and intellectuals and it was the latter who, in the next two to three years, gravitated towards socialism. The transition was effectively made not so much with the change of nomenclature in 1884 as with the appearance, in August of the previous year, of the manifesto *Socialism made Plain*.[2] By that time Marx had been dead for five months, but Engels, in a letter to August Bebel, gave the manifesto a heavily qualified welcome. It was good to the extent that its authors were 'obliged openly to proclaim our theory', but unfortunately the initiative had come from 'a crowd of young bourgeois intelligentsia' and not from the working-class members, who 'for the most part only accept the new programme unwillingly and as a matter of form'. Of course, the socialist intellectuals might succeed 'since they have accepted our theoretical programme and so acquired a basis, but *only* if a spontaneous movement breaks out here among the workers *and* they succeed in getting control of it'.[3] However, in a letter written during the last year of his life, Engels was still hoping that a genuine workers' party would be established since 'The Social-Democratic Federation ... has managed to transform our theory into the rigid dogma of an orthodox sect.'[4]

It is the purpose of this essay to find out in what way and, perhaps, why the S.D.F. succumbed to the 'rigid dogma' which partly stultified the activities of England's first Marxist party. For Marx, despite a certain flair for vituperation, was very far from being a dogmatist, and Engels, though sometimes accused of being over-schematic, was flexible in most respects, including his account of historical materials and his advice on political tactics. If the S.D.F. succumbed, as it did, to a narrow and unimaginative interpretation of Marxism, this was its own doing and, as it turned out, its own undoing.

What Marx and Engels created for the international labour movement was a body of writings encyclopedic in scope which exemplified a theory and a method rather than a doctrine. As Karl Korsch has pointed out,[5] the concept of 'critique' played

---

[2] *Socialism made Plain. Being the Social and Political Manifesto of the Democratic Federation. Educate. Agitate. Organise* (1883).

[3] Engels to Bebel, 30 August 1883.

[4] Engels to F. A. Sorge, 10 November 1894.

[5] K. Korsch, *Karl Marx* (1938), pp. 101–9. According to Mr. C. Abramsky Korsch was the first writer to discuss the full significance of this concept.

a peculiar and probably unique part in the development of Marx's thought. As early as 1844 Marx had contributed an *Introduction to the Critique of Hegel's Philosophy of Law* and Engels his *Outline of a Critique of Political Economy* to the *Deutsch-Französische Jahrbücher*. The first joint published work by Marx and Engels was *The Holy Family* in 1845, subtitled sardonically *A Critique of Critical Critique*, presenting an early version of historical materialism in opposition to the insistence of Bruno Bauer and his friends that the way to social progress lay exclusively through the battle of ideas. When the first volume of *Capital* appeared in 1867 it was, in turn, subtitled *A Critique of Political Economy*, of which an earlier draft of the first three chapters had been published in 1859 as *A Contribution to the Critique of Political Economy*. Marx's last major work, written in 1875, appeared posthumously in *Die Neue Zeit* of 1891 as *Critique of the Gotha Programme*, directed against the Lassallean elements in the programme of German Social Democracy, and Engels's most successful work of popularisation, *Socialism, Utopian and Scientific*, of which the first English edition appeared in 1892, was based on an earlier critique of the Positivist philosopher Eugen Dühring.

In short, there was no finished body of doctrine, containing a set of propositions, to which the name 'Marxism' could be attached. There was instead – and as was embedded in the 1844 *Theses on Feuerbach* – a dialectical concept of a world in process of eternal change with which humanity was engaged in permanent creative conflict. In Marx's view, philosophy and, a little later, politics, were aspects of the struggle to subjugate the world to human purposes, with humanity and purposes alike developing in the course of the conflict. Appropriately, the concept of 'critique' was itself dialectical, embodying the notion of development through conflict. 'Marxism' did not develop merely *in conflict with* but also *in relation to* Hegelian philosophy, the capitalist system and conflicting trends within the socialist movement. The concept of 'critique' is complex and subtle, and it is incompatible with the presentation of a systematic body of teachings to be accepted by disciples.

'Marxism' at the death of Marx and Engels, therefore, was unfinished, in fact unfinishable. And the ambiguities and uncertainties which perplexed future generations of followers

GARDNER WEBB COLLEGE LIBRARY

arose from this situation and not necessarily from lack of clarity in the teachings themselves. Take, for example, the notion of immiseration, or the inevitability of increasing poverty for the workers under capitalism. When Eduard Bernstein attacked this view and was himself attacked by Plekhanov and others for repudiating a basic tenet, he turned to the appropriate chapter of *Capital* and concluded that 'One can interpret this chapter in very different kinds of ways.' There were conflicting tendencies within the process of 'capitalist accumulation' and the outcome, which was not to be deduced from first principles, would be determined in the ensuing class struggle. 'Engels,' added Bernstein, 'has never expressed himself against this interpretation of mine.'[6]

The Bernstein who considered Marx's view on immiseration to be ambiguous had been, for many years, a close personal friend of Engels, who nominated him his literary executor. And it seems probable that Marx's theory of the long-term trend of wages under capitalism was not so much ambiguous as, down to the time of his death, incomplete. The question, however, was to cause a good deal of trouble to the S.D.F. and to many future generations of Marxists.

Another problem which perplexed the heirs of Marx and Engels, including the S.D.F., was the question of how far the materialist conception of history implied a rigid determination which both guaranteed victory to the cause and laid down, within very narrow limits, the strategy and tactics to be employed. By 1890, when the S.D.F. had been in existence for six years and when the materialist conception of history had become a central topic of discussion in the Socialist movement of Germany, misunderstanding of what the theory implied had become so rife that Engels felt obliged to write a series of letters[7] explaining the difference between the views which he and Marx had propounded and the crude, one-sided interpretations which had become prevalent in and around the Social Democratic Party. In accepting a good deal of blame for the misunderstanding, Engels argued that he and Marx, because

[6] *Evolutionary Socialism* (1st edn., 1899).
[7] See especially Engels to C. Schmidt, 5 August 1890; to J. Bloch, 21–22 September 1890; to C. Schmidt, 27 October 1890; to F. Mehring, 14 July 1893.

of the circumstances in which their views had developed – that is, in reaction to the idealism of Hegel which his disciples in the 1840s were taking to fantastic lengths – *'were bound to'* over-emphasise the role of the economic base in determining the political, legal, moral and cultural characteristics of society without, in their earlier presentation, stressing sufficiently the element of feed-back.

In short, 'Marxism' as interpreted by both its founders was a body of theory developed by revolutionaries in response to specific challenges and particular situations. But it was not so interpreted by its disciples, either here or abroad. Among the most salient features in the history of 'Marxism', exemplified in the story of the S.D.F., has been the tendency to repeat and the reluctance to develop what was taken to be the body of truths revealed by the founders. 'No disciple,' writes Walter Kendall, 'interprets his master's doctrine in an entirely authentic fashion,'[8] but for most of the theoretical questions considered by the S.D.F. in their attempts to operate as Marxists under British conditions, there was no 'authentic' doctrine to interpret, but rather a view of the world in terms of dialectical change, a theory of historical development, an analysis, in general terms, of the dynamics of capitalist society and a method to apply well or badly.

Lastly, a study of the theory of the S.D.F. should help to explain something of the achievements and limitations of early British 'Marxism'. Theodore Rothstein, who joined the S.D.F. in 1895 and served on its Executive from 1901 to 1905, considered retrospectively that the failure of the S.D.F. to exercise more influence on the development of Britain's labour movement could not have been avoided, however inspired the leadership, because of the favourable economic situation of British capitalism during the period.[9] No doubt this is true in the sense that the British workers were unlikely in any event to become revolutionary. On the other hand, superior leadership could unquestionably have given the S.D.F. far greater success and made it far more influential in the wider labour movement

---

[8] W. Kendall, *Revolutionary Movements in Britain 1900–1921* (1969), p. 3.

[9] *From Chartism to Labourism* (1929), pp. 255–80.

than it ever became.[10] We shall be looking, for the remainder of this essay, at the use made by the S.D.F. of its Marxist inheritance. Without entering into the broader question of the relation between political theory and practice, it is likely that the successes and failures of a party depend, to a significant extent, on its underlying philosophy, its view of society and its conception of its own role in conserving or changing that society.

II

Among the earliest introductions to socialist theory made available by the S.D.F. in popular form was *The Socialist Catechism* which J. L. Joynes had written for *Justice* and which he expanded into a sixteen page pamphlet in 1885, at a time when works by Marx in English were all but unobtainable.[11] In this pamphlet thousands of Englishmen for the first time encountered the idea that the exploitation of labour was not incidental but built into the capitalist system, since it stemmed, of necessity, from the private ownership of the means of production. Joynes explained clearly and simply the concept of surplus value, based on the distinction between necessary and surplus labour, and of class conflict, reaching back to the beginnings of civilisation. What was distinctive in capitalism, Joynes argued was not exploitation as such, which had also existed in slave and feudal societies, but exploitation arising out of the operation of market forces rather than established custom. Again, compared with previous forms of society, he went on, capitalism was dynamic since it constantly raised labour productivity through technological progress, although this did not benefit the worker, whose wages remained at or close to subsistence level.

Joynes referred explicitly, as did other S.D.F. writers of the period, including Hyndman, to the 'iron law of wages', not realising that this Lassallean concept had been explicitly repudiated by Marx in his confidential comments on the 1875 Gotha programme of the German Social Democrats. And, though Marx's

[10] E. J. Hobsbawm, *Labouring Men: Studies in the History of Labour* (1968 edn.), p. 237.

[11] For a list of the earliest writings of Marx and Engels available to those members of the S.D.F. who read only English, see Dona Torr, *Tom Mann and His Times* (1956), p. 326.

comments were reprinted in the *Neue Zeit* in 1891, *A New Catechism of Socialism*, which appeared in 1901, written by Belfort Bax and Quelch, restated the old view with even more emphasis, asserting that 'the "Iron Law of Wages" ... stands as firmly today as when stated by Lassalle'. This is all the more surprising since Bax was fluent in German and since an earlier criticism by Marx of the 'iron law' as pronounced by the Owenite Weston, in 1865 had been published in English by his daughter Eleanor in 1898. It was not as though the leaders of the S.D.F. were exercising their right to disagree with Marx's views; they were simply unaware of them, and F. C. Watts, writing in the theoretical journal of the S.D.F. as late as September 1903, drew members' attention to Marx's theory, which was that, while market forces tended to pull wages down to subsistence, ideas of what constituted subsistence depended on custom and expectation and could be modified, at least up to a point, by trade-union pressure.[12] This story seems to suggest a rather low level of theoretical alertness, all the more unfortunate in a party which laid such stress on theory.

Belief in the iron law was linked, of course, to the party's view of the general uselessness of trade unions; Joynes's *Socialist Catechism* does not mention them and there was no suggestion of any way open to the workers to affect the level of their wages. It followed from this that the strike weapon was ineffective, a view which was to persist as a kind of malign obsession throughout the history of the party. In the first issue of the *Socialist Annual*,[13] Dan Irving, a former railwayman and later M.P. for Burnley, referred to the strike weapon as being antiquated. Hyndman, who held this view as consistently as any other of his views, may have derived it initially from his study of Lassalle, whom he described with admiration as 'essentially a national Socialist',[14] but when he turned from Lassalle to a study of the Chartists and their contemporaries he came across very similar ideas. Summing up a lifetime's experience in 1915, he felt that Marx had been wrong in ever expecting trade unionism to become a revolutionary force in Britain: Bronterre O'Brien had been right in saying that the unions represented merely an

---

[12] *Social Democrat*, September 1903.
[13] Ed. Theodore Rothstein (1906).
[14] C. Tsuzuki, *H. M. Hyndman and British Socialism* (1961), pp. 30–1.

'aristocracy of labour'.[15] The Webbs drew attention to the great similarity between the views of the S.D.F. and those of the Owenites of the 1830s,[16] and O'Brien, who blended many elements of Owenism into his Chartist theories, may have posthumously influenced the S.D.F. through his close friends James and Charles Murray, who joined the Democratic Federation when it was founded in 1881.

In any case, the Democratic Federation and the S.D.F. were formed at a time when it was an incontrovertible fact that trade unions in Britain did represent only a small minority of better-paid workers in skilled trades. And it was not only the English socialists of the 1830s but also Engels, writing in 1881, who urged the working class to realise that 'the present movements for higher wages and shorter hours exclusively keep it in a vicious circle out of which there is no issue; that it is not the lowness of the wages which forms the fundamental evil, but the wages system itself'; and drew the conclusion that over and above 'the Unions of special trades there must spring up a general Union, a political organisation of the working class as a whole'.[17] Engels and the S.D.F. were at one, in fact, in holding that the trade-union fight for improved wages and hours was inadequate. Yet while Engels believed that this limited fight would *develop into* a wider movement for political power, the S.D.F. thought that the first would be *superseded* by the second. This difference, which became crucial with the development of the 'new unionism' at the end of the 1880s, might well have escaped trade unionists who read Engels's articles and later joined the S.D.F.

As E. J. Hobsbawm has pointed out, Hyndman failed to carry the S.D.F. with him in such quirks as chauvinism and anti-semitism,[18] but unfortunately the party's attitude to the relationship between trade unionism and the wider political movement for socialism was exactly the same as his. The reason was partly the O'Brienite background of such veterans as the Murrays, already referred to, and partly the outlook of John Sketchley, who during the late 1870s contributed to German

[15] H. M. Hyndman, *The Future of Socialism* (1915), pp. 182–3.
[16] S. and B. Webb, *The History of Trade Unionism*, (1950), pp. 409–11.
[17] Engels, in *Labour Standard*, 4 April 1881; reprinted in F. Engels, *The British Labour Movement* (1934), pp. 20–1.
[18] *Op. cit.* p. 234.

Socialist papers and was deeply influenced by the Lassallean Gotha programme.[19] All three played a prominent part in the formation of the Democratic Federation, and Sketchley's *Principles of Social Democracy* was the means by which some the key socialist pioneers of the early 1880s made the transition from republican radicalism. It must also be noted that when such men as these turned from bourgeois radicalism to socialism, they saw in Gladstonian Liberalism the main obstacle to an independent workers' movement and in the leaders of trade unionism the main working-class allies of Gladstone. It was Hyndman's view that as allies of Liberalism the unions had consistently 'acted as a bulwark of capitalism'.[20]

III

What was strange and, from the standpoint of S.D.F. prospects, sad, was not that the Party believed in 1884 that partial strikes, by which they meant anything short of an international general strike, were harmful to the workers[21] but that the view persisted for the next quarter of a century. A more alert, less blinkered party would have responded enthusiastically when, at the end of the 1880s, trade unionism began to break through its narrow craft barriers and the 'new unionism' started among gasworkers, dockers and others who were classified as unskilled. But while 'new unionists', like Will Thorne, John Burns and Tom Mann, played leading parts in the movement, the official view was that there was no significant difference between the new unionism and the old and that such movements as the great dock strike of 1889 represented merely 'a lowering of the flag, a departure from active propaganda, and a waste of energy'.[22]

Of course, the S.D.F. encouraged its members to join trade unions and agreed that strikes were often necessary to prevent a worsening of the worker's conditions. But because of the inexorable economic pressures of capitalism, as interpreted by the

---

[19] E. P. Thompson, *William Morris, Romantic to Revolutionary* (1955), p. 322, and John Eichmannis, 'The Activities of the Social-Democratic Federation, 1881–1901' (M.A. thesis, Guelph, 1968), f. 8.

[20] *Ibid.*

[21] The S.D.F. manifesto to the trade unions was published in *Justice*, 6 September 1884.

[22] *Ibid.* 3 May, 1890.

S.D.F., strikes could do nothing to raise wages to any significant or lasting extent and socialists were expected to work in their unions mainly to explain to fellow-members that the money spent on strike pay would have been better devoted to socialist propaganda. When the Taff Vale judgement severely weakened the right to strike, the S.D.F., far from demanding an all-out struggle for legal reforms, felt that the judgement might do more good than harm if it helped convince the unions that their future lay in political *as opposed to* industrial action.[23]

The prevailing view in the S.D.F. was put most succinctly by Hyndman in an article which he wrote for a Russian socialist periodical towards the end of 1900.[24] Marx and Engels, he believed, had so far been proved wrong and Bronterre O'Brien and Ernest Jones proved right in their assessment of the potentialities of trade unionism in Britain. Here and there, perhaps, pressure by trade unions for improved conditions might have done limited good, but to be of value in the future the unions would have to learn various 'lessons'. One of these was that 'unless the workers in a free country use the political forms as a class-conscious whole, in order to obtain their economic emancipation, there is a poor prospect for the obtainment of any real freedom', another was that 'strikes' should never be entered upon, if it were possible to avoid them. 'The money and sacrifices involved by them – even when successful – would secure much more important results if applied in other directions.'

As we have seen, this view was retained and repeated in more or less the same form at literally every stage of the party's history – the 1880s, the 1890s and the 1900s up to and beyond the outbreak of the First World War. It was by far the most important cause of weakness and stagnation and caused the early defection of such 'new unionists' as Burns and Mann. And, as the Webbs maintained, 'With the defection of the New Unionists, revolutionary Socialism ceased to grow.'[25] The Webbs were misleading, however, when, later in the same work, they referred to the S.D.F. as being 'outspokenly contemptuous of

[23] *Social Democrat*, August 1901 and February 1903.
[24] The article was not published at the time but was reproduced by Andrew Rothstein in the *Quarterly Bulletin* of the Marx Memorial Library, October–December 1966, from a photocopy supplied by the Institute of Marxism–Leninism, Moscow.
[25] Webb, *op. cit.* p. 412.

the whole trade-union movement as a mere "palliative" of the Capitalist system'.[26] For the S.D.F. was never, at any time, opposed to palliatives. In the manifesto *Socialism made Plain* already referred to, the Democratic Federation had announced, for the first time, its objective of transferring the 'means of producing and distributing wealth' to public ownership. But it went on immediately to announce a list of 'stepping-stones to a happier period' drawn up for 'immediate adoption'. The immediate programme called for (1) the public provision of low-cost housing, (2) free, compulsory education with free school meals, (3) an eight-hour day, (4) progressive income tax, (5) nationalisation of railways, (6) nationalisation of banks, (7) extinction of the National Debt and (8) land nationalisation. In common with other extreme radical programmes of the nineteenth century this one has been substantially realised in Britain – specifically, the first six points. More important, however, was the fact that the Democratic Federation from the beginning envisaged a period of transition in which reforms of a generally progressive nature, but stopping well short of complete socialism, 'would be secured. The term 'stepping-stones' implied the transitional nature of the programme, which was taken over intact by the S.D.F. as measures which would 'palliate the evils of our existing society'. In fact the inclusion of 'palliatives' was one of the reasons for the first split in the party which led to the breakaway of William Morris and others to form the Socialist League at the end of 1884.[27]

IV

Nor is there any doubt about the sincerity with which the S.D.F. worked for its short-term aims. As against the faction which came ultimately to dominate – and destroy – the Socialist League, the S.D.F. believed genuinely in Parliament and in the possibility of using it to win social reforms, even while society remained capitalist. The programme of the Democratic Federation included adult suffrage, annual parliaments, payment of M.P.s, abolition of the House of Lords and Church disestablishment. The programme of the S.D.F., on the other hand, was

26 *Ibid.* p. 652.
27 Thompson, *op. cit.* pp. 387–95.

more methodically set out. It began with a list of political and social aims culminating in the collective ownership of 'The Means of Production, Distribution and Exchange'. There followed the transitional programme of palliatives, after which, 'As means for the peaceable attainment of these objects,' it listed the democratic reforms taken from the programme of the Democratic Federation, beginning with adult suffrage and ending with disestablishment.

In short, the S.D.F. took seriously both parliamentary democracy and the possibility of using it for social reform. Nor is there anything surprising in this. It is logically possible for revolutionaries to take other views, for example that partial reforms are unattainable because the ruling class will refuse them, or, if attainable, undesirable because they will make existing society more tolerable to its victims. This was, at times, the view of William Morris and the section which came to control the Socialist League and, perhaps logically, to carry it over to anarchism and disintegration. It was never the view of the S.D.F., and in this the party followed in the traditions of Marx, who had laid great stress on the value of legally limiting the working day and who had more than once referred to the possibility of a peaceful change in a country such as England, where the workers possessed political and democratic rights. Marx had said as much to Hyndman when they met in 1880 and Hyndman saw no reason to dissent.[28] On occasions Hyndman went further than, perhaps, the majority of his comrades in arguing that even non-socialist governments were liable to be compelled, by the sheer 'pressure of current events,' to take increasingly collectivist measures, though everyone agreed in the possibility of a transition to full socialism 'without bloodshed and bitter war'.[29]

A New Catechism of Socialism which Bax and Quelch published in 1901 explained that palliatives were justified for two reasons. In the first place reforms such as the eight-hour day, better housing and school meals made workers fitter and, to that extent, more energetic and effective fighters in the class struggle. Secondly, they somewhat changed the character of

[28] H. M. Hyndman, *Record of an Adventurous Life*, quoted in Tsuzuki, *op. cit.* p. 34
[29] H. M. Hyndman, *Commercial Crisis of the Nineteenth Century* (1932), p. 9. The book was first published in 1892.

society by shifting the balance between private and public sector to the benefit of the latter. Thirdly, since most workers were in any case at subsistence level, taxation was paid entirely out of surplus value. Social benefits financed out of the rates and taxes were, therefore, an effective means of redistributing real incomes, if only to a modest extent.

With this neat piece of logic the S.D.F. reconciled the two disparate sides of its theory about the nature of the class struggle under capitalism. Of course some members were not rigidly committed to a 'biological subsistence' theory of wages. These would accept the more sophisticated analysis supplied by Karl Kautsky, according to which wages oscillated between a theoretical upper limit at which surplus value would be zero and the lower limit imposed by biological subsistence with some tendency to secular growth resulting from the rise in productivity.[30] But they took it for granted that these oscillations and trends resulted from blind market forces about which unions could do nothing.

At this point it is worth stopping to ask why the S.D.F. believed so firmly in the value of campaigning politically for palliatives while at the same time proclaiming ' the utter hopelessness of strikes'.[31] It was not the only possible position for revolutionaries to adopt. A generation later, the syndicalists adopted exactly the opposite position. To some extent, as has already been suggested, Hyndman and his followers took over the view of strikes propagated earlier by Owenites and O'Brienites. To some extent also they were conditioned by the fact that the S.D.F. was born at a time when trade unionism in Britain was at an unusually low ebb and was failing notably to cope with the problems of the 'Great Depression'. But it was not difficult to derive the outlook of the S.D.F. from the writings of Marx himself. In 1885, two years before the *Communist Manifesto* became generally available to English readers and a year before the first English edition of *Capital*, J. L. Joynes, whose *Socialist Catechism* has already been mentioned, published his translation of *Wage-Labour and Capital*,[32] and it is clear that the first genera-

[30] Karl Kautsky, *The Proletariat* (1908). This was one of a series by Kautsky explaining the Erfurt programme of 1891.
[31] H. Quelch, in *Social Democrat*, October 1897.
[32] The English edition appeared first in *Justice* and was published

tion of British Marxists derived its notion of political economy mainly from this source. The pamphlet presents a model of capitalist development in which 'the faster productive capital increases, the more does the division of labour and the employment of machinery extend. The more the division of labour and the employment of machinery extends, so much the more does competition increase among the labourers and so much the more do their average wages dwindle ... thus the forest of outstretched arms by those who are entreating for work becomes ever denser and the arms themselves grow ever leaner.'

Nowhere does *Wage-Labour and Capital* suggest that the workers can modify these pressures through trade-union organisation or by any other means. Nor did it seem particularly likely, in the conditions of the 1840s, that they could in fact do so. Referring to trade-union struggles in the 1848 *Communist Manifesto*, Marx and Engels had written that 'Now and then the workers are victorious, but only for a time. The real fruit of their battle lies, not in the immediate result, but in the ever-expanding union of the workers.' And this union, they went on to say, would lead to a directly political conflict culminating in the triumph of the workers.

For any member of the S.D.F., reading the *Manifesto* in 1888, when it became generally available in English, these passages would come as no surprise. On the contrary they would seem entirely in line with what their party was saying – that strikes could do no lasting good and that the unions should turn to political struggle instead. Moreover, when the S.D.F. had been formed in 1884 the most effective unions were still those of the skilled craftsmen, and, as *Wage-Labour and Capital* made clear, these very skills were being constantly undermined by mechanisation which hurled the craftsmen down into the ranks of the unskilled, and through increasingly intense competition forced the independent small masters and businessmen down into the ranks of the proletariat. According to this analysis the strike weapon really did look puny and inadequate, and Marx's *Capital*, which appeared a year later, while not asserting an iron law of wages with any Lassallean rigidity, contained few references to trade unions and none from which any very encourag-

---

separately as a pamphlet five years before its first appearance as a separate work, edited by Engels, in German.

ing conclusions might be drawn. By contrast, the S.D.F. member who read *Capital* in 1887 would find glowing references to the 'physical and normal regeneration of the factory workers'[33] resulting from the Ten Hours Act and favourable treatment of the movement for an eight-hour day, which featured prominently among the S.D.F. 'palliatives'.

V

Taking account, then, of the ideological background of British socialism, the state of trade unionism when the S.D.F. was founded and those writings of Marx which were available to its members, a dichotomy in attitude towards palliatives and strikes becomes readily understandable. Moreover, the depressed economic conditions of the 1880s made agitation among the unemployed seem more useful than strike action, while the 1888 reform in local government and the increased powers secured by elected school boards and local authorities during the next few years provided the S.D.F. with a field in which it could campaign for palliatives with, here and there, some chances of limited success. Members and ex-members of the party were able, for example, to exert pressure for school meals on local authorities. John Burns, who was elected to the L.C.C. for the Borough of Battersea in 1889, soon resigned from the S.D.F. after a quarrel with Hyndman. This was not an unusual experience for S.D.F. members, and Burns was still regarded as a standard-bearer of socialism in the government of London. In a pamphlet issued by the S.D.F. in 1893 it was said of him that 'his Socialistic work on the London County Council greatly exceeds in importance any work he has done, is doing, or is ever likely to do, as an organiser of labour unions'.[34] The local authorities were also regarded as a promising field for the development of working-class power independent of and sometimes in opposition to the capitalist state.

A year or two before the creation of the L.C.C., Hyndman had put forward a plan for rationalising the government of London and giving the new corporation power not only to provide public works for the unemployed and a network of social

[33] *Capital* (1889 edn.), p. 282.
[34] James Leatham, *A Socialist View of the New Trade Unionism* (1893).

services but also to 'carry on certain productive business' by employing direct labour,[35] and in a subsequent pamphlet he pointed with pride to the achievement of socialist representatives on the Paris Municipal Council.[36] The S.D.F. view was put more comprehensively by William Morris and Belfort Bax in 1893 when they said that the road to socialism was via the eight-hour day, a legal minimum wage and the price control of necessities, 'since otherwise, prices would rise in some sort of proportion to the higher wages *enforced by the new legislation*'. Municipal enterprise was praised as a way of decentralising control to offset the current trend towards bureaucracy, as undesirable in a socialist as in a capitalist society. The only substantial reference to trade unionism was a vague statement about the desirability of unions transcending national limitations by forming international associations of miners, masons, cotton operatives, etc.[37] Ten years later the same view was being expressed more lucidly by Theodore Rothstein, who listed the advantages of municipal enterprise as being (1) a countervailing force against monopoly, (2) a source of revenue from municipally owned undertakings available for public use, (3) a practical demonstration of the efficacy of public ownership and (4) a training ground to prepare socialists for a take-over on a wider scale. With all their admitted limitations, he concluded, the local authorities could be used as a source of 'democratic and non-capitalist' power against the State.[38]

Given this general outlook, it is easy to see why the S.D.F. was able to throw itself so vigorously and, up to a point, successfully into the movement of the unemployed which began in London at the beginning of 1886 and culminated in 'Bloody Sunday' on 13 November 1887. This was the biggest mass movement in which the S.D.F. was ever involved and it earned for it a reputation which, had it been consolidated, might well have established the party as a considerable force in a labour movement which was approaching its turning-point. Police repression at first increased support for the S.D.F. By the end of

[35] H. M. Hyndman, *A Commune for London* (n.d.).
[36] H. M. Hyndman, *General Booth Book Refuted* (1890).
[37] William Morris and E. Belfort Bax, *Socialism, Its Growth and Outcome* (1893), pp. 277–83.
[38] *Social Democrat*, April 1903.

the year, indeed, even Engels, highly critical as he was of the S.D.F. in general and of Hyndman in particular, wrote somewhat reluctantly that the Federation was 'beginning to become a power'.[39] The savage attack by the police in Trafalgar Square on 13 November 1887, brought the movement to a climax. Many, like Bernard Shaw, were impressed by the ease with which a disciplined force of police could dispose of 'a band of heroes outnumbering their foes at 1,000 to 1.'[40] Some drew the conclusion that Fabian gradualism was a better bet than revolution. Political agitation, it seemed, was no match for police truncheons. But what if, alongside political activity, the workers began to use their economic strength in industrial action? The question was not academic, for in May 1888 – six months after 'Bloody Sunday' – the match girls at Bryant & May's were led by socialists in a successful strike. In July 1889 the London gasworkers, led by an S.D.F. member, Will Thorne, won a big reduction in hours and organised themselves into the Gasworkers' and General Labourers' Union with Thorne as General Secretary. In August the great dock strike broke out and was brought early in the following month to a triumphant conclusion. The S.D.F. gave tepid and equivocal support, while Burns and Mann, who had both quarrelled with Hyndman, threw themselves into the leadership of the struggle.

Engels's account of the position in a letter to Laura Lafargue revealed an attitude completely at variance with that of Hyndman and a majority of the S.D.F. Engels did not want to tell the dockers that the fight for sixpence an hour was almost a waste of time which would be better spent campaigning for socialism. For him the decisive thing was 'That these poor famished broken down creatures who bodily fight amongst each other every morning for admission to work, should organise for resistance, turn out 40–50,000 strong, draw after them into the strike all and every trade of the East End in any way connected with shipping, hold out above a week, and terrify the wealthy and powerful dock companies,' a development he was proud to have lived to see, adding that 'all this strike is worked and led by *our* people, by Burns and Mann, and the Hyndmanites are nowhere

[39] Engels to Laura Lafargue, 24 November 1886; *Engels–Lafargue Correspondence* (1959 edn.), i, p. 396.
[40] Shaw to William Morris, quoted in Thompson, *op. cit.* p. 585.

in it'.[41] It was an attitude in harmony with that which he and Marx had expressed in the *Communist Manifesto* and applied consistently throughout their lives, an attitude of support for what they regarded as every genuine workers' movement, whatever they considered to be its limitations. This was what Marx's position in the days of the First International had been, and this was what Engels advised his followers to do when the Independent Labour Party was founded in 1893, in contrast, once again, to the 'benevolent neutrality' advocated by Hyndman.[42] It was this attitude which enabled Marx and Engels to remain alert to new developments which no amount of theory would enable them to predict. Commenting on the American scene in a letter to Mrs. Wischnewetzky of 28 December 1886, Engels had said that 'A million or two of workingmen's votes next November for a *bona fide* workingmen's party is worth infinitely more at present than a hundred thousand votes for a doctrinally perfect platform.' Hyndman would have put it just the other way round.

VI

The S.D.F. thus became sealed off from the opportunities of wider development which opened up at the end of the 1880s and the early 1890s. It was not opposed, however, to unity with other socialist organisations, and a few months before the foundation of the I.L.P. had published a joint *Manifesto of English Socialists* together with the Fabian Society and William Morris's Hammersmith Socialist Society. The *Manifesto*, printed by the S.D.F.'s Twentieth Century Press, included a demand for 'Municipalisation' and for a number of the familiar palliatives 'not . . . as solutions of social wrongs, but as tending to lessen the evils of the existing *regime*', so that the workers, 'having more leisure and less anxiety', could put more energy into the fight for fundamental change.

There were no further developments towards unity between the S.D.F. and the Fabians, but in 1898 James Macdonald, a member of the S.D.F. and Secretary of the London Trades Council, initiated talks intended to lead to a merger with the I.L.P. The S.D.F. had nothing against the proposal, and it was

[41] *Engels–Lafargue Correspondence*, ii, p. 304: Letter of 27 August 1889.
[42] Tsuzuki, *op. cit.* p. 95.

the I.L.P. which finally withdrew from negotiations.[43] However, in the following year, on I.L.P. initiative, the Plymouth Conference of the T.U.C. carried the historic resolution which led to the establishment of the Labour Party, and both the I.L.P. and the S.D.F., together with the Fabians, were represented on the Labour Representation Committee set up in 1900.

The actual events which led to the withdrawal of the S.D.F. in the following year were of no great moment in themselves, but Harry Quelch, who had been largely instrumental in bringing it about, defended the decision[44] as the inevitable result of trade-union affiliation. The I.L.P. presented no problem, he explained, since the S.D.F. was in favour of unity with other socialist parties. But it would be wrong for the S.D.F. to establish a permanent alliance with such non-socialist bodies as trade unions. The S.D.F. should co-operate with unions but not enter into a formal relationship with them, at least until they accepted socialism. Later in the same year the Blackburn conference of the S.D.F. endorsed this standpoint while trying to make it clear that this implied no hostility towards the unions. On the contrary, 'it was for us to conciliate and not to antagonise the organised workers' and since trade unions were showing signs of becoming more political, socialists should work inside them 'to turn this political action in a socialist direction'. In this the S.D.F. was only carrying further the policy which had weakened its influence in London local government, when it broke off negotiations with the I.L.P. and the London Trades Council for a joint campaign in the L.C.C. elections. At a time when Labour was starting to establish itself as a force in local government, winning control of West Ham in 1898, the S.D.F., by refusing to support trade-union candidates, left the field clear for the I.L.P.[45] By the early 1900s some twenty members of the S.D.F. had won seats on the local authorities, but the party made little headway.

Nevertheless, many S.D.F. members worked actively in their unions. They were particularly prominent on the Aberdeen

[43] I.L.P. *Conference Report* (1898), pp. 5–6 and 25–8; S.D.F. *Conference Report* (1898), pp. 11–15; H. W. Lee and E. Archbold, *Social-Democracy in Britain* (1935), p. 159.
[44] *Social Democrat*, May 1902.
[45] [George Tate] *London Trades Council, 1860–1950. A History* (1950), p. 83.

Trades Council and also on the London Trades Council, securing a majority on the latter's Executive in 1891. In Lancashire, where the party was relatively strong, it had influence in the Nelson Weavers' Association from the early 1890s, and one of its members became Vice-President of the Burnley Weavers' Association in 1895.[46] But in the mind of the trade union members who belonged to the S.D.F. there was generally a clear division of labour between party and union. The Hackney and Kingsland (Dalston) Branch had members who were active in the tramway workers', bookbinders' and glassblowers' unions, but it never seems to have considered giving support to the local union branches in their efforts to get better wages or shorter hours. The S.D.F. branch campaigned locally for such 'palliatives' as public works for the unemployed, free meals for school children, secular education (which again became topical with the 1902 Education Act) and the eight-hour day. On one occasion, when they did protest against sweated labour in the post and telegraph services, they characteristically added a demand for *legislation* to secure a weekly minimum wage of thirty shillings.[47]

The peculiar position the S.D.F. took up in relation to trade unions was a disaster in more ways than one. It restricted the possibilities of growth in the trade-union field directly and in the Labour Party by extension. It was disastrous even in the sphere of Marxist propaganda and education which the S.D.F. made particularly its own. The greatest upsurge of Marxist education among the working classes came when the revolt of Ruskin students established the Plebs League in 1908 and the Central Labour College in 1909. Although a few of the Ruskin students were members of the S.D.F. (most of the remainder being I.L.P.ers and Clarionites, with one member of the Socialist Labour Party)[48] there seem to have been no further links between the Labour College and the S.D.F. and W. W. Craik's history of the Central Labour College does not even mention the Federation after the Ruskin strike of 1909. A more alert and flexible organisation than the S.D.F. would have made strenuous attempts to make contact with and offer service to workers who

[46] Eichmannis, *op. cit.* p. 104.
[47] Andrew Rothstein, *Our History. An S.D.F. Branch, 1903–1906* (History group of the Communist Party of Great Britain).
[48] W. W. Craik, *The Central Labour College, 1909–29* (1964), p. 52.

were not only receptive to but stridently demanding Marxist education. But the Central Labour College depended mainly on the support of trade-union branches and, at a national level, on the South Wales Miners' Federation and the National Union of Railwaymen. In fact, both the Central Labour College and the syndicalist movement of the period grew from the same rich soil – soil in which the S.D.F. never managed to take root.

The change of name from Social Democratic Federation to Social Democratic Party in 1909 signified little, but its development into the British Socialist Party in 1911 marked the start of a new phase which ended with the formation of the Communist Party of Great Britain in 1920. From 1911 onwards the pressure of syndicalism and industrial unionism became significant and party attitudes began to change. At this point the S.D.F., which had existed remarkably unchanged, not to say suspiciously unchanged, for over a quarter of a century, began half-consciously to adjust itself to new pressures.

VII

What had been achieved during that quarter of a century was the establishment in England of a Marxist presence which, if it made little progress, at least showed no sign of dying. Its membership was overwhelmingly working-class and 'like the Owenites and the Secularists, who were their ancestors, the men in the S.D.F. tradition wanted to read, study and discuss, and to work out a general theory of the workers' lot and the world in general by systematic thought'.[49]

This essay has been concerned with the nature of that theory in its domestic aspect (in relation to problems of capitalism and of labour unity), where it exerted a crucial influence on the tactics and destiny of the S.D.F. Yet as a self-conscious part of the world-wide socialist movement and an affiliated section of the Second International the S.D.F. was, of course, concerned with international and colonial affairs, and Theodore Rothstein published an outstanding contribution on British colonialism, especially in its economic and financial aspects.[50] And in domestic

[49] Hobsbawm, *op. cit.* p. 235.
[50] Theodore Rothstein, *Egypt's Ruin* (1910) with introduction by Wilfred Scawen Blunt.

politics S.D.F. theory was not as rigid or sectarian as has sometimes been claimed. Just as the Socialist League broke away in
1885 in part because the S.D.F. believed in fighting for reforms
within the framework of capitalism, so the Socialist Labour
Party broke away in 1903 because it found the S.D.F. too willing
to co-operate with the Labour Party and insufficiently critical of
its trade-union leadership. The fact that the S.D.F. members
fought locally for the unemployed and for school meals and that
they *did* join unions and participate in strikes (with whatever
theoretical reservations) meant that the party never became just
another sect whose members, cut off from the outside world,
spent all their time talking to each other.

But if the S.D.F. was not *just* a sect it was *partly* a sect and
the reason for that is linked closely with its disbelief in the possibility of effective industrial action. This disbelief stemmed from
a too literal, restricted and inflexible interpretation of Marxist
economics which led the party to entertain illusions about the
inevitable and more or less automatic collapse of capitalism. A
member of the Battersea branch of the S.D.F., who later became
secretary of the Fabian Society, explained in retrospect how
he had 'learned as a result of my study of the Marxian system
that man is entirely a creature of external circumstances; that
social and economic evolution takes its own course regardless of
man's will or desire, and that he cannot broadly speaking affect
it in any way, at least consciously' but that the contradictions in
the system would continue to deepen until 'the great mass of
disinherited workers ... would discover the power of numbers,
rise up in their myriads, violently expropriate the handful of
expropriators, and establish the Socialist Commonwealth'.[51] Another S.D.F. member, John E. Ellam, who later turned to syndicalism, expressed a common enough view at the time when he
wrote of the lack of effective demand under capitalism, aggravated by technological unemployment giving rise to a situation
in which socialists might confidently 'wait for the capitalist system to break down under its own weight'.[52] There were, indeed,
enough passages from Marx which, if quoted out of context and
without the qualifications he was always careful to insert, could
be taken to imply a theory of automatic collapse. Simplified

[51] W. Stephen Sanders, *Early Socialist Days* (1927), p. 29.
[52] *Social Democrat*, April 1899.

reliance upon the theory would, in itself, help to explain both the staying power and the stagnation of the S.D.F., since a belief in inevitable victory can keep men going through years of discouragement. On the other hand, no revolutionary party can thrive by simply preaching revolution and waiting for it to break out.

While the theory of 'Marxism' as applied by the S.D.F. was in many ways close to that of European Socialist parties in the Second International, particularly the German, in three respects the position of the Europeans was more favourable. First, 'Marxism' only appeared in Britain when the trade-union movement was firmly established : in Europe trade unionism was often created by Marxist parties. That this contrast might put British Marxists at a disadvantage and even require them to develop their own original tactics was sometimes dimly, but only dimly, perceived, and no new tactics emerged.[53] Indeed when new tactics did emerge outside the S.D.F., they took the over-compensatory form of syndicalism. Second, the S.D.F. came a very poor second to the Fabians in the fight to establish a following among the intellectuals, whereas in Germany by 1890 Marxism had no serious rival. Third, many of the key works by Marx and Engels only became available in English in the late 1890s or not until the twentieth century. *Value, Price and Profit* appeared only in 1898 and then attracted little attention. Many oher works, including *Class Struggles in France* and *The Eighteenth Brumaire of Louis Bonaparte* had no English edition until after 1900. Had they been available earlier, as they were in Europe, they would have presented the English reader with models of political analysis which were rich, complex and multi-faceted and which would have helped to offset the dogmatic lifelessness of so much English Marxist writing.

Had the Marxism of the S.D.F. been more open to novelty and change, had it kept some of the spirit of *Critique* discussed at the beginning of this essay, had it, in short, been less didactic and more dialectical, the S.D.F. might have been a more effective force within a different political atmosphere.

[53] See reply by Harry Quelch to Theodore Rothstein in a discussion on unions and strikes, *Social Democrat*, July 1900.

4

J. E. WILLIAMS

THE LEEDS CORPORATION STRIKE IN 1913

A GREAT deal of attention has very properly been focused on the lock-out of the Leeds gasworkers in 1890 as a landmark in the development of the 'new unionism'.[1] The Leeds municipal strike of 1913, with the gasworkers again as its spearhead, was another local dispute which assumed national importance. It was, in a sense, the logical outcome of the events of 1890, but developments both in the labour movement and in society at large had been rapid since 1890 with the result that the dispute of 1913 posed new problems, more familiar to the trade unionist of today than those which faced the gasworkers in 1890.

In 1890 the Leeds gasworkers were fighting to establish an effective union. By 1913 they were well organised. The Leeds branch of the Gasworkers' and General Labourers' Union had about 3000 members employed by the Corporation, of whom just over a third were gasworkers.[2] Moreover, the growth of municipal enterprise throughout the country had rapidly created a situation in which workers employed by local authorities were beginning to think of themselves as a group with common interests. In Leeds the first step towards the 1913 dispute was taken by forming a Federal Council of Municipal Employees to put forward a demand for increased wages.[3] The Council, with eight affiliated unions, was initiated by the Tramway and Vehicle

[1] E. P. Thompson, 'Homage to Tom Maguire', in Essays in Labour History, ed. Asa Briggs and John Saville (1960), p. 299; H. Pelling, A History of British Trade Unionism (1963), p. 97; E. J. Hobsbawm, Labouring Men (1964), p. 169; H. A. Clegg, A. Fox and A. F. Thompson, A History of British Trade Unions Since 1889, (Oxford, 1964), pp. 69–70.

[2] Leeds Corporation, Report of Special Committee on the Strike of Municipal Workmen, 11 December 1913, to 13 January 1914 (Henceforward cited as Report), p. 10.

[3] Ibid., p. 8.

Workers' Union, which defected in the early stages of the strike, leaving the Gasworkers' and General Labourers' Union in control.[4]

Another important change concerned the attitude and composition of the Leeds Trades Council. In 1890 the new unions still remained outside the Trades Council, whose annual report for that year did not even mention the gasworkers' dispute.[5] In 1913 the strikers had the full support of the Trades Council,[6] and its president, Arthur Gill, of the Street Masons' and Paviors' Society, was also president of the Federal Council. When the strike was over, he bitterly attacked the Tramway and Vehicle Workers' Union for its defection at a meeting of the Trades Council: 'These tramway men had acted as traitors and had betrayed them. . . . As far as the Federal Council was concerned it was "as dead as Queen Anne", and they would give due notice of its termination.'[7]

The dispute of 1913 was also different in its political context from that of 1890. The Liberal-dominated Leeds municipal council of 1890, for reasons of local politics, avoided total war, yet the experiences of that year led many skilled unionists in Leeds to turn away from Liberalism.[8] The rise of the I.L.P. and, later, the Labour Party made it increasingly difficult for the Liberals to present themselves as the champions of the working man. At the November elections in 1913, at which the wages question was the main issue, the Labour Party gained three seats and returned to the council Walt Wood, the local organiser of the Gasworkers' and General Labourers' Union. At the by-elections following on the aldermanic elections there was a further Labour gain.[9] Labour then had 17 representatives in the council, the Liberals 18 and the Conservatives 33. During the dispute there was close co-operation between the Labour group and the Trades Council,[10] but the Conservatives had the full support of the Liberals. The special committee of five appointed by the

[4] *Ibid.*, p. 125.

[5] Thompson, *loc. cit.* p. 297.

[6] Minutes of the Leeds Trades and Labour Council, 13 December 1913.

[7] *Ibid.*, 25 February 1914; *Report*, p. 125.

[8] Thompson, *loc. cit.* p. 301.

[9] Arthur Greenwood, 'The Leeds Municipal Strike', *Economic Journal*, xxiv (1914), pp. 138–9.

[10] Minutes of the Leeds Trades and Labour Council, 13 December 1913.

council to deal with the strike consisted of three Conservatives and two Liberals, and was notable for its intransigence.

One of the issues in the dispute was the relationship between the wages of municipal workers and those of workers employed by private enterprise. Alderman C. H. Wilson (later Sir Charles Wilson), the Conservative leader in the council and chairman of the special committee, stated: 'It was sought to place Corporation workmen in a privileged position – privileged in the sense that they were to be paid higher wages than a similar class of men in other employ. The time had now arrived when they must say "No" to the men's demands for they might be certain of this – that if they gave way now there would be a further demand for a minimum 30s. a week before long.'[11] One member of the Leeds Chamber of Commerce said: 'It would be a good thing if the Corporation employed fewer men, and gave the traders of the city an opportunity to do more work.' Another asserted: 'Wherever Socialism arose it must be met by force, if reason did not prevail.'[12] According to Arthur Greenwood, it was alleged that the special committee was supported by 'powerful industrial interests'.[13]

The intransigence of the special committee was no doubt reinforced by the hardening of public opinion against increasing trade-union militancy. Although the cost of living was increasing more rapidly after 1909, every strike was branded as 'syndicalist' by the anti-labour newspapers. 'The hotheads amongst the Corporation employees appear to have been permeated with Syndicalist ideas, and to have been very anxious to put their wild, anarchical theories to the test,' stated the *Yorkshire Post*.[14] In October 1913, even before the strike had started, W. W. Macpherson had written to the Press urging the formation of a Citizen's League of Law and Order such as existed in Liverpool, where 1600 men were said to be enrolled 'for the purpose of acting in emergencies', and in the early days of the dispute he took active steps to form a Citizens' League in Leeds.[15] The *Yorkshire Post* opened a fund for non-strikers which by the end of the strike, and with the help of contributors such as 'Practical

[11] *Yorkshire Post*, 13 December 1913.
[12] *Ibid*. 17 December 1913.
[13] Greenwood, *loc. cit.* p. 139.
[14] *Yorkshire Post*, 16 December 1913.
[15] *Ibid*. 15 October, 12 and 16 December 1913.

Sympathy', 'Live and Let Live' and 'Anti-Syndicalist No. 1', had reached £450.[16]

Just as the municipal workers were beginning to realise an identity of interest as a result of the growth of collectivism, so were their employers. The *Yorkshire Post* commented: 'It is well known that the trouble in Leeds is regarded in Labour circles as a sort of "test strike".... Notices of a somewhat similar character in Blackburn expire on Wednesday.'[17] A London correspondent reported: 'In official and administrative quarters in London there is the greatest admiration for the way in which the citizens of Leeds have risen to the occasion. It is recognised that they have not merely saved their own town from the designs of the most Syndicalist of trade unions, but have performed a real service to the whole country.'[18] Civic dignitaries such as Alderman Sir Joseph Rymer, a former Lord Mayor of York, publicly expressed their satisfaction with the policy of the Leeds Corporation, and Haldane, described by the *Yorkshire Factory Times* as 'that fat and highly placed Lord Chancellor', compared the situation in Leeds with that in South Africa. 'No person could threaten the State,' he said. 'The State must protect itself.'[19]

Yet another change which had occurred since 1890 and had relevance for the 1913 dispute was the establishment of a civic university in Leeds in 1904. While some of the more progressive members of the academic staff publicly supported the strikers, the Vice-Chancellor found himself in the position of justifying to an irate labour movement the use of undergraduate labour in the municipal gasworks and electricity stations. In the nineteenth century trade unionists and employers alike were accustomed to the intervention of churchmen, civic dignitaries, lawyers and politicians in industrial disputes, but the idea of academics and their students, partially financed from local rates and benefactions, taking sides in a strike was relatively new and proved to be highly controversial.

[16] *Ibid.* 15 December 1913, 8 and 12 January 1914.
[17] *Ibid.* 15 December 1913.
[18] *Ibid.* 19 December 1913.
[19] *Ibid.* 17 and 18 December 1913, 16 January 1914; *Yorkshire Factory Times*, 22 January 1914.

I

The origins of the dispute are to be found in a strike of 150 paviors' labourers in June 1913. They were immediately joined by 750 scavengers, 150 park employees and 150 permanent way workmen. According to the report of the special committee appointed to deal with the December dispute, the city council 'conceded in large measure the improved pay and conditions of labour demanded.'[20] Altogether some 867 workers received increases ranging from one shilling a week to two shillings and over.[21] Then, again according to the committee, the Federal Council formulated 'a general demand for an all-round advance of 2s. a week for each workman throughout the Corporation services, irrespective of ... advances which the City Council had previously granted'.[22] This statement, published weeks after the strike, was untrue. Walt Wood and others had pointed out during the dispute that the Federal Council was asking for a single increase of two shillings a week on the pre-June wage rates for every worker,[23] but D. B. Foster, a Labour councillor who took an active part in the strike, partially attributed its failure to the confusion surrounding the men's demand.[24] The unions based their claim on the increased cost of living and the fact that many men had not had wage increases for a considerable number of years.

At a meeting of the city council on 3 September 1913, Alderman C. H. Wilson, chairman of the Finance Committee and leader of the Conservative group, moved that consideration of the unions' claim should be deferred until after 9 November. 'In view of the facts,' stated the special committee, 'that during the year considerable concessions had been made in the way of advances of wages, amounting approximately to 1d. rate, and that for some years applications for increased pay had been made immediately before the November elections, the resolution was moved with the object of challenging the principle as to whether there should

[20] *Report*, p. 7.
[21] The summary tables given in the text of the report of the special committee do not agree with the more detailed statistics given in Appendix E. The figures given here are based on Appendix E.
[22] *Report*, p. 8.
[23] *Yorkshire Post*, 12 and 20 December 1913.
[24] *Ibid*. 19 January 1914.

be any advance of wages before the elections.'[25] After a prolonged debate the resolution was carried.

On Sunday, 21 September, there was a mass meeting of the Gasworkers' and General Labourers' Union at which it was decided to write to Wilson, as chairman of the consultative committee appointed by the council in 1912, asking him to arrange a meeting to discuss the wage claim. It was also decided that if satisfactory arrangements were not made the men should cease work not later than 15 October. These decisions were confirmed by a ballot on 30 September. Of the 3000 members of the Gasworkers' Union employed by the Corporation, 2023 voted in favour of a strike and 138 against.[26]

Meanwhile, on 26 September, there had been a meeting of the Federal Council at which it was decided to ask the city council to rescind its previous decision and 'to provide for a meeting being arranged between all parties to such application, thereby preventing any possible dislocation of the City's services.'[27] The Federal Council claimed to represent 'all sections of Corporation employees'. The total number of Corporation workmen was about 4500, and of the 1500 who were not organised by the Gasworkers' and General Labourers' Union the majority were members of the Tramway and Vehicle Workers' Union. The tramwaymen had a wage agreement with the Corporation which did not expire until 4 August 1914. However, they had joined the Federal Council in the hope that they would receive its support when the time came for them to negotiate a new agreement.[28] The remaining members of the Federal Council were craft unions. Although they represented only a small minority of Corporation workers, the unity of the skilled and unskilled workers gave additional strength to the Federal Council. Since many of the craftsmen, such as the paviors, had already received increases and the tramwaymen were working under an existing agreement, the struggle of 1913, started in the name of the Federal Council, was basically between the Gasworkers' and General Labourers' union and the Corporation.

At the September meeting of the city council Labour members

[25] *Report*, p. 8.
[26] *Yorkshire Post*, 1 October 1913.
[27] *Ibid*. 27 September 1913.
[28] *Ibid*. 15 December 1913.

had urged the abolition of the consultative committee and the setting up of a new committee to conduct a full inquiry into wages and hours and 'to make such recommendations to the Council as they may decide to be just and equitable at the earliest possible date'.[29] When the council met again on 8 October the Labour group returned to the attack, arguing that the matter had now become much more urgent as a result of the decision of a very large majority of the workmen to strike.[30] Nevertheless it was decided that the men's claims should be considered under the existing procedure after the municipal elections, and the pledge was given that 'any applications which may be agreed to shall be dated back to 1 October'.[31]

There was a further mass meeting of the men on Sunday, 12 October. Two days later, on the eve of the threatened strike, the Lord Mayor, A. W. Bain, and the Town Clerk, Sir Robert E. Fox, received a deputation and explained the meaning 'in its legal and general aspect' of the council's decision. Later in the day the Lord Mayor and members representing the city council met J. R. Clynes,[32] Will Thorne,[33] Walt Wood, three members of the local executive committee of the Gasworkers' Union and three members of the Federal Council. After this conference the Federal Council recommended that the men should 'proceed with their claims before the Committees after 10 November'.[34] At a subsequent mass meeting the strike was called off.

The newly elected city council, of which Walt Wood was now a member, duly appointed its committees on 10 November.

[29] *Report*, p. 9.
[30] *Ibid.* p. 11.
[31] *Ibid.* p. 12.
[32] J. R. Clynes P.C. (1869–1949): organiser, National Union of Gasworkers and General Labourers, 1891–6; Secretary for Lancashire district, 1896–1914; President, 1914–37 (the union becoming successively the National Union of General Workers and the National Union of General and Municipal Workers); Labour Party Executive Committee, 1904–39; M.P., 1906–31, 1935–45; Parliamentary Secretary to the Ministry of Food, 1917–18; Food Controller, 1918–19; Lord Privy Seal, 1924; Home Secretary, 1929–31.
[33] Will Thorne, P.C. (1857–1946): General Secretary, National Union of Gasworkers and General Labourers, later National Union of General Workers, later National Union of General and Municipal Workers, 1889–1934; Parliamentary Committee, later General Council, Trades Union Congress, 1894–1934; M.P., 1906–45.
[34] *Report*, p. 12.

Detailed information from a number of towns[35] had already been collected for comparative purposes, and the various committees immediately considered the applications received from the men. On 3 December the city council approved the recommendations of the committees, the increases to date back to 1 October 1913. The statistics given for these wage increases are not very meaningful since some of the workers who had received an advance before 1 October now received a second one. However the net effect of both operations was to give increases of two shillings and over to 1202 workers, from 1s 6d. to 1s 11d to 94, and from one shilling to 1s 5d to 1449. Of the 2984 involved, 239 received no increases.[36]

On 7 December a mass meeting of the men resolved that they were not satisfied with the concessions granted by the city council and gave three days' notice of a strike. They repeated the demand for an advance of two shillings a week for every municipal workman. On the following day Alderman Wilson had an interview with Will Thorne, the General Secretary of the Gasworkers' and General Labourers' Union, whose part in the 1890 lockout had earned him the approval of Engels.[37] Wilson offered to refer the dispute to the arbitration of 'any fair-minded person outside Leeds and more particularly, if the workmen so desired it, to Sir George Askwith as the sole arbitrator'.[38] The proposal was rejected by the union. According to the report of the special committee dated 9 March 1914, 'many workmen who went on strike were, and even at this day are still ignorant of the fact that arbitration was refused by their leaders without their having been consulted'.[39] This seems unlikely since Arthur Gill, at a public meeting in the Leeds Town Hall on 12 December, referred to the men's refusal to accept arbitration and commented

[35] Birmingham, Bolton, Bradford, Bristol, Leicester, Liverpool, Manchester, Salford, Sheffield and Stoke-on-Trent (City of Leeds, *Information as to the Rates of Pay, Hours of Labour and Holidays of Workpeople Employed by Leeds and other Corporations*, November 1913).
[36] *Report*, p. 14. The errors in the summary table have been corrected.
[37] Pelling, *op. cit.* p. 97.
[38] *Report*, p. 12. Sir George, later Baron, Askwith (1861–1942): Assistant Secretary of Railway Branch of Board of Trade, 1907–9; Controller-General, Commercial, Labour and Statistical Department of Board of Trade, 1909–11; Chief Industrial Commissioner, 1911–19.
[39] *Ibid.* p. 16.

boldly: 'We can be the arbitrators',[40] Arthur Greenwood writes:
'The employees rejected this eleventh-hour proposal, partly because they felt that matters had gone too far for appeal to an
external authority and partly because they felt that the suggestion
was prompted by fear, no proposal of the kind having been made
during the months the men's demands were before the council.'[41]

There were further last-minute negotiations on 10 December.
A letter from the Lord Mayor, E. A. Brotherton, proposing a
conference on the following day and urging a postponement of
the strike, was read to a crowded meeting in the Albert Hall at
10.15 p.m. The workers refused to call off the strike but replied: 'We are very sorry the chairmen of the respective committees have not thought it worth while to meet the representatives of the men, which might have averted a stoppage of work,
and we regret to say that the letter from the Lord Mayor came
to the Federal Council too late, but a deputation are still prepared to meet the chairmen of the committees and the representatives of the three parties in the Council at 2.30 tomorrow, as
per the Lord Mayor's letter of tonight.'[42] This proposal was
ignored.

I I

The strike began on Thursday, 11 December. With the exception of the tramways, all branches of municipal enterprise were
affected. It was estimated that some 3000 trade unionists were
on strike and that in various ways about 1000 other employees
of the Corporation were thrown idle. The strike committee of
eighteen members representing the different sections of the workmen made its headquarters in an office in Hunslet Road. From
there it got to work early in the morning, sending out pickets for
duty and advising them to keep strictly within the letter of the
law.[43]

On the following day, 12 December, the enginemen and other
workmen in the electricity stations for the tramways and street

[40] *Yorkshire Post*, 13 December 1913.

[41] Greenwood, *loc. cit.* p. 143. For a full discussion of the reasons for the
declining popularity of arbitration, see J. H. Porter, 'Industrial Conciliation and Arbitration, 1860–1914' (Ph.D thesis, Leeds, 1968).

[42] *Report*, p. 17; *Yorkshire Post*, 11 December 1913.

[43] *Ibid.* 12 December 1913.

lighting also ceased work. Meanwhile, the tramwaymen, who were bound by a wage agreement until 4 August 1914, were considering their part in the dispute. In the People's Hall, Albion Street, Councillor G. H. Pearson, the local secretary of the Tramway and Vehicle Workers' Union, and Councillor D. B. Foster addressed a crowded midnight meeting at which the result of a strike ballot was announced. Of the 1229 members entitled to vote, 955 were in favour of striking if non-union labour was brought into the power station and only 51 were against.[44] The cessation of work by the tramwaymen on Saturday, 13 December brought the number of strikers to an estimated total of 4292.[45]

The strike was now at its height. On the Corporation side, the chairman of the principal labour-employing committees and the heads of departments were struggling to maintain the municipal services. Clerks, supervisory staff and volunteer labour were being pressed into service to replace the strikers. According to one Corporation clerk, he and his colleagues were being 'coerced into working as blacklegs, under the threat of dismissal' by Alderman Wilson, who relied 'on some of the Tory and Masonic officials in the various offices for information concerning the clerks'.[46]

The men employed in the gasworks and the waterworks were subject to the provisions of the Conspiracy and Protection of Property Act, 1875,[47] which made breach of contract a criminal offence. Of about 600 men at the gasworks some 200 were required to give notice to cease work. The stokers, firemen and coal wheelers gave twenty-eight days' notice, and the enginemen and exhaustmen seven days' notice.[48] However, on the first day of the strike a foreman at the Meadow Lane gasworks sprayed water on to some coke, which was normally a labourer's job, and the whole of the men left the works.[49] On the following day the enginemen, firemen, boiler and retort men at the York Street and New Wortley gasworks also stopped work and the

[44] *Ibid.* 13 December 1913.
[45] *Report*, p. 18.
[46] *Yorkshire Post*, 13 December 1913.
[47] 38 and 39 Vict. ch. 86.
[48] *Yorkshire Post*, 11 December 1913.
[49] *Ibid.* 12 December 1913. Although these men were liable to prosecution the Corporation appears to have taken no action.

city's supply of gas was entirely dependent on such emergency arrangements as could be made by the Corporation. At the New Wortley works, the most important of the city's gas plants, a few non-strikers were assisted by clerks from the Education, Poor Rate, Water and Gas Offices who were paid 7s 6d a day and promised compensation for spoilt clothing. Food, sleeping accommodation and police protection were provided at the works to avoid clashes with the pickets.[50]

The waterworks were not seriously affected by the dispute. Of the 125 men employed, 85 had already received wage increases of two shillings or more a week. Only 33 workers, mainly turn-cock men and waste inspectors, broke their agreements, but they soon returned to work.[51]

Breach of contract by workers in the Electricity Department was not governed by the Conspiracy and Protection of Property Act,[52] and the whole of the enginemen, stokers and cleaners employed at the Corporation's electricity generating stations ceased work at the beginning of the strike despite their agreements to give notice.[53] However, the Whitehall Road plant, manned by volunteers, continued to operate and there was no serious shortage of electricity.[54]

The most serious problem for the Corporation in the early days of the strike was the inadequate supply of gas, despite the efforts of the volunteers. Thousands of Leeds workers were on short time because their factories depended on gas for illumination. The greatest inconvenience was felt in the clothing trade, where gas was used for heating the pressing irons. In some engineering works and boot and shoe factories, where gas engines provided the motive power, there was unemployment and short-time working. Cafés and restaurants were also affected. Gas lighting in homes, shops and offices was supplemented by oil lamps and candles. At night many of the streets were in darkness. There were many other minor inconveniences such as unswept streets and unemptied dustbins.[55]

[50] *Yorkshire Post*, 13 December 1913.
[51] *Report*, pp. 18 and 51.
[52] Section 4 of the Act was extended to persons employed in the supply of electricity by the Electricity (Supply) Act, 1919, 9 and 10 Geo. V, ch. 100.
[53] *Report*, p. 18.   [54] *Yorkshire Post*, 15 December 1913.
[55] *Ibid.* 12 and 13 December 1913.

When the tramway workers joined the strike on 13 December, only about 100 men reported for duty. With the help of clerks, inspectors, electricians and other grades, they maintained a skeleton service. The men were accommodated at the depot in Kirkstall Road to avoid clashes with the pickets, and the trams were protected by police who had been brought in at the beginning of the strike from Liverpool, Huddersfield, Bradford, Hull and Sheffield. There were a number of clashes in which constables were assaulted, strikers were arrested and tram windows were broken by stone-throwing. A more serious form of sabotage occurred in Hunslet Road, where the supply of current to the trams was cut off by tampering with a section box.[56]

The use of non-union labour was the main source of provocation to disorderly behaviour among the strikers. Three or four hundred strikers, led by C. A. Glyde, a well-known Bradford socialist, marched to the Gas Offices on Ludgate Hill where relief labour was being taken on for the New Wortley gasworks. The demonstrators were scattered by mounted police, who charged from both ends of the thoroughfare. Constables on foot used their batons to disperse the crowd and some of the strikers were arrested. The New Wortley gasworks were virtually in a state of siege, with food being brought in for workers and policemen guarding the premises. The Leeds Trades Council protested to the Home Secretary and the Chief Constable about 'the provocative attitude of the police'.[57]

III

No steps were taken during the first two days of the strike to bring the contending sides together other than a request on the second day by five Labour members (Councillors G. H. Pearson, G. Thaxton, L. Verity, D. B. Foster and W. Benton) for a special meeting of the city council to be held on Wednesday, 17 December, at which they promised to produce a scheme to bring about a settlement.[58] At the meeting, which lasted only five

[56] *Ibid.* 15 and 16 December 1913; *Report*, p. 56.
[57] Minutes of the Leeds Trades and Labour Council, 13 and 31 December 1913; *Yorkshire Post*, 16 December 1913.
[58] *Yorkshire Post*, 13 December 1913; *Report*, p. 19.

minutes, the Labour group was hopelessly outmanoeuvred. The Lord Mayor called upon Alderman C. H. Wilson to bring forward a Conservative proposal for the establishment of the special committee with full powers to deal with the strike. The members were to be two Conservative aldermen, F. M. Lupton and R. A. Smithson, and two Liberal aldermen, J. R. Ford and F. Kinder, with Wilson as chairman. Arthur Gill agreed with the Labour members that 'the procedure of the Lord Mayor was most unfair', but thought them 'slow in bringing forward their proposition'.[59]

The special committee went into session immediately after the council meeting and sat continuously from day to day throughout the strike. It discovered that there were 4434 men on strike and issued a statement instructing the chief officers of the various departments 'to receive up to 6.30 p.m. on Friday, the 19th December, 1913, applications for reinstatement from the employees who were engaged in their respective departments at the date of the strike, and who have not since returned to work'.[60]

Walt Wood described this ultimatum as 'the worst possible decision if it is hoped to bring about a peaceable settlement of the dispute'.[61] Its immediate effect, however, was to destroy the unity of the strikers. On Thursday, 18 December, a mass meeting of the tramwaymen decided to return to work if allowed to do so in a body and on the understanding that they would not be asked to do any work at the power stations. The Gasworkers' and General Labourers' Union, on the other hand, decided not to comply with the terms of the Corporation's ultimatum but reasserted its willingness 'to enter into conference with the Special Committee'.[62]

By 6.30 p.m. on Friday, 19 December, when the ultimatum expired, 2028 workers, mostly tramwaymen, had been reinstated, leaving 2965 men, mainly members of the Gasworkers' Union, still on strike. The special committee then gave an extension of time for those wishing to return to work until 10 a.m. on Monday, 22 December, 'after which time all applications will be con-

[59] Minutes of the Leeds Trades and Labour Council, 17 December 1913; *Yorkshire Post*, 18 December 1913.

[60] *Report*, p. 24.

[61] *Yorkshire Post*, 19 December 1913.

[62] *Ibid*.

sidered entirely on their merits, and quite apart from previous service'.[63]

There followed a period of nineteen days in which no further progress was made in settling the dispute because the special committee continued to refuse to negotiate in a normal manner. Not only had the strikers repeatedly requested a full conference but outsiders had also made strenuous efforts to bring the contending parties together. On 19 December, when the special committee was considering the results of its ultimatum, the meeting was interrupted by the arrival of a deputation consisting of the Vicar of Leeds (Dr. Bickersteth), the ex-Lord Mayor (A. W. Bain) and Charles Lupton. Later Bain stated in a letter to Owen Connellan, the Secretary of the Trades Council, that the deputation had 'every reason to believe that if the men themselves ask for an interview it would be granted'.[64]

On the following day, Saturday, 20 December, the special committee met the representatives of the men at the Great Northern Hotel. They were in the same room for less than an hour, and the remainder of the negotiations, which continued on Monday, 22 December, were conducted by the exchange of typewritten statements, the two sides sitting in separate rooms.[65] This peculiar procedure was subsequently justified by the special committee 'because of the serious misunderstandings and misrepresentations which invariably arise owing to written records of what had actually occurred not being in existence'.[66] Naturally, negotiations of this kind produced no useful results and were soon broken off. The special committee then issued a statement to the effect that 'the men may come back on individual application'.[67]

The denial of a free and full conference and the offer of individual reinstatement struck at the roots of collective bargaining, and the question of trade-union recognition became an additional issue in the dispute. At a mass meeting called to discuss the negotiations on Monday, 22 December, Will Thorne described the members of the special committee as 'five little Czars' and asserted that 'the fight was now for the trade unionist movement

[63] *Report*, p. 25.
[64] *Yorkshire Post*, 20 December 1913.
[65] Greenwood, *loc. cit.* p. 144; *Report*, pp. 24–5.
[66] *Report*, p. 24.
[67] *Report*, p. 28.

throughout the country'. He recalled the violence of the 1890 dispute in which he had taken part and ended his speech with the words: 'There is a lot of street sweeping ... going on every night. Turn out tonight, and do your duty like men, and not allow your wives and children to be victimised while these scally-wags are taking the bread out of their mouths. Do your duty and fight as men should fight, as Yorkshiremen fought in days gone by. You will have to use both hands and your feet on this occasion.'[68]

Provoked by Thorne's violent speech, the special committee alleged that the negotiations had been misrepresented to the men and resolved 'that all future representations should be made in writing only'.[69] Meanwhile, with Christmas close at hand, the men were drifting back to work. On Christmas Eve the special committee instructed the chief officers of the various departments 'to fill up as quickly as possible all vacancies in their staffs'. By Christmas Day about 300 men had made formal application for reinstatement at the New Wortley gasworks, new labour had also been recruited wherever possible, and only 1000 vacancies remained to be filled.[70]

On 29 December the National Executive Council of the Gas-workers' Union held a special meeting in Leeds and discussed the situation for four hours. Eventually it was agreed that the weekly strike payments should be increased from 12s. 6d. to 15s. and that an appeal for financial assistance should be sent to trade unionists throughout the country. J. R. Clynes, the union's President, was requested 'to intimate publicly our readiness to discuss immediately the points of difference with a view to an early settlement of the dispute'. The special committee's reply was merely that it was prepared to consider any points of difference which were stated in writing.[71]

The Federal Council was now facing defeat, and on 31 December offered to recommend a resumption of work on the basis of an advance of one shilling a week for those who had not already been given that amount, the proposal being subject to all men being reinstated and to concessions already made being adhered

[68] *Yorkshire Post*, 23 December 1913.
[69] *Report*, p. 24.
[70] *Ibid.* pp. 32–3.
[71] *Ibid.* p. 34; *Yorkshire Post*, 30 December 1913.

to.[72] The special committee replied that it was unable to accede to any of these requests. For men who were now reinstated such increases as had been granted on 3 December were to be paid from the time of reinstatement and not retrospectively to 1 October as had been the case for those who had responded to the Corporation's ultimatum.[73]

On 1 January J. Buckle, a Labour councillor, made an unsuccessful attempt to arrange an interview between Clynes and the special committee. Clynes himself then wrote to the committee proposing a conference. The committee refused on the ground that 'we have already replied at length to the points raised.... Having nothing further to add, we fail to see any advantage in a conference which we gather would not only be attended by you, but by others who have already attended before the Committee.' Clynes replied briefly: 'I regret the terms of your note of January 1st. Cases are numerous where no advantage can be seen from a conference till after the conference has taken place.'[74]

The special committee's refusal to accept the strikers' conditions for a resumption of work led Arthur Gill and Walt Wood, on behalf of the Federal Council, to send a lengthy letter to the committee expressing 'disgust and disappointment ... at the un-Englishlike methods of the special committee in dealing with its employees, which is a disgrace to all British justice and fair play'. The Federal Council objected strongly to the committee's ruling that such men as were now reinstated would not be paid retrospectively to 1 October if they were entitled to wage increases: 'The communication from the Special Committee has evidently been composed in the offices of the Free Labour Association, and breathes right through with the spirit which animates Mr. Murphy and his *confrères* in Dublin, and in [sic] behalf of the men we represent we now accept the challenge to call upon all members to resent this calculated insult to the organised workers of this City, which insult is a menace to British Trade Union liberty.' The letter ended by asserting that 'the Committee's action is an organised attempt to crush trades unionism in the City of Leeds' and calling for a plebiscite of the

---

[72] *Report*, p. 35; *Yorkshire Post*, 1 January 1914.
[73] *Report*, pp. 36–7.
[74] *Ibid.* pp. 37–8.

citizens 'so that the methods of Czarism adopted by the Committee may be submitted to the judgment of public opinion'.[75]

Further letters were exchanged between the special committee and the Federal Council, which again called for a conference. At this stage the Federal Council, with the support of Will Thorne, tried to extend the area of the strike. The attempt was unsuccssful, but violence and disorder began to increase. Strikers were imprisoned for assaulting or intimidating blacklegs. On 6 January some explosive was thrown at the door of the boiler-house in an attempt to wreck the Crown Point electricity station. On the following night a bomb was thrown at Harewood Barracks.[76]

Meanwhile Clynes had been active and had made it known to Alderman Kinder, a Liberal member of the special Committee, that he would 'personally like to meet' the committtee. Clynes, alone, proved to be more attractive to the committee than had been the case when he had proposed to head a deputation. The committee decided, 'in view of the known moderation of Mr. Clynes, to make this variation from their settled policy to negotiate in *writing* only, and to admit Mr. Clynes to an interview'.[77] Clynes met the special committee on four occasions, on 7, 8, 9 and 12 January. He began his negotiations by insisting on the three conditions which had been put forward by the Federal Council on 31 December. On all counts he was eventually obliged to capitulate. The special committee's only concession was that it would not further prejudice the chances of former workmen being restarted by engaging any more fresh men 'unless essential to the needs of a particular case'.[78]

Amidst shouts of 'Twister!' and 'White Flag!', Clynes reported the terms of the settlement to a mass meeting of the men at 9 a.m. on 13 January. By accepting these terms the meeting accepted defeat. The strike was officially ended, and Clynes lost no time in leaving Leeds by the 11 a.m. train. Among the small party bidding him farewell at the Great Northern Station were three members of the special committee, Aldermen Lupton, Ford and Kinder.[79]

Reinstatement, which raised the whole question of trade-union

[75] *Ibid.* pp. 39–41.
[76] *Ibid.* p. 43; *Yorkshire Post*, 5, 6, 7 and 8 January 1914.
[77] *Report*, p. 44.
[78] *Ibid.* p. 45.
[79] *Yorkshire Post*, 14 January 1914.

recognition and collective bargaining, had been the important issue in the final settlement. Clynes, on his own admission in a letter written to the special committee after his return to London, had stated the terms of the settlement to the strikers 'in some of the more generous language used by members of your Committee during our recent discussions'.[80] Clynes did not tell the mass meeting that the committee saw no hope of restarting about half of the 2000 strikers. In the event the committee did rather better than promised. By 3 February 1386 strikers had been reinstated since the settlement, leaving about 700 who were not reappointed.[81]

'There is no cock-crowing,' said Will Thorne. 'We haven't won a victory and we don't think the Corporation have.'[82] But Thorne's success as a strike leader in 1890 had not been matched by his performance in 1913–14. The reaction against trade unionism during the 1890s had left its mark.[83] In a municipal strike the odds against the men were even greater than usual, since the public were the employers and public opinion was therefore biased. The anti-labour newspapers were a powerful weapon against the strikers, and the economic issues became confused with political ideas. These factors, in turn, reinforced the obstinacy of the special committee, which on more than one occasion during its negotiations with Clynes reminded him that it could not reverse its previous public statements without loss of face. Strikes were now becoming increasingly sophisticated affairs in which members of universities became involved and in which the methods of 1890 advocated by Will Thorne were less likely to be successful.

IV

The intervention of the university, although not one of the most important factors in the dispute, was certainly one of its more controversial aspects. Requests for assistance came from some of the municipal departments on the second day of the strike. Students were informed of these requests and advised to

[80] *Report,* p. 46.
[81] *Ibid.* pp. 46–7; Greenwood, *loc. cit.* p. 139.
[82] *Yorkshire Post,* 14 January 1914.
[83] See John Saville, 'Trade Unions and Free Labour: The Background to the Taff Vale Decision', in *Essays in Labour History,* pp. 317–50.

consult their parents before reaching a decision. Eventually about 200 of them volunteered their services.[84] On 14 December a number of students began work at the New Wortley gasworks and by 18 December about 140 were employed at the Meadow Lane gasworks.[85] Others were employed at the electricity stations. Some senior members of the university also gave their services.[86] Like other non-union workers, the students were accommodated at their place of work.[87]

At this time the formation of students' political societies at Leeds was forbidden by both Senate and Union rules[88] and it is difficult, in such a 'non-political' atmosphere, to gauge the attitude of the students. The *Gryphon*, the student periodical, commented: 'We were sympathising with the workers, or with their employers, or with both; for the subject of the dispute had never been made clear, and in any case, clear or not, a University, if it means anything, means freedom of thought.'[89] It was not until after the strike that some of the students were helped to clarify their thoughts by a debate in the University Working Men's Club where it was pointed out 'that the action of "black-legging" is one of the very worst things a Trade Unionist can think of and that the volunteer workers did not realise the awful seriousness of the work they were doing'.[90] The 200 students who volunteered their services represented a substantial proportion of the 663 full-time students, of whom at least 130 were women and therefore ineligible.[91] At this time most of the university's students lived at home and one of them suggested that pressure to volunteer came from parents rather than from the university.[92]

Hostility to the university quickly mounted. The Trades Council decided to send a deputation to the Vice-Chancellor 'to

[84] *Gryphon*, xvii, No. 3 (1914), p. 35.
[85] *Yorkshire Post*, 15 and 19 December 1913.
[86] M. E. Sadler, 'Note on Mr Greenwood's Article on the Leeds Municipal Strike', *Economic Journal*, xxiv (1914), p. 147.
[87] For a full account of 'A Day in the Gas Works', see *Gryphon*, xvii, No. 3 (1914), pp 35–6.
[88] See a letter, 'Leeds Incident', by Mr William Pickles, *The Times*, 10 May 1968.
[89] *Gryphon*, xvii, No. 3 (1914), p. 35.
[90] *Ibid.* No. 4 (1914), p. 60.
[91] University of Leeds, *11th Annual Report, 1913–14–15*, p. 109.
[92] *Yorkshire Post*, 23 January 1914.

make representations to him regarding the blackleg labour of students'.[93] Waring, a student employed at the New Wortley gasworks, prematurely abandoned by his police escort, was savagely attacked at Holbeck station and sustained a fractured skull.[94] The decision of the University Senate to make special provision for students who were absent from terminal examinations[95] led to further charges that the university was 'encourging blacklegging'.[96]

On 19 December the Pro-Chancellor of the university, A. G. Lupton, brother of Alderman Lupton, and the Vice-Chancellor, Dr. M. E. Sadler (later Sir Michael Sadler), received a deputation from the Trades Council consisting of Owen Connellan, the Secretary, with R. M. Lancaster and J. Hills, members of the executive committee. Connellan asked whether the students had discussed the merits of the dispute before they volunteered their services and pointed out that the University was partially financed 'by the ratepayers of the city, of whom the workers were a part'. Lancaster argued that the situation was 'fraught with serious consequences to the further education of the working people.... The working man would have none of the education that had come to work out as that had been worked out there.'[97]

In a lengthy reply the Vice-Chancellor reiterated his already publicly expressed view that while the university had not acted officially, individual members had a right and indeed a duty, like other citizens, to ensure the maintenance of the public services. 'They recognised,' he said, 'that of the income of the University about one-third came from the rates, and they desired to act as trustees for the whole community which in part enabled them to do their work.' Sadler then went on to discuss the position of public employees in general and propounded a view similar in some respects to that of some present-day advocates of an incomes policy. He believed that 'every worker engaged in competitive industry had the moral right to strike' but this right did not extend to the employees of public monopolies. For them

---

[93] *Ibid.* 17 December 1913; Minutes of the Leeds Trades and Labour Council, 16 December 1913.
[94] *Yorkshire Post*, 19 December 1913.
[95] University of Leeds, Minutes of the Senate, 23 December 1913.
[96] *Yorkshire Post*, 1 January 1914.
[97] *Ibid.* 19 December 1913.

there was a great need 'for furnishing ... some right of easy appeal to a tribunal so constituted as to command general respect and armed with such powers of extensive inquiry and report as would enable it to review, and then bring before the public, whatever needs to be changed in the condition of employment'.[98]

The Leeds Trades Council remained unconvinced, as did other trades councils.[99] The Vice-Chancellor received many letters of protest from local labour organisations, and the matter was taken up nationally by the Parliamentary Committee of the T.U.C. In his reply to C. W. Bowerman, the secretary, Sadler used the arguments which he had presented to the Leeds Trades Council and concluded: 'We have done our utmost, privately and publicly, to promote a spirit of conciliation and mutual understanding, and to urge upon all concerned the importance of sympathetic inquiry into grievances felt in our public service.'[100]

Labour members of local authorities also protested.[101] J. Badlay, a former Leeds Labour alderman and a member of the University Court, pointed out that when in the past Alderman Wilson had tried to stop the city's grant to the university he had been strenuously opposed by the Labour representative on the Finance Committee.[102] Herbert Smith, the President of the Yorkshire Miners' Association, unsuccessfully urged the West Riding County Council, of which he was a member, to suspend all grants to universities 'until an agreement has been arrived at between the County Council and such universities that in any future trade dispute the authorities of the universities shall take no action on one side or the other'.[103]

The bitterest protest of all came from the Workers' Educational Association. Sadler, who had been associated with adult education since 1885 and a member of the Leeds branch of the W.E.A. since 1905, had been chosen as its President in the autumn of 1911, soon after he became Vice-Chancellor.[104] In

[98] *Ibid.*; Sadler, *loc. cit.* p. 150.
[99] *Bradford Pioneer*, 13 February 1914; *Yorkshire Factory Times*, 8 January 1914; *Yorkshire Post*, 31 December 1913.
[100] University of Leeds, Minutes of the Council, 21 January 1914.
[101] *Yorkshire Post*, 3 and 9 January 1914.
[102] *Ibid.* 31 December 1913.
[103] *Ibid.* 13 January 1914; *Yorkshire Factory Times*, 22 January 1914.
[104] Lynda Grier, *Achievements in Education: The Work of Michael Ernest Sadler, 1885-1835* (1952) p. 4; J. F. C. Harrison, *Workers' Educa-*

February 1914 the branch, meeting under the chairmanship of
Dr. Moorman, condemned the attitude of its President during
the strike and demanded his resignation.[105]

Sadler was unrepentant on the issue of volunteer labour. He
said so publicly on several occasions, and on 17 December, in a
formal letter to the city council, described the actions of the
strikers as amounting to 'acts of brigandage'.[106] On the other
hand he was opposed to the intransigence shown by the city
council. In a letter to his son on the second day of the strike he
wrote: 'The trouble is partly due to the Lord Mayor's abrupt
Norman Warrior manner.'[107]

Although Sadler's actions were approved by a resolution of the
University Council,[108] there was some dissent even within the
university. Notable among the dissenters were the economists
Professor D. H. MacGregor, Henry (later Sir Henry) Clay and
Arthur Greenwood. On 26 December, in an attempt to break
the deadlock between the strikers and the special committee,
they published a letter urging nine reasons for a full conference[109] As W.E.A. tutors, they also played a leading part in
arranging an informal meeting between the Vice-Chancellor and
members of the Leeds branch to discuss the situation. A W.E.A.
student who was present wrote of Sadler: 'He took the whole
responsibility for what had happened. He is well paid for his
work, he is well supported by the master-class. His opinions
were endorsed by the Pro-Chancellor, whose brother has become
one of the five dictators of Leeds.'[110]

The intervention of MacGregor and his colleagues led to
further controversy. The *Yorkshire Post* expressed surprise and
disgust that 'there are Professors in a University in receipt of
public money from the ratepayers and from endowments provided by wealthy citizens who think it wrong that certain

*tion in Leeds: A History of the Leeds Branch of the Workers' Educational
Association* (Leeds 1957), p. 7.
[105] Harrison, *op. cit.* p. 8.
[106] Michael Sadleir, *Michael Ernest Sadler (Sir Michael Sadler, K.C.S.I.)
1861–1943: A Memoir by his Son* (1949), pp. 258–9.
[107] *Ibid.* p. 259.
[108] University of Leeds, Minutes of the Council, 21 January 1914.
[109] *Yorkshire Post*, 26 December 1913.
[110] *Bradford Pioneer*, 9 January 1914. A. G. Lupton, the Pro-Chancellor,
was the brother of Alderman F. M. Lupton, a member of the special
committee.

students in the University should come to the rescue of the city to whom they owe so much.... Judging by what is reported, Mr. MacGregor seems to have believed that Economics ought to be taught from the standpoint of the Trade Unions and Syndicalists, possibly of Mr. Sidney Webb and Mr. Henry George.'[111] Sadler, who was extremely jealous of the university's reputation, was now under attack from both sides.[112]

Lynda Grier, in her biography of Sadler, has underestimated the importance of this episode both for Sadler and for the university.[113] A. N. Shimmin took the view that the incident 'might easily have ruined Sadler's career in Leeds'.[114] Certainly the strain on the loyalty of outside organisations was greater and more lasting than Lynda Grier suggests. As late as September 1945 Sadler's nephew, John Harvey, wrote that 'his action then as V.C. still arouses comment in some quarters'.[115]

Sadler himself recognised that he had made matters difficult for the infant university. On 29 December 1913 he wrote: 'The Leeds–Bradford plan [for a joint civic university] is knocked on the head I fear.'[116] He consoled himself with the thought that he had struck a blow for academic freedom: 'I'm really quite pleased at having carried off this piece of academic booty from the stricken field – tho' the first use of it is apparently against myself.'[117] Shimmin's comment that 'it did not need a strike to establish that right: it was there all the time' is somewhat naïve. The price of university autonomy and academic freedom is eternal vigilance. Unfortunately for Sadler he was not in search of this particular 'piece of academic booty' when he intervened in the strike and would not have succeeded in carrying it off but for the action of MacGregor and his colleagues.

[111] *Yorkshire Post*, 27 December 1913.
[112] Sadleir, *op. cit.* pp. 162–3.
[113] Grier, *op. cit.* p. 178.
[114] A. N. Shimmin, *The University of Leeds: The First Half-Century* (1954), p. 40.
[115] Sadleir, *op. cit.* p. 263.
[116] *Ibid.* p. 262.
[117] *Ibid.* pp. 261–2.

V

As in many major industrial disputes, the political controversy surrounding the Leeds municipal strike tended to obscure the basic economic issues. The strikers argued, not unnaturally, that their wages were lower than those of municipal workers in other towns. The Corporation held the view that wage rates in Leeds compared favourably with those of other corporations and that the strikers were attempting to establish a precedent which would be detrimental not only to other corporations but also to private employers in Leeds and, ultimately, elsewhere.

Neither of these propositions was easy to substantiate or as simple as it appeared. There were about 280 different grades of worker employed in Leeds, some of which did not exist in other towns. Moreover, where the grades were comparable there were differences in hours of work and holidays. The true facts of the situation were further obscured by the publication, on 23 December 1913, of *The Corporation's Case*, which compared current rates in Leeds with average rates in ten other towns based on the November survey. This comparison showed that of the 2813 men affected, 2387 were receiving higher rates than the average in the ten towns, 135 were receiving the same and 109 were receiving less. It was also stated that 182 cases were not comparable.[118] The Corporation was thus comparing Leeds rates which had been increased as a result of the first phase of the dispute with rates which had been paid in other towns before the dispute began.

By 23 December, when *The Corporation's Case* was published, it was quite clear that the union had already met with considerable success and wished to do even better by securing for every worker the full advance of two shillings. If the strike had been successful, every wage rate paid by the Leeds Corporation would have been higher than the average in the other towns and in some cases considerably higher. The concessions dating from 1 October, which were those included in *The Corporation's Case*, had been gained merely by threatening to strike. The subsequent strike for the award of the full two shillings to every worker achieved neither wage increases nor complete recognition of the principle of collective bargaining.

[118] *Yorkshire Post*, 23 December 1913.

Indeed, some of the ground which had been gained was now lost as a result of the Corporation's decision not to reinstate 700 workers.

An analysis of wage rates paid by the Leeds Corporation before the dispute began shows that even then the Leeds rates were generally higher than the average in the other towns.[119] For the purpose of this comparison, instead of the weekly rates used by the corporation hourly rates have been used to eliminate the difficulties caused by differences in hours of work.[120] Because of the nature of the data this method cannot be applied to all of the 2813 cases reported by the Corporation but of the 2494 cases examined, hourly rates were higher in Leeds in 1937 cases, the same in 54 cases and lower in 503 cases. There were 210 cases which were not comparable.

It is clear from this analysis that the Leeds gasworkers saw themselves once again as the spearhead of their union as they had been in 1890.[121] But just as the social and political context of strikes had changed, so had the economic climate surrounding the gasworkers. As Dr. Hobsbawm has shown, the gas industry became increasingly capital-intensive in the period 1873–1914, partly as a result of greater labour militancy.[122] The Leeds Gas Department provides a further illustration of his thesis. Before the strike 947 experienced workmen were employed in actual gas making in the various works. Just before the strike was settled the same amount of gas was being made by 708 men, half of whom were volunteers and therefore not originally experienced gasworkers. The special committee commented: 'This clearly proves that the various gasworks have been over-manned in the past and that the system of "go easy" has been in operation.' The committee was advised that it was possible to introduce improved forms of gas plant 'which would return the whole capital expenditure in about four years'. The introduction of one vertical retort plant at Meadow Lane had enabled 12 men to produce 1·25 million cubic feet of gas daily while other processes still obtaining in the works required 60 men for the same

[119] I am indebted to Mr C. G. Bamford for assistance with this statistical work.

[120] No adjustment has been made for holidays, since it was found that they made no significant difference to the final result.

[121] Hobsbawm, *op. cit.* p. 169.

[122] *Ibid.* pp. 158–78.

output. The committee therefore recommended 'that the whole of the gas plant should, by the adoption of the most efficient equipment, be thoroughly modernised'.[123]

The committee made similar recommendations for other departments. It pointed out that an annual saving of £6000 could be made by installing an automatic lighting system for gas lamps at a cost of £19,000. Automatic controllers for electric arc lamps at a cost of £500 were estimated to bring about an anuual saving of £500. The Cleansing Department, 'with competent organisation, direction and supervision', could be efficiently carried on with 300 fewer men, giving an annual saving of £21,000. There was need for co-ordination between the Highways and Tramways Departments and between the Parks Department, where the demand for labour was seasonal, and other departments.[124]

The extent to which real wages were depressed in this period by the low level of home investment has been much discussed. Whatever may have been the case in industry, there is general agreement that overseas investment deprived the home market of funds for such bodies as local authorities. The Leeds Corporation workers, and particularly the gasworkers, were helping to remedy this situation. In at least one, though untypical, sector of the economy, the employers were being compelled by trade-union militancy to abandon their sluggish ways in favour of modernisation and reorganisation.

[123] *Report*, pp. 53–4.
[124] *Ibid.* pp. 52–5.

5

PHILIP S. BAGWELL

THE TRIPLE INDUSTRIAL ALLIANCE, 1913–1922*

THE period between the Boer War and the First World War in Great Britain was one of increasing industrial concentration, rising prices, a falling standard of living for a majority of the wage earners and an intensification of class conflict.

Consolidation in business management had reached a very advanced stage in the railway industry. A confidential report to the Cabinet, written in July 1913, contained the blunt statement that 'competition amongst railway companies is dead or dying' and that it was 'quite impossible to resuscitate it'.[1] Similar trends were observable in other forms of transport. In 1909 the establishment of the Port of London Authority, whose board was dominated by representatives of the ship owners, merchants, wharfingers and owners of river craft, carried a stage further the concentration in management begun in 1890 with the creation of the Shipping Federation. In road goods haulage a notable amalgamation took place in 1912 between Carter Paterson, the London Parcel Delivery Company, Beams Express and Pickfords. Although the British coal-mining industry was remarkable for the survival into the 1920s of a large number of small independent firms, the South Wales region provided an important exception before 1914. D. A. Thomas's Cambrian Combine by 1911 controlled an impressive network of collieries, ironworks and importing and brokerage agencies.[2]

* I should like to thank the staff at Transport House, the L.R.D., Unity House, the N.U.M. Headquarters and Congress House for help with access to records, and the members of postgraduate seminars at the Institute of Historical Research and the Polytechnic of Central London for comments on an earlier version of this essay.

[1] 'Enquiry into the railway companies of Great Britain', P.R.O. CAB 37/116, M/6, July 1913.

[2] G. R. Carter, *The Tendency towards Industrial Combination* (1913), p. 289.

The wage earner who lived through these changes was finding it increasingly difficult to make ends meet. A Board of Trade inquiry into the cost of living revealed that over the years 1905–12 food prices rose by 12·8 per cent while in five major trade groups the highest increase in wages was 5·5 per cent.[3]

During a period of rising profits and falling real wages it is scarcely surprising that the number of industrial disputes rose sharply. In 1913 the number of disputes was more than double the average of the preceding twenty years. In both 1912 and 1913 the number of working days lost in strikes was greater than in any previous year with the exception of 1893 and 1898.[4] A remarkable feature of these turbulent years was the nation-wide scale of some of the strikes. In railways the first national strike in the history of the industry took place in August 1911. The coal strike which began on 1 March in the following year was not only the first nation-wide dispute in that industry but also the greatest industrial conflict so far experienced in British history.

In an attempt to match the growing power of capital the trade unions sought to enhance their strength by federation and amalgamation. In September 1910 the leading unions in transport (other than railways) associated together for the first time in the National Transport Workers' Federation. In 1913 three of the five principal unions in the railway industry merged to form the National Union of Railwaymen. Although there were no structural changes of comparable importance in coal-miners' unions the authority of the Miners' Federation of Great Britain was enhanced through the part it played in securing the Eight Hour Act in 1908 and the introduction of district minima for miners' wages in 1912.

In the case of three leading industries the occurrence of a strike in any one of them immediately caused unemployment in the other two. No doubt it was true that a strike of miners, railwaymen or transport workers would, before long, bring about a closure of factories and plants in a wide range of industries through a breakdown in the source of power or failure to get

[3] *Railway Review*, 10 October 1913, quoting a Board of Trade inquiry into the cost of living.
[4] Memorandum on the conditions of labour and trade at the beginning of 1914, Board of Trade, P.R.O. CAB 37/118, No. 19, p. 11.

goods to the markets. But a closure of the pits brought an *immediate* reduction in the demand for rail, road and water transport. Likewise a transport strike directly affected employment in the mines since there were severe limits to the quantity of coal that could be stored at the pithead. When the railwaymen withdrew their labour in August 1911 the jobs of many thousands of miners were immediately threatened. On the occasion of the national coal strike in 1912, although the railway companies were not in dispute with their employees, the south Wales district organiser of the Amalgamated Society of Railway Servants reported that 'notices to terminate engagements had been given to practically all employees of the local railways'.[5] A week later the Middlesborough No. 2 branch of the same union reported 'many members laid off'.[6] All told, compensation payments to members affected by the coal strike cost the A.S.R.S. £94,000. In the same year the repercussions of transport strikes in Dublin and London cost the railwaymen's union a further £36,000.[7] More than a quarter of the £437,121 in the union's funds at the end of 1911 had been drained away a year later as a result of disputes in other industries.

In view of this uneconomic dissipation of union funds, it is not difficult to understand why demands were voiced for closer collaboration between the organisations serving the miners, railwaymen and transport workers. Hitherto the Miners' Federation has been credited with taking the initiative to remedy the situation. Its annual conference at Scarborough in October 1913 carried a resolution moved by the delegates from south Wales:

> That the executive of the Miners' Federation of Great Britain be requested to approach the executive committees of other big trade unions with a view to co-operative action in support of each other's demands.[8]

However, it would be quite misleading to suggest that the miners were alone in realising the need for co-operation. In the

[5] *Railway Review*, 8 March 1912.

[6] *Ibid.* 15 March 1912.

[7] Statement made by Thomas at a conference at No. 10 Downing Street, 22 March 1919, P.R.O. CAB 21/169, GT 7021. A.S.R.S. President's address to the A.G.M., 1912, *Railway Review*, 11 October 1912.

[8] M.F.G.B., *Annual Conference Report* (1913), Resolution 27.

course of 1911 and 1912 the executive of the A.S.R.S. was inundated with requests from branches seeking authority for sympathetic strike action in support of the transport workers and miners. A resolution passed by a mass meeting of Sheffield railwaymen, at the time of the national coal strike, was typical of many passed at numerous well-attended meetings throughout the country:

> That this meeting ... calls upon the joint E.Cs. of the railway unions and the transport workers to take up the fight for a living minimum wage for all workers in the event of the miners calling them to their aid.[9]

The A.S.R.S. was no less concerned than the M.F.G.B. to end the wastefulness of unco-ordinated industrial action. But at first it sought a different solution. Two years before the Scarborough conference of the miners, its annual general meeting at Carlisle resolved to appeal to the Parliamentary Committee of the T.U.C. to consider 'the many and varied circumstances in which railwaymen are involved in trade disputes' and to make recommendations for 'uniform policy and concerted action' with other trade groups.[10] The appeal met with no success. At the T.U.C. in 1912 a resolution on trade-union consolidation was whittled down into ineffectiveness, while in the following year the plan of the National Labourers' Union for an industrial committee to co-ordinate the work of the unions was defeated on a card vote. In view of the failure of their own plan, the railwaymen welcomed the letter from Frank Hodges (on behalf of the M.F.G.B. executive) suggesting closer co-operation between the miners, transport workers and railwaymen, and they readily agreed to a meeting of the three executives.[11]

The transport workers, though not so well organised as the other two groups, were as keenly aware of the drawback of unilateral action. While the campaign for a minimum wage for miners was still in its early stages, the first annual general council meeting of the National Transport Workers' Federation, in June 1911, agreed to a resolution moved by Will Thorne:

[9] *Railway Review*, 15 March 1912.
[10] A.S.R.S., A.G.M., 1911, p. 9, Resolution 20.
[11] N.U.R., E.C., March 1914, Resolution 75.

That it be an instruction to the general council to get in touch with the miners' federation with a view to giving whatever assistance they may consider necessary.[12]

Thus when a letter from the miners, similar to that sent to the railwaymen, was received by Robert Williams, the N.T.W.F. secretary, early in 1914, the proposals it contained for a meeting of the three executives were accepted 'very readily'.[13]

II

The three organisations whose executives met together for the first time on 23 April 1914 were of very unequal strength. The senior partner of the three, the M.F.G.B., possessed a membership of 870,000, which was double that of the combined membership of the other two organisations. Although the Federation was the most powerful of the three bodies, the district miners' associations still retained great influence. They had made it a Federation rule that before a national strike could be called a ballot of the membership would have to be held. Only when two-thirds of those voting approved was a strike permissible. The N.U.R., with 268,000 members at the end of 1913, was the only organisation of the three consciously formed on industrial unionist lines. Its rules permitted the executive to call a strike without the preliminary of a ballot vote although, when it was in session, the annual or special general meeting took over the powers of the executive. The weakest partner of the three, the N.T.W.F., was formed in 1910 as a loose alliance of twenty-six unions, of which the more important were Thorne's Gasworkers and General Labourers' Union, Ben Tillett's Dock, Wharf, Riverside and General Labourers' Union and Harry Gosling's Amalgamated Society of Watermen, Lightermen and Bargemen.[14] Its membership at the close of 1913 was no more than 163,000. At this time the General Council of the Federation had the power to call a strike of the members, but in 1919 the

[12] N.T.W.F., *Report of the First Annual General Council Meeting* (Liverpool, 1 June 1911).

[13] N.T.W.F. *Report of the Second Annual General Council Meeting* (London, 4–7 June 1912), p. 15.

[14] N.T.W.F. *Report of the Third Annual General Council Meeting* (Newport, Mon.), 5–6 *June* 1913, 'Constituent Bodies in the N.T.W.F.'

annual meeting was to decide that majority approval by ballot vote was needed before a strike could be called.

The conference of the three executives held on 23 April appointed a committee comprising the President and General Secretary of each of the three organisations. Bob Smillie and Hodges represented the miners; J. H. Thomas and Arthur Bellamy the N.U.R.; and Williams and Gosling the transport workers. Writing the draft of a constitution and consulting the constituent bodies kept the committee occupied for the rest of 1914 – with the First World War intervening – and for most of 1915, but on 9 December 1915 a delegate meeting of miners, railwaymen and transport workers held in the Westminster Palace Hotel formally approved the constitution, which was as follows:

1. That matters submitted to this joint body, and upon which action may be taken should be those of a national character or vitally affecting a principle, which in the opinion of the executive making the request, necessitates combined action.
2. The co-operation of the joint organisation shall not be called upon, nor expected, unless and until the matter in dispute has been considered by and received the endorsement of the national executive of the organisation primarily concerned, and each organisation instituting a movement which is likely to involve the other affiliated organisations shall, before any definite steps are taken, submit the whole matter to the joint body for consideration.
3. For the purpose of increasing the efficiency of the movement for combined action, periodical meetings of the full executives shall be held at least half yearly.
4. There shall be appointed a consultative committee of six, composed of two members chosen from each of the three bodies, whose duty it shall be to meet from time to time, and who shall be empowered at any time to call a conference of the executives of the three bodies if, in their opinion, such a conference be necessary. That a meeting be called on application made by any one of the three bodies.
5. With a view to meeting all management expenses incurred each affiliated body shall contribute a sum of 10/- per

   1000 members per annum, or such sum as may be decided upon from time to time.

6. Simultaneously with these arrangements for united action between the three organisations in question, every effort shall proceed among the three sections to create effective and complete control of their respective bodies.

7. Complete autonomy shall be reserved to anyone of the three bodies affiliated to take action on their own behalf.

8. Joint action can only be taken when the question at issue has been before the members of the three organisations and decided upon by such methods as the constitution of each organisation provides. A conference shall then be called without delay to consider and decide questions of taking action.

9. No obligation shall devolve upon any one of the three bodies to take action unless the foregoing conditions have been complied with.[15]

The wording of the constitution suggests that its framers were more concerned to maintain freedom of action for each union than they were to establish an instrument for the conquest of industrial power. Certainly clause 7, granting complete autonomy to each union to act in isolation from its partners, was to give J. H. Thomas the means to undermine the unity of the Alliance. Both in the committee and in the delegate conference in December 1915, however, the greatest controversy centred round the crucial clause 8. At first the miners' delegates proposed that their own rule of a ballot vote with a two-thirds majority needed for strike action should also apply to the other partners of the alliance. They urged that whenever strike action was contemplated a ballot should be conducted in each of the three organisation and that a two-thirds majority in at least two out of the three should be a precondition for a strike of the whole alliance. Such a rule would prevent them from being dragged into a strike when their own interests were not directly at stake. The railwaymen and transport workers successfully resisted this proposal. For the N.U.R. Bellamy said:

[15] 'Constitution of the Triple Industrial Alliance of Miners, Railwaymen and Transport Workers', N.T.W.F., *Report of the Sixth Annual General Council Meeting* (Glasgow, 8 June 1916), p. 28.

We have not got all the men working at a pit where we can have a pithead meeting ... we have stretches of country, hundreds of miles in extent, where we have very few men working: and it very often means if we take a ballot of our members it takes not days but weeks to get an accurate return.... You are insisting on something that even our own organisation does not insist upon with its executive.

His colleague 'Charley' Cramp, commented that the N.U.R. 'could get men to strike much easier than it could get them to vote'. The work situation of the unions was fundamentally different. The effectiveness therefore of a coal strike would increase each day it continued since a rush of volunteers to dig coal was highly improbable. On the railways, however, the strike 'would have to be used as quickly as possible to be effective' as engine driving was a favourite occupation for amateurs.[16] In 1915 the compromise in clause 8 – 'by such methods as the constitution of each organisation provides' – only papered over the cracks. The different rules of the Alliance partners remained to engender suspicion and create disunity after 1918.

For what purpose was the new instrument of the Alliance created? Were its leaders to be 'the general staff of labour' who directed strategic operations in the struggle to overthrow capitalism or were they to be the instruments of industrial harmony?

Only a small minority of the leaders ever considered that the purpose of the Alliance was to bring about revolutionary change. Williams, described by the labour correspondent of *The Times* as 'one of the wildest speakers in the labour movement',[17] was, for a time, one of them. In 1920 he wrote:

When the workers are negotiating with the employers or with the government which invariably represents the employers, they invariably exercise a greater influence when they speak in terms of industrial strength and power than when they speak politically.... Before the general strike the general election pales into insignificance.[18]

[16] Triple Industrial Alliance, *Minutes of Proceedings at a Conference of the M.F.G.B., N.U.R. and N.T.W.F. at Westminster Palace Hotel, London, Tuesday 9 December 1915.*

[17] *The Times*, 27 November 1919.

[18] Robert Williams, *The New Labour Outlook* (1921), pp. 139, 192.

Cramp of the N.U.R. also took a syndicalist view. He believed that 'the centre of gravity was passing from the House of Commons to the headquarters of the great unions'. This was a welcome change since the 'ultimate aim' of the Alliance was 'the control of industry'.[19] The man most distrustful of the Alliance was Cramp's colleague Thomas, a Member of Parliament, who held that the strike weapon should only be used as 'the last, and absolutely the last, resource when every other means had failed'.[20] It would only be necessary for the strike to be used once effectively. The fear of it would be 'sufficient for all time after'.[21]

The majority of the leaders of the Alliance would have accepted the strictly limited statement of aims given by Smillie:

> The predominant idea of the alliance is that each of these great fighting organisations, before embarking upon any big movement, either defensive or aggressive, should formulate its programme, submit it to the others, and that upon joint proposals joint action should then be taken.[22]

Certainly Thorne was of this opinion. In June 1914 he told the annual general council meeting of the N.T.W.F. that 'it should be an understanding that all agreements should terminate at the same time'. If this were done the number of spasmodic strikes would be reduced.[23] It was this plan which Hodges had in mind when he supported the proposal for the Alliance at the M.F.G.B. conference in 1913. In the past the struggles of the miners, railwaymen and transport workers had been left to 'hazard and chance'. What was needed was 'co-operative action in supporting each other's demands in a uniform movement'.[24] And yet, significantly, the constitution of the Alliance made no mention of the simultaneous termination of contracts.

The standpoint of Gosling, President of the N.T.W.F., was

[19] Presidential address to the A.G.M. of the N.U.R. reported in *Railway Review*, 20 June 1919.

[20] Triple Industrial Alliance, *Minutes of Proceedings at a Conference of the M.F.G.B., N.U.R. and N.T.W.F. at Westminster Palace Hotel, London, Tuesday 9 December 1915.*

[21] *Railway Review*, 9 January 1920.

[22] Labour Year Book (1915).

[23] N.T.W.F., *Fourth Annual General Council Meeting* (Hull, 11 June 1914), debate on the resolution welcoming the alliance.

[24] M.F.G.B., A.G.M., October 1913, *Report*, p. 139.

greatly influenced by his experience of the dock strike in London and on the Medway in 1912. Although the Federation had issued a strike call to affiliated unions, a number of them had decided that they would first sound the opinion of their members in a ballot. They still managed their members' funds and they were all too well aware that they were not in a position to sustain a prolonged strike. When Gosling commended the Alliance to the annual meeting of the Federation in June 1914 he expressed the hope that the unity of the organisation would be strengthened by association with the better organised miners and railwaymen:

> There was some suggestion that the transport workers ... were by no means as effectively organised as were the railwaymen and the miners. I feel that if we apply ourselves to the difficulties of organisation which immediately confront us, we shall be helped in no small degree by our association with two powerful organisations like those with whom we have been conferring.[25]

It is apparent from their different statements that the leaders were by no means of one mind about the purposes to be served by the Alliance.

III

Several meetings of the joint executives were held in the years 1916–18, but although these had some importance the war years provided no real test of the effectiveness of the Alliance because of the existence of an industrial truce from 25 August 1914. The three major tests of the value of the Alliance came within three years of the signature of the armistice. They were the national railway strike of September–October 1919, the miners' 'datum line' strike of October 1920 and the miners' lock-out which began on 31 March 1921. It is worthwhile examining each episode in some detail.

At the beginning of 1919 each constituent body of the Alliance proceeded to negotiate for its own programme without

[25] N.T.W.F., *Fourth Annual General Council Meeting* (Hull, 11 June 1914); H. Gosling, *Up and Down Stream* (1927), p. 172.

any serious attempt being made to dovetail the content or timing of the demands. It is true that a memorandum prepared by the joint executives was read by Thomas to the National Industrial Conference on 27 February, but this four point programme was expressed in very general terms.[26] There was no hint of a concerted plan to press the particular demands of each industrial group. Such practical steps were never taken.

Although the post-war demands of the miners attracted most press publicity, the demands of railway labour brought division of opinion to a head in the Cabinet as early as 30 January 1919. The Railway Clerks' Association claimed the right to represent stationmasters and other supervisory grades in negotiations with the Railway Executive Committee. Despite the assertion of Sir Albert Stanley, President of the Board of Trade, that conceding these demands would create an 'impossible situation' and an assurance by Sir Eric Geddes that a strike 'could be faced' on this issue, the majority of the Cabinet heeded words of caution from Bonar Law:

> Trade union organisation was the only thing between us and anarchy, and if trade union organisation was against us the position would be hopeless.[27]

The decision to recognise the R.C.A. which followed was the first of a number of major concessions to railway labour designed to wean the N.U.R. away from the Alliance. It was a remarkable victory for moderation and good sense which also helped to convince Thomas that much might be attained through unilateral negotiations with the Cabinet.

In the ensuing weeks of February and early March substantial progress was made in further negotiations between the Railway Executive Committee and the railway unions. By 19 March Sir Albert Stanley was won over to the policy of concessions. He advised that terms offered the railwaymen 'should be as generous as possible and should go a little further than in ordinary circumstances.... It was worthwhile paying something

---

[26] T.U.C. Library, HD 6664, typescript on the Triple Industrial Alliance (n.d.).

[27] P.R.O. CAB 23/9, War Cabinet 522, 30 January 1919, 4 February 1919.

to avoid the threatening catastrophe.' With prophetic insight, in the light of the railwaymen's lukewarm support for the miners in 1920 and 1921, Sir Robert Horne was convinvced that

> it was worth while to pay the extra cost of the railwaymen's demands in order to secure their support.... If the miners came out on strike the railwaymen might come out too, but with this difference, that if the above concessions were now granted, they would be striking without a grievance.[28]

Meanwhile at Unity House the executive of the N.U.R. was listing, in the form of a resolution, some of the impressive advances made during the recent negotiations. They included:

> the eight hour day, a guaranteed week, a guaranteed day, each day to stand by itself, extra remuneration for night duty, twelve hours rest with nine hours minimum, a week's holiday with one year's service, time and a quarter for overtime and time and a half for Sunday duty, the principle of standardisation and the principle of sharing in the control.[29]

On 20 August, when the principle of 'standardisation upwards' (i.e. that to the War wage should be added the best rate paid on any railway in the United Kingdom in July 1914) was applied to the footplate grades, it seemed that the settlement with the railwaymen was nearing completion.[30] But appearances proved deceptive.

What made the government's generosity fade after 20 August, when negotiations began for the standardisation of pay for other grades in the railway service? The answer lies in the evidence of disunity and lack of resolution in the Triple Alliance.

A delegate meeting of the Alliance held in Southport on 16 April 1919 demanded that the Parliamentary Committee of the T.U.C. should convene a special national conference of unions to consider how to compel the government to withdraw conscription, recall British troops from Russia, raise the blockade on Germany and release imprisoned conscientious objectors.

[28] P.R.O. CAB 23/9, War Cabinet 546, 19 March 1919, Minutes, *et seq.*
[29] N.U.R., E.C., 18 March 1919, Resolution 18.
[30] J. R. Raynes, *Engines and Men* (1921), p. 259.

The Parliamentary Committee secured an interview with Bonar Law, but refused to summon a conference of unions. At a further delegate conference of the Alliance on 23 July the ineptitude of the Parliamentary Committee was condemned and it was agreed that the three prepare to take industrial action to enforce their demands.[31] At their annual conference in Keswick the miners endorsed the four demands but decisively rejected an attempt to streamline their rules concerning strikes, for the benefit of the Alliance. A resolution moved by Warne from Northumberland authorising the committee of the Federation or a national conference of miners to call a strike without going through the procedure of a ballot was rejected by an overwhelming majority after W. Brace, M.P., had declared that the proposed change would be 'an abandonment of democracy'.[32] The conference of the National Transport Workers' Federation held in Swansea on 5 June changed the earlier rule empowering the executive to call a strike, to a requirement that each affiliated union should conduct a ballot before a Federation strike could be called. The executive of the N.U.R. retained its right to call members out on strike, but there was a mixed reaction in the branches to the proposal for industrial action in support of the political demands of the Alliance. Of 218 branches reporting resolutions to headquarters by 6 August, 100 endorsed the Alliance call for action, 68 demanded a ballot of the whole of the members, 44 objected to using industrial action for political purposes, four declined to take any action on the Alliance resolution and two others endorsed it provided English troops were withdrawn from Ireland.[33]

Information about these hesitations of the rank and file reached the Cabinet through the weekly reports of the Ministry of Labour on the labour situation and from the report of the Directorate of Intelligence on 'Revolutionary organisations of the United Kingdom'. This latter report, dated 14 August, noted 'the change of feeling which has undoubtedly taken place amongst the rank and file of the component unions'. There was a 'considerable aversion from direct action' in many districts.[34]

[31] T.U.C. Library, HD 664, typescript on the Triple Industrial Alliance.
[32] M.F.G.B., *Annual Conference Report* (Keswick, July 1919), p. 6.
[33] N.U.R., E.C., 6 August 1919, Report of General Secretary.
[34] Directorate of Intelligence, 'Report on Revolutionary Organisations in the United Kingdom' (14 August 1919), P.R.O. CAB 24/86.

The virtual collapse of the police strike by 7 August and the decision of the Lancashire and Cheshire Miners' Federation two days later to oppose direct action, helped to persuade the conference of the Triple Alliance, meeting on 12 August, to postpone the ballot on the question of a strike of the Alliance in support of the four political demands. The explanation given out was 'the changed attitude of the government towards the proposals of the triple alliance', yet this was only one of the reasons. An important influence on the delegates was the change of feeling that had taken place in the rank and file.[35]

The Geddes brothers and others in the Cabinet who had at first opposed concessions to the railway clerks earlier that year, now determined to resist the application of the principle of standardisation upwards to the other grades of railwaymen. They calculated that the footplatemen would not come to the aid of the N.U.R. and that support from the Triple Alliance was, to say the least, uncertain.

Why was it that on 26 September Thomas and the executive of the N.U.R. brought the union out on strike without first consulting the other members of the Triple Alliance? The reason that Thomas gave to the meeting of the Alliance convened on 27 November, some weeks after the strike had been called off, was that 'the railwaymen sought a settlement right up to the last moment, and when the breakdown came it was too late to utilise the machinery of the triple alliance in any effective manner'.[36] This cannot be accepted as a complete explanation. A railway strike to be effective needed to be a sudden, sharp blow. The miners had recently rejected proposals which would have made possible a prompter response to a call for help from the railwaymen; and because of their change of policy towards the ballot at their annual conference three months earlier the response of the transport workers was likely to be more dilatory. In any case Thomas had no relish whatever to extend the strike. When the Associated Society of Locomotive Engineers and Firemen threw in its lot with the N.U.R. on 26 September he commanded all the power that he needed for the

[35] Directorate of Intelligence, 'Survey of Revolutionary feeling during the year 1919', P.R.O. CAB 24/96, CP 462.
[36] N.T.W.F., *Tenth Annual General Council Meeting* (Southampton 3–4 June 1920).

limited purposes he had in view. When the N.U.R. executive met Lloyd George on 3 October in an endeavour to reach a settlement, Thomas assured the Premier that 'he had refused repeated offers of assistance from other trade unionists'. He wanted a settlement because he 'wished to prevent circumstances and consequences far worse'.[37]

The unilateral action of the railwaymen in September 1919 reduced the chances of a strike of the Triple Alliance at some future date. The seeds of distrust were sown among the leadership. Soon after the settlement of the railway strike, Robert Williams, speaking at Newport (Mon.), complained that the railwaymen had not used the machinery of the Alliance and that from 'a common courtesy standpoint' the Alliance should have been informed. This outburst led to an exchange of abusive letters between Thomas and Williams.[38]

Although Thomas had not even notified the other partners of the Alliance that a strike was imminent, despite instructions from his executive that he should do so, the strike was ended by the intervention of a mediation committee of fourteen leading trade unionists who helped to negotiate a settlement. This committee later reported to the Parliamentary Committee of the T.U.C. that a more permanent 'general staff of labour' should be established within the T.U.C. The ultimate outcome of these recommendations was the formation in 1921 of the General Council, which was assigned the task of 'co-ordinating industrial action'. After its foundation the authority of the Triple Alliance was weakened as the moderate trade-union leaders were able to argue that the Triple Alliance was now superfluous.

During the railway strike the government mobilised the services of 6000 servicemen and 2500 military lorries to maintain the distribution of essential supplies. Civilian volunteers who maintained a skeleton railway service were paid standard rate, plus overtime, plus a bonus of 50 per cent of total earnings. They had no complaints to make about their pay! A proposal of the Cabinet strike committee that the strikers should be prose-

[37] 'Shorthand notes of the proceedings of a conference between the Prime Minister and the Executive Committee of the N.U.R., 3 October 1919', P.R.O. CAB 27/61.
[38] Philip S. Bagwell, *The Railwaymen* (1963), p. 400.

cuted was vetoed by Lloyd George, and another proposal that strikers should be denied the use of telephone and telegraph services and forbidden to purchase petrol was rejected by the committee itself, as likely to cause a sympathetic strike of the post office workers 'which would not be worth the trouble it would undoubtedly cause'.[39] In calling a railway strike on 26 September Thomas did the government a good turn by providing the occasion for a dress rehearsal of organisation to meet the emergency of a Triple Alliance strike, should one occur in the future. It is not surprising that on 14 October 1919 the Cabinet decided to continue the strike committee in being, though under the different name of the Supply and Transport Committee.[40]

IV

Both on 20 March and 23 June 1919 a majority of the members of the Coal Industry Commission (the Sankey Commission) had reported in favour of some form of national ownership of the mines. The government declined to act on these recommendations, using the excuse of the lack of unanimity of the members of the Commission. Between September 1919 and March 1920 an intensive political campaign sponsored by the T.U.C. and the Miners' Federation in favour of nationalisation of the mines failed to have much impact on either the government or the public. On 12 February 1920 the Directorate of Intelligence reported to the Cabinet that, despite the distribution of ten million leaflets, the campaign had met with an apathetic response from the public.[41]

In view of the fact that after the failure of political action the miners might be expected to ask their partners in the Triple Alliance to support them in industrial action, it is significant that they were themselves divided on the question of a strike. The delegate conference of the Miners' Federation on 9 March 1920 approved by 524,999 votes to 344,000 'a general trade union strike', but included in the large minority were the block

[39] 'Review of the work of the strike committee' (27 September 1919), P.R.O. CAB 27/60.
[40] P.R.O. CAB 3/12, War Cabinet meeting 630 of 14 October 1919.
[41] Directorate of Intelligence, 'Report on revolutionary organisations in the United Kingdom' (12 February 1920), P.R.O. CAB 24/98.

votes of the Yorkshire and Durham miners as well as those from seven other smaller districts.

In the meantime a sharp rise in the cost of living in the early months of 1920 brought an understandable preoccupation with wage negotiations. The broader issues of public control tended to take a back seat. On 26 July the government rejected the miners' proposal for a reduction of 14s. 2d. a ton on the price of domestic coal combined with an increase in wages of two shillings a shift. The reaction of the special miners' conference on 12 August was to order a ballot of the full membership of the M.F.G.B. The result, declared on 31 August, showed 845,647 in favour of a strike and 238,865 against. The response of the Triple Alliance was lukewarm. Although the conference held later on 31 August promised the miners 'all possible support', the officers of the Transport Workers' Federation warned that they could only recommend a strike to the constituent unions, they could not order one. Thomas emphasised his union's willingness to open direct negotiations.[42]

The miners, in conference on 2 September, issued a call for a national coal strike to start on 25 September. But less than a fortnight later they abandoned their 'invisible' demand for a reduction in the price of household coal when the government published a statement revealing a sharp fall in the profits of the industry over recent weeks. The miners' change of tactics contributed to the hesitations of the N.U.R., which held a special general meeting on 23 September. By 28 votes to 27, with 2 neutral and 2 absent, the delegates turned down a resolution calling for a sympathetic strike of railwaymen to start at midnight on 25–26 September.[43] At the same time Gosling had to confess to a meeting of the Alliance that the transport workers were as yet undecided on what action to take.[44]

The miners, concluding that they could not count on the support of their Alliance partners, accepted Lloyd George's offer to reopen negotiations. On 30 September Smillie placed the Cabinet's final offer before the conference delegates. If the output of coal reached a rate of 242 million tons a year – the

[42] G. D. H. Cole, *Labour in the Coal Mining Industry* (1923), pp. 122–40.
[43] N.U.R., S.G.M., 23 September 1920, Resolution 6.
[44] Cole, *op. cit.* p. 151.

'datum line' – the miners would be given an increase of one shilling a shift. At a rate of 250 million tons the increase would be two shillings and at 260 millions three shillings. On 14 October another special conference of the miners learnt that the proposals had been rejected by 635,098 votes to 181,428. A national coal strike therefore began two days later. On 21 October the S.G.M. of the N.U.R., which barely a month before had rejected a proposal for a sympathetic strike, carried by 33 votes to 24, with 3 neutral, a proposal that a national railway strike in support of the miners should start on 24 October.[45]

This gesture proved sufficient to cause a reopening of negotiations between Lloyd George and the miners, who in the meantime asked the N.U.R. to postpone its sympathetic strike. On 28 October the miners' leaders decided to submit the government's offer – a rise of two shillings per shift to remain in force until the end of 1920 and the resumption of negotiations on a longer-term plan for wages settlement in the industry – to a ballot of the membership. As the result announced on 2 November – 338,045 for acceptance and 346,504 for rejection of the government's offer – did not show the necessary two-thirds majority required by the Federation's rules, it was decided to recommend a return to work the following day. The 'datum line' strike was over. The Triple Alliance had again revealed its ineffectiveness.

There were many reasons for the failure of the Alliance to function in the autumn of 1920. Hodges was no more anxious than Thomas had been the year before to accept outside advice on when to strike and on what issues the strike should be fought. At the full meeting of the Alliance on 23 September Thomas made it clear that if the railwaymen were expected to strike in sympathy with the miners they would require that control over policy should pass from the M.F.G.B. to the whole of the Alliance.[46] This was not a proposal that the miners found palatable. They were aware that in November 1919 Thomas had struck a bargain with Lloyd George. In return for abandoning nationalisation of the railways and workers' participation in management, the railway unions were promised equal representation with the companies on central and national wages

[45] N.U.R., S.G.M., 21 October 1920, Resolution 5.
[46] Cole, *op. cit.* p. 150.

boards which would settle wage rates and other conditions of service.[47] Thomas considered that as the railwaymen had found it necessary to compromise in order to gain important immediate concessions, the miners should have followed Smillie's advice and accepted Sir Robert Horne's proposals of 3 September to submit their wage claim to arbitration. However, the majority of the miners' leaders had not altogether abandoned plans for the public ownership of the mines, and on wages they felt they could do better by direct negotiations with the government without the interference of their Alliance partners.

Ernest Bevin felt considerable sympathy for Thomas's arguments. In December 1919 Williams had consulted the miners and railwaymen on the best means of advancing the dockers' claim for an increase in wages, and Smillie had replied that it was 'a very inopportune time' to call a strike as the miners were engaged in 'the fight of their lives'. It had required the exercise of all Bevin's persuasive powers to induce the seventy delegates attending the N.T.W.F. conference on 30 December to vote for a court of inquiry rather than an immediate stoppage of work.[48] In this case sending the dispute to the arbitrament of a court had paid dividends. At the end of March 1920 Lord Shaw's court had awarded the dockers the sixteen shillings a day minimum and forty-four-hour week that they had been demanding.[49] Since in their own case the transport unions had abandoned the strike in favour of arbitration, they were reluctant to strike in sympathy with the miners who had just rejected an offer of arbitration. In characteristically forthright language Bevin asked the miners' delegates at the conference of the Alliance on 23 September: 'Why, seeing we had to use considerable influence to get our people to accept a court of inquiry, we have to use our influence now to get them to strike because you will not accept a court of inquiry?' He knew that only ten of the thirty-two unions affiliated to the Federation were prepared to give plenary powers to the executive to call a strike in support of the miners.[50]

[47] Bagwell, *op. cit.* p. 408.
[48] N.T.W.F., 'Report of a meeting of delegates, 30 December 1919'; Directorate of Intelligence, Report No. 36 (9 January 1920), P.R.O. CAB 24/96.
[49] A. Bullock, *The Life and Times of Ernest Bevin* (1960), i, pp. 131–2.
[50] *Ibid.* pp. 151–2.

Many railwaymen and transport workers still did not appreciate that the miners were no longer the privileged group they had been in 1913 when their average weekly earnings were the highest, while the railwaymen's earnings were among the lowest and their hours of work the longest, of any major industrial group. At the conference of the Alliance on 23 September Thomas mentioned newspaper reports of the fat wage packets of the miners. Hodges explained that the figures cited were quite unrepresentative and often referred to the earnings of a limited class of privileged 'buttymen'. But more railwaymen read the *Daily Mail* which published these stories than the *Daily Herald* which controverted them.[51]

Influencing the more cautious views of Thomas, Smillie and Hodges was the belief in the imminence of a Labour electoral victory and a desire not to queer the pitch of growing middle-class support by over-hasty industrial action. Although coalition candidates had swept the board in the general election of December 1918, the Labour vote had risen to 2,385,472 compared with only 371,772 in December 1910. In the immediate post-war years the by-elections revealed a strong leftward tide. In April 1920 J. Mills gained Dartford for Labour with a vote that exceeded the combined votes of the other four candidates. In the rural constituency of Woodbridge, four months later, the Labour candidate came within 192 votes of defeating the coalitionist.[52] The respect which Thomas expressed for the British constitution was enhanced with each by-election victory for his party. The scent of Cabinet office was in the air. A Lancashire miner, Sutton, sized up Thomas when he said that the railwaymen's leader 'had the weight of empire on his shoulders and wanted everything possible to be done to prevent

[51] A. L. Bowley, *Wages and Income in the U.K. since 1860* (1937), pp. 50–1; B. Mitchell and P. Deane, *Abstract of British Historical Statistics* (1962) p. 351.

[52] D. Butler and J. Freeman, *British Political Facts 1900–1960* (1963); *The Annual Register* (1919, 1920); Directorate of Intelligence, Report No. 36 (9 January 1920), P.R.O. CAB 24/96. After E. Montagu and Viscount Haldane had considered, with Frank Hodges and R. H. Tawney, the threat of a Triple Alliance strike, they told Tom Jones, Assistant Secretary to the Cabinet that both men 'seemed anxious to move on constitutional lines in view of the bye-election successes'; T. Jones *Whitehall Diary*, i (1969) p. 104.

a stoppage'.[53]

The subtle influence of recent piecemeal gains in wages, working conditions and job security made the rank and file of the railwaymen more reluctant to throw in their lot with the miners. Thomas's statement to the meeting of the Alliance on 23 September that there was some doubt, even if a strike were called, as to the response of the railwaymen, was not without some foundation. The response of the branches to the plan for a sympathetic strike was patchy. Many of the south Wales branches were 'clamouring for a strike' and there was similar enthusiasm in most parts of Lancashire. Support for the strike was also expressed by the Sheffield, north Wales and Chesterfield district councils of the N.U.R. In the south and south-west, on the other hand, members were far more cautious. Of 91 branch reports summarised in the *Railway Review* on 1 October, 46 expressed support for the strike while 11 were opposed or were hesitant. Perhaps more realistic than many branch reports was that from Lydney: 'A resolution to support the miners was carried by a majority of one, as many remaining neutral as voted.' One of the elements of uncertainty was how the footplatemen's union would act. The remarkable goodwill between the N.U.R. and ASLEF displayed in the railway strike had soon eroded. By April 1920 Thomas and Bromley were at daggers drawn, Bromley threatening to return the gold medal and the vellum address in a £50 gold frame presented to him by the N.U.R. less than six months before.[54]

Undoubtedly the miners would have had a stronger incentive to seek the support of their Alliance partners if there had been any serious likelihood of blackleg labour being recruited for the mines; but there was never the remotest possibility of this happening. The Supply and Transport Committee of the Cabinet, after persistent inquiry, came to the reluctant conclusion 'that it would be impossible to recruit volunteers to work the mines'.[55] It was the contrast between the blackleg-proof coal mines and the vulnerable transport industry which galled Williams:

[53] Lancashire and Cheshire Miners' Federation, *Report of a Special Conference* (Bolton, 25 September 1920), p. 3.

[54] Directorate of Intelligence, Report No. 50 (15 April 1920), P.R.O. CAB 24/103.

[55] Supply and Transport Committee, Report 14 (October 1920), P.R.O. TC 171, CAB 27/73.

The miners have not, during the past twenty years had a single dispute broken by the importation of scab labour. The whole of London is an armed camp. Regents Park and Kensington Gardens were fitted up with an improvised transport service.... The government was spending half a million a day, not to break up the miners' dispute, but to break the threatened transport workers' dispute.[56]

Had the three parties to the Alliance been able to resolve their differences in September 1920, they might well have been in a stronger position to put pressure on the government than they had been the year before. Because of the effects of rapid demobilisation the Minister of Transport felt obliged to warn the Cabinet in December 1919 that if an Alliance strike occurred, the government would be 'in an infinitely worse position than in the case of the recent railway strike' since the representatives of all three fighting services had warned him that they 'could give but little help'.[57] This was one reason for the hasty passage of the Emergency Powers Bill, which passed through all its stages in Parliament between 25 and 29 October.

V

By the time the next crisis came in the coal industry and in the affairs of the Alliance in April 1921 the British economy had taken a sharp downward plunge. The short post-war replacement boom came to an abrupt end in the closing weeks of 1920.

This time the issue was not whether the railwaymen and transport workers should support the miners' claim for an increase in wages but whether they could be wise enough to stand together to resist a drastic cut in miners' pay which was seen as the prelude to a general attack on wages.

The average price of British coal for export in the last quarter of 1920 was 83s. 2d. a ton. By January revived competition from the European mines had brought the price down to 65s. 4d. and by March of the same year to 43s. 6d.[58] It was this collapse

---

[56] N.T.W.F., *Eleventh Annual General Council Meeting* (Edinburgh, 9–10 June 1921).
[57] Minutes of Cabinet Meeting, 10 December 1919, P.R.O. CAB 23/18.
[58] P.R.O. CAB 21/190 (April 1921).

which stampeded the Cabinet, by 22 February, into announcing that government control over the coal-mining industry would end on 31 March 1921 instead of 30 June 1921, as previously promised. The mine owners reacted by declaring that from the beginning of April there would be a return to district wage agreements and that in most districts substantial wage reductions, amounting in the south Wales and Cumberland districts to between 40 and 50 per cent of previous rates, would be introduced at the time of decontrol.[59] As the miners refused to agree to these proposals a lock-out of the coal-mining industry began on 1 April. The M.F.G.B. accepted the necessity for some reduction in wages, but demanded the continuation of national agreements to be applied through a national wages board and a national pool whereby the more profitable coalfields would subsidise wages paid in the poorer fields. Since in prolonged negotiations at No. 10 Downing Street the government refused to consider a wages pool or a postponement of the wage reductions, the conference of the Triple Alliance, meeting on 8 April, resolved to call a strike of the Alliance on 12 April unless, in the meantime, the government reopened negotiations with the miners. The government agreed to hold further meetings with the mine owners and miners on 11 April and the strike notices were cancelled, but when these further talks broke down new notices were sent out to take effect from 15 April.

During the evening of 14 April Hodges was asked to explain the miners' point of view to a meeting of M.P.s in the House of Commons. After consultations with Smillie (the President) and James Robson (the Treasurer) of the M.F.G.B., it was agreed that all three men should attend the meeting, Hodges acting as spokesman. No newspaper reporter was present. After the meeting was over, second-hand and, according to Hodges, garbled versions of what was said were passed on to the press by excited coalitionist M.P.s. Eight days later, speaking at a special conference of miners' delegates, Hodges gave his own version of what he had said in answer to questions. He affirmed that the miners' executive was prepared to 'hear and consider any proposal as to wages' provided it was 'clearly understood that any such consideration was not dependent on giving up fundamental principles' for which miners stood. In view of newspaper reports that an offer to

[59] Cole, *op. cit.* p. 197.

return to district wage agreements had been made, Hodges's version of what transpired at this crucial point of the meeting is worth quoting:

> I was then asked: 'Suppose an offer was made to effect a temporary settlement on the basis that wages shall not fall below the cost of living, what would be our attitude?' I replied: 'Any such offer coming from an authoritative source would receive very serious consideration at our hands,' and I repeated 'that we had only had one proposal from the government, that is a permanent settlement on a district basis; they refused any temporary national settlement'.

Hodges afterwards explained to the miners' delegates that he had answered the above question 'eagerly' because 'any temporary settlement of a national character ... implied a continuance of financial control of the industry by the government – one of the foremost objectives of the miners at that time'.[60]

In the absence of a verbatim report of what was said at the fateful House of Commons meeting it seems reasonable to accept Hodges's version of what was said as being nearest to the truth. The two principal officers of the M.F.G.B. were sitting beside Hodges both on the occasion of the questioning by M.P.s and when he spoke to the miners just over a week later. On 14 April they gave the Commons meeting no hint of disagreement with their General Secretary's exposition of executive policy. On 22 April they did not challenge the accuracy of his report to the miners' delegates. As to the discrepancy between the press reports of the meeting and Hodges's version, one explanation could be that M.P.s who spoke to press reporters mistook Hodges's reference to government proposals for a district wages settlement for a willingness on the part of the miners to consider such a retrograde step.

No sooner had the House of Commons meeting ended than Lloyd George was informed that a loophole existed for a last-minute renewal of the discussions with the miners. He therefore wrote inviting the miners' executive to meet him on the morning of 15 April. The miners were sharply divided on how to

[60] M.F.G.B., *Report of a Special Conference, Memorial Hall, Farringdon St.* (22 April 1921).

reply, but after two hours' discussion decided by a majority of one to decline the Premier's offer of fresh talks. Sensing that this decision amounted to a repudiation of his actions of the previous evening, Hodges handed in his resignation, but was persuaded by the unanimous vote of the miners' executive to continue as Secretary 'for the sake of the mining community'.

After the miners had announced their refusal to renew discussions with the government their Alliance partners made a last, fruitless effort to persuade them to change their minds.

In default of a verbatim report of what was said when the railwaymen and transport workers renewed separate discussions on their own later that morning, it is only possible to conjecture what were the immediate reasons given for the decision, reached by 32 votes to 12, to call off the Triple Alliance strike.

On the day following, Black Friday, the executives of the N.U.R., ASLEF and the N.T.W.F. issued a statement in explanation of the decision made on the previous day. In view of the 'confusion' which confronted them because of newspaper hints that the Alliance strike was not likely to take place, 'no reasonable hope remained of securing spontaneous and united action of the three bodies which was so essential to give the Miners' Federation the assistance they sought'. Nevertheless there were many deep-seated reasons why the miners were left to continue their struggle alone until returning to work on the employers' terms on 1 July 1921. The speech by Hodges in the House of Commons and what immediately followed it was the occasion, rather than the cause, of the breakdown of the Alliance.

Writing two months after Black Friday, G. D. H. Cole attacked the

> convenient theory that a few leaders alone were wicked while the hearts and wits of all the others were in the right place. There was present among the executive members who made their momentous decision at Unity House, an unaccredited delegate who cast his vote against the vote of loyalty and good sense. And that delegate's name was Panic.[61]

Among the influences that had sent the delegate Panic to the Black Friday conference of the Alliance was the exceedingly

[61] G. D. H. Cole, 'Black Friday and After', *Labour Monthly*, i, No. 1 (July 1921).

rapid growth of unemployment. The Ministry of Labour returns showed no less than 1,615,000 persons out of work on 8 April 1921, a figure 109,000 larger than that of the previous week and more than double that of December 1920. The transport workers and railwaymen who were being asked to strike in sympathy with the miners had a much greater cause to fear permanent loss of employment in April 1921 than they had had in September 1920. District reports on the employment situation reaching N.T.W.F. headquarters in January 1921 provided gloomy reading. In Cardiff trade was 'exceptionally bad'; Workington was 'very quiet'; unemployment in Bristol was 'very acute'; and London reported a 'severe depression'. Only Middlesbrough and Salford sent in more cheerful accounts of the labour market.[62] On the railway stations of the south and south-west there was evidence that the 'dare to do spirit of the rank and file was curbed by the enormous number of unemployed to be found in every town and village'.[63]

This sudden change in the state of the labour market had its influence on union branch discussions. Although a majority of the branches of the N.U.R. that reported decisions would have been prepared to back an Alliance strike, the enthusiasm which was present in the branches in September 1919 was notably absent. Typical of the cautious branches was Kidderminster, whose secretary wrote: 'In view of the present state of the labour market, we think that the time is not opportune to take drastic action, but we are prepared to support the miners financially'. Of the 1500 branches of the N.U.R. 471 replied to a questionnaire sent out by Cramp. Of these 130 specified that they were willing to withdraw their labour in support of the miners. A further 172 indicated that they would support any action the executive thought appropriate. Branches which were definitely against a strike or which said 'We want a ballot' or 'We want the ASLEF in this' numbered 156. Thirteen other branches wanted reference of the dispute to the T.U.C. or to arbitration. It was by no means a wholly encouraging response.[64]

The leaders of the N.T.W.F. had little doubt that the dockers would back a strike of the Alliance, but after the crisis had passed

---

[62] N.T.W.F., *Minutes of the Emergency Committee* (6 January 1921).
[63] A. E. Rochester writing in the *Railway Review*, 29 April 1921,
[64] *Railway Review*, 15 April 1921.

Bevin disclosed that the response of the road transport workers had given cause for 'serious anxiety'.[65] Nevertheless, at least on the railways it is highly probable that a large proportion of the waverers would have fallen in with the majority and supported the strike if they had been given firm encouragement by their leaders.

Thomas's speeches were designed to have the exactly opposite effect. He warned the railwaymen that if they left their work in support of the miners they would lose the guaranteed week. He claimed that only 70 per cent of the railwaymen would come out and that this would not worry the railway companies, which could provide a skeleton service with less than 30 per cent of the labour force employed.[66] Thomas disliked the idea of the pool as he held that it was political in its implications. It was an attempt to get nationalisation by the back door. Since he had given up trying to get the railways nationalised it would have been illogical of him to have supported this part of the miners' programme.

By 1921 Thomas's colleague, Cramp, had also lost most of his revolutionary fervour. At the time of the railway crisis in September 1919 the press had suggested that he had been the main influence in stampeding the N.U.R. into calling a strike during the temporary absence of Thomas in America. At the Downing Street conference which ended the strike, Cramp made a personal statement claiming that he had acted with strict impartiality as President of the N.U.R. Lloyd George's acceptance of the explanation – 'I am sure he is one of the most respectable citizens of this land. I am sure he intends no harm to the constitution of this country and least of all to the present government' – was spoken with tongue in cheek and greeted with laughter. But the assertions it jokingly contained were nearer the truth than must have seemed likely at the time to many of Lloyd George's Cabinet colleagues.[67]

Bevin's Black Friday decision to vote against the strike sprang not from any tender regard for the British constitution but from

[65] N.T.W.F., *Eleventh Annual General Council Meeting* (Edinburgh 9–10 June 1921), p. 31.

[66] N.U.R., A.G.M. (Newcastle), reported in *Railway Review*, 15 July 1921.

[67] 'Shorthand notes of the proceedings of a conference between the Prime Minister and the Executive Committee of the N.U.R., 10 Downing Street, 5 October 1919', P.R.O. CAB 27/61, f. 34.

disgust with the gross inefficiency of the Alliance as an organisation. When sumoned to one of its meetings on 29 March 1921 he 'did not know, other than from the press, what was to be discussed' and entered the conference room without an agenda. Along with the other leaders of the railwaymen and the transport workers, he was simply told that the miners were coming out on strike and that they were appealing for the support of their Alliance partners. There had been no prior consultation.[68]

The miners' leaders were not of one mind on the wisdom of continuing to demand the pool. Hodges believed it was necessary to keep the issues simple and clearly understood. In the other unions there were 'men who were prepared to go all the way with the miners if wages and wages only had been the consideration upon which the strike was to be declared', but who had little sympathy for or understanding of the pool and the national wages Board.[69] Herbert Smith, Vice-President of the Federation, agreed. He admitted to the delegates at the annual conference in August 1921 that the miners 'did not seek support on simple and elementary things but urged compliance with us on a much more involved and political claim, namely that of the Pool'.[70] A leading member of the Lancashire and Cheshire Miners' Federation held the opinion in April that if they struck 'until next Christmas Day' they would still not get a national pool,[71] while Jack Lawson of the Durham Miners' Federation found the idea of the pool 'too abstract'.[72] It is certainly arguable that there would have been more widespread enthusiasm for the strike of the Alliance if the issue had been the simple one of resistance to the savage cuts in miners' wages. Hodges was undoubtedly thinking along these lines when he made his famous statement in the House of Commons on 14 April.[73]

The tendency of the miners to treat the Alliance as something of a last resort precluded any serious attempt to reform its structure and procedures. On 26 November 1920 Bevin wrote to

[68] Dock, Wharf, Riverside and General Workers' Union, Executive Council Minutes, 12 May 1921, N.T.W.F., *Eleventh Annual General Council Meeting* (Edinburgh, 9–10 June 1921).

[69] M.F.G.B., *Report of a Special Conference* (22 April 1921), p. 8.

[70] M.F.G.B., *Annual Conference Report* (17 August 1921), pp. 12–13.

[71] Lancashire and Cheshire Miners' Federation, *Report of a Special Conference* (18 April 1921), p. 9; speech of Mr McGurk.

[72] J. Lawson, *The Man in the Cap* (1941), p. 148.

[73] M.F.G.B., *Annual Conference Report* (1921), p. 8.

Robert Williams and to the Secretaries of the M.F.G.B. and N.U.R. requesting a meeting which would reorganise the Alliance so that its constitution would provide 'for the promotion of agreed programmes and policies'. But despite all his efforts there was 'no meeting, no discussion, no exchange of opinion' on proposed reforms. During the crisis of April 1921 Bevin drew the attention of the miners to the fact that he had met with no positive response, but was told that nothing had been done because the miners 'did not think that the triple alliance would again function'.[74]

The failure of the Alliance to embrace all organised workers in the three major groups of coal mining, railways and transport undoubtedly reduced its appeal to the rank and file. The committee of the Alliance first considered broadening the basis of membership as early as April 1914, but Thomas effectively thwarted a proposal to bring in ASLEF, the R.C.A. and other transport unions by the unhelpful suggestion that the first two could be represented 'through the N.U.R.' and the other transport unions through the N.T.W.F.[75] The consequence of this shortsightedness, which sprang from inter-union jealousy, was the weakening of the Alliance challenge to the mine owners and government in 1921. As late as 8 April 1921 Bromley, the Secretary of ASLEF, stated in a circular to union branches that members were to take no action in the forthcoming strike as the union 'had not been approached or consulted in any way'.[76] It is true that at the eleventh hour ASLEF joined the Alliance and Bromley issued a circular on 13 April calling upon footplatemen to support the strike. But this move came too late to influence the decisions of many N.U.R. branches, and in the discussions of the Alliance before 13 April Thomas was able to point to the understandable fear of many members of the N.U.R. that large numbers of enginemen would continue at work as justification for not giving all-out support for the miners.

Despite all these divisions and weaknesses within the organisation, an Alliance strike might still have happened in April

[74] Dock, Wharf, Riverside and General Workers' Union, Executive Council Minutes, 12 May 1921.

[75] Triple Industrial Alliance, *Report of Conference* (23 April 1914), p. 31.

[76] Supply and Transport Committee (8 April 1921), P.R.O. CAB 27/73, TC 280.

1921 if the Cabinet had acted clumsily and provocatively. Instead it again displayed remarkable cool-headedness and circumspection in dealing with the crisis. Three days before Black Friday, when there might have been every excuse for panic, it decided 'that any action which might be regarded and quoted afterwards as provocative' was to be avoided.[77] A few days earlier the Supply and Transport Committee of the Cabinet had considered whether, in the event of the miners' strike, the railwaymen's guaranteed week should be suspended. The Committee concluded that to rescind the guaranteed week would be to invite railway workers 'to throw in their lot with the miners'.[78] It is indeed likely that if tens of thousands of men had been told that they would, in any case, lose their jobs in the event of a miners' strike, the 'dare to do' spirit whose absence had been noted by A. E. Rochester would have returned. A strike in support of the miners would then have been regarded as a worthier alternative to unemployment.

VI

In the view of Williams, one of its keenest supporters, the Triple Alliance was 'irretrievably broken' after the fiasco of Black Friday.[79] The other leaders would not have quarrelled with this verdict.

Even the belated efforts of the railwaymen and transport workers to mitigate their betrayal of the miners by helping in other ways than by striking seemed only to add to the bitterness between the unions. On 22 April a conscience-stricken N.U.R. executive ordered an embargo on the transport of coal for commercial uses. The transport workers followed suit. But when some of the members of the N.U.R. in Glasgow and elsewhere were dismissed by the railway companies – though the men concerned were quickly reinstated – it was decided to lift the embargo. It was an ignoble retreat which caused Hodges to tell the miners that the attitude of the other unions was largely a 'sham' one since their main concern was 'how to save themselves

[77] Cabinet 19 (21) of 12 April 1921, P.R.O. CAB 23/25.

[78] Supply and Transport Committee (1 April 1921), P.R.O. CAB 27/73, TC 249.

[79] R. Williams, 'Black Friday and After', *Labour Monthly*, i, No. 2 (August 1921), p. 102.

from a general strike in consequence of the victimisation of their members'. While the embargo was still the official policy of the transport workers, men belonging to Havelock Wilson's National Sailors' and Firemen's Union, which was affiliated to the N.T.W.F., were employed in Belgian ports loading coal for export to Britain even though the Belgians themselves had at first refused this work out of sympathy for the British miners.[80] In the light of such manifestations of disunity it is scarcely surprising that many months elapsed before any attempt was made to renew co-operation between the unions.

When a new start was made by the miners early in 1925 they made proposals for an industrial alliance more comprehensive in scope than the Triple Alliance had been. The foundry workers, engineers and shipbuilders as well as the three railway unions, the miners and the Transport and General Workers' Union were all represented at a plenary meeting held in London on 4 June 1925 to devise a constitution for the proposed alliance.

At the second plenary meeting on 17 July the prospects for creating a strong organisation looked promising when the following was agreed as one of the clauses in the constitution of the alliance:

> The conditions of membership of this alliance shall involve the allied organisations in definitely undertaking, notwithstanding anything in their agreements or constitutions to the contrary, to act as directed by the general conference of the alliance.[81]

It seemed that the lessons of past disunity had been learnt, and it would not be fanciful to claim that this new evidence of the unions' willingness to stand together helped to persuade Baldwin's Cabinet to capitulate on Red Friday – 31 July 1925 – and to offer the mine owners a nine months' subsidy to stave off the proposed cuts in miners' wages. But as the months of summer passed it became all too clear that the attitude of Thomas, spokesman for the N.U.R., was making it impossible for agreement to be reached. At a delegate meeting on 5 November he proposed that a commitment to a policy of industrial unionism

[80] M.F.G.B., *Annual Conference Report* (1921), p. 35.
[81] R. Page Arnot, *The Miners: Years of Struggle* (1953), p. 373.

should be a precondition of membership of the industrial alliance even though he was fully aware that such a policy was anathema to ASLEF and other craft unions. When the N.U.R. proposal was decisively defeated its delegation withdrew from the conference. Formal withdrawal from the alliance was announced by the executive of the N.U.R. later that month. This action 'put paid to the alliance'.[82]

VII

In September 1920 Bevin warned a delegate conference of the Triple Alliance that unless they overhauled the organisation to make it capable of speaking with one voice it would be revealed as a 'paper alliance' when the testing time came.[83] Such proved to be the case both in September 1920 and in April 1921. Gosling held much the same opinion when he wrote that 'the alliance was not a compact body and never acted as such'.[84] But had the leaders of the railwaymen, miners and transport workers made any effort to dovetail their industrial programmes they would have seen to it that a closely knit organisation was created to ensure success. When he looked back at the failures of the years 1919–21 Hodges quite rightly went beyond questions of organisation to more fundamental reasons of weakness. He told the annual conference of the miners in August 1921 that it was impossible for the Alliance to function until each party was affected 'simultaneously by the same questions', had 'the same claims maturing at the same moment' or were 'attacked by jointly organised capitalism at the same moment'.[85] None of these preconditions existed. The unions were of such unequal strength and their leaders' personalities and policies were at such great variance that no common industrial programme for the Alliance was ever attempted. Consequently no organisation suitable for enforcing such a programme was created. Even so the Alliance might have been bludgeoned into unity by the stupidity of government policy. But whenever there were signs of a common front by the trade unions the coalition govern-

---

[82] H. J. Fyrth and H. Collins, *The Foundry Workers* (1959), p. 179.
[83] Bullock *op. cit.* p. 152.
[84] Gosling, *op. cit.* p. 176.
[85] M.F.G.B., *Annual Conference Report* (1921), p. 21.

ment studiously avoided provocation. The skill displayed by the Cabinet in treating the railwaymen more generously than the miners undermined fatally the unity and fighting spirit of the Alliance and saved the day for both the government and the propertied classes.[86]

[86] The article by G. A. Phillips, 'The Triple Industrial Alliance in 1914', *Economic History Review*, second ser., vol. xxiv, no. 1 (February 1971), pp. 55–67, appeared after this essay was sent to the press. With the conclusions set out on pp. 66–7, I am in general agreement.

6

C. L. MOWAT

RAMSAY MACDONALD AND THE LABOUR PARTY

S I N C E his death in 1937, Ramsay MacDonald has not attracted much attention from historians and might seem to have fallen into an oblivion unparalleled among the Prime Ministers of the twentieth century.[1] It is true that the centenary of his birth in 1966 did not pass unnoticed; indeed the Prime Minister, Harold Wilson, spoke at a lunch to mark it, which suggested that a reconciliation between the Labour Party and MacDonald's shade was in the making. The forthcoming biography by David Marquand may well succeed in rehabilitating him as one of the Labour Party's great figures, second only to Keir

[1] In his lifetime there were biographies of MacDonald by Mary Agnes Hamilton (pseud. 'Iconoclast'), *The Man of Tomorrow* (1923), *James Ramsay MacDonald, 1923–1925* (1925), both reprinted as *J. Ramsay MacDonald* (1929), and H. H. Tiltman, *J. Ramsay MacDonald: Labor's Man of Destiny* (New York, 1929). L. MacNeill Weir, *The Tragedy of Ramsay MacDonald* (1938) is a sustained attack, concentrating on the 1931 crisis. His friend Godfrey (Lord) Elton published *The Life of James Ramsay MacDonald (1866–1919)* in 1939, but a second volume has never appeared; Lord Elton also wrote the article on him in the *Dictionary of National Biography, 1931–1940*. More recent work on him includes Reginald Bassett, *1931: Political Crisis* (1958); R. Skidelsky, *Politicians and the Slump; The Labour Government of 1929–1931* (1967); R. W. Lyman, *The First Labour Government* (1957) and his very perceptive article 'James Ramsay MacDonald and the Leadership of the Labour Party, 1918–22', *Journal of British Studies*, ii (November 1962) pp. 132–60; Francis Williams's sketch in *A Pattern of Rulers* (1965) is penetrating. Benjamin Sachs, *J. Ramsay MacDonald in Thought and Action* (Albuquerque, New Mexico, 1952) is an anthology of his ideas. MacDonald appears in many memoirs, especially Philip Snowden's *Autobiography* (1934) and Beatrice Webb's *Our Partnership* (1948) and *Diaries, 1912–1924* and *1924–1932* (1952–6). Mary Agnes Hamilton's *Remembering My Good Friends* (1944) contains the best character sketch of him. Lord Vansittart's *Mist Procession* (1958) and Leonard Woolf's *Beginning Again* (1964) are also useful – the latter unflattering in its examples of MacDonald's vanity and 'treachery' and his 'tortuousness of mind' (pp. 217–26). But Vansittart wrote of him: 'a fiery tongue went with a gentle nature' (p. 323).

Hardie among the first generation; meanwhile a provisional estimate may be worth attempting. For the trouble has been that MacDonald's action in forming the 'National' Government in 1931 left him in a biographical limbo, a renegade in Labour's eyes and a very short-lived hero to his new friends among the Conservatives and Liberals. The last six years of his long political life cast a blight over his previous record, causing it to be read largely by hindsight. He left few champions, either from right or left, to cherish his memory.

MacDonald's association with the labour movement began in 1894, when he joined the Independent Labour Party, though he was already a Fabian. He had then been in London for eight years, having arrived, a penniless Scot of 20 from Lossiemouth, in 1886. How he supported himself – for a time he was clerk in a warehouse earning fifteen shillings a week – how he began to be known, to be taken up by people of the middle class (the Fabians mistook him for an army officer), to become Private Secretary to Thomas Lough, a Radical-Liberal candidate for Parliament: these things remain obscure.[2] He earned something by writing, even including articles for the *Dictionary of National Biography,* then in course of publication. In 1888 he was writing from Kentish Town to Keir Hardie, transmitting, as Secretary, a resolution in support of Hardie's candidacy at Mid-Lanark from the London Committee of the Scottish Home Rule Association.[3] His decision to join the I.L.P. followed a by-election at Attercliffe (Sheffield) in which the Liberals gave great offence by refusing to accept the Trades Council candidate. His application – often quoted before – is worth quoting in full, since it shows both his reluctant conversion and his prior acquaintanceship with Hardie.

> 20 Duncan Buildings,
> Baldwin Gardens, E.C.
> 15th July 1894.

My dear Hardie,
   I am now making personal application for membership of the I.L.P. I have stuck to the Liberals up to now, hoping

---

[2] In spite of what information is to be found in Lord Elton's *Life.*
[3] W. Stewart, *J. Keir Hardie* (1921), p. 42 (cf. Lloyd George's early parliamentary career as a Welsh nationalist).

that they might do something to justify the trust that we had put in them. Attercliffe came as a rude awakening and I felt during that contest that it was quite impossible for me to maintain my position as a Liberal any longer. Calmer consideration has but strengthened that conviction, and if you now care to accept me amongst you I shall do what I can to support the I.L.P.

Between you and me there was never any dispute as to objects. What I could not quite accept was your methods. I have changed my opinion. Liberalism, and more particularly local Liberal associations, have definitely declared against Labour, and so I must accept the facts of the situation and candidly admit that the prophecies of I.L.P. relating to Liberalism have been amply justified. The time for conciliation has gone by and those of us who are earnest in our professions must definitely declare ourselves....[4]

Having declared himself, MacDonald played his part in the great though unspectacular campaign of the next few years to win supporters for Labour : the long week-end train journeys, the speeches to small gatherings of the faithful in the back streets. He was soon a member of the National Administrative Council of the I.L.P.

The most important event in his career at this time was, however, his marriage to Margaret Gladstone, daughter of Professor J. H. Gladstone, F.R.S., and a grand-niece of Lord Kelvin. Her work as a school manager in Hoxton, where she also served the District Nursing Association and the local Charity Organisation Society committee, had led her to socialism. When MacDonald stood for Southampton in 1895 she sent him a contribution. They met soon afterwards. By this marriage MacDonald vaulted into the middle classes. His wife brought him affection and happiness, and also status and income (supplementing his journalistic earnings). Though by birth a member of the working class he had not, since leaving Lossiemouth, lived as such, and he never worked with his hands. His marriage, we may say, confirmed him as a gentleman in the sense in which he applied the term to Keir Hardie : 'the true gentleman

[4] *Ibid.* pp. 96–7.

131

is he who acts like a gentleman unconsciously'.[5] It put him among the middle-class men whose revolt against the Establishment of late-Victorian Britain took on the form of socialism and made the labour movement more than a working-class movement. The MacDonalds' home, 3 Lincoln's Inn Fields, became a place where socialists gathered – from London and throughout the country, from the Continent, from India.

At the conference at the Memorial Hall, Farringdon Street in February 1900 at which the Labour Representation Committee was founded and MacDonald's political career was launched, MacDonald was one of the I.L.P. delegates. At Hardie's request, he had drafted a constitution for the new party.[6] He was certainly in agreement with its objectives: an independent Labour group in Parliament, free of the old parties, supported by the socialist societies (I.L.P., Social Democratic Federation, Fabians) and the trade unions, and not formally committed to socialism. In this form the L.R.C. emerged from the conference, with MacDonald as its unpaid Secretary. His work during the next few years helped to swell its membership, as trade unions were persuaded to affiliate; the Taff Vale decision was also a powerful agent for recruitment. The secret 'entente' with the Liberals, by which Liberals and L.R.C. promised each other a clear run in a number of constituencies, was negotiated with Herbert Gladstone, the Liberal Whip, by MacDonald, with Hardie's blessing.[7] In 1906 MacDonald entered Parliament as one of the beneficiaries, elected for the double-member constituency of Leicester along with a Liberal.

The twenty-nine Labour M.P.s of 1906 were a mixed bunch to which no system of classification really does justice: trade unionists, intellectuals, moderates, socialists, I.L.P.ers and Fabians. Included within Labour's first generation were older men already well known such as Hardie, Will Crooks, 'Mabon', Will Thorne and Arthur Henderson, and the new members such as MacDonald, Snowden, Jowett, Clynes. There was a good deal of mutual suspicion among them: Snowden complained of the trade-union group, who were mostly not politicians; 'elderly trade unionists spending much time in the

[5] His introduction to Stewart, *op. cit.* p. 20.
[6] *Ibid.* p. 163.
[7] Frank Bealey and Henry Pelling, *Labour and Politics 1900–1906* (1958).

smoking room' was another complaint; another damned Mac-
Donald and Snowden as intellectuals with no connection with
organised labour, men who had no hesitation in rapping their
leaders over the knuckles, even in public.[8] At the conference of
1907, after the L.R.C. had become the Labour Party, two
motions were defeated: the first (heavily) to confine the party
to socialists, the second (moved by Ben Tillett) to confine it to
trade unionists. All they could agree on was their independence
and their 'Labour' name; objectives must be limited, partly to
serving as watchdog for the interests of trade unionism.[9]

The years 1906–10 brought out the conflict of aims. There
were real achievements: over the Trades Disputes Act and
the legislation for school meals and workmen's compensation.
Conflict was most apparent in the annual conferences of the
Labour Party and the I.L.P. over the party's programme:
should it be long-range or limited? should it demand 'the
socialisation of the means of production, distribution and exchange'? The last was narrowly carried at the Labour Party
Conference in 1908, but on other occasions such motions were
defeated. In 1909 MacDonald discouraged a long-range programme with the ingenious argument that it must either be so
far ahead that neither Liberals nor Tories could steal it, in
which case the party would become an ineffective fighting force;
or it must be so practical that both could steal it if they liked,
in which case it would be impossible to maintain our independence.[10] At this same conference Tillett's attack on the party,
Is the Parliamentary Labour Party a Failure? (in which he criticised members as 'toadies', 'liars at five and ten guineas a time')
was keenly debated, but a motion of lack of confidence in the
leaders was defeated. Perhaps the vigour of Tillett's language
spoilt his case.[11] In the I.L.P. conferences the clashes were even
sharper, exacerbated by the controversy caused by Victor Grayson's election, without endorsement, as 'Socialist Labour' Member for Colne Valley, and his subsequent performances in Parliament on behalf of the unemployed.

[8] Elton, *op. cit.* p. 133; John Scanlon, *Decline and Fall of the Labour
Party* (1932), pp. 24–5.
[9] J. H. S. Reid, *The Origins of the British Labour Party* (Minneapolis,
1955), pp. 120–1.
[10] *Ibid.* p. 120.
[11] *Ibid.* pp. 199–200.

MacDonald was Chairman of the I.L.P. in 1906–9, and his restraining influence in the chair hardly added to his popularity with his critics. Matters came to a head at the 1909 conference, when a motion that the I.L.P. should secede from the Labour Party was defeated but MacDonald, Bruce Glasier, Snowden and Hardie felt obliged to resign from the N.A.C. MacDonald's farewell speech emphasised his faith in parliamentary methods: violence would only breed counter-revolution. But his argument, sound if hard, was not made more palatable by his characteristic tone:

> I sometimes receive resolutions beginning in this way. 'Seeing that the Unemployed are of more importance than the rules of the House of Commons –'. You know the rest. If I said that I see nothing of the kind I would, of course, be misunderstood. So I shall put it this way. The opposition between Parliamentary procedure and the question of how to deal with the unemployed is purely a fictitious one. The unemployed can never be treated by any Parliament except one which has rules of procedure, and those rules must prescribe majority responsibility. Every facility given to a minority to impose its will upon the majority is a facility which any minority could use, and not merely a Labour or a Socialist minority. To protect the conditions and the existence of democratic government is just as essential to the building up of a Socialist State as is the solution of the problem of unemployment. . . . The Party which propose to strike at the heart of democratic government in order to make a show of earnestness about unemployment, will not only not be tolerated by the country, but does not deserve to be.[12]

In Parliament the position of the Labour Party was changed as a result of the two general elections of 1910, which destroyed the Liberals' majority and made them dependent on Labour or Irish Nationalist votes for their continuance in office. This might be thought to have given Labour increased bargaining power;[13] instead, it seemed to increase its subservience. Was it symbolic that, because of the enlarged size of the opposition, Labour

[12] *Ibid.* p. 178; Elton, *op. cit.* pp. 151–4.
[13] Ralph Miliband, *Parliamentary Socialism* (1961), p. 23.

members were asked to occupy seats on the government side of the House? The change was followed by MacDonald's election as Chairman of the Parliamentary Labour Party in 1911, a position he retained until the War. Henderson succeeded him as Secretary of the party, and MacDonald took Henderson's place as Treasurer. A new, firm leadership, less trade-unionist than before, was thus installed at a critical time when divisions within the party were enlarged by the great public issues of the time: the Parliament Bill, Home Rule, votes for women, syndicalism and strikes, the effects of the Osborne decision upon trade unions, the National Insurance Bill (but syndicalism, which they generally opposed, tended to draw Labour members together).

Why was MacDonald chosen as leader? His predecessors were Hardie, Shackleton, Henderson and Barnes; a spell of ill-health made Barnes's continuance as Chairman impractical In some ways his temperament made MacDonald unsuited to the task. In 1910, when he foresaw that he might succeed Barnes, he was writing to Glasier:

> I can see nothing but storms and heartaches ahead. I shall not lead as a great many people want, because I shall say what I mean, whereas so many of our folk want declamation, stage dressing, paint and daggers in the belt. I can fight that battle more effectively as a non-official than as a chairman.[14]

The tendency to self-pity, and the tone of vehement moderation which he often sounded in public, were hardly the best equipment for a leader. Yet he had many qualities which made him the obvious choice. His very moderation made him acceptable to the majority in the middle of the Parliamentary Party, in which he had at first been identified with the leftward I.L.P. members. As early as 1908, Max Beer, the historian of socialism, had written in the *Labour Leader*: 'I cannot help perceiving that his general policy is at present thoroughly in conformity with the mental condition of the British Labour Movement. Any other policy might at the present juncture spell disruption.'[15] In 1913 the *Labour Leader* endorsed his continuation as Chair-

---

[14] Elton, *op. cit.* p. 190.
[15] Quoted in Stewart, *op. cit.* p. 293.

man, declaring 'Mr. MacDonald can best maintain the unity of the Party as it is now constituted.'[16] Moreover, he was a figure of international standing, an important delegate each year to the International and other meetings. He was well-travelled, had visited Canada and Australia and India in 1906 on a round-the-world tour, and published a prophetic book, *The Awakening of India* (1910), after a subsequent visit. He was an able parliamentarian: though this was a double-edged quality if playing the parliamentary game became an end in itself, not a means to the advance of Labour policies. His long service to the party as Secretary gave him an undoubted claim to his turn as leader. Beyond this there was a certain aura of greatness about him: his bearing, his handsome mien, his assurance, his magnetic power as a platform speaker, in short what Lord Elton calls 'his mysterious personal distinction.... He was widely recognised as a figure both challenging and formidable.'[17]

MacDonald was also a prolific writer on socialism, and this alone increased his standing both in the party and among the wider public. Some examination of his writings is essential to an understanding of his strength and weakness as leader of the Labour Party. The principal ones are: *Socialism and Society* (1905), which is volume 2 of the 'Socialist Library' edited by MacDonald and published by the I.L.P.; *Socialism* (1907) in Messrs. Jack's 'Social Problems' series; and his important *Socialist Movement* (1911) in the Home University Library. His introduction to William Stewart's *Life of Hardie* (1921) also deserves notice, for much which he there attributes to Hardie he is really saying of himself.

One's first impression of MacDonald's socialism is that it is romantic, abstract, airy, not practical and immediate: a rosy glow in the sky. There is some, but not the whole, truth in this. Of Hardie he wrote:

> ... his Socialism was not an economic doctrine, not a formula proved and expressed in algebraic signs of x and y. He got more Socialism from Burns than from Marx; 'The Twa Dogs' and 'A Man's a Man for a' that', were more prolific text books for his politics than 'Das Kapital'.[18]

[16] Elton, *op. cit.* p. 219.
[17] *Ibid.* p. 144.
[18] Stewart, *op. cit.* p. 23.

In *Socialism* he calls socialism 'a theory of Social organisation, which reconciles the individual to Society' (p. 3), and concludes with ringing eloquence (p. 124):

> ... where life alone will be valued as treasure, and the tyranny of the economic machine will no longer hold spiritual things in subjection. That State I call Socialism.

Hence he has no use for Marxist theory: 'the industrial and economic inevitability of Socialism is a mere fancy'.[19] Equally he rejects utopian and revolutionary socialism, anarchism, communism and class war. The function of the socialist theory is to guide. With typical indulgence of his love of metaphors he writes:

> The seaman in his voyages across the sea steers by certain marks, and at certain points alters his course and follows new marks when the old can lead him no further. So with Socalism. Its method is not the architectural and dogmatic one of building straight from bottom to top, but the organic and experimental one of relieving immediate and pressing difficulties *on a certain plan, and in accordance with a certain scheme of organisation.*[20]

Here we reach, in his earliest work, his 'organic concept of society' which he called the most fruitful. Elsewhere he declares that 'the Socialist method is the Darwinian method'.[21] Or, to quote *Socialism and Society* again: '*Solvitur ambulando*, not *sic volo* – laboratory experiment, not revolution – is the method of Socialism emerged from the Utopian and pseudo-scientific stages.'[22] In the *Socialist Movement* he is rather more definite:

> Socialism is the creed of those, who recognising that the community exists for the improvement of the individual and for the maintenance of liberty, and that the control of the economic circumstances of life means the control of life itself, seek to build up a social organisation which will include in its activities the management of those economic instruments

[19] *Socialism and Society*, p. 125.
[20] *Ibid.* p. 178.
[21] *Socialist Movement*, p. 115.
[22] *Socialism and Society*, p. 179.

such as land and industrial capital that cannot be left safely in the hands of individuals. This is Socialism. It is an application of mutual aid to politics and economics. And the Socialist end is liberty, the liberty of which Kant thought when he proclaimed that every man should be regarded as an end in himself and not as a means to another man's end. The means and the end cannot be separated. Socialism proposes a change in the social mechanism, but justifies it as a means of extending human liberty. Social organisation is the condition, not the antithesis, of individual liberty.[23]

As for equality under socialism, its meaning is 'that the inequalities in the tastes, the powers, the capacities of men may have some chance of having a natural outlet, so that they may each have an opportunity to contribute their appropriate services to society'.[24]

What did all this imply for MacDonald in practical application? He was uncompromising in his criticism of capitalist production and distribution, quoting impressively the facts and figures of poverty and wealth, of monoplies and large profits and bonus shares.[25] In the *Socialist Movement* he demanded 'municipalisation and nationalisation in every shape and form, from milk supplies to telephone', at once adding that state capitalism is not socialism and that socialists strive to make the state a model employer, working co-operatively with its employees.[26] Rent and large private profits should be taxed for the benefit of the community, large estates should be broken up, monopolies ended. In *Socialism: Critical and Constructive* (a later work, published in 1921) he supported workshop control and the proposals of the railwaymen and the coal miners for the nationalisation of their industries. On one thing he was explicit: 'The Labour Party is not Socialist. It is a union of Socialist and trade-union bodies for immediate political work. . . . But it is the only political form which evolutionary Socialism can take in a country with the political traditions and methods of Great Britain'.[27]

[23] *Socialist Movement*, p. 11.
[24] *Ibid.* p. 139.
[25] In the *Socialist Movement* and *Socialism: Critical and Constructive* (1921).
[26] *Socialist Movement*, p. 157.
[27] *Ibid.* p. 235.

MacDonald's powers of leadership were tested to the full in the parliamentary situation of 1911–14, amid peculiarly distressing circumstances. For Margaret MacDonald fell ill in 1911, and died before the year was out. For a man of MacDonald's sensitive, withdrawn temperament it was a hammer-blow of fate; he was, perhaps, never a whole man again.[28] That part of his nature which was warm and sympathetic, and which few but his family ever saw, was blunted, though his affection and care for his children burnt as strongly as ever. But the loneliness of his nature, his self-centredness and self-pity, were reinforced; his touchiness at criticism now found no anodyne; more and more he became an actor on the public stage.

It is an open question whether MacDonald's leadership in those very difficult pre-war years made things better or worse within the party. In Parliament members were divided and voted in opposing divisions on several issues. The National Insurance Bill found MacDonald supporting and others opposing the contributory principle; on one division thirteen members voted one way and sixteen the other, and members opposed each other in seven divisions in a single day; an amendment by Snowden got thirty-four votes but was opposed by MacDonald and two others. The question of votes for women found Hardie supporting the militant suffragettes while MacDonald and the majority preferred the various compromise proposals which proved equally barren. Labour Members voted with the government on the second reading of the Home Rule Bill in 1913, but only twenty-five of them supported the party's protest against police brutalities in the Dublin transport strike.[29] Outside Parliament the failure of the national executive to nominate Labour candidates against Liberals in several by-elections aroused opposition. Instances of this went back to 1906 and included the Colne Valley election in 1907. MacDonald's statement (or alleged statement) when Tillett stood against Sir Alfred Mond at Swansea, 'Had I a vote in Swansea it would not be given to Tillett,' was much resented; when Labour did not nominate at a by-election at Leicester in 1913 MacDonald's defence was brushed aside as evidence of an alliance to safeguard his own

[28] See his moving yet curiously impersonal memoir of her: *Margaret Ethel MacDonald* (1912 and several later editions).
[29] Reid, *op. cit.* pp. 161–5, 200–2; Elton, *op. cit.* p. 209.

seat.[30] No wonder the Labour Party and I.L.P. conferences became increasingly acrimonious, with charges that members gave in too much to 'parliamentary exigencies and parliamentary expediency'. Will Thorne accused MacDonald of making 'bargains behind the Speaker's chair', something Hardie had never done as leader; Hardie supported the charge. Hostile resolutions were defeated or shelved, but it was significant that the Labour Party held a special conference on 27 January 1914 to discuss the party's tactics in Parliament.[31] There is much truth in Professor Reid's conclusion that the party was drifting into an almost impossible situation, 'in danger of losing the support of both militant socialists and dissatisfied trade unionists', and that the outbreak of war was in one sense a blessing in disguise, providing a 'period of grace'.[32] One may only speculate whether under some other leader the party would have had a smoother or a more disastrous passage.

August 1914 ended all lesser controversies and provided the first great challenge to MacDonald's career. His opposition to the War, the most surprising action of his life, influenced his entire future. It made him seem what he never was, one of the extremists, drawing him back to the I.L.P. and making him in 1922, when disillusionment about the War was widespread, acceptable to both left and centre of the party as leader. At the same time it broadened his circle of acquaintances and widened his beliefs, for it threw him into the company of those, Liberals and some Conservatives as well as Labour, who saw that the War must be used as a means for building a better world order and a just and durable peace. He was one of the four signatories of the letter which invited support for what became the Union of Democratic Control. He prepared the way for the influx of Liberals such as Ponsonby, Trevelyan, Wedgwood, Addison and Haldane into the Labour Party. And yet all this was done without making between him and the Labour Party any real split — a situation due as much to his colleagues' magnanimity and solidarity as to his own good sense. The division of the party in 1914 was thus quite different from that of 1931. It never got beyond a difference of emphasis.

[30] Reid, *op. cit.* pp. 194–8; Elton, *op. cit.* p. 213.
[31] Reid, *op. cit.* pp. 180–1, 201–4. Cf. Miliband, *op. cit.* pp. 29–38.
[32] Reid, *op. cit.* p. 204.

To understand MacDonald's position we must remember that on 30 July 1914 the Parliamentary Labour Party passed a resolution in favour of Britain staying out of the War, even if war should come, and that on 2 August Hardie and Henderson both spoke at a large meeting in Trafalgar Square, demanding peace. MacDonald's speech in Parliament on 3 August, after Grey's speech justifying the declaration of war, was, therefore, in conformity with what was still the party's policy. Yet it was a confused speech. If Grey had said the country was in danger, 'we would be with him and behind him'. If the nation's honour were at stake, 'we would be with him' (immediately cancelled by his remark that there had never been a crime committed by statesmen without appealing to the nation's honour). If Belgium were in danger, 'we would support him'. His opposition was based on three points: (1) '... You are engaging in a whole European war which is not going to leave the map of Europe in the position it is now'. (2) 'We want to try to find out what is going to happen, when it is all over, to the power of Russia in Europe, and we are not going to go blindly into this conflict without having some sort of a rough idea as to what is going to happen'. (3) 'Finally, so far as France is concerned, we say solemnly and definitely that no such friendship as the Right Hon. Gentleman describes between one nation and another can ever justify one of those nations entering into war on behalf of the other' (to which he strangely added 'If France is really in danger ... then let him say so'). He concluded:

> So far as we are concerned, whatever may happen, whatever may be said about us, whatever attacks may be made upon us, we will take the action that we will take, of saying that this country ought to have remained neutral, because in the deepest parts of our hearts we believe that that was right and that that alone was consistent with the honour of the country and the traditions of the party that are now in office.[33]

Two days later the Parliamentary Labour Party, though re-iterating its opposition to the War, refused to follow MacDonald in opposing Asquith's demand for a war credit of £100 million. He at once resigned the chairmanship, though he remained Treasurer of the party.

[33] *Parl. Debates*, 5th ser. lxv, 1830–1.

Though MacDonald's resignation seems precipitate, it could probably not have been long delayed. Once the party was strongly drawn into support of the War a leader who opposed the War would be in an impossible position. And once the break was made, circumstances were bound to perpetuate it. A prominent opponent of the War would naturally be drawn, as MacDonald was, into new associations and movements which most of his colleagues avoided or opposed. MacDonald's own views naturally became clearer and sharper as the War continued. What were they?

He was never a pacifist. He believed that the War, once begun, must be fought through: 'whatever our views may be of the origins of the war, we must go through with it'.[34] Over recruiting, where his conduct has been most criticised, his position was that 'those who can enlist ought to enlist'; he refused to appear on recruiting platforms, saying that enlisting was a matter for individual judgement.

A mature statement of his position can be found in a book he published in 1917, *National Defence: A Study in Militarism*. This not only condemns militarism: armies always produce war, and they threaten democracy and working-men's organisations in peace-time. He condemns the old diplomacy also, for it operates by secrecy and deception. Alliances, entered into for defence, always become offensive. The nation was kept asleep before 1914 as to its entanglements: 'our honour had been privately bound to see France through a war with Germany', and France, under its alliance with Russia, was bound to fight Germany if Russia fought. Thus it was not Germany, nor the invasion of Belgium, which brought on the War, but the alliances and the armies behind them. MacDonald feared that conscription would become a permanent condition for Britain; the wartime alliances would continue with larger commitments, and defence would become all the more onerous. He had little faith in the American idea of a league to enforce peace by an international army (this would be militarism enlarged) and was shrewd about the impossibility of economic sanctions as an

[34] At Leicester, 7 August 1914, quoted by Elton, *op. cit.* p. 252. See *ibid.* pp. 256–66 for MacDonald's attitude to the War, and especially the summary of his article in the *Labour Leader*, 13 August 1914, on responsibility for the War, which elaborates the points made in his speech of 3 August.

alternative to war. A peace imposed by victors could not be lasting; defeated Germany, even if it became a democratic state, would continue to nurse its grievances. 'When the best and the worst have been done, Germany will still have it in her power to stir up strife and fear or accept peace.' The only hope was in a negotiated peace, leading to a co-operation of states.[35] Above all, policy must come into the control of the people :

... the State is less democratic than the nation. Now, the Army is the servant of the State, not of the nation. That is the fundamental fact which we have to bear in mind. If this distinction between State and nation were removed by democratic Governments, international diplomacy would be so altered that armies would be altogether unnecessary.[36]

These views were close to those of the U.D.C., whose aims were the parliamentary control of foreign policy, open negotiations and an end to the War on terms that would not lead to another.[37]

MacDonald's independence drew him into many organisations besides the U.D.C. He wrote constantly for the *Labour Leader*, the *Socialist Review*, *Forward* and the U.D.C.'s own magazine; he contributed one of the U.D.C.'s pamphlets, *War and the Workers*. He was equally active in the I.L.P., the War Emergency Workers' National Committee, in which Labour supporters and trade unionists of differing opinions co-operated, and in the National Council of Civil Liberties, another all-party organisation which defended freedom of public meetings, opposed police raids on U.D.C. and other offices, and criticised the Military Service Act. In Parliament he repeatedly questioned the treatment being meted out to conscientious objectors and other men affected by conscription.[38]

His public meetings, his writings and speeches, his committee work kept MacDonald's name before the public, and brought him many new political friendships. He was not unpopular in

[35] J. R. MacDonald, *National Defence: A Study in Militarism* (1917), pp. 42, 128, *passim*.
[36] *Ibid.* p. 101.
[37] See H. M. Swanwick, *Builders of Peace: being Ten Years' History of the Union of Democratic Control* (1924).
[38] See his very cogent speech on 19 October 1916: *Parl. Debates*, 5th ser. lxxxvi, 802–15.

the labour movement generally: indeed, he was warmly received as fraternal delegate to the 1915 T.U.C. and at the 1916 Labour Party Conference. It was his enemies who turned him into a seeming martyr and revolutionary, ignoring the continuing moderation of his views. Several of his meetings were broken up by organised violence, for instance an N.C.C.L. meeting at Cardiff in November 1915; and after the prearranged tactics – forged tickets, stink bombs, the platform stormed before the meeting began – had prevented a big meeting from being held in Memorial Hall, London that same month, this form of campaigning was abandoned. But the strategy of the war patriots boomeranged. When MacDonald came to speak at Plumstead Common near Woolwich in the summer of 1918 a number of Scottish soldiers accompanied him and made sure that he was allowed to speak. Horatio Bottomley's action in publishing in *John Bull* a copy of his birth certificate, showing his illegitimacy, had the opposite effect to that intended.[39]

MacDonald's importance was both demonstrated and increased by events in 1917 which in their turn changed both the Labour Party and MacDonald's relationship to it. The Russian Revolution in its first phase roused general enthusiasm at the ending of Czarist autocracy. MacDonald was one of twelve Labour and trade-union leaders (others were Snowden and Smillie) who as the United Socialist Council summoned the famous meeting at Leeds on 3 June 1917 to '*hail the* Russian Revolution *and* to Organise *the* British Democracy *To follow Russia*'. MacDonald moved the first of the four resolutions (the one giving the hail).[40] From Leeds he was to go, with Jowett, to Russia as a delegate from the national executive of the Labour Party to prepare the ground for the projected conference of socialists at Stockholm. The mission had the government's approval but not that of Havelock Wilson's Seamen's Union, which refused to allow the delegation to sail. A little later Arthur Henderson, Labour member of the War Cabinet, was tripped up by the same abortive Stockholm conference. After an official

[39] Elton, *op. cit.*, Snowden, *op. cit.*, and Fenner Brockway's *Inside the Left* (1942) are useful in recalling the side of the War in which MacDonald played his part.

[40] Beside Elton's and Snowden's accounts of the Leeds Convention, see Allan Bullock, *Life and Times of Ernest Bevin*, i (1960), pp. 74–6, and Woolf, *op. cit.* pp. 210–13.

visit to Russia he supported the plans for the conference and
persuaded a special conference of the Labour Party to do so.
Lloyd George, however, changed his mind about its desirability,
and Henderson's resignation from the Cabinet followed. Now
MacDonald and Henderson, long-time colleagues in the party
organisation but recently divided (however narrowly) in their
attitude to the War, could combine forces in the party's cause.
Labour had gained greatly in strength and confidence from the
War, whether from experience in office or in opposition, whether
as trade unionists finding themselves accepted as essential
partners in the war effort or as men and women concerned to
fight for civil liberties and a just peace.

The new collaboration between Henderson and Sidney Webb
and MacDonald soon had notable results. The Labour Party
got a new constitution which committed it to socialism and
opened it to individual members alongside those belonging
through membership of affiliated bodies such as trade unions,
the Fabian Society and the I.L.P.; it became, in fact, a normal
political party. Here, and particularly in the very vagueness of
the celebrated clause 4, MacDonald's moderate philosophy and
his commitment to parliamentary methods received confirma-
tion; nor did he find the new programme, 'Labour and the New
Social Order', any less palatable. By the War's end MacDonald
was back in the inner circle of the party's leaders, but with new
contacts and wider experience which had made him, more than
any of his rivals except perhaps Henderson, a national figure.
His loss of Leicester in the 'coupon election' of 1918 was thus
unimportant, all the more since Labour men who had supported
the War, including Henderson himself, were buried under the
electoral landslide along with the hated 'pacifists'.

During the critical years of the post-war coalition of 1918–22
MacDonald re-established his claim to the leadership of the
party. It has been argued that his election as Chairman in 1922
by a narrow margin was an accident, caused by the late arrival
of some trade-union M.P.s who were pledged to support
Clynes.[41] Alternatively he was accused (long afterwards, by
Snowden in his autobiography)[42] of having played up to the left
wing; this because Clydesiders, who soon regretted it, nomi-

[41] Scanlon, *op. cit.* pp. 32–5.
[42] Snowden, *op. cit.* ii, p. 574.

nated him for the chairmanship. His popularity in Glasgow was
nothing new. It was he who delivered the memorial eulogy to
Keir Hardie in St. Andrew's Hall in 1915. He had many friends,
notably the Robertons, founders of the Orpheus Choir. He contributed a fortnightly column to Tom Johnston's *Forward*, and
was grateful for its hospitality in the War years. But there was
much more to it than this.

MacDonald's return had, in fact, a certain inevitability about
it.[43] With the division of the Liberals and the near-annihilation
of Asquith's 'wee frees', the place of the opposition was waiting
for Labour, but its members in Parliament, under the mild
leadership of Adamson and Clynes, seemed unwilling to take it.
MacDonald's criticism, in *Forward* and the *Socialist Review*,
could not but make the contrast between the present leadership
and the past, for all that it was moderately expressed. He pointed
to the ignorance of the Parliamentary Party over parliamentary
procedure (in fact, J. H. Thomas proposed that he be made an
adviser to the group but this, not surprisingly, fell through).
In his column in *Forward* he commented on the use of 'direct
action' or the threats of it in these years, which included the
'Jolly George' incident, the succession of strikes in 1919–21
and the collapse of the Triple Alliance. He did not condemn
direct action outright nor exalt consitutionalism at any price;
but he argued that force could only be used in exceptional circumstances, and always carried the danger of defeating itself.
His language on any political subject was often strong, particularly in denouncing the government; but the message itself was
much more emollient. Professor Lyman gives an instance from
the *Socialist Review* for April 1920, when MacDonald commented on a suggested Liberal–Labour government:

> The political imbecility of such a forecast and of such
> complacency is a colossal betrayal which will be challenged
> so long as a remnant of the Independent Labour Party hangs
> together. Coalitions there may have to be, but a coalition like
> this with 'comparatively little matter' who is Prime Minister
> – never.[44]

[43] The ensuing argument is based chiefly on Lyman's cogent article in
Journal of British Studies, ii (1962), pp. 132–60.
[44] *Ibid.* p. 158.

MacDonald, in fact, in his busy writing of these years, followed his characteristic style, rich in qualifications and saving clauses, which reflected the bent of his thinking.

At the same time MacDonald was extremely active in the I.L.P. Here, too, his restraining counsel, however beneficial to the labour movement in the long run, must have irritated many members, but it demonstrated his continuing importance. He was determined that the campaign for 'Socialist unity' (spurred on by the need to end Allied intervention in Russia) should not lead to any acceptance of Communism. In 1920 the I.L.P. voted to secede from the Second International, but MacDonald's eloquence helped to prevent it from resolving to join the Communist International – a decision confirmed at the Southport conference in 1921, when a disgruntled delegation returned from Moscow. MacDonald worked hard to revive the Second International, serving for a time as its Secretary (on the nomination of the T.U.C. side of the International Joint Committee of the T.U.C. and the Labour Party).[45] In all this MacDonald and Snowden, who was Chairman at the time, helped to keep the I.L.P. in step with the Labour Party and prevent any dangerous fissures within the movement from widening. MacDonald had, indeed, a foot in both camps. He was still Treasurer of the Labour Party; and he had his own 'cell' in the I.L.P., the Information Department of which he was Chairman, with Ernest Hunter and Mary Agnes Hamilton as important members. At this time MacDonald used to frequent the '1917 Club' at No. 4 Gerrard Street in Soho, a haunt of authors, pacifists and Labour people (there is an odd story somewhere of MacDonald dropping in for lunch, as he used frequently to do, on the day when he became Prime Minister, and never coming there again).[46] The Woolwich by-election in 1921 completed the process of recovery for MacDonald. He stood for Will Crooks's old seat, and lost to the unknown Captain Gee, V.C., by 683 votes. Bottomley spewed forth more of his poison against the 'traitor', but equally effective in rousing sympathy and support for MacDonald was the opposition of the Communists.

When the greatly enlarged Parliamentary Party met after the

[45] *Ibid.* p. 145.
[46] Woolf, *op. cit.* p. 216.

general election of 1922 to elect a Chairman, MacDonald (returned to Parliament for Aberavon) was chosen by sixty-one votes to fifty-six. Professor Lyman's comment, 'the remarkable thing is not that MacDonald won, but that the vote was so close',[47] seems justified. In a great many contexts MacDonald was the most prominent Labour figure of the day. His writings (including *Socialism: Critical and Constructive*, published in 1921), his speeches, his membership of innumerable committees,[48] his standing among international socialists, testified to and enlarged his reputation. He appealed equally to the left and and to the centre. There may have been some campaigning to secure his election, but the Clydesiders and I.L.P. alone could not have given him a majority: he needed and received the votes of a number of the trade-union M.P.s.[49] Dissatisfaction with Clynes's leadership was one factor; the new members had no cause to re-elect him out of past loyalty. Time was to show that MacDonald's personality and manner, uncongenial to many before the War, were obstacles to unity and firm purpose within a Labour Cabinet and the party. At the time he possessed, in Professor Lyman's words, 'an array of talents unmatched by any potential rival'. As the *New Leader* put it (24 November 1922), 'By his ability to give, in initiative, in speech, in tactics, a powerful expression to the will and the ideals of the whole party, MacDonald will infallibly become the symbol, the personification, which we have hitherto lacked.'[50]

This mood could not be maintained; but MacDonald did give the Labour Party the leadership and sense of direction which it needed in the next few years. He led it from the centre and he confirmed it as a party of the centre. When the indecisive election of 1923 gave Labour the opportunity of forming a minority government he accepted it; indeed, its minority position suited and justified his role as moderator. His Cabinet included only two men of the left, Wheatley and Jowett, and several ex-Liberals and non-party men; but the trade-union side was quite well represented. MacDonald's first Labour government settled three things of importance for the future: that a Labour Prime

[47] Lyman, *loc. cit.* p. 155.
[48] *Ibid.* p. 149.
[49] *Ibid.* pp. 153–5.
[50] *Ibid.* p. 160.

Minister would choose his own Cabinet and not follow the advice of a party caucus;[51] that a Labour government was quite capable of governing, at least as well as a Tory or a Liberal government; and that Labour could, as MacDonald told Lord Parmoor he intended to do, 'gain the confidence of the country'. Even the shabby fall of the government over the Campbell case and its defeat in the 1924 election did not seriously weaken MacDonald's hold on the party; the Zinoviev letter, however ineffective in fact, was a useful alibi for defeat. There were, naturally, murmurings against his leadership; but where were the alternatives? Henderson brusquely declined Snowden's suggestion that he take the hot seat, observing that MacDonald was the party's strongest figure and the only man with a real following in the country.[52] Labour has never had much use for king-makers. MacDonald's position was made easier once the I.L.P. went into the wilderness with Maxton after Clifford Allen had given up the impossible task of yoking it to two horses, socialism and MacDonald; MacDonald (and Snowden too) had already drawn away from it, particularly over its programme 'Socialism in Our Time'. He showed his power, which was much more than the power of an orator, at successive Labour Party Conferences; at the Liverpool conference of 1925 after the defeat in the previous general election, for example, or the Birmingham conference in 1928, when 'Labour and the Nation' was debated and MacDonald, knowing exactly what he wanted, resisted successfully all the amendments he disliked as making the programme more specific. And as Leader of the Opposition he continued to show his mastery of parliamentary tactics.

In the second Labour government MacDonald's weaknesses were more apparent than his strength. When it came to acting a public part of dignity, such as presiding over the first India Round Table conference, he was still magnificent; when it came to dealing with everyday politics in the setting of world depression and menacingly swelling unemployment, he could supply no leadership. He was irritated by dependence on the votes of the unstable and disintegrating Liberals. He was held back from bold measures against unemployment by the wooden-

---

[51] See Lyman, *First Labour Government*, ch. vii.
[52] M. A. Hamilton, *Arthur Henderson* (1938), pp. 256–7.

ness and bad judgement of Snowden and the Treasury officials.[53] His fatal lack of hard knowledge and his reluctance to admit it, his scorn of experts, worked against him. Having appointed his Economic Advisory Council in 1930, he made little use of it. At one of its monthly meetings he asked whether the Council could not present the unemployment figures so as to make them look better. 'It's not the figures but the facts,' J. H. Thomas replied. At which Keynes leant over to Thomas and whispered: 'Leave him alone; he'll overcome unemployment quicker that way than any other.'[54]

MacDonald was, thus, helpless when the crisis of August 1931 came upon him. Faced with horrendous tales of the flight from the pound, he could only accept the 'safe' advice of economists, including a cut in unemployment pay, and was encouraged in this by the Conservative and Liberal leaders whom he had prematurely consulted. He could understand neither the passion of those members of his Cabinet who obstinately balked at reducing unemployment pay nor the mild heterodoxies of other proposals for balancing the budget. He must have his way or throw all away – as in a different sense he had done in 1914 and 1924. Yet, had he been content with the resignation of his government, he would have remained, certainly for a time, the leader of the party and might still be a Labour hero.

His decision was hardly surprising to a man of his temperament. He did not foresee more than a temporary breach between himself and the party – something like that of 1914. He was easily persuaded that only the economies under a National government could overcome a crisis which threatened working men as much as the rest of the community. The appeal of the King (who 'trusted there was no question of the Prime Minister's resignation') was bound to touch his innermost feelings, those of the outsider who longed to be inside;[55] here was the greatest role which life would ever give him to play, the saviour putting country above party. Moreover, leadership of an emergency all-party government was consistent with the moderate, generalised, almost non-party spirit of his ideas. Yet to condemn him on his action in 1931 alone is to misjudge both him and the party.

[53] Skidelsky's *Politicians and the Slump* brings this out very clearly.
[54] Information from the late R. H. Tawney.
[55] Francis Williams, *op. cit.* p. 64.

If the Labour Party condemns MacDonald it condemns itself, for having chosen and retained him as leader. Whether it likes it or not, the party still has its heritage from him. He helped to found and organise it, to win members for it. He expressed its hopeful, sentimental, intangible socialism, which means to each member what he wants it to mean. He kept it on the path of moderation and of constitutional method, particularly in the uneasy days of 1919–21. He maintained its longing for peace, its hatred of war, its fraternal links with European socialism. He helped to make it a national party, not class-bound but appealing to men and women in all walks of life, an alternative to the Conservatives when the Liberal Party faltered. He showed that Labour could form a government and that a Labour Prime Minister need fear comparisons with few of his predecessors and successors. In none of this was he alone: Hardie, Henderson, Snowden, Clynes, Thomas, most of the other Labour leaders of his generation shared the same ideas and reinforced them. But he embodied them; his *persona* attracted the general public to them.

At the same time it is clear that Labour's 'split personality' is due in some measure to MacDonald. He never gave up his platonic affair with socialism, and so could not lead his party towards a purely reformist policy, Liberal in spirit, Labour in emphasis; and he never had the passion for socialism which might have made his Labour Party socialist. Perhaps it is as well that the Labour Party has never reconciled the two sides of its personality, liberalism and socialism. But it does not make for a united and self-confident party; it fosters the minority complex, the death-wish. MacDonald had the stature within the party to make it one thing or the other; he lacked the character to do so. Even today Labour pays tribute to him in its predilection for leaders endowed, not with the doctrinaire spirit which was alien to him but with his moderation and his dislike of class-consciousness. Henderson and Lansbury, Attlee and Gaitskell and Harold Wilson are all of a kind. Only under a different kind of leader will Labour have exorcised MacDonald's influence.

7

JAMES HINTON

THE CLYDE WORKERS' COMMITTEE AND THE DILUTION STRUGGLE

'S E L D O M has a prominent politician, a leading representative of the Governing class, been treated with so little respect by a meeting of the workers. It is evident that the feeling of servility towards their masters no longer holds first place in the minds of the Clyde workers....'[1] This was the revolutionary John Maclean's comment in his short-lived paper, the *Vanguard*, on the meeting of 3000 engineers which Lloyd George addressed in the St. Andrew's Hall, Glasgow, on Christmas Day, 1915. The same dominant emphasis on working-class audacity permeates William Gallacher's portrayal of the Clydeside unrest of 1915–16.[2] These judgements seem to catch the authentic tones of Red Clydeside.

Yet Red Clydeside, in these years at least, is something of a myth. Both Maclean, in the heat of the moment, and Gallacher, on mature reflection, were guilty of evoking misleading impressions, heroic fantasies which obscured the real import of these early struggles on the Clyde. What really happened can best be reconstructed from the Ministry of Munitions papers in the Public Record Office and the Beveridge Collection on Munitions in the British Library of Economic and Political Science. The story, though less heart-warming than Gallacher's own account, remains of the greatest historical interest.

[1] Ministry of Munitions papers in Public Record Office: Mun. 5.70, extracts from the suppressed issue of *Vanguard*, 30 December 1915.
[2] W. Gallacher, *Revolt on the Clyde* (1936).

I

When Lloyd George decided to visit the Clyde during December 1915, the Clyde munitions workers, led by the Clyde Workers' Committee (C.W.C.), appeared to be the major obstacle to the government's campaign to increase the output of war material by introducing less skilled men and women into jobs previously the preserve of the craftsmen – i.e. dilution. The Minister's reception confirmed this opinion, and on 21 January he announced the government's intention of pushing ahead with dilution without permitting any further delay 'on any ground whatever'.[3] To give effect to this policy special Dilution Commissioners were dispatched at once to the Clyde. (And also to the Tyne, another troublespot.) The Clyde Commissioners were remarkably successful both in introducing dilution and in destroying the C.W.C. By August 1916, 7436 skilled engineers had been transferred to new jobs as a result of dilution,[4] at a time when there were 17,500 members of the skilled engineering unions on Clydeside.[5] By April 1916 the C.W.C. had been broken and its leaders deported from the area or imprisoned.

The suppression of the C.W.C., as this essay will demonstrate, was the result of a well-planned offensive directed by the Labour Department of the Ministry of Munitions. It is, perhaps, significant that the principal officials concerned were a group of civil servants recruited from the Board of Trade's Labour Exchange and Unemployment Insurance Departments.[6] These men had been prominent before the War in the making of the new Liberal welfare legislation which, from Hilaire Belloc to J. T. Murphy, chief ideologist of the shop stewards' movement, had been seen by some of its opponents as a milestone on the road

[3] Parl. Debates, 5th ser. lxxviii, 765–6.
[4] Mun. 2.27, 'Secret Weekly Reports of the Labour Department of the Ministry of Munitions' (5 August 1916).
[5] Amalgamated Society of Engineers (A.S.E.), *Monthly Journal and Report*, January 1916; B. Drake, *Women in the Engineering Trades* (1916), p. 127.
[6] These were the men to whom Ernest Bevin referred in September 1916: 'Behind the Minister [Lloyd George] was a sinister crowd of Civil Servants ... the Labour Exchange crowd, Mr. Beveridge, Llewellyn Smith and the rest.' Quoted in W. Beveridge, *Power and Influence* (1953), p. 127.

to the 'Servile State'.[7] The story of the dilution struggle on the Clyde can be read as a central incident in a repressive phase of the 'New Liberalism'.

William Beveridge[8] was, during 1915–16, an Assistant General Secretary in the Ministry of Munitions, responsible initially for the Labour Department and the Secretariat, and, from March 1916, for Labour Regulation. Charles Rey,[9] also an Assistant General Secretary, was in charge of Labour Supply. Consolidating the Board of Trade influence was Sir Hubert Llewellyn Smith,[10] General Secretary of the Ministry, with special responsibility for the Labour Department and the Secretariat.[11] Together with Lloyd George, Llewellyn Smith, Beveridge and Rey were the prime movers in the offensive against the C.W.C. One other man, who played a major role, should be

[7] H. Belloc, *The Servile State* (1913), *passim*. For Murphy's views, see, for example, *Solidarity*, March 1917. The C.W.C. shared this outlook. Thus, at Christmas 1915, the Committee's spokesman explained to Lloyd George: 'You have to remember that for some years past there has been considerable nibbling at the individuality of the worker. During all his working hours he is merely a cipher – known by a check number. At the Labour Exchange he has a number, and when he is ill, under the State Insurance, he is also known by a number. The Munitions Act and the Defence of the Realm Act have divested him of the last shreds of individuality, and it begins to look to him as if they were gone permanently ...' *Worker*, 15 January 1916.

[8] William, later Lord, Beveridge (b. 1879). From 1909 Director of Labour Exchanges at the Board of Trade. Helped to establish Ministry of Food after leaving Munitions. Director of London School of Economics, 1919–37, and Master of University College Oxford, 1937–45. Author of the Beveridge Report, 1942.

[9] Charles Rey (b. 1877) had joined the Board of Trade staff in 1900. One of the officials sent to study the German Labour Exchanges, he was appointed General Manager of Labour Exchanges in 1909. In 1912 he became General Manager of Unemployment Insurance. After his time at the Ministry of Munitions he returned to the Board of Trade. In 1918 he became Assistant Secretary to the new Ministry of Labour. Subsequently his interests took him to Africa, where he became Resident Commissioner in Bechuanaland, 1930–7. In 1968 he was still alive, resident in Cape Town.

[10] Sir Hubert Llewellyn Smith (1864–1945): Oxford and Toynbee Hall. Wrote *The Story of the Dockers Strike* with Tillett in 1890. Joined the staff of the Board of Trade in 1893, and was Permanent Secretary from 1907. After the War he became Chief Economic Adviser to the government. Retired in 1927, and subsequently directed the *New Survey of London Life and Labour* (1928–35).

[11] There were other ex-Board of Trade officials in the Labour Department who did not play a leading role in the Clyde affair, notably H. Wolfe and J. B. Adams.

mentioned. William Weir[12] was a Glasgow businessman and, from July 1915, Director of Munitions for Scotland. If ever there was an interested party it was Weir, whose factory, G. & J. Weir of Cathcart, was a major stronghold of the Clyde Workers' Committee.

The Dilution Commissioners, upon whose tact and discretion the success of the government offensive ultimately depended, were chaired by Lynden Macassey, K.C., who had been a member of an earlier comission[13] dispatched to the Clyde during the troubles of the autumn of 1915, and who was an experienced industrial arbitrator. The other two members were Isaac Mitchell, who had risen from the shop floor via the secretaryship of the General Federation of Trade Unions to become an Assistant Industrial Commissioner at the Board of Trade, and Sir Thomas Munro, County Clerk of Lanarkshire and a figure of local weight and influence.[14]

I I

When the Dilution Commissioners arrived on the Clyde, they soon discovered that the C.W.C., though it was supported by a large minority on the district committee of the chief engineering union, the Amalgamated Society of Engineers (A.S.E.), in their own words, 'has not effective control over the workers in more than five or six shops'.[15] The leading figures in the Committee were representative of these factories: David Kirkwood[16]

[12] William Weir (1877–1959). Not to be confused with Andrew Weir (Lord Invernorth), who became Minister of Munitions in 1919. William Weir was Director-General of Aircraft Production at the Ministry of Munitions from 1918. During the inter-war years he was Chairman of the Advisory Committee on Civil Aviation. In 1939 he became Director-General of Explosives at the Ministry of Supply, and in 1942 Chairman of the Tank Board. He was also, for a time, Hon. President of the British Employers' Confederation.

[13] See *Report by Lord Balfour of Burleigh and Mr. L. Macassey, K.C. on ... Munitions Workers in the Clyde District* (P.P. 1914–16, Cd. 8136).

[14] For biographical details of the Commissioners, see *The Times*, 24 January 1916.

[15] Mun. 5.73, memorandum by Macassey, 9 February 1916; Beveridge Collection on Munitions, vol. iii (hereafter Bev. iii), p. 355, memorandum by Mitchell, 21 February 1916.

[16] David Kirkwood (1872–1955). Worked at Parkhead since 1910. Joined I.L.P., having originally been a member of the S.L.P., early in the War. Subsequently a member of the I.L.P. National Administration Committee,

and Tom Clark from Beardmore's Forge at Parkhead, William Gallacher[17] from the Albion Motor Car factory in Scotstoun, John Muir[18] from Barr & Stroud in Anniesland, James Messer and Arthur MacManus[19] from Weir's in Cathcart. The Committee also had influence in Beardmore's shipyard and marine engineering works at Dalmuir and, more questionably, at the Coventry Ordnance Works and one or two smaller sub-contracting shops in Scotstoun.

Apart from the concentration of influence in the Scotstoun–Anniesland area to the west of Glasgow, these works were widely dispersed throughout the city: Parkhead in the East End, Dalmuir nine miles away on the lower reaches of the Clyde and Weir's in the south. It was not location but output that these factories had in common: by 1915 they were all substantially employed on munitions contracts.[20] This is significant, since the production of munitions – shells, guns, tanks, aircraft engines, etc. – played a subordinate role on the Clyde. Shipbuilding and marine engineering predominated.

Since the 1870s shipbuilding and marine engineering had been the most dynamic sector of the metal industries on the Clyde, directly employing, by 1921, over one-third of their workers.[21] A handful of firms dominated this sector, four of them employing 20,000 workers, perhaps half the total, by 1915.[22] There were many smaller shipbuilding and marine engineering firms clustering particularly in the central Govan–Finneston

and M.P. for Dumbarton, 1922–51. Created Baron Kirkwood of Bearsden in 1951.

[17] William Gallacher (1881–1965). Worked at Albion since 1913. Joined S.D.F. in 1905. Subsequently founder member of Communist Party, and M.P. for West Fife, 1935–50.

[18] John Muir (1879–1931). Member of S.L.P. Editor of *Socialist* and *Worker*. Subsequently joined I.L.P. and became M.P. for Maryhill in 1922. Parliamentary Secretary to the Ministry of Pensions, 1924. Later, General Secretary of the Workers' Educational Association.

[19] Arthur MacManus (1889–1927). Member of S.L.P. and editor of *Socialist*. Elected President of National Administrative Council of Shop Stewards' Movement in August 1917. First President of the British Communist Party.

[20] For a detailed analysis of the Glasgow metal industries at this time, see my Ph.D. thesis, 'Rank and File Militancy in the British Engineering Industry, 1914–1918', (London, 1969) ch. v, sec. ii.

[21] *Report of the Thirteenth (1921) Decennial Census of Scotland*, vol. iii; *Occupations and Industries* (1925), Industry Tables.

[22] Bev. v, p. 76 'Report on Labour in Controlled Establishments'.

area. At the beginning of 1915 Glasgow was firmly in the grip of the Admiralty, and the only firms on munitions work apart from Beardmore's and his sub-contractors were 'a few sub-contractors of English firms'.[23] From August 1915, however, the Ministry of Munitions began to press contracts upon Glasgow firms. William Weir was appointed Director of Munitions for Scotland, his job being to carve out an area in the metal trades to be devoted to munitions production, while taking care not to step on the toes of the Admiralty.[24]

Weir's greatest success was in promoting shell production, which, by 1916, had cut deeply into the hegemony of the ship-yards in Glasgow.[25] This sector is, however, only of marginal importance in relation to the themes of this essay, since less than 10 per cent of shell workers were engineering craftsmen.[26] In the struggle over dilution shell production was not at issue. No shells had been produced on the Clyde before the War, thus no men were directly replaced by women, and, in the change-over to peace-time production, the manufacture of shells and the dilution associated with it were expected to disappear.[27] It was in the heavier branches of munitions production, where a very high proportion of skilled labour was initially employed, that dilution met with the fiercest resistance; and the largest firms (with one or two exceptions) on this type of work were those affiliated to the C.W.C.

An analysis of A.S.E. branch membership figures over the five years 1914–19 indicates a close correspondence between these figures and the emergence and rapid growth of the muni-tions sector, on the one hand, and the relatively sluggish ex-pansion of the shipbuilding and marine engineering sector on the other. In the East End, dominated by Parkhead Forge, A.S.E. membership grew by 358 per cent. In Scotstoun and Anniesland, the home of Albion, Barr & Stroud, and the Coventry Ordnance Works it grew by 266 per cent. On the other

[23] W. R. Scott and J. Cunnison, *The Industries of the Clyde Valley During the War* (Oxford, 1924), p. 113.
[24] *History of the Ministry of Munitions (1920–1924)*, vol. 2, pt. ii (here-after *M.M.* 2, ii), pp. 131–2.
[25] Based on material in *M.M.* 2, ii, p. 161; *M.M.*8, ii, pp. 133, 137; Bev. v, p. 76; Scott and Cunnison, *op. cit.* pp. 112–15.
[26] Bev. v, p. 79.
[27] *M.M.* 4, ii, p. 49; Scott and Cunnison, *op. cit.* p. 98.

hand, in the whole central area of Glasgow – Govan, Partick, Finneston – dominated by shipbuilding and marine engineering firms, the A.S.E. grew by only 51 per cent. These areas, between them, account for over half the total A.S.E. membership in Glasgow. The same correspondence carried through the rest of the district, though less strikingly and with some exceptions.[28]

By 1919, 20 per cent of A.S.E. members belonged to the expanding branches of the localities dominated by munitions firms, and it was from these firms that the C.W.C. had emerged. There is no direct evidence that this 20 per cent of engineering workers worked in the munitions firms, but it seems unlikely that the coincidence between the location of an expanding munitions sector and the location of the fastest-growing A.S.E. branches could be explained in any other way.

The figure of 20 per cent of the A.S.E. membership thus provides a (very crude) indicator of the basis of support immediately available to the C.W.C. One major problem for the Committee would therefore be to extend its influence beyond the sector of its origin into the sector dominated by shipbuilding and marine engineering which employed the great majority of Glasgow engineers. This it failed to do: indeed, the history of militancy on the Clyde between the strike of February 1915 and the deportations of March 1916 is, in part, a history of the progressive isolation of this militant vanguard in the munitions factories.

III

The C.W.C. was formed in the last week of October 1915, but the origins of local rank-and-file organisation based in the workshops are to be sought in the strike of February 1915. A demand for an increase of twopence per hour was first put to the employers in December 1914 on the expiration of a three-year wages agreement. The employers turned it down, and by the end of January an overtime ban was being imposed by

[28] A.S.E., *Monthly Journal and Report* (1914–17, 1919); Fabian Research Department, *Gazetteer of Trade Union Branches* (1918); *Kelly's Directory of the Engineering Trades* (1917); Glasgow Chamber of Commerce, *Handbook* (Glasgow, 1919).

workers in all the principal Glasgow factories. On 16 February 2000 men at Weir's struck over a local issue. This ignited unrest throughout the district and within four days 10,000 skilled engineers had joined the strike demanding payment of the two-pence an hour increase. The great majority remained out for nearly two weeks, until 3 March.[29]

This solidarity was achieved despite the opposition of the A.S.E. district committee, which, though sympathetic to the overtime ban, denounced the strike and ordered the men back to work.[30] In place of the district committee a Clyde Labour Withholding Committee – so named in order to avoid trouble under the Defence of the Realm Act – was formed, composed largely of A.S.E. shop stewards who had previously met together in an officially recognised local Vigilance Committee.[31]

Gallacher described the organisation in his memoirs as follows:

Every morning mass meetings were held in the areas and the discussions and decisions of the previous day's committee meeting were reported. Every afternoon and evening the committee was in session, taking reports from the areas and considering ways and means of strengthening and extending the strike. For a fortnight, under the most terrific barrage ever directed against a strike, we kept going without a break of any kind, despite the fact that not one striker was receiving a penny of strike pay or relief.[32]

Although most of the shop stewards did not represent fully fledged workshop organisations, the leading group within the Labour Withholding Committee came from those factories where workshop organisation was already established as a bargaining force – Messer, the Secretary, from Weir's; Gallacher, the Chairman, from Albion; David Kirkwood and Tom Clark

[29] *M.M.* 4, ii, pp. 36–8; A.S.E. *Executive Minutes*, cxc (28 January 1915); Board of Trade, *Labour Gazette*, March 1915; *Herald*, 6 March 1915; *Glasgow Herald, passim; Glasgow District Record, passim.*
[30] *Glasgow Herald*, 18–19 and 25–26 February 1915.
[31] Labour Party, *Report of Special Committee ... upon the Circumstances which resulted in the Deportation in March 1916 of David Kirkwood and other Workmen ...* (1917), p. 12.
[32] Gallacher, *op. cit.* p. 47.

from Parkhead.[33] From the start the factories which were to provide the basis for the C.W.C. were in the lead.

The vanguard role of these factories became even more evident during the last days of the strike. On Friday, 26 February the government intervened, demanding a return by the Monday and offering arbitration. Over the week-end, union and government officials mounted a large-scale campaign to get the men back to work, with a liberal application of threats and bribes: the men would get strike pay if they went back, strikes would be made illegal and arbitration compulsory if they did not. Under this barrage the Labour Withholding Committee decided to recommend a return on the Thursday while maintaining the overtime ban and threatening a stay-in strike if the twopence were not granted by a specified date. When this resolution was put to mass meetings in the localities on Tuesday, 2 March a general separation of the more from the less militant engineers took place. Nearly 40 per cent of those voting rejected the Committee's recommendation and returned to work the next day. Foremost among these were the workers in the shipbuilding and marine engineering area of Govan and Finneston. The areas which remained most solidly behind the Committee were (with the exception of Weir's, where the strike crumbled on the Wednesday) those which were to provide the backbone of the C.W.C. – Dalmuir, Scotstoun, Parkhead.

As soon as the men returned to work, the authority of the Labour Withholding Committee evaporated. The overtime ban was partial from the start and the stay-in strike never materialised.[34]. The eventual award of one penny an hour (a farthing more than the employers had offered shortly before the strike broke out) was accepted without protest.[35] But while the Labour Withholding Committee had failed to establish itself as a permanent local rank-and-file organisation independent of the officials, the idea of such an organisation had now been created,[36]

[33] *Ibid.* p. 43; *Herald*, 16 October 1915. The organisation at Albion may still have been unrecognised by the management.

[34] *Glasgow Herald, passim; Glasgow District Record, passim.*

[35] Board of Trade, *Labour Gazette,* May 1915; *Glasgow Herald,* 25 March 1915.

[36] The leading theoretician of the shop stewards' movement was later to see in the February 1915 strike the decisive transition from 'pressure on the executives' to 'action in spite of the executives': J. T. Murphy, *Preparing for Power* (1934), p. 111.

and a small group of leaders – 'the most trusted men of the labour movement in Glasgow'[37] – remained in contact, ready when an appropriate issue arose, to call the rank-and-file movement into being.[38]

The opportunity arose with the passing of the Munitions Act in July 1915. Yet it was not until the end of October that the C.W.C. was formed, too late to assert any effective leadship of the widespread unrest occasioned by the Munitions Act during the previous three months. The explanation of this failure again points to the narrowness of the C.W.C. base in the munitions firms.

The Munitions Act was designed to reinforce employers' control of labour against the pressures of war-time full employment and to facilitate the introduction of diluted labour. To this end strikes were made illegal, restrictive practices suspended and the free movement of labour restricted by the device of the 'leaving certificate'. Munitions Tribunals were established to enforce the workshop rules, which, under the Act, the Minister of Munitions was empowered to lay down; to hear appeals against the withholding of leaving certificates by employers; and to deal with workers striking in defiance of the Act. The immediate effect of the Munitions Act of the Clyde was to enhance greatly the disciplinary powers of the employers: managers and foremen became 'more autocratic and dictatorial in their treatment of the men'.[39]

Matters came to a head early in September when seventeen shipwrights employed at Fairfield shipyard (Govan) were fined for leading a strike against an abuse of the leaving certificate system. Three of these men refused to pay the fines and, on 6 October, were jailed. Co-ordinated by the Govan Trades Council, preparations were made for a strike, but at the last moment the government intervened, appointing a Commission of Inquiry. Strike action was staved off with promises until, on 27 October, the government finally agreed to release the men.[40]

[37] *Vanguard*, October 1915.
[38] *Worker*, 29 January 1916.
[39] *M.M.* 4, ii, p. 61.
[40] For this and the following paragraph, see *M.M.* 4, ii, pp. 50–60; *Glasgow Herald*, 4 September 1915, 12, 14–16 October 1915, 14 April 1916; *Forward*, 18 September 1915, 9, 23 October 1915, 18 November 1915; *Vanguard*, October, November 1915; *Herald*, 23, 30 October 1915; *Worker*,

Simultaneously with these events the A.S.E. shop stewards were agitating against the 'Slave Clauses' of the Munitions Act, and on 2 October had decided to set up 'a strong representative committee ... [to] organise the prevailing opposition to the operation of the Act'.[41] When this committee, which included delegates from unions other than the A.S.E., met on Saturday, 16 October it appeared that the Fairfield men had been released, so no action was taken. The men had not, in fact, been released, and the militants suspected that the rumour of their release had been deliberately put about by the authorities to prevent an outburst on the sixteenth.[42] Shortly afterwards the union officials paid the fines, and the crisis ended.

The leaders of the unofficial committee felt they had allowed themselves to be bamboozled by the government and the trade-union officials.[43] The moment for independent action had passed unexploited. The rank-and-file initiative had remained with the Govan Trades Council, itself too geographically limited a body to lead effectively. Underlying this situation was the uneven impact of the Munitions Act on the Clyde. It fell hardest on the shipyards and left virtually untouched the central core of militancy – the engineers in the munitions firms. No member of the A.S.E. or of any of its closest allies among the smaller engineering unions had come before the Munitions Tribunal for striking, though three short strikes were settled without prosecutions.[44] The engineering employers had learned their lesson in February and they were wary of provoking their workers. As one Glasgow A.S.E. militant wrote a year later:

Owing to the fact that the stop stewards were linked together, and had already proved that they had the men in the

---

29 January 1916; Mun. 5.79, 'Threatened Clyde Strike' (16 October 1915); Bev. iii, p. 79, 'Circular Issued by Govan Trades Council' (n.d.); A.S.E., *Executive Minutes*, cxcii (1 October 1915); A.S.E., *Monthly Journal and Report*, October 1915; Gallacher, *op. cit.* pp. 64–5.

[41] *Forward*, 9 October 1915.

[42] *Herald*, 23 October 1915; *Forward*, 23 October 1915. The Fairfield shipyard workers were threatening to strike unless the men were released by the sixteenth. The official papers do suggest that the rumour may have been put about deliberately, see Mun. 5.79, 'Threatened Clyde Strike' (16 October 1915).

[43] Gallacher, *op. cit.* p. 65; *Vanguard*, November 1915.

[44] Bev. ii, p. 99, 'Report on Strikes and Lockouts' (to 13 November 1915); *Glasgow Herald*, August–October 1915, *passim*.

workshops behind them, prepared to take action if necessary, the Act was very lightly administered in the Clyde area. In fact while members of the A.S.E. in every other district of the country were groaning under the slave clauses of the Act, the Clyde district as far as the engineers were concerned was practically free.[45]

Shortly after the C.W.C. was formally established a new convulsion seized Clyeside. Yet again the militant workers in the munitions factories who had led in February failed to take the initiative. One of the hoariest legends about the C.W.C. is that it led the Rent Strike of the autumn of 1915.[46] At the climax of that struggle, however, when eighteen tenants were summoned before the Small Debts Court for rent arrears, it was the men from the five largest shipyards in central Glasgow who struck work to demonstrate in their support. The only munitions workers who came out were those at the Coventry Ordnance Works, the others – the backbone of the C.W.C. – being represented, if at all, by deputations.[47] The rent issue arose most acutely in Govan and Partick,[48] and support from the industrial workers came predominantly not from the munitions sector, whose workers were not so badly affected, but from the shipyards of Govan which had led the way in the Fairfield case. The Rent Strike may well have been the Clyde workers' greatest victory of the war,[49] but the C.W.C. as such had nothing whatsoever to do with it.[50]

[45] *Trade Unionist*, October 1916.
[46] This legend is largely based on Gallacher's account in *Revolt on the Clyde*, pp. 54–5: 'From far away Dalmuir in the West, from Parkhead in the East, from Cathcart in the South and Hydepark in the North, the dungareed army of the proletariat invaded the centre of the city ... leaving the factories deserted, shouting and singing.' In its combination of verve and inaccuracy, this passage is typical of Gallacher's account of the events covered in this article as a whole. According to the Ministry of Munitions' records not one of the factories referred to by Gallacher struck work.
[47] Mun. 2.27 (20, 27 November 1915); *Trade Unionist*, December 1915; *Herald*, 20, 27 November 1915.
[48] *M.M.* 4, ii, p. 104.
[49] Murphy, *op. cit.* p. 118.
[50] John Maclean was fiercely critical of the Committee's inactivity during the Rent Strike: *Vanguard*, December 1915.

IV

The C.W.C. was, from the start, quite clear about its status, asserting roundly the principle of independent rank-and-file organisation that had been implicit in its predecessor's activity during February 1915:

> We will support the officials just so long as they rightly represent the workers, but we will act independently immediately they misrepresent them. Being composed of Delegates from every shop and untrammelled by obsolete rule or law, we claim to represent the true feeling of the workers. We can act immediately according to the merits of the case and the desire of the rank and file.[51]

In fact the 200-300 people who attended the weekly meetings of the Committee were not strictly speaking delegates – 'You could represent a minority in the Shop just the same as a majority, even though the minority was one' – though members indicated whom, if any, they claimed to be representing when they spoke.[52]

The Committee was not seeking either to take over existing trade-union structures, or to construct a new 'dual' organisation entirely outside these structures. Its aim, rather, was to build a local organisation based directly on the workshops (and therefore more representative than district committees elected from the sparsely attended branches), an organisation which would permanently coexist with the official structures, superseding their authority only in moments of crisis when it was felt that the officials ceased to 'rightly represent the workers'. Thus, at the height of the dilution crisis, it was reported that: 'The Clyde Workers' Committee initiates its own programme; lays down its own policy; submits, through the shop stewards in the various shops, their own demands and issue privately their own orders, including decisions to strike, to enforce these demands.'[53] When the crisis was over, so the statement implied, the Com-

---

[51] Bev. iii, p. 96, 'Fellow-workers', the C.W.C.'s first leaflet (?November 1915).

[52] Labour Party, *Report ... upon ... Deportations*, pp. 13–14.

[53] Bev. iii, p. 355, memorandum by Mitchell, 21 February 1916.

mittee would be content to relinquish the leadership and retire to a ginger group position within the unions pending the next crisis.

This formulation represented the most important contribution made by the C.W.C. to the shop stewards' movement that developed in other munitions centres following the débâcle on the Clyde in March 1916.[54] In some of these centres, notably Sheffield, the Workers' Committee was to all intents and purposes 'composed of Delegates from every shop'. This, however, must not be allowed to obscure the fact that on the Clyde the independence that was actually established was not the independence of the rank and file as such from the officials, but the independence of a militant vanguard among the rank and file from officials who derived their authority from a relatively apathetic majority. Within this vanguard was the 'small leading committee' elected at the delegate meeting, which did the day-to-day work of the C.W.C. and was largely responsible for the formulation of its policy.[55]

Most of the leaders of the C.W.C. were revolutionaries, conscious of belonging to a political vanguard. Although the Independent Labour Party (I.L.P.) was the dominant socialist party on the Clyde, only two of the Committee's leaders, Messer and Kirkwood, belonged to it, and neither of them was of any importance in the party hierarchy. James Messer, the organisation man of the C.W.C., apparently contributed little to its policy. Assiduous attempts were made to build up David Kirkwood as the leading figure in the rank-and-file movement,[56] but although convenor at the largest factory in Glasgow he was far from being the Committee's leader. Parkhead, under Kirkwood, was on more than one occasion the weakest link in the militants'

[54] J. T. Murphy's pamphlet *The Workers' Committee* (Sheffield, 1917, 18 pp). was based on this idea. In December 1917 the pamphlet was accepted as official policy by the National Administrative Committee of the Shop Stewards' Movement. (*Solidarity*, January 1918).

[55] Labour Party, *Report ... upon ... Deportations*, p. 13; Gallacher, *op. cit.* p. 58.

[56] Cf. Gallacher, *op. cit.* p. 127: 'The whole apparatus of the I.L.P., including *Forward*, was brought into play to boost him. Soon all others were forgotten; Kirkwood, *the* deportee was established.' The I.L.P.'s success is clear from the full title of the Labour Party's Report, see p. 159, n. 31 above. For earlier I.L.P. boosting of Kirkwood, see *Forward*, 21 August 1915.

chain,[57] and Kirkwood, far more the labour aristocrat than the revolutionary,[58] accepted neither the authority nor the policy of the Committee. In this he was in tune with his party, whose paper, *Forward*, was consistently hostile to the C.W.C.'s claim to independence of established trade-union authority.[59]

It was from the revolutionary parties of the left that the C.W.C. drew its leaders. Muir, MacManus and Clark were all leading members of the Socialist Labour Party (S.L.P.), whose sectarian commitment to dual unionist ideas[60] was already weakening before the War, when the party headquarters shifted from Edinburgh to the more proletarian atmosphere of the Clyde. The S.L.P. gave consistent support to the Committee[61]. Gallacher was a member of the British Socialist Party and a follower of John Maclean,[62] whose lectures on Marxist economics could fill large halls with engineering workers. The John Maclean group formed, for a time, a small but vocal element in the weekly meetings of the C.W.C.[63]

These political groups from which the leadership was drawn were minute. The dominant faction, the S.L.P., had about 100 members in Glasgow in 1915 though the emphasis on educational work no doubt created a politically conscious vanguard of workers considerably larger than the formal membership of the

[57] Kirkwood 'broke the front' in December 1915 by agreeing to meet Lloyd George, and again in January 1916 by agreeing to meet the Dilution Commissioners. On both occasions the C.W.C. had decided on a policy of non-co-operation at factory level designed to force the authorities to negotiate directly with the Committee: *Worker*, 8 January 1916; Labour Party, *Report ... upon ... Deportations*, p. 9; Gallacher, *op. cit.* pp. 79, 103.

[58] T. Bell, *Pioneering Days* (1941), p. 98.

[59] *Forward*, 13 March 1915, 1 April 1916. The paper even refused to report strike action in war-time: *ibid.* 6 March 1915, 5 February 1916, 26 January 1918. This record of isolation from the industrial struggle is possibly explained by the Glasgow I.L.P.'s largely non-proletarian membership. See A. Marwick, *The Deluge* (Pelican edn., 1967), p. 74.

[60] Members were forbidden to stand for trade-union office, since the existing unions were seen as an integral part of capitalism: D. M. Chewter, 'The History of the Socialist Labour Party of Great Britain from 1902 to 1921' (B.Litt, thesis, Oxford, 1965), p. 48; Bell, *op. cit.* p. 42.

[61] Chewter, *op. cit.* pp. 116–7, 120, 127, 129, 184.

[62] John Maclean (1879–1923). Schoolteacher. Joined S.D.F. in 1902. Led anti-war agitation in Glasgow. Jailed 1915, 1916 and again in 1918. Left B.S.P. in 1920 and refused to join the Communist Party.

[63] Bell, *op. cit.* pp. 26, 57; Gallacher, *op. cit.* pp. 27, 58–9.

parties.[64] The C.W.C. represented for its leaders a dramatic breakthrough from propagandist politics to leadership in a genuine mass movement. Leadership, however, raised unfamiliar problems; problems which long immersion in the abstract clarities of propaganda had not equipped the revolutionaries to solve.

When the Committee was formed, the struggle against the Munitions Act was uppermost in their minds. 'The support given to the Munitions Act by the Officials,' declared the Committee's first leaflet,[65] 'was an act of Treachery to the Working Class. Those of us who refuse to be *Sold* have organised the above Committee ... determined to retain what liberties we have, and to take the first opportunity of forcing the repeal of all the pernicious legislation that has recently been imposed upon us.' After the Fairfield case, however, no opportunity to mobilise the workers against the Munitions Act as such arose on the Clyde for several weeks. During the last two months of 1915 it was the government's campaign to impose dilution that occupied the thoughts of the C.W.C. The leaflet quoted above went on to identify the foremost change of the War as 'the scrapping of Trade Union rules', and set the Committee the task of making good the failure of the officials 'to grasp the significance of these changes, and ... to formulate a policy that would adequately protect the interests of the workers...'.

The revolutionaries, who had always been fiercely critical of craft unionism and of the labour aristocratic outlook associated with it, were now faced with the task of 'formulating a policy that would adequately protect the interests' of the craft workers threatened by dilution. This they did in a document presented by John Muir to a meeting of the C.W.C. in December 1915.[66] The initial step was to reject the protective reflex of the craftsmen, hostility to dilution as such. 'We regard [dilution] as progressive from the point of view that it simplifies the labour process, makes labour more mobile, and tends to increase output. In short it is a step in the direct line of industrial evolution.'

[64] Chewter, *op. cit.* pp. 2, 23, 25–8, 101, 129; Bell, *op. cit.* pp. 38, 55, 57.
[65] Bev. iii, p. 95.
[66] Published in *Worker*, 15 January 1916.

Accepting dilution in principle, the statement went on to argue that its progressive character would be lost to the community unless organised labour had a share in controlling its introduction.

But how could organisations of skilled workers which excluded the potential 'dilutees' from membership hope to secure control of the process of dilution? In the long term, the obvious answer was to do away with sectional trade unionism altogether: 'The *ultimate aim* of the Clyde Workers' Committee,' wrote Gallacher in January 1916, 'is to weld these unions into one powerful organisation that will place the workers in complete control of the industry.'[67] More immediately, control over dilution could best be achieved by building up an all-grades organisation in the workshops, thereby reconstructing the trade-union movement from the base upwards.[68] In practice, however, the workshop organisation they built could only reflect the organised strength which already existed, and organisation was still, in the Clyde munitions factories, very largely confined to skilled workers.[69]

Faced with the urgent problem of dilution the C.W.C. had to formulate a polcy that was based on the real *craft* strength of its members. The difficulty was that the defence of craft unionism by craft unionists alone against the threat inherent in dilution was all too likely to submerge the long-term aim of replacing craft by industrial organisation. The revolutionaries attempted to break out of this vicious circle by adopting an ambitious programme of nationalisation and workers' participation in management: 'that all industries and national resources must be taken over by the Government – not merely "controlled", but taken over completely – and organised labour should be vested with the right to take part directly and equally with the present managers in the management and administration in every deparment of industry'. And Muir added, 'I have used the word "demand" advisedly, as this is no propagandist statement. It is our fixed decision to force this matter to an issue.'

[67] *Worker*, 29 January 1916.
[68] *Ibid.* See also Bev. v, pp. 38–9 'C.W.C. Scheme for Dilution of Labour' (February 1916).
[69] The strength of the general unions in the Glasgow engineering industry is discussed in my thesis, chapter vi, section ii.

When Muir put this policy to the Committee, no one challenged the irresistibility of dilution. But the demand for nationalisation and workers' participation in management raised a storm of argument. Peter Petroff,[70] Maclean's closest associate, launched an attack on the policy in the course of which, apparently, he implied that Muir was an *agent provocateur*. Gallacher, formerly a member of the Maclean group, sided with Muir and, as Chairman, expelled Petroff from the meeting. This ended the Maclean group's participation in the C.W.C. and left the S.L.P. in control.[71]

There is no direct record of the debate, but its content can be reconstructed from other sources. Maclean attacked Muir's policy at two points. In the forefront was the issue of the War. The S.L.P., after some confusion during the first months, had come down firmly in opposition to the War.[72] On the C.W.C., however, their members, in particular John Muir, appear to have pushed a line of neutrality. They were neither for nor against the War: they were concerned only to defend the workers against the threats to their organisation brought about by the War. To John Maclean such 'neutrality' was hypocritical and a betrayal of socialism.[73] The dilution policy would give this betrayal concrete form. The workers in question were, after all, munitions workers. They had a responsibility not only to themselves but also to the soldiers being killed in a war whose continuance the munitions workers facilitated in their everyday work. 'If the Clyde Workers took part control of the munitions work they would thus accept part responsibility for the War.'[74]

[70] Peter Petroff, a Russian, was jailed for his role in the 1905 revolution. He escaped, and reached Britain in 1907. He became a prominent member of the London S.D.F. In 1915 he joined Maclean on the Clyde. Interned for his anti-war activities, he was deported to Russia after the February Revolution, where he became, for a time, a Soviet diplomat. In January 1916 a local Munitions official informed his superiors about 'Peter Petroff, a Russian Socialist of a very dangerous type. The easiest thing to do with Petroff is to have him re-patriated, when, from all that I am told, he will be shot within 24 hours of landing in Russia.' Bev. iii, p. 111, Patterson to Llewellyn Smith, 17 January 1916.

[71] Gallacher, *op. cit.* pp. 59–62; interview with Mr. H. McShane on 15 September 1965.

[72] Chewter, *op. cit.* pp. 125–7.

[73] Interview with Mr. H. McShane on 15 September 1965. See also *Glasgow Herald*, 14 April 1916.

[74] Mun. 5.70, extracts from the suppressed issue of *Vanguard*, 30 December 1915. Gallacher claims that 'despite trouble over Petroff' there was no

Maclean's second line of attack exposed the failure of the S.L.P. leadership to transcend the narrow craft basis of the C.W.C. Muir's policy, the *Vanguard* alleged, demanded nationalisation and workers' participation in management *only* for the munitions factories.[75] The C.W.C. repeatedly denied this,[76] but the very vigour of its denial indicated that the charge had struck home. And so it would. The policy of nationalisation and workers' participation in management was unoriginal. What was new was Muir's transformation of the argument from a propagandist point into a negotiating stance over the issue of dilution. For the C.W.C. leadership, 'forcing this matter to an issue' became the central task of the Committee. 'The S.L.P. section declare that they would not strike for anything short of this.'[77]

This single-minded concentration on the dilution policy had fatal implications for the development of the C.W.C. as a revolutionary vanguard on the Clyde. At this stage dilution was being proposed as an urgent measure only in the munitions factories. Whatever the leaders said, therefore, their policy was only of direct relevance to the munitions workers. Taken at face value the dilution policy committed the munitions workers, alone in any position to negotiate about dilution, to enter a fight to blackmail the government into effecting a social revolution relying entirely on their own resources. Instead of the political vanguard trying to use its position in the leadership of the rank-and-file movement to broaden that movement out beyond a militant section of the labour aristocracy, the vanguard was proposing to bring the entire weight of the class struggle to bear on that section alone. While they were right to see the skilled engineers, in war conditions, as the key section of the workers, they were quite wrong to assume that this section was so strong that it had no need to draw other sections into the struggle. As J. T. Murphy later commented, Muir's policy was 'either

---

cooling off between Maclean and himself: Gallacher, *op. cit.* pp. 67, 115.
But his whole account is most improbable, and Harry McShane told the author that Maclean attacked Gallacher publicly on the War issue, just as he did Kirkwood; cf. D. Kirkwood, *My Life of Revolt* (1935), pp. 114, 118.
[75] Mun. 5.70.
[76] *Socialist*, February 1916; *Worker*, 8 January 1916.
[77] Mun. 5.70.

window-dressing propaganda, or a complete over-estimation of the power and extent of the influence of the Clyde Workers' Committee.[78]

That Muir's policy tended to reinforce the narrowness of the C.W.C. became clear in the struggle over conscription during January 1916. Following the St. Andrew's Hall meeting the Committee was left with a deep sense of foreboding. 'Every effort will be made to crush us,' warned Gallacher.[79] The shape of the offensive, so the C.W.C. leaders thought, soon made itself clear. On 5 January, after weeks of rumour, Asquith introduced the first Military Service Bill in the Commons. This was seen on the Clyde not as a measure dictated by military necessity, but as an attempt to establish indirectly 'the military control of industry and consequently the abolition of the functions of our trade unions'.[80]

In the fight against conscription during January 1916 the C.W.C. had a chance to broaden its base among the Clydeside workers. Well aware of the need to do this, it nevertheless failed. Underlying this failure was the continuing commitment of the Committee to Muir's dilution policy. Two quite distinct elements appeared in the C.W.C. propaganda against conscription. On the one hand, it talked of a last-ditch struggle in defence of democracy: 'The whole British constitution is in the melting pot. . . . The next few weeks may decide the fate of democracy.'[81] On the other hand the struggle was seen exclusively in terms of the dilution policy. At Christmas Muir had told Lloyd George that if his policy were adopted 'the coming fight on conscription would be avoided, because conscription would be absolutely unnecessary'.[82] Conscription was seen purely as a weapon which the government would use to tighten its control over the workshops, for the specific purpose of imposing dilution. Hence a policy designed to meet the threat of dilution, and argued out and popularised in terms of that threat, was simply switched to meet the conscription threat. The relevance of the C.W.C.'s proposals continued to be limited, therefore, to the skilled engineers who alone were faced with the threat of

[78] Murphy, *op. cit.* p. 121.
[79] *Worker*, 8 January 1916.
[80] C.W.C. resolution, quoted in Gallacher, *op. cit.* p. 116.
[81] *Worker*, 8 January 1916.
[82] *Worker*, 15 January 1916.

dilution. The nearest body the C.W.C. had to an ally in the industrial field, the Glasgow Trades Council, with which it organised a large demonstation on Glasgow Green at the end of January,[83] never even debated, let alone approved, the Committee's 'only alternative to Industrial Conscription'.

V

It was not only John Maclean and his group who had declined to accept Muir's dilution policy. Although they made less noise about it, this was also true of Kirkwood and his allies in the I.L.P. For this section the argument for workers' participation revolved solely around the need for the skilled workers to have a say in the introduction of dilution if a flood of cheap labour was to be avoided.[84] The demand for nationalisation had, from the start, left them cold. It is this attitude that explains the position of leadership in the rank-and-file movement gained by Kirkwood and John Wheatley[85] for a couple of weeks at the end of January 1916.[86]

Soon after the Dilution Commissioners arrived on the Clyde,

[83] Glasgow Trades Council Minutes (Mitchell Library, Glasgow), 3, 19 January and 9 February 1916; *Worker*, 29 January 1916; *Herald*, 22 January 1916.

[84] *Forward*, 1 January, 5 February 1916; Kirkwood, *op. cit.* p. 118; Labour Party, *Report ... upon ... Deportations*, p. 17.

[85] John Wheatley (1869–1930). Son of Irish labourer, miner until aged 24, small grocer, journalist. In 1912 started successful publishing business. Joined I.L.P. in 1908. Founded Catholic Socialist Society in Glasgow. Glasgow City Council, 1910–20, for Shettleston ward. M.P. for Shettleston from 1922 until his death. Minister of Housing, 1924.

[86] The role of Kirkwood and his mentor Wheatley in the C.W.C. has been overestimated both by Marwick in *The Deluge* pp. 75–8, and by R. K. Middlemas in *The Clydesiders* (1965), pp. 66–7. Both Gallacher, *op. cit.* pp. 126–7, and Bell, *op. cit.* p. 98, testify that Wheatley's undoubted influence over Kirkwood (see, for example, Kirkwood's *My Life of Revolt*, p. 82) was used to draw him away from the C.W.C. leadership. It is true that Wheatley did retain sufficient influence with Gallacher and Muir for them to pay great attention to his views during the deportation crisis (Gallacher *op. cit.* p. 107), but Marwick's claim that he was 'the political genius in the background' is certainly unfounded. Middlemas is probably a great deal nearer the truth in his assertion that Wheatley used his influence to 'undo the extremists' *op. cit.* pp. 68, 72). The present writer is, however, unaware of any materials that could shed adequate light on Wheatley's motives. For a full catalogue of Middlemas's errors in his partisan treatment of this period, see J. Hinton, 'The Clydesiders', *New Left Review*, No. 37, pp. 74–7.

they 'decided that our right procedure was to convert and persuade the men in say half-a-dozen of the principal establishments to the principle of dilution, then arrange a scheme for
each establishment thoroughly effective and efficient in all its
details, get it started and from time to time thereafter fix and
adjust the minor inequalities that emerge ...'. Problems about
the detail of wages 'arise very quickly and acutely within a few
days after the scheme's commencement and if not immediately
disposed of may lead in one hour to a strike'. 'To avoid that,'
Macassey went on, 'I have made it a condition of each scheme
that a Joint Shop Committee be formed of Employers and Shop
Stewards to discuss and adjust any difficulties in regard to the
working out of dilution.'[87] The C.W.C. leaders, who had failed
to force the Commissioners to negotiate centrally with themselves,[88] were thrown into confusion by these tactics. While all
their attention had been focused on the threat of conscription,
the offensive had suddenly materialised from an unexpected
quarter. Muir's demand for nationalisation and workers' participation in management was shattered overnight and vanished
without a trace : 'The full and free discussions we have with the
men,' Macassey wrote 5 February, 'are entirely modifying their
outlook and modifying their temper.'[89]

While the C.W.C. leadership was forced to recognise the failure of Muir's dilution policy, Kirkwood and the I.L.P. section
remained unalarmed. The Commissioners' recognition of workshop organisation to negotiate grievances arising out of dilution
appeared as a victory for their policy. This is what they had
meant all along by workers' control. The Parkhead agreement,
written, at Kirkwood's request, by Wheatley,[90] was welcomed
by Patrick Dollan, the industrial correspondent of *Forward*, as
admitting 'the principle of control by the workers for the first
time in an industrial agreement'.[91]

Partly, no doubt, as a result of the I.L.P.'s interpretation of
the C.W.C.'s dilution policy, the conciliatory aspect of the
Dilution Commissioners' role has been greatly exaggerated.
G. D. H. Cole, for instance, whose account has been generally

[87] Bev. v, p. 14, memorandum by Macassey, 5 February 1916.
[88] Gallacher, *op. cit.* p. 103.
[89] Bev. v, p. 14.
[90] Kirkwood, *op. cit.* pp. 115–18.
[91] *Herald*, 5 February 1916.

accepted, explained the appointment of the Commissioners in the following terms:

> However precisely the national conditions [for dilution] might be formulated, there remained inevitably countless points of detail which had to be adjusted separately for each works or department. General regulations for the introduction of dilution were found either to remain inoperative, or to serve as a source of constant friction, unless a definite procedure was laid down for applying their provisions to each individual case. The consciousness of this fact, and the certainty that dilution would prove effective only when it was introduced with the consent, and, if possible, the willing co-operation, of the skilled workers affected, were the causes which led to the appointment of the Dilution Commissioners for the Clyde and Tyne.[92]

In fact, the conciliation on which Cole lays exclusive stress was only one element, and a subordinate one, in the government's intentions.

The decision to appoint Dilution Commissioners arose from the government's awareness that employers would not, left to themselves, introduce dilution on a large scale. As yet unconvinced of the value of dilution, employers were not prepared to force it through against the wishes of their men and at the risk of provoking extensive strike action. This was particularly the case on the Clyde, where the munitions workers had thoroughly intimidated their employers;[93] and from the start the government was aware that it would have to take the initiative against the C.W.C. The first mention of the Committee in the official government papers, on 24 November 1915, was unequivocal: 'To obtain a reasonably smooth working of the Munitions Act, this committee should be smashed.'[94] By 17 January 1916 the idea of using the anticipated strike against the enforcement of dilution as the occasion to deport the C.W.C. leaders from the district was being strongly canvassed within the Ministry of

[92] G. D. H. Cole, *Workshop Organisation* (1923), p. 50.
[93] Mun. 5.73, 'Memorandum on the Dilution of Labour', by Patterson (18 December 1915).
[94] Bev. iii, p. 94, Bartellot to Third Sea Lord, 24 November 1915.

Munitions.[95] Two days earlier in a memorandum approved by representatives of both Vickers and Armstrong Whitworth, Adams argued:

> It is my view, and I have suggested it to others in the Ministry, and it is backed up by the biggest employers who are having trouble in this connection, that dilution in cases where there is obstruction should be taken out of the hands of the employers altogether and that it should be done by the Ministry. I mean to say that employers should be relieved of all responsibility in this matter and that the Ministry should accept it and the consequences it involves.[96]

William Weir, part-owner of Weir's of Cathcart and since August 1915 Director of Munitions for Scotland, had long been identified with such a policy. In May 1915, following a dispute over dilution at his works, Weir had called on the government to intervene directly with the 'arbitrary justice' appropriate to war-time. He argued that since 'as a general proposition ... the existing skilled men, organised as trade unionists, are uncontrollable by the employer', the State should take the employers' disciplinary functions on itself.[97] After the passing of the Munitions Act, itself a major step towards the industrial compulsion preached by Weir, he continued to assail the government for its 'want of sincerity', for dragging its feet on dilution. 'Every delayed decision,' he wrote in October, 'shows to the working man that the State – or rather its leaders and advisors – are not in earnest. The effect of this is unrest and ferment in the shops....' In December, taking his stand with the compulsionist critics of Asquithian 'drift', Weir attacked the government for its negotiations and compromises with the trade unions. 'The fallacy was the belief that bargaining was necessary ... the bargaining spirit becomes rife. The actual position was that the men would have loyally done whatever the country required of them, if the position had been clearly put to them, as they have done as soldiers.'[98]

By mid-January the Ministry of Munitions was prepared to

[95] *Ibid.* pp. 111–14, Patterson to Llewellyn Smith, 17 January 1916.
[96] *Ibid.* p. 224, memorandum by J. B. Adams, 15 January 1916.
[97] *Glasgow Herald*, 21 May 1915.
[98] Mun. 5.73, 'Memorandum on the Dilution of Labour', by Weir (n.d.)

give definite orders for dilution and to take the consequences. A detailed scheme for the introduction of dilution and contingency plans to deal with strike action were to be prepared: 'Plans must be laid very carefully as to the whole procedure in order that the thing may be carried out on well thought out lines, quickly and firmly, so as to give no time for opposition to be engineered.'[99]

Weir was the man for the job.

A paper Weir prepared and submitted to Lloyd George on 18 January was the basis, with minor modifications, of the scheme that was finally adopted.[100] Three Commissioners were to be sent to both the Clyde and Tyne, where they would check that the dilution schemes already prepared by leading munitions firms were suitable. Having done this, the Commissioners would arrange to meet the shop stewards' committee, together with the management, at the firm in question. The workers would be informed of the scheme and given two days in which to 'consult' with the management further on the scheme, though any refusal to acquiesce in dilution at all would be ignored. On the third day, whatever issues had been raised in consultation, the scheme in its final form would be carried into force.

In the event of a strike, the immediate reaction would be to provide 'police and military protection to all who are willing to work'; to make sure, if necessary by injunction, that trade-union funds were not used to support the strikers; and to 'deport and bring to trial under the Defence of the Realm Regulations any person inciting to strike'. Further measures would depend on the dimensions of the strike. The strikers themselves (as distinct from their leaders) would only be prosecuted if the strike was a small one. A large strike would 'have to be left to take its course', though once it started to weaken 'the process can be hastened by prosecuting those who hold out'. Finally, the condition of withholding the use of the Munitions Act in such a case was that there should be 'no parleying or negotiation with the strikers, either directly or through the Labour Advisory

---

[99] Bev. iii, p. 222, Rey to Lloyd George, 18 January 1916.

[100] Bev. iii, pp. 267–8, 'Summary of Dilution Programme as Based (with modifications) on Mr. Weir's Memorandum' (22 January 1916). Unless otherwise noted the following section is based on this document.

Committee'.[101] On 20 January Lloyd George told his friend Lord Riddell that 'he intends to take a firm line and would rather have a six weeks' strike now than later on'.[102]

If it is difficult to recognise Cole's account of the government's motives in all this, that is evidence of the success with which the government covered its tracks.[103] In so far as the Clyde Commissioners operated a conciliatory policy, they were doing so within a firm framework of repression. The Commissioners themselves never forgot this, and their early success in getting dilution underway by use of a conciliatory tactic by no means weakened their intention to smash the C.W.C.

VI

The reasons for the Commissioners' delay in attacking the C.W.C. were summarised by Isaac Mitchell on 21 February: 'I early arrived at the conclusion that a fight was inevitable, and was anxious that it should be on a question which would divide the employers from the men and split the men into sections.'[104] It was the first of these conditions that held up the Commissioners initially. The employers were not, as they had been led to believe, 'ready and able forthwith to accept dilution'.[105] Employers' dilution schemes were ill-prepared, and, more important, many employers remained hostile to dilution itself. Unconvinced of the value of women workers, they feared the loss of scarce skilled labour to competitors implied in the government's intention of concentrating craftsmen where they were most needed. It was as important for the Commissioners to convert the employers as to convert the men. In this situation they realised that any precipitate confrontation with the C.W.C.

---

[101] This quotation is taken from a handwritten outline of the scheme by Sir Hubert Llewellyn Smith, in Bev. iii, p. 218 (n.d.).

[102] Lord Riddell, *War Diary* (1933), pp. 150–1.

[103] Piecing together the Beveridge Papers with what is available in the Public Record Office, i.e. the papers made available to the official historians of the Ministry of Munitions, proved an intriguing exercise. The clearest evidence of the government's repressive intent is in the Beveridge Papers, a fact which leads one to speculate that Beveridge himself was the original censor.

[104] Bev. iii, p. 357, 'The Clyde Position', by Isaac Mitchell (21 February 1916).

[105] Bev. v, pp. 14–15, memorandum by Macassey, 5 February 1916.

over the principle of dilution would be fatal to their mission.[106]

Two further opportunities arose for the Commissioners to implement the repressive policy outlined in their instructions during their first weeks on the Clyde. In both cases they were divided over whether to take action. The first, a strike against dilution at Lang's was unsuitable both because at this time (2–7 February) the policy of conciliation was working well in the main Glasgow factories, and because to escalate the Lang's strike by deporting its leaders would be unlikely to provoke the C.W.C. out on to the necessary limb. The Committee had little influence at Lang's, a machine-tool works at Johnstone, seven miles west of Glasgow, and was uneasy about the narrow craft outlook revealed by the strike.[107]

The second opportunity was more appropriate. On 2 February the police raided the Socialist Labour Press, broke up the machinery, and suppressed the forthcoming issue of the C.W.C. paper, the *Worker*.[108] Five days later Gallacher, Muir and Bell, the printer, were arrested, charged under the Defence of the Realm Act, and refused bail.[109] Immediately strikes broke out at Weir's, Albion, Barr & Stroud, Coventry Ordnance Works and Dalmuir – all the leading constituents of the C.W.C. with the exception of Parkhead.[110] With this pressure, the court changed

[106] Bev. iii, p. 357; *ibid.* p. 151, 'Memorandum on Skilled Labour' (n.d.); M.M. 4, iv, p. 91.

[107] Bev. v, p. 18, memorandum by Macassey, 5 February 1916; Bev. iii, pp. 355–8, 'The Clyde Position', by Isaac Mitchell (21 February 1916).

[108] The suppression of the *Worker*, following the suppression of the *Vanguard* early in January 1916, left the C.W.C. and the anti-war forces on the Clyde without a public platform. John Maclean, whose phenomenal agitational energy was worth several newspapers to the revolutionaries, was arrested at the same time as Gallacher and Muir, but not released on bail. It is interesting that *Forward*, which had been suppressed on 1 January, was allowed to reappear at the beginning of February. The timing may have been coincidental, or it may, as T. Brotherstone has suggested, have been deliberate: 'It was clearly in the government's interest ... that the *Forward*, already a moderating (or confusing) influence – and now further emasculated – should reappear.' On the whole curious story of the suppression of the *Forward*, see Brotherstone's article of that title published in *Bulletin of the Scottish Society for the Study of Labour History*, No. 1 (May 1969).

[109] Mun. 5.73, report from Rey, 7 February 1916; *Herald*, 12 January 1916; *Glasgow Herald*, 4, 8, 9 February 1916.

[110] Mun. 2.27. 'Secret Weekly Reports of the Labour Department of the Ministry of Munitions' (12 January 1916); Mun. 5.73, memorandum by Macassey, 9 February 1916; A.S.E. *Executive Minutes*, 9 February 1916.

its mind about bail and the arrested men were released on the morning of 9 February.[111]

At this point Macassey saw his opportunity to 'strike a sharp line of cleavage' between 'loyal' workers and the subversives. By the morning of the ninth some of the workers were returning, and more were expected to go back on the tenth. Those who remained out, demanding withdrawal of the charges against the accused men, could be assumed to be the hard core of the C.W.C. The deportation of the agitators would catch the Committee disunited and enable the government to break it up without further trouble.[112] At the last moment, however, the hunter was deprived of his prey. The C.W.C. leaders, seeing the weakness of the strike, called it off, and, at some cost to their own prestige, persuaded the more obdurate strikers to return to work[113]. Although its paper was gone and the threat of a long prison sentence hung over the heads of Gallacher and Muir, the Committee survived. It may even have recovered somewhat during the next few weeks, although the evidence on this point is conflicting.

The reports of the Dilution Commissioners suggest a consolidation and extension of the Committee's powers. On 9 February, for example, Macassey warned that 'spurred into fresh activity . . . its tentacles now fairly widespread and growing', the C.W.C. was dispatching its emissaries to the workshops to induce the men, apparently with considerable success, to repudiate agreements already signed by their shop stewards with the Commissioners.[114] It is true that a new and more realistic policy on dilution was formulated and that on 18 February Messer, claiming to speak for twenty-nine shops and yards on the Clyde, demanded a meeting with the Commissioners to discuss this policy.[115] But it seems that Messer was putting on a brave face and that Macassey was exaggerating, for the success of the Com-

[111] *Forward*, 19 February 1916.

[112] Mun. 5.73, memorandum by Macassey, 9 February 1916. The final sections of this document are missing from the Public Records, the last extant page being torn in half. But the drift of the argument is clear, and is fully corroborated in Mitchell's report of 21 February: Bev. iii, pp. 355–58.

[113] *Herald*, 19 February 1916; *Forward*, 19 February 1916; *Trade Unionist*, October 1916; Murphy, *op. cit.* pp. 121–2.

[114] Mun. 5.73, memorandum by Macassey, 9 February 1916.

[115] *Herald*, 26 February and 4 March 1916; Labour Party, *Report . . . upon . . . Deportations*, pp. 15–16.

missioners at Parkhead had initiated a profound fragmentation of the C.W.C.'s base.

The dilution agreement reached at Parkhead was open to serious criticism both on account of the wages rates it laid down for 'dilutees', and on account of its failure to guarantee the Convenor's right to enter any department of the works to check how the agreement was operating.[116] At Albion and Barr & Stroud far more successful dilution agreements were negotiated. United in their wish to avoid the intervention of the Dilution Commissioners, management and shop stewards at both these firms negotiated model agreements, guaranteeing that dilutees be paid, after a short period, the 'full rate for the job', and fully recognising the Convenor's right 'to go into any department to enquire into alleged grievances'.[117] Kirkwood, demonstrably preferring the advice of Wheatley and the I.L.P. to that of the C.W.C. leadership,[118] could expect little sympathy from the latter when the inadequacies of the Parkhead agreement made themselves felt. Gallacher recalled that shortly after signing the agreement, Kirkwood 'declared he was concerned with Parkhead alone and as this agreement had safeguarded the Parkhead workers he was satisfied. This statement went circulating around the Clyde and caused incalculable harm. The whole front started cracking up.'[119] The isolation of Parkhead was astutely exploited by the Commissioners.

Their opportunity came at the end of February when Sir William Beardmore, the patriarch of Parkhead, suddenly decided to revoke Kirkwood's *de facto* right as Convenor of Shop Stewards to move freely about the works.[120] No convincing explanation can be found for this provocation, unless it be that

---

[116] Kirkwood, *op. cit.* p. 118, Middlemas, *op. cit.* p. 66, and Marwick *op. cit.* p. 77 are quite wrong in praising this agreement. It demonstrates, not Wheatley's intelligence, but his ignorance of the workshop situation. The agreement is discussed in my thesis, ch. vii, sec. ii.

[117] *Glasgow Herald*, 14 April 1916; Gallacher, *op. cit.* p. 105; letter from two shop stewards at Barr & Stroud to H. E. R. Highton, 27 October 1917, in Highton Collection, Glasgow University Library; Labour Party, *Report ... upon ... Deportations*, p. 63.

[118] It does appear, however, that after signing the agreement as drawn up by Wheatley the Parkhead shop stewards allied with those at Weir to get the wage clauses renegotiated: *Herald*, 5 February 1916; A.S.E. *Monthly Journal and Report*, February 1916.

[119] Gallacher, *op. cit.* p. 105.

[120] Labour Party, *Report ... upon ... Deportations*, pp. 22, 37.

Beardmore had agreed to give the Commissioners their opportunity to break the C.W.C. For two weeks the Parkhead engineers negotiated, with no success, and on 17 March they struck. Although informed, the Commissioners made no attempt to intervene, a paralysis which contrasted strangely with their attitude in other disputes. (On 5 February Macassey had reported: 'On the mere suggestion of a strike I am down on the spot, at all hours of the day and night.')[21] By the twenty-third the strike had spread to two other works, where the men had been given work transferred from Parkhead.[122]

Late on 23 March Macassey finally set the wheels in motion, wiring the Ministry of Munitions: 'We should deport the whole of the C.W.C.' The next day, 'after various frenzied telegrams from the Commissioners, recommending first one thing and then another, we decided ... that we would agree to the deportation of certain leaders'.[123] Three Parkhead stewards were arrested, including Kirkwood, together with two other C.W.C. leaders, Messer and MacMannus (who worked at Weir's, which was not on strike), and all five were deported from the area. The deportations provoked an immediate extension of the strike. The original strikers from Parkhead, Dalmuir and the North British Diesel Engine works in Scotstoun were joined by men from Weir's, Coventry Ordnance Works, Albion and two other works. Two more Parkhead stewards were deported, including Tom Clark, and three more from Weir's.[124]

Immediately the deportations started posters were put up threatening the strikers with prosecution under the Defence of the Realm Act and the Munitions Act, and promising that no action would be taken against workers who returned to work at once. On Thursday, 30 March, thirty men from three leading factories on strike were prosecuted under the Munitions Act and fined £5 each. In the final days of the strike rumours, no doubt inspired, of the impending declaration of martial law circulated through the district.[125]

[121] Bev. v, p. 17, memorandum by Macassey, 5 February 1916.
[122] Labour Party, *Report ... upon ... Deportations*, pp. 18–26, 43; *Glasgow Herald*, 30 March 1916.
[123] C. Addison, *Four and a Half Years* (1934), pp. 184–5.
[124] Labour Party, *Report ... upon ... Deportations*, pp. 18–19.
[125] Mun. 5.79, 'Papers re. Clyde Strike' (March 1916); *Glasgow Herald*, 27, 30 March and 1, 3 April 1916; *Socialist*, April 1916.

The government used its emergency powers further to prevent any direct press reporting of the strike until 30 March, and meanwhile put out its own version of events. On the twenty-eighth Christopher Addison, Parliamentary Secretary at the Ministry of Munitions, explained that the strike was 'a systematic and sinister plan' controlled by the C.W.C. to blackmail the government into repealing the Munitions Act and the Military Service Act by bringing out men 'engaged upon the production of a particular heavy gun and gun-mounting for which we are receiving the most urgent demands.'[126]

The Commissioners could not have chosen a better issue on which to attack the C.W.C. The strike was small and partial even in the firms which did come out. At its peak (29–30 March) there were probably not more than 4500 workers on strike, compared with at least 10,000 in the strike of February 1915.[127] The C.W.C. leaders cannot have been unaware that this was the general offensive against the Committee which they had anticipated ever since Christmas 1915, but they were reluctant to resist. Within hours of the first deportations the Committee met. 'So keen was the indignation that a motion was submitted that the C.W.C. should declare a strike in the Clyde District. The Chairman, William Gallacher, ruled this motion out of order as it was against the accepted aims of the C.W.C. This aim was the building of an industrial organisation in the engineering industry. The members of the committee could inform their fellow workers in the shop where they worked as to what happened at the Forge, but beyond this the C.W.C. had no jurisdiction. No further discussion about the possibility of a strike took place at the meeting.'[128] What lay behind this timidity was not, as might appear, a doctrinaire industrial pacifism, but rank-and-file hostility towards Parkhead.[129] Indeed, Gallacher and Muir issued a statement to the press on 30 March which disassociated the Committee from the Parkhead strike and emphasised that 'the shops in which the president and other officials of the Committee are employed find that dilution is

[126] Reproduced in C. Addison, *Politics from Within* (1924), pp. 291–2.
[127] Labour Party, *Report ... upon ... Deportations*, p. 18; Board of Trade, *Labour Gazette*, May 1916.
[128] Quoted in Murphy, *op. cit.* p. 123.
[129] Cf. Gallacher, *op. cit.* p. 107: 'Parkhead had broken the front. Parkhead could take the consequences. Such was the situation we were facing.'

working smoothly and without a hitch'.[130] The C.W.C. had not recovered from the fragmentation caused by the collapse of its original, ill-considered policy on dilution.

The extent of this fragmentation is illustrated by the attitude of the workers at Barr & Stroud. When Muir, the Convenor, was arrested on the *Worker* charges on 7 February, the Barr & Stroud workers struck. Subsequently a dilution agreement was negotiated. So smoothly did this agreement work that, at Muir's trial in April, his managing director could testify: 'As Convenor of shop stewards he exercised his influence for the good, and his employers had every confidence in him. . . . He had also done his best to carry out the scheme for the dilution of labour.[131] Satisfied with their agreement, the Barr & Stroud workers looked with disdain and hostility on the troubles at Parkhead. Not only did they not strike in sympathy but a large majority of them voted (according to a report in the *Glasgow Herald*) to repudiate 'the frantic effort of a small percentage of the workers to retard by strikes' the production of munitions.[132] To the extent that the workers elsewhere shared these views it is not surprising that the C.W.C. leaders accepted defeat.

The deportations broke the Committee. The remaining leaders, Gallacher and Muir, made little effort to extend the strike, and when, on Friday, 31 March, a mass rally called by the local officials in connection with a joint wages movement[133] turned into a demonstration against the deportations, the C.W.C. had no further action to propose.[134] The return started, at Weir's, on 30 March. On Sunday, 2 April, the strike committee handed over its authority to the district committee of the A.S.E.[135]. On 13 April a further batch of strikers were prosecuted and fined from £5 to £25 each. The same day, in Edinburgh, Gallacher and Muir were sentenced to a year in jail on charges arising from the suppressed issue of the *Worker*.[136] They were released,

[130] *Glasgow Herald*, 30 March 1916.
[131] *Ibid.* 14 April 1916. When he came out of jail nine months later, Muir was immediately reinstated at Barr & Stroud! Gallacher, *op. cit.* p. 138.
[132] *Glasgow Herald*, 1 April 1916.
[133] Mun. 5.81, memorandum by Sir George Gibb, 21 February 1916; *Glasgow Herald*, 5, 22, 24 February and 9 March 1916.
[134] *Glasgow Herald*, 1 April 1916.
[135] Labour Party, *Report . . . upon . . . Deportations*, p. 18; *Glasgow Herald*, 1–6 April 1916, *passim*.
[136] *Glasgow Herald*, 14 April 1916.

with remission, in February 1917, but the ten deportees did not return to Glasgow until the summer of 1917. It was eighteen months before the shop stewards' movement was re-established on the Clyde.

During the twelve months following February 1915 the Clyde was characterised by a continuing state of unrest over a wide range of issues. The C.W.C. stood at the centre of this unrest. Through the C.W.C. the largest of the revolutionary parties gave leadership to the most powerful and most militant section of the local working class. Nevertheless the Committee failed to become an effective vanguard for the local working class as a whole. Even the revolutionaries could not escape entanglement in the protective reflexes of the craftsmen, and it was a narrow and self-isolating path that they cut through the turmoil on the Clyde. The Committee was easy prey for the government. In the dilution struggle the tortuous self-deceptions of the revolutionaries contrasted vividly with the actions of the government. The Ministry of Munitions and the Dilution Commissioners directed an offensive remarkable for its clarity of aims, its flexibility, its ruthlessness, and for the careful planning of the means. Gallacher, Kirkwood, Muir and the rest were amateurs in class warfare in war-time beside Lloyd George, Llewellyn Smith, Beveridge, Rey, Weir and Macassey. Not the least of the victories of the latter was their ability to conceal this fact for more than fifty years.

8

SIDNEY POLLARD

THE FOUNDATION OF THE CO-OPERATIVE PARTY*

A T its meeting in Swansea in May 1917 the Co-operative Congress voted by an overwhelming majority to seek 'direct representation in Parliament and on all local administrative bodies'. By October of that year a National Emergency Conference had enthusiastically endorsed this decision and had set up machinery to implement it. The Co-operative Representation Committee (later prefixed 'National') fought its first by-election in January 1918, opposing the official coalition candidate, and at the coupon election it fielded ten candidates, of whom one, A. E. Waterson, was successful. By 1919 the N.C.R.C. had become the Co-operative Party.

The most striking feature of this sudden incursion into politics and the alliance with Labour was the fact that right up to 1917 the Co-operative Congress and the movement generally had repeatedly and decisively rejected both developments. The complete about-turn which occurred in 1917 is generally ascribed to specific and immediate business grievances against the government of the day, against which political pressure was to be mobilised by the new initiative. Among the chief of these complaints were unfair treatment over the allocation of food, particularly of sugar and wheat; biased and hostile decisions by the military selection tribunals over the deferment of staff; the application of the Excess Profits Duty to Co-operative dividends, though they had for many years been recognised by the revenue authorities to be rebates rather than profits; and the persistent slighting and neglect of Co-operators in the manning of

* Research on which this paper is based was made possible by a grant from the Knoop Fund of the University of Sheffield. I am most grateful for the kind attention by the following Librarians: Mrs. I. Wagner of the Labour Party, Mr. Desmond Flanagan of the Co-operative Union and Mr. Brian Reith of the Co-operative Party.

Ministries and local tribunals dealing with distributive matters. 'The essential point to observe here,' wrote G. D. H. Cole, following a long tradition of similar views, 'is that what brought the Co-operative Movement into politics was not a conscious will to unite on a common political programme or to form a new party in any ordinary sense, but a feeling of acute grievance and a disbelief that co-operation could ever look for fair treatment from Governments unless it took matters actively into its own hands.'[1]

It is the argument of this paper that this view, while formally and superficially correct, omits the decisive underlying development that converted the ingrained hostility of the movement towards political involvement into its eager acceptance: this was the general swing to the left of all sections of the labour movement in 1917. The specific events which led to the formation of the organisation which soon after became the Co-operative Party cannot be properly understood unless they are seen against this background.

I

The political evolution of the rest of the labour movement was so much in line with the conversion of the Co-operators that it is rather surprising that the parallel was not drawn by other observers almost as a matter of course. Yet there is virtually no reference to it in the Co-operative literature, and we must begin by examining some of the reasons for this neglect.

The main source for the traditional view lies in the contemporary pronouncements of the Co-operative leadership itself. Almost from the outbreak of the war onwards, and increasingly so in later years, the pages of the *Co-operative News* were filled with detailed and practical complaints, and by 1917 these had become crystallised into the demand for greater political power

---

[1] G. D. H. Cole, *A Century of Co-operation* (1944), p. 269. Very similar views will be found expressed in all other standard accounts, e.g. Arnold Bonner, *British Co-operation* (Manchester 1961), pp. 140–3; W. G. Rhodes, *Co-operative–Labour Relations, 1900–1962* (Co-operative College Papers No. 8, 1962), pp. 15–17; S. and B. Webb, *The Consumers' Co-operative Movement* (1921), pp. 245–7, 266, 352–5; Burt Williams, *The Case for Co-operative Representation and How to Obtain It* (Manchester, 1918), pp. 20–4; Tom Carbery, *Consumers in Politics* (1968), ch. 2.

by direct representation in Parliament. Similarly, the Congresses of 1916 and 1917 and the Emergency Conference of October 1917 were dominated by statements linking directly the specific grievances of local societies with the entry into politics. An editorial entitled 'Direct Representation in Parliament', for example, in the *Co-operative News* of 28 April 1917, commenting on 'the remarkable change in opinion throughout the Co-operative movement during recent years in the question of direct representation in Parliament', stated categorically that

the 'right about turn' on this matter has been brought about by the way the movement is being menaced by vested interests, and the manner in which it has been ignored during the period of the national crisis.

William Maxwell, the Scottish leader, who had worked for political representation for twenty years, and who greeted the Emergency Conference with the words: 'This is, I think, the happiest day of my career', admitted that 'the change that has come over the movement has been largely due to the circumstances of the past three years'. From the other extreme, J. Maton, of Edmonton, describing himself as one who had always opposed the entry into politics in the past, explained that he had now changed his mind because: 'We, today, are faced with the threat of annihilation.' He was echoed in October by Aneurin Williams: 'During the twenty-five years I have worked with the Co-operative movement, I have been consistently against the entrance of the movement into politics ... [but now] we have been driven into political action.'[2]

Moreover, it was also true in the long prehistory of attempts at Co-operative politics[3] that it was usually practical and *ad hoc* experience rather than permanent ideological conviction which

[2] *Report of the Co-operative National Emergency Conference, 1917* (Manchester, 1917), pp. 89, 114; *Co-operative Congress Report* (1917), p. 556. See also the explicit statements in the Co-operative Union leaflet: *Why Co-operators have entered into Politics* (n.d. but 1917).

[3] Good accounts will be found in Cole, *op. cit.* pp. 312 ff.; A. Barnes, *The Political Aspect of Co-operation* (Manchester, 1926, first edn. 1923), pp. 10 ff.; Carbery, *op. cit.* ch. 2; B. J. Youngjohns, *Co-operation and the State* (Co-operative College Papers No. 1, 1954), pp. 54 ff.; Rhodes, *op. cit.* pp. 5–11; Peter Shea, '*Times Past*'. *Paragraphs on the History of the Co-operative Party* (195), pp. 9 ff.

had released such clamour in favour as there was. Perhaps the clearest case was in 1897 when Maxwell carried his resolution in favour of direct parliamentary representation at the Perth Congress, only to be followed by overwhelming opposition or apathy on the part of individual societies in the following year when the decision had to be implemented. On that occasion the immediate cause had been the attempted boycott of Co-operative meat supplies by Scottish butchers and the attempt by traders to get the dividend taxed as 'profit'. At other times the issue was usually raised after some rebuff received by the Joint Parliamentary Committee, a body set up by 1880 and recognised in 1892, in the course of its lobbying of Members of Parliament on behalf of Co-operative demands. After the turn of the century Co-operative Congresses passed resolutions on numerous political (though not necessarily party-political) matters,[4] and the men who had to attempt to bring these before Parliament, by lobbying friendly M.P.s, were among the most persistent in demanding more directly responsive Co-operative representation so that they would not always be in the posture of abject petitioners.[5] The example of the trade unions was often quoted before 1914, and in 1917 the phrase 'the Co-operators' Taff Vale' was on many lips.[6] At the same time the argument of the opponents of direct representation was not so much that political influence was unnecessary as that it was better exercised through a pressure group on M.P.s of all parties than through a small number of committed Co-operative members.[7]

[4] See list in Barnes, *op. cit.* App. i.

[5] This is much of the burden of Tweddell's paper read to the 1905 Congress and published (to be republished in 1918) under the title *Direct Representation in Parliament*. See also annual report of the J.P.C., *Co-operative Congress Report* (1913), p. 90.

[6] 'There was a likelihood,' said Purdie of the Scottish Section at a Central Board Meeting in April 1917, 'that they were about to receive their Taff Vale, and he hoped co-operators, like trade unionists, would rise to the occasion': *Co-operative News*, 28 April 1917; for other occurrences of the phrase, see W. C. Anderson's article in the series 'Co-operative Reconstruction', No. ix, *ibid.* 31 March 1917; W. R. Allan, in *Co-operative Congress Report* (1917), p. 551.

[7] *Co-operative Congress Report* (1917), pp. 552–3.

II

Yet this kind of explanation, which seeks to isolate changes in Co-operative opinion as if it were not part of working-class opinion, is in conflict with much of the evidence. In particular, it assumes a sudden interest in politics, whereas in fact there was a long and logical tradition of political involvement and a steady and natural growth of the demand for direct representation of the Co-operative movement as a working-class organisation.

The Congress votes themselves show a clear line of evolution. The vote of 1897 in favour of direct representation, and (after rejection in the localities) the negative vote in 1900 of 409 : 905 were taken before the Labour Party had entered the lists as a possible contender. No attack on the existing party system could therefore have been intended. By 1905, the next major debate, the vote for political involvement was reversed, to 654 : 271 in favour, but now the new element, the attempt to link involvement specifically with the Labour Representation Committee (there was no thought of affiliation at that time) suffered an overwhelming defeat of 807 : 135. By 1913, the last important occasion before 1917 when the matter was discussed – and by then an alliance with the Labour Party was implicitly understood – the adverse vote had fallen to 1346 : 580, showing a substantial growth of the minority view. At the same time a majority voted for closer links with the trade-union movement as the other main working-class representative organisation.

This slow *rapprochement* was on the face of it a full seventeen years behind, and in sharp contrast with, the action of the trade unions, many of whom had affiliated to the L.R.C. in 1900, while only a single small Co-operative Society, Tunbridge Wells, had done so. In fact, however, all three sections of the organised working class – the unions, the party and the co-operatives – moved forward in a twilight of unresolved issues. It is now widely recognised, for example, that many of the trade unionists who nominally supported the L.R.C. and the Labour Party, including even those who stood for election under their auspices, did not think that they were thereby totally breaking their links with Liberalism: the Labour Party, for them, was a sectional pressure group rather than a contender for office in opposition to the two 'real' parties. Nor could the Labour Party programme be said to be explicitly socialist before 1918, or its acceptance by all the trade-union leadership to be certain afterwards. All three organisations contained a small, though active, minority of socialists; all three contained larger numbers of members who wished to see working-class interests more powerfully represented. At the same time each of the three contained a solid core of older men tied to the Liberal–Nonconformist tradition, particularly in the north, while the tradition was weaker, and radicalisation easier, in Scotland and in the south. And if one or other of the three pulled slightly ahead of the rest, it was because tactically and temporarily it found itself under the necessity of doing so. Taken together they all represented the same people, the same sector of the population, the skilled and semi-skilled workers and some labourers and their sympathisers.

Throughout this period Co-operative sentiment became more explicitly and more articulately one of defending 'working-class' interests against an indifferent or hostile government. There was no great clarity and there was certainly no agreement as to future tactics in relation to a two-party or even a three-party system. Yet there was genuine disappointment with the record of Liberal administrations, from whom a great deal had been expected.

In some respects, indeed, Co-operators were ideologically more advanced than either the Labour Party or the unions. Even those of their active members who voted Liberal and Conservative were committed to the 'Co-operative Commonwealth', a concept which was comfortably nebulous yet clearly implied some kind of socialism. When Margaret Llewelyn Davies read her paper on 'Relations between Co-operative and Socialistic Aspirations' at the 1890 Congress, maintaining that these two had a close kinship, even her sharpest critics, like Holyoake, could allege only that the one assumed State intervention and that the other was individual and voluntary, without being able to challenge the basic similarity of ultimate aims.[8] It was the practical experience of the years between then and 1917 which was to prove that Holyoake was wrong, and that even Co-operators could not do without positive action by the State.[9]

[8] *Congress Report* (1890); Youngjohns, *op. cit.* pp. 55–7.
[9] Rhodes, *op. cit.* p. 15; Margaret Llewellyn Davies, A. Honora Enfield

Co-operative socialism, however, was pie-in-the-sky for most Co-operators, even among the leadership. What was much more immediate and effective was the consciousness of the inevitable common interests of the working people as a class, over against other classes, irrespective of party allegiance and loyalty. 'We have in our ranks', declared T. Tweddell in 1905, in the lecture already noted, 'upwards of three millions of the steadiest, most thrifty and, I believe, the most thoughtful of the working people of this kingdom', and they no longer feel represented by the two parties, 'neither of whom cares a rap for their interests'. The trade unions, after Denaby Main and Taff Vale, had decided in large numbers to join the new L.R.C.

> Its ideal is that of a party which ... shall specially represent the workers.... It is in the interest of the great array of workers which the people's party will specially represent in that great struggle between capital and labour upon which we have entered, and round which more and more as the years roll by political combinations will be compelled to group themselves.[10]

In 1905 Tweddell's initiative – and that of the Joint Parliamentary Committee – to join forces with the L.R.C. was defeated, Fred Maddison, a co-operator who had been elected a Liberal M.P. for Brightside, Sheffield, declaring that the 'L.R.C. are entirely opposed to the essentials of our movement'.[11] Yet in the following years the movement came to assume without question that in the alignment on class lines, which was coming to be the one that mattered most, not only the trade unions but also the Labour Party were 'natural allies'. Within a short period, and by imperceptible steps, the alliance with Labour came to be taken totally for granted – even when it was being denied for tactical reasons by its own supporters.

Most of this was germinating quietly within the movement without necessarily coming into the open, helped along by political experience and socialist propaganda. There were some

and Lilian Harris, *Co-operation and Labour Unrest* (Manchester, 1919); J. Young, in *Co-operative Congress Report* (1913), pp. 495–6.

[10] *Co-operative Congress Report* (1905), pp. 421, 426, 427.
[11]*Ibid.* p. 447.

societies (as there were some trade unions), like Stratford, Plymouth or Manchester and Salford, in which the leadership appears to have been far to the left of the membership in this respect; but in most others – and again trade-union parallels might be found – the positions were reversed. There was, in the pre-war years, a good deal of suspicion among Labour supporters of the political leanings of much of the Co-operative leadership, and it was well expressed by W. C. Robinson in a confidential memorandum to Arthur Henderson composed in February 1913 as a result of an initial meeting with Co-operative leaders:

> I have very little confidence in the men who are leading the Co-operative Movement ... the rank and file are in advance of their heads and officials.... The objects of the two movements are very similar, both seek to raise the condition of the workers. We are both trying to obtain a greater share of the wealth of which the workers were producers. The two movements both in aim and practice are one, both denounce the capitalist trader, but unfortunately like many of our trade-union members they applaud the capitalist politician.... I wish it were possible to realise some hope, but personally my experience of these managers and committees of co-ops are [sic] of the narrow radical type. [There might be collaboration on food prices and on housing] if we had not so many men who had property interests on our co-operative management committees.[12]

This meeting, significantly, had arisen out of the increasingly violent industrial unrest and a major speech on the topic by William Maxwell following a lecture by Rae at the 1912 Portsmouth Co-operative Congress. After due consideration, the Board of the Co-operative Union took the initiative in September 1912 to approach the Labour Party and the Parliamentary Committee of the Trades Union Congress 'with a view to considering whether co-operation between the three bodies is

[12] Robinson lived in Heywood, Lancashire: 'Labour and Co-operative Union' file in Labour Party Muniments (referred to below as L.P.M.). It is only fair to add that the other Labour representatives, in their memoranda, were much more optimistic over the potential of the Co-operative Movement for Labour interests.

possible, and if so, to what extent and in what manner. It should be understood that if such a conference is arranged it would be of a non-committal character, and simply with the object of the question being considered in a free and friendly manner.'[13] The agenda proposed by the Co-operative side contained the following four points:

(1) 'How best can the forces of the Co-operative trade-union and labour movements be utilised to raise the economic status of the people?'
(2) To help the trade unions to invest their funds securely in Co-operative Societies, 'and at the same time gradually placing in the hands of the workers to a much greater extent the control of the sources of supply, production and distribution.'
(3) Mutual assistance in 'their propaganda and educational work'.
(4) To devise a 'practical scheme ... whereby the Co-operative Movement may be able to render greater assistance to the labour force in time of industrial dispute.'

The subsequent story has often been told. A meeting took place on 8 February and resolved:

That this joint Conference of Representatives ... is of opinion that in order to assist in the promotion of the social and economic conditions of the people, it is advisable that there should be closer mutual effort – educational and practical – between the three sections represented at the Conference.

However, when the issue of this collaboration was raised at the 1913 Co-operative Congress, it was heavily defeated by the Liberals led by Greening.[14]

[13] A. Whitehead, General Secretary of the Co-operative Union, to Henderson, 27 September 1912, L.P.M.

[14] It has often been noted that even then, the clash was partly between age groups as well as between political allegiances. E. O. Greening, leader of the Liberal, anti-Labour faction, was aged about 77 in 1913; and it was ironic that he himself had stood as a working-class candidate, opposed both by the Conservatives and by a large proportion of Liberals, at Halifax at the general election of 1868, forty-five years earlier: Tom Crimes, *Edward Owen Greening* (1924), pp. 84–9.

Yet two other significant developments should be marked. The first was the close collaboration between Co-operatives and trade unions. Even Greening's hostile amendment included the proviso that

> Whilst approving of concerted action with trade unions and other organised bodies for raising the status of Labour, [this Congress] cannot sanction union with the political Labour Party.'[15]

During the years of pre-war 'unrest', 1912 and 1913, numerous local links were forged between unions and consumer societies, particularly during strikes. At such times the Co-operatives allowed strikers' families to draw on their shares or to anticipate dividends, lowered prices of coal or food for them, contributed to strikers' relief funds, and, when commercial banks on various pretexts, froze union funds during the strikes, saw to it that the C.W.S. bank advanced them the necessary strike pay.[16] Indeed, the unanimity with which even Liberal Co-operators saw themselves as part of the labour movement was evident when the directors of the C.W.S. (a body not normally found among the radical wing of the movement) decided on their dramatic action of sending a food ship to Dublin to relieve the starving families of the locked-out workers in 1913.

The second was that the natural groundswell which drove the Co-operative movement into the arms of the Labour Party seemed to be irresistible, no matter how many victories Greening and his forces managed to win on the surface. Thus, despite the apparently adverse vote, the negotiatons with the T.U.C. and the Labour Party went on, the Board declaring blandly that only a full union had been explicitly rejected, not a working alliance among independent bodies. Greening sounded the alarm in the *Co-operative News*, when he learnt of the next meeting

[15] The original hostile amendment, proposed by Warrington Society, had been even milder: 'That this Congress, whilst recognising the efforts of the trade unions and the National Labour Party [sic] for the uplifting of the workers, yet considers that it is unwise, in the interests of the co-operative movement as a whole, that it should be identified with any political party or section.' *Congress Report* (1913), pp. 488 ff.

[16] F. M. Eddie, *Co-operation and Labour Uprisings* (Women's Guild, Hull, 1912); also *Joint Builders. How Co-operators and Trade Unionists should Work Together* (Pamphlet, Women's Guild, n.d. but 1912 or 1913).

of the three parties, held on 30 May, which had proposed a 'United Co-operative and Labour Board' and had drawn up a list of eight common objectives; and as a result of this adverse publicity the Board lay low for a while.[17] But in November the Co-operative Union again took the initiative, proposing to make the first moves confidentially by the United Board, which had only 14 members, before putting it before the Central Board, which had 72.[18] The proposal for a joint committee, in which Co-operators would have half the seats, was raised again at the Dublin Congress of 1914. However, it was shelved owing to insufficient preparation, and after getting some indecisive but generally hostile reactions from the sections, it was defeated in 1915.[19]

III

Meanwhile, the outbreak of war forced each working-class organisation to face almost at once the issue of its primary allegiance. As early as 6 August 1914, Henderson had called an emergency meeting which set up the War Emergency Workers' National Committee (W.E.W.N.C.), consisting of representatives of the Labour Party, the T.U.C. and individual trade unions, the Co-operative movement, and other similar organisations. The original objectives of the Committee included the relief of cases of hardship and general legislation to protect working people from the ill-effects of war, and in the early years most of the Committee's herculean labours were in the fields of aid and advice on legislation regarding pensions, prices, housing and rent, relief, and other individual problems.[20] Later on, however, it became caught up in the general Labour campaigns about the conduct and objectives of the War.

The Committee was quickly loaded with an immense amount of work, much of it carried by its Secretary, J. S. Middleton,

[17] *Co-operative News*, 14 June 1913; Whitehead to Henderson, 6 June 1913, L.P.M.
[18] Whitehead to Henderson, 25, 28 November 1913, L.P.M.
[19] A good summary will be found in Rhodes, *op. cit.* pp. 10–12, and Barnes, *op. cit.* pp. 16–21.
[20] W.E.W.N.S., *Report August 1914 to March 1916* (1916), copy in L.P.M.; W. H. Brown, 'Co-operation as the only Hope', *Co-operative News*, 30 January 1915.

and its record is discussed fully in another essay in this volume.[21] Its membership was somewhat fluctuating. Originally, four Co-operators had been invited, two from the Co-operative Union and two from the wholesale societies, but the latter turned down the invitation on grounds of overwork. The Union, on the other hand, considered that the War over-rode the adverse Congress vote which had rejected any link-up with the Labour Party, and appointed Mrs M. A. Gasson and B. Williams.[22] Other representatives were found from the Women's Guilds and from London (Stratford) Societies, and there were thus usually four or five Co-operators on an executive committee of around thirty. In the concrete reality of the Committee's work for the victims of war, the qualms about political independence were quickly forgotten and common and basic class interests were recognised.

As early as 1915, the Joint Parliamentary Committee in its report to the Co-operative Congress called the W.E.W.N.C. 'the most representative National Committee ever appointed in the interests of the working classes' and declared that it 'has been useful in demonstrating the advantages which might be obtained from a properly organised union of working-class forces'.[23] But as year was added to weary year, the weaknesses of Labour in the war situation became more apparent than its advantages. During the course of the War, the Government was assuming control over prices, supplies and distribution of an ever-growing range of commodities, including consumer goods. Yet the increasingly powerful State was essentially still the servant of profit-making industry and trade; and, as a matter of course, its new apparatus was built up largely by drawing on the personnel of the businesses to be 'controlled', on men who were often still paid their salaries by their own private firms. The role of this 'businessmen's government' was enlarged to scandalous proportions after Lloyd George took over,[24] and the bias and discrimination it exerted against the Co-operative

[21] [See below, pp. 211–59, for the essay by Royden Harrison.]

[22] Whitehead to Middleton, 11 August 1914, Brodrick to Middleton, 21 August 1914, 'W.N.C. – Co-operatives file', L.P.M.

[23] *Co-operative Congress Report* (1915), pp. 148, 120–1.

[24] Beveridge in his standard history, called this phase, somewhat whimsically, 'the expert in charge': *British Food Control* (1928), ch. 4. See also his *Power and Influence* (1953), p. 142.

Societies, against the consumer, and against Labour, came to be considered to be intolerable in all sections of the movement.

Between December 1916, when the reshuffle began, and May 1917, when food and other shortages, aggravated by U-boat sinkings,[25] were added to selfishness, greed and mismanagement at the top, the Co-operative movement exploded with anger, looking naturally to its allies who were suffering and reacting in similar fashion. The W.E.W.N.C., for example, sent its very first deputation to Lord Devonport, the Food controller (and owner of a large grocery chain), to complain about the allocation of sugar, which formed one of the chief grievances of the Co-operative Societies. Again, on the invitation of the Labour Party, a Conference on Food Prices was held, at which about half the delegates were Co-operators, and its resolution, offered in the name of 'this Conference, representative of national labour organised on both its wage-earning and consumer sides', urged the government to step up its measures of price control, central purchasing, and allocation of supplies of food, coal and other consumption goods. Throughout 1917 there were protest meetings in all large towns and Food Vigilance Committees were set up in many centres in June–July 1917, drawn mostly from local Co-operative Societies, trades councils and Labour Parties; and towards the end of the year a National Convention on Food Supply reiterated the demands for tighter control. In June a powerful delegation, led by J. R. MacDonald, saw Lord Rhondda, the new Food Controller, and obtained important concessions from him, placing great weight on the Co-operative grievances. In all these actions the Co-operative Societies took their place as a matter of course by the side of other Labour organisations. Locally as well as nationally there was an intense feeling of solidarity[26]

Even at the beginning of the year Scotland, politically always the most advanced section of the Co-operative movement, was certain not only that Co-operation needed political influence

[25] E.M.H. Lloyd, *Experiments in State Control. At the War Office and the Ministry of Food* (Oxford, 1924), pp. 156 ff., 231 ff.; Beveridge, *Food Control*, pp. 91 ff., 123 ff., 134 ff.; Arthur Marwick, *The Deluge* (1965), pp. 206–9.

[26] 'Conference–Food', and 'Food' files, L.P.M.; *Manchester Guardian*, 22 June 1917; *Co-operative Congress Report* (1917), pp. 146, 240.

but that it also needed an alliance with the Labour Party through
a proposed 'United Co-operative and Labour Committee'.[27]
Elsewhere, too, class-consciousness was growing as attacks
mounted on an establishment which appeared under different
guises – those of the trader, politician or military officer. Mass
meetings, resolutions and common action with trade unions and
socialist groupings on issues such as food prices, food allocation
and profiteering were reported in every issue of the *Co-operative
News* from December 1916 onwards. Shedding its official
political neutrality, the paper introduced its report of the Labour
Party Conference with these words: 'As members of the same
class – the working class – co-operators were interested in all
the resolutions which came before the annual meeting of the
Labour Party last week....'[28] P. S. Urell, Secretary of the
Plymouth Trades and Labour Council, indeed, declared that
the application of the Excess Profits Duty to Co-operative dividends 'was nothing more nor less than a capitalist plot to stab the
Labour Party in the back by crippling the co-operative societies'.
The town had already proposed a local electoral pact between
them, to be called the Labour and Co-operative Representation
Association.[29] Strong support for political intervention also came
from Wales, from the West Riding, from Manchester, Tyne-
side and many other areas. The disillusionment, frustration and
newly strengthened feeling of class solidarity were perhaps most
succinctly expressed in a reply to Greening's plea in the *Co-
operative News* against political involvement. The War, it declared, had been the great educator:

Conscription at a shilling a day for the private soldier;
excess profits for the manufacturer and dealer. Suppression
for the workers' papers: licence for the Harmsworth press.
Tall prices for producers: queues for consumers. Imprisonment for strikers: autocracy for a War Cabinet of three.[30]

[27] *Co-operative News*, 13 January, 21 April, 28 April 1917.
[28] *Ibid.* 3 February 1917.
[29] *Ibid.* 17 February and 5 May 1917.
[30] Anonymous article: 'Why Should we Wait?', *ibid.* 26 May 1917. T. W.
Mercer put it that by the War, 'as in a flash of lightning', the whole social
horizon was illuminated, and the structure of modern society revealed:
The Co-operative Movement in Politics (Manchester, 1920), p. 6.

When Congress met in Swansea on 28 May 1917, the atmosphere was electric from the beginning. An activist group, the Manchester and District Defence Committee, had prepared the ground well, and apart from the Parliamentary Committee's own resolution for direct parliamentary representation, no fewer than 104 Societies had agreed beforehand to sponsor an even more explicit motion, which extended the demand for representation to 'all local administrative bodies' also. Those who sponsored it knew that they carried the large majority of Congress with them, while the movers of the amendment, E. O. Greening and F. Maddison, were wholly on the defensive. In fact it proved difficult to balance the debate, since so few speakers could be found to support their amendment. As one participant remembered it,

> There could have been no greater evidence of the immense change of thought among co-operators than the difference between the effectiveness of Mr. Greening's speech at Aberdeen in 1913 and the ineffectiveness of his remarks at Swansea, 1917. While in 1913 ... he rang a chord with his fear of political dissension, in 1917 ... [he] had an air of unreality, and no link with living issues.[31]

The Manchester resolution was passed by the overwhelming majority of 1979:201 votes.

There had been no mention in the resolution – and little in the supporting speeches of its sponsors – of a link with the Labour Party: the wording was merely for independent representation of the Co-operative movement. Yet there was never any doubt in the minds of both supporters and opponents that that was what was implied. It would have been quite unthinkable on any realistic assessment to split the working-class vote, or to find any major divergence of interest between the two sections.

Even before the meeting, the Joint Parliamentary Committee had recognised in its report that

> immense charges are upon us in every department of our national life ... unless we are alive to the trend of events, we

---

[31] Barnes, *op. cit.* p. 29.

shall find ourselves in the backwash of the revolution, instead of on the crest of its foremost waves.

The government's decisions about income tax and the E.P.D., declared F. Ireland of the Plymouth Society,

have demonstrated to us that politicians, whether Liberal, Conservative or Unionist or any other – when it comes to working-class politics – are united in their determination to exterminate us. I am surprised to see so old a champion of the working-class emancipation as Fred Maddison stand here still and ask us to put our trust in the capitalist domineering political party. He knows that in the House of Commons there are no Liberals or Conservatives when it is a capitalists' question. . . . What we want in the House of Commons is a body of intelligent co-operators . . . realising that the time must come when these organised working-class associations must have control not only of the industrial and economic institu-tions of the nation, but of its legislative assembly as well.'

Other speakers were equally clear that the issue was larger than Co-operative war-time grievances.

Stand together, working men, use your intelligence. Go forward and reform the Poor Law and all abuses in the country and you will never regret the vote you give today. (D. McCarthy, Leicester)
You must choose a man in favour of the nationalisation of the mines, railways and canals, and of banking, by both the State and the municipality. (J. Johnston, North-Western Section)
We want a People's Party up against the privileged classes. (E. Brennan, Darlington)

It had been put in a nutshell by a member, Mr. King, at a sectional conference at Norwich before Congress:

It was no use expecting the wolf to legislate fairly for the lamb.[32]

[32] *Co-operative Congress Report* (1917), pp. 137, 554, 557, 559; *Co-operative News*, 26 May 1917.

Meanwhile, as prices rose, queues lengthened and the sense
of frustration increased, Lloyd George committed the grave
error of repeatedly refusing to see a Co-operative delegation, on
the grounds that the conduct of the War took up all his time,
while the movement believed he had found sufficient time to see
a deputation of the Jockey Club. This deliberate slight was the
last straw, and drove even life-long Liberals into supporting
political action. At the Emergency Conference of October 1917,
at which the decisions of the Swansea Congress were to be
turned into concrete policies, the major resolutions were passed
unanimously, and the sentiments became even less distinguishable from those of the more militant Labour supporters. Below
the bitterness over the immediate grievances and the studied
insult by the Prime Minister, lay a matured ideological and
class-based political philosophy.

In his opening address the Chairman, T. W. Allen, referred
to the failures of food controls: their 'net result', he averred,
'was to preserve inviolate the profits of a class which have been
fleecing the people from time immemorial':

> Man has to be freed from the intolerable burden of being a
> producer of profits for others, and for this tremendous effort
> every democratic force must march side by side in mutual
> understanding. Our first effort is in the direction of a fuller
> understanding with the trade unionists ... Both movements
> have made up their mind that industry in all its forms shall be
> for public service, and not for the growth and further en-
> trenchment of capital.... Today the State in its final analysis
> is the expression of the will of capital ... but it is capital as
> profiteer that has been proved our greatest enemy. The evil
> is known. One form or other of collective control is now in-
> evitable.... Let us away with that nest of parasites who in-
> trude themselves into the processes of production and
> distribution.[33]

Such views, which expressed something very different from
simple fear over specific measures, the fear which has tradition-
ally been made responsible for the Co-operative entry into

[33] *Report of the Co-operative National Emergency Conference, October
1917*, pp. 8, 10, 11, 13, 14.

politics, were echoed consistently by the delegates from the floor. 'Never again,' cried Gordon of the Plymouth Society to great applause, 'shall the profiteer in the capitalist and landlord fatten or batten on the sufferings of the people. . . . In the words of Prince Kropotkin we shall declare, "Never again must this happen." '

Seconding the resolution on closer collaboration with the trade unions, Stubbs of the Cambridge Society was quoted as saying:

> I second this resolution because I believe it will set up a thorough working-class party. The trade union movement and the Co-operative Movement have one common enemy, and it is the duty of the two movements to join hands and close their ranks against the common enemy of the working classes. (Applause) The time is coming when these two movements must stand shoulder to shoulder against that dominant capitalist class and the profiteering class. . . . I hope the Co-operative Movement will rise now, as it has never risen before, and show to its enemies the power of the working classes. (Applause) We have a world to win, but we will only win it by a united effort by the trade union and Co-operative Movements. (Loud applause)

He was supported by Pickles of the Pendleton Society:

> I am a Socialist, a trade unionist, and a co-operator. I am attending meetings one night as a Socialist, another as a trade unionist, and another as a member of a co-operative board, but I am working for democracy in sections. . . . It is high time now that we sought democracy – not co-operation, or trade unionism, or socialism, but democracy. (Applause) Let us put all our cards on the table, stand together, and go forward for democracy – (applause) – triumphant democracy.[34]

The resolutions passed at that meeting were mostly on practical issues of trading, taxation and recruitment, but in the final provisional political programme agreed to, only two out of eleven points had a directly Co-operative slant, the other nine

[34] *Ibid.* pp. 33, 74–5.

being on general political matters, including the ending of profiteering, the democratisation of education, of the civil service and of foreign policy, policies on housing, credit and agriculture, and other far-reaching social reform.[35] The second of the two specifically Co-operative resolutions ran:

> 2. That eventually the processes of production, distribution and exchange (including the land) shall be organised on co-operative lines in the interests of the whole community.

The echo of the Labour Party's first socialist platform is unmistakable, and Cole may have been right in his surmise that at this point the Co-operatives were ahead of the other wings of the labour movement, and may have had some influence in hastening the plans of Sidney Webb and Arthur Henderson for introducing the new Labour Party constitution and programme.[36]

At the May Congress and in the sectional meetings preceding it there had still been loud voices warning against any alliance with socialists, and some supporters had played down any such possibility in order to disarm the opposition. By the October Conference, however, attended by over 1000 delegates from over 500 Societies, most of these inhibitions had been dropped. Arthur Henderson, addressing it as a fraternal delegation, was cheered to the echo by the assembled Co-operators at the very mention of his presence, and his speech was repeatedly interrupted by loud applause:

> I never like to think of the Co-operative Movement and the trade-union movement and the political side of the trade-union movement – the Labour Party – as being separate forces. (Applause) Our ideals ought to be same if they are not. (Hear, hear) One of the things we ought to be determined to accomplish – and to accomplish with all possible speed – is that when this War is ended the 'have-nots' are given a greater opportunity than they have ever previously enjoyed. (Loud applause) ... I do not mean that I am here asking that the Co-operative Movement should at once affiliate with the Labour Party. I am treating the matter from

[35] *Ibid.* pp. 109–11; Bonner, *op. cit.* p. 143.
[36] Cole, *op. cit.* p. 317.

a higher standpoint. (Applause) I would be prepared to advise that the Labour Party as known should cease to exist if by so doing we could combine the whole of the democracy. (Loud applause)[37]

When, in January 1918, a vacancy occurred at Prestwich, a Manchester constituency, the Labour Party gave H. J. May, Secretary of the N.C.R.C., a free run as 'consumers' candidate' to oppose the coalition nominee. He had been adopted on the initiative of nine Manchester Co-operative Societies, who resolved on 12 January 'that provided there is no other democratic candidate in the field, we go forward with the candidature of a Co-operative Representative'.[38] Polling 2832 votes against 8520 for the victor (a son of the former M.P., who had been elevated to the peerage as Lord Cawley), he had clearly collected most of the Labour vote. Even though some C.W.S. directors were said to have dragged their feet over this by-election, *the Co-operative News* supported May in an article entitled 'By Their Deeds Ye shall know Them, or What Has Lord Cawley done for the Workers?'[39]

By this time a joint committee of the C.P.R.C., the Parliamentary Committee of the T.U.C. and the Labour Party Executive had been set up to avoid electoral clashes,[40] and the *Co-operative News* was somewhat ingenuous when it reacted to the information that the Liberal Party had mounted a major campaign to capture the Co-operative vote by stating that 'the decision of the Swansea Congress – confirmed by the London Emergency Conference ... was arrived at on the distinct understanding that there should be no alliance with any existing political party, be it Liberal, Labour or Conservative'.[41] At the general election later in the year the N.C.R.C. fielded ten candidates, none against Labour opposition, though there had been some friction in some constituencies,[42] and its one successful

[37] *Emergency Conference Report*, pp. 96–7.
[38] *C.P.R.C. Minutes*, 22 January 1918.
[39] Shea, *op. cit.* p. 16.
[40] Cole, *op. cit.* p. 319; Barbara Smith and Geoffrey Ostergaard, *Constitutional Relations between the Labour and Co-operative Parties* (Hansard Society, ?1960), p. 5.
[41] *The Times*, 22 January 1918.
[42] N.C.R.C. (Co-operative Party) Minutes, e.g. 8, 20 August 1918. The Labour Party had left the N.C.R.C. an option on twelve constituencies.

candidate, A. E. Waterson, had in fact been jointly sponsored by Co-operators and Labour at Kettering, and at once joined the Labour group in the House. The 1919 Co-operative Congress instructed the newly named Co-operative Party to open negotiations with the other two wings of the labour movement 'with the ultimate aim of a united Democratic or People's Party', but the actual terms for a 'Labour and Co-operative Political Alliance' were rejected by the 1921 Congress by a tiny margin of 4 in a vote of 1682 : 1686, the adverse vote being cast largely by Societies which had not contributed financially to the Co-operative Party.[43] The steam had gone out of the leftward movement, and it was not until 1927 that relations between the Labour and Co-operative Parties were formalised.

IV

The sharp increase in political awareness and the marked shift to the left which occurred among Co-operators in 1917 was not, of course, unique. It could also be observed among the other sections of the labour movement, where it had equally far-reaching effects. This was the period of the rise of the power of the shop stewards and of Guild Socialism, of the widespread support for the Stockholm Conference and of a peace without annexation and indemnities, of plans for soviets in Britain, and of the new constitution and new socialist programme of the Labour Party. There is no space here to enlarge on these powerful parallel developments,[44] nor on the strikingly parallel substantial increases in membership among the different sections of the organised labour movement in the war, but it will be useful to examine some of the causes of this rousing of the working classes in Britain and, indeed, in all the belligerent countries.

Some of them, undoubtedly, had their base in the realm of ideas. They included revulsion against crude war propaganda, cynicism over repeatedly broken promises and hypocritical statements of governments regarding their war aims, and feelings of solidarity with suffering soldiers and workers of the enemy

[43] Webb, *op. cit.* pp. 269–70; W. H. Watkins, *The Co-operative Party: Its Aim and Work* (Manchester, 1921).

[44] For a competent account, see Paul W. Kellogg and Arthur Gleason, *British Labor and the War* (New York, 1919), and M. A. Hamilton, *Arthur Henderson* (1938), pp. 168 ff.

nations and the examples and ideas provided by the Russian revolutions. But many of them were more concretely based, or nurtured in more concrete experience: sheer weariness due to overwork and poor diet, horror at the human sacrifice demanded, resentment at the disruption of normal life. Above all, the contrast between profiteering and luxury among the rich and shabby treatment of the workers, even when they were praised as war heroes, struck a chord among those who had at any time listened to the teaching of the socialists in the pre-war years. By and large, their description of the State as a bourgeois instrument of exploitation seemed to fit the facts with increasing accuracy.

As always, the question of the fall of real wages, expressed in this case in rising prices of necessities, lay near the heart of the working-class revolt. The eight committees set up to inquire into 'industrial unrest' in June–July 1917 came up with staggering unanimity with the same answer from every major region of Britain: its chief cause was the rising price of food.[45] Among other causes quoted were shifting wage differentials, poor housing and welfare facilities, military comb-outs, maldistribution of food, profiteering, dislocation, overwork and uncertainty about future legislation affecting them. One complaint very high on the list, the repeated breaches of solemn undertakings regarding labour by the government, the committees found difficult to circumscribe, since the chief culprit was the Prime Minister, to whom the reports were technically addressed.

It is clear that the Co-operative Societies were at the very centre of this web of dissatisfaction, disillusionment and distrust, which lay behind the 'unrest' and the leftward shift in labour politics.[46] They felt directly much of the burden of unfair distribution of food, unfair taxation and call-up, the official hostility to collective and non-profit-making enterprises and neglect by government authorities, and as for profiteering, much of their time was spent fighting price increases which they found unnecessary and which, they alleged, could have been desired only by profiteering suppliers. If it is thought that the co-operative protest was earth-bound by comparison with the high-minded ideological conversion of the Labour Party and its socialist

[45] (Cd. 86629–9 1917). *Commission of Enquiry into Industrial Unrest.*
[46] E.g. 'Special Commissioner', 'Why there is Labour Unrest', *Co-operative News*, 7 July 1917.

societies, it is worth pointing out how much of that conversion, too, was due to the painful concrete day-to-day experiences of the working classes in Britain.

V

There are several subsidiary developments which also point in the same direction, to a major ideological conversion rather than a series of *ad hoc* complaints as the real basis of the Co-operative entry into labour politics, and they will be mentioned here only briefly. One important pointer was the remarkable collaboration which developed with the trade unions and which fits the point of view advanced here much better than the traditional one.

Like the leftward movement itself, the trade-union-Co-operative link had developed in the immediate pre-war years,[47] but it was greatly and remarkably strengthened during the War. In 1916 the Birmingham T.U.C. had declared 'that the development of the Co-operative Movement is essential to an active Trade Union Movement' and had proposed a 'National Advisory Council'. This was endorsed with enthusiastic unanimity by the Swansea Co-operative Congress of 1917, and the Council, consisting of six members from each side, was quickly formed and drew up a 'statement' which was later amplified into detailed plans for joint action both at national and at regional and local levels. In a pamphlet entitled *Trade Unionism and Co-operation: The Union of Forces*, the N.U.A.C. declared in 1919:

> The activities of organised capital have shown most conclusively that the closest possible union of the two organisations is essential for the protection of the interests of the workers as producers and consumers. By the making of vast profits, the piling up of large reserves, by amalgamation, combination, and federation, by manipulation of the Press, by securing panic legislation, by direct and indirect influence over Governments, and by the exploitation of patriotic sentiment capitalist and profit-making interests have strengthened, and are daily strengthening their resources.... We believe in the reconstruction of society on the basis of the Co-operative

---

[47] See p. 194 above. Also Women's Co-operative Guild, *Joint Builders. How Co-operators and Trade Unionists Should Work Together* (1913).

ownership and control of all things socially necessary. This is the policy which inspires joint action between the leaders of the Trade Union and Co-operative Movements; and it is this policy which we propose to carry out in the creation of a state of society in which mutual aid will replace competition and give to the workers a just and equitable share of the wealth their hands and brains produce.[48]

Again, there was much of practical interest behind this collaboration: the banking of trade-union funds with the C.W.S., common educational schemes, and support for strikes by Co-operative Societies. In the railway strike of 1919 the workers received perhaps greater help from the Co-operatives than in any major dispute before or since. It would clearly be inadequate to derive these major and ideologically based plans for collaboration from the sudden discovery of only minor practical common interests.

Secondly, it is significant that by the last quarter of 1917 and early 1918, when the Co-operative political reaction had just begun to get into its full stride, many of the immediate grievances were in fact being met. Lloyd George did receive a deputation and promised to look into the worst abuses later, in October 1917; Rhondda had always been sympathetic, and attempted as far as lay in his power to ensure that Co-operators were represented on local food committees.[49] The Consumers' Council, on which his Ministry came to lean heavily, was almost entirely a working-class affair, chaired by Clynes, with T. W. Allen, Chairman of the October Co-operative Conference, as Vice-Chairman, and with a strong Co-operative contingent of 6 out of 20, plus 3 from the W.E.W.N.C. Following Rhondda's illness and death, J. R. Clynes, a Labour representative, took over his duties. The regular, and less biased, civil service came into its own again in 1917–18 in the Ministry of Food. Finally, food rationing began in earnest in the spring of 1918, and most profiteering was brought under control, or at least very heavily taxed. Some grievances, particularly regarding taxation, and

[48] The best account will be found in Webb, *op. cit.* pp. 275 ff. See also F. Hall and W. P. Watkins, *Co-operation* (Manchester, 1934), pp. 345–6; *Emergency Conference Report*, pp. 70 ff.; Barnes, *op. cit.* pp. 43–4.

[49] Ministry of Food Circular M.G.3 (1917). Also 'Consumer Council' file in L.P.M.

the distribution of sugar, wheat and coal, remained; yet if they had been the sole cause of the entry into politics, one would have expected the impetus to decline in 1918–19 instead of reaching its climax.

Thirdly, the solution proposed – that of sending Co-operative M.P.s to Parliament – did not seem to meet the immediate grievances, even if it is conceded that the frustration and impotence of the War years forced Co-operators to clutch at any visible straw. No one could have hoped for much direct representation in war-time, when only by-elections offered an opportunity to test public opinion; but even in the middle distance of the immediate post-war years, with a general election in the offing, it is not clear what a handful of M.P.s could have accomplished: few thought of more than a handful, although one reader of the *Co-operative News* stated that 'we ought to have at least forty members in the House of Commons alongside of the other Labour members'.[50] It is difficult not to have some sympathy with the arguments of the Liberal opponents, who pointed out that the small number of Co-operative M.P.s envisaged would always be outvoted, would not be amenable to discipline on questions not relating to Co-operation, and would become indistinguishable from the other M.P.s of the larger group they would be forced to join, to the point even of accepting office and forgetting their election pledges, as some Labour M.P.s had done in war-time.[51] In the event, these reservations have proved to be realistic, and it would be hard to maintain that it has been easier to get Co-operative grievances relieved by Parliament since the foundation of the Co-operative Party than it was in the pressure-group days before. Specific short-term grievances alone would not have called such a party into being.

VI

It has been customary to underrate the role of the Co-operative movement in the past (and, indeed, in the present) perhaps mainly because it works in the provinces rather than in London,

---

[50] Letter by F.H.W., 3 March 1917.

[51] E.g. Greening, Maddison and E. J. Hill at the Swansea Congress, *Co-operative Congress Report* (1917), pp. 552–4, 558; letter by F.J.N. in *Co-operative News*, 28 April 1917.

by piecemeal advances rather than by spectacular leaps, and by voluntary accession rather than by legal compulsion. But part of the fault lies with Co-operators themselves, who too easily accept a subordinate position for their movement, and with Co-operative historians, who fail to see its crucial role in the evolution of the organisation of labour. Quite apart from the solid achievement of a £1000 million business without the profit motive, the movement can also claim with some justice that without its defence of working-class families as consumers, and without its own specific critique of society, the labour movement and its members would have been much poorer and much less effective in the past.

The suggestion which is often made in standard histories, that during the First World War, and particularly during the critical years 1917–18, Co-operative organisations were concerned merely with pounds of sugar or the dignity of representation on local bodies while the rest of the labour movement determined fundamental historical issues, is not untypical of the treatment to which Co-operative effort is frequently subjected, if indeed it is given any treatment at all. In fact, the role and contribution of the Co-operative movement were as significant as those of the other sections of the labour world. Alfred Barnes alone seems to have grasped this at the time :

> Surveying the Co-operative and Trade Union Movements, with their later political developments, the Labour Party and the Co-operative Party, we can trace their origin to the same source – the revolt of labour against the licence and tyranny of capitalism, their object being the creation of a workers' Commonwealth.[52]

The language has the now somewhat dated fervour of the post-war years, but the historical analysis implied in it has stood the test of time better than that of the traditional historians of Co-operation.

[52] Barnes, *op. cit.* p. 76.

9

ROYDEN HARRISON

THE WAR EMERGENCY WORKERS'
NATIONAL COMMITTEE, 1914–1920

T H E War Emergency Workers' National Committee is generally remembered only for the ironic circumstances associated with its formation. It arose from a conference summoned by Arthur Henderson, who hoped to supply a united proletarian response to the threat of war. Acting on behalf of the Labour Party, Henderson sent out invitations to the principal institutions of organised labour and to a large number of prominent personalities in the trade-union and socialist world. When the conference met on 5 August 1914, the United Kingdom had already declared war on Germany. The meeting wasted no time reflecting upon its original purpose: it spared no thought for the implications of the Stuttgart Resolution of the Second International. It rather addressed itself to the matter in hand, resolving to establish a committee which would be responsible for safeguarding working-class interests during the 'Emergency'. And it stuck to its last.

At this point the historians have stopped.[1] According to taste

[1] G. D. H. Cole. *Labour in War Time* (1915) is still the best account, although it necessarily deals only with the early, formative stage of the Committee's work. M. A. Hamilton, *Sidney and Beatrice Webb* (n.d. ?1933), pp. 222–8, also provides an incomplete, but generally reliable account.

I am deeply indebted to the Labour Party and in particular to its Librarian, Mrs. Irene Wagner, for allowing me to consult the records of this Committee which are held in the strong-room of Transport House. J. S. Middleton placed the correspondence and proceedings of the Committee in boxes in alphabetical order by subject. Thus the files run from 'Admiralty', 'agriculture', 'air-raids', 'aliens', 'apprentices', 'asylums', 'Belgian refugees', 'the blind', 'banking' and so on down to 'War', 'War Office' and beyond. Each box has, therefore, to be identified by its starting and finishing subject or by its number – if it has one. While the research upon which this essay is based was in progress, the collection was being systematically ordered by archivists. Where a particular item had been classified by the archivists I adopted their mode of reference, but most of the items in the they pause to commend the incomparable realism and common-sense of the Labour leaders, or else they deplore the insufferably pedestrian and parochial spirit which reduced Labour in wartime to nothingness. Yet neither within the language of praise nor of blame has justice been done to a committee which was at once the most, and the least, representative ever established in the British labour movement: uniquely close to the experience of the rank and file and yet extremely dependent upon established bureaucracies; formative of crucial new departures, but pathetically responsive to events over which it made no pretence of control.

I

The membership of the Workers' National Committee was determined by nomination, election and co-option. The Parliamentary Committee of the T.U.C., the Management Committee of the General Federation of Trade Unions and the National Executive Committee of the Labour Party, the three organisations united in the Joint Board, each nominated three members of the new body. They supplied the new Committee's principal officers and most of its funds. From the T.U.C. came C. W. Bowerman, H. Gosling and J. A. Seddon: Seddon becoming Vice-Chairman. The G.F.T.U. sent W. A. Appleton, who became Treasurer, along with Ben Cooper and Ben Tillett. The Labour Party nominated W. C. Anderson, John Hodge and Arthur Henderson, Henderson serving as Chairman until he entered the government in 1915. The Labour Party's Assistant Secretary, Jim Middleton, became the Secretary of the new organisation. Middleton brought with him the entire staff of the Labour Party with the exception of one organiser who went off to aid military recruitment.[2]

collection had not been so treated while I was at work. Although my gratitude is particularly due, in this instance, to the Labour Party, I welcome the opportunity of acknowledging the generous assistance of the library staff at the London School of Economics, at Nuffield College, Oxford, and elsewhere. The Passfield Trustees, who invited me to write the *Life and Times of Sidney and Beatrice Webb*, will, I hope, forgive me for making this short excursion away from the strict line of my proper studies. Mr. David Martin, my research assistant, has checked numerous references, and made some helpful suggestions.

[2] J. S. Middleton to J. T. Abbott, 28 February 1917 ('Executive–Food'

One of the advantages of setting up a new committee rather than relying upon the Joint Board to organise Labour's response to the War was that the Board lacked any independent administrative or clerical resources. However, there were other, and more compelling, reasons which account for Henderson's decision to extend invitations not only to the constituent organisations of the Joint Board, but to a number of important trade unions, socialist societies and co-operative institutions. The slow and cumbersome workings of the Joint Board were inappropriate to an emergency which called for prompt action. Although it was nominally the most representative institution in the Labour world, it could not claim to speak authoritatively on behalf of women workers or working-class consumers, groups of citizens whose interests were to be vitally affected by the War. Nor did the Board enjoy the entire confidence of the powerful unions which had formed the Triple Industrial Alliance. The miners contended that they were under-represented upon the Parliamentary Committee of the T.U.C., and they had been in bitter dispute with the G.F.T.U., which they saw as a centre of narrow craft conservatism and factionalism.[3] Henderson overcame these difficulties by allowing the inaugural conference directly to elect six members to the Committee in addition to the nine nominated by the three organisations associated with the Joint Board. The persons elected were all well-known figures in the movement. Their presence made the Committee more representative and more authoritative than it would otherwise have been. At the same time the directly elected members were not effectively accountable to anyone. They helped to give the Committee an independent character and they were responsible for most of its effectiveness. The first elected member was Robert Smillie of the Miners' Federation. He topped the poll on 5 August with 62 votes and eventually succeeded Henderson and Seddon as Chairman. Since Albert Bellamy of the N.U.R. also secured

---

box): 'The fact that at the outbreak of war the political truce was entered into led, of course, to the suspension of all our Labour Party activity. Mr. Peters threw himself into the recruiting campaign while I, in common with the rest of the staff, very rapidly became immersed in our War Emergency work. All the administrative work of the Committee has been done at this office. . . .'

[3] B. C. Roberts, *The Trades Union Congress, 1868–1921* (1958), pp. 264–5.

election, the claims of the industrial unions were accorded some practical recognition. Sidney Webb, with 55 votes, was joint runner-up to Smillie. He rapidly established his intellectual ascendancy within the Committee and was the principal author of all its proposals.[4] He shared second place with an old student of his from the London School of Economics, Dr. Marion Phillips, an energetic Australian who had already established herself as the leader of the Women's Labour League. Beatrice Webb respected her and found her handsome – 'in a coarse and sumptuous way'.[5] Mary MacArthur, the wife of W. C. Anderson and a prominent figure in the Women's Trade Union League, tied for the last place on the Committee with Bellamy and she helped to ensure that the interests of women workers received due attention. The remaining directly elected member was H. M. Hyndman, who came in fourth with 43 votes.[6] Hyndman was a most industrious member of the Committee and his record of attendances was second only to that of Middleton. In general, it was the elected rather than the nominated members who shouldered the main burden of the work.

The Committee established on 5 August was given powers of co-option and it exercised them vigorously. Its membership rose from the original fifteen to between thirty and forty. Co-option was immediately used to secure Co-operative representation, and Mrs. M. A. Gasson and B. Williams of the Co-operative Union were soon numbered among the most diligent attenders. They were joined by H. J. May of the Co-operative Congress Parliamentary Committee and W. H. Brown of the Stratford Co-operative Society. Women's representation was enlarged by Margaret Bondfield (Women's Co-operative

[4] J. S. Middleton, 'Webb and the Labour Party', in M. Cole (ed.), *The Webbs and Their Work* (1949), p. 171. Middleton might simply have been rising to the occasion for this memorial volume, but Mrs. Lucy Middleton confirms that he always held that Webb was the architect of the Committee's main proposals. Max Beer's estimate of Webb's leading position on the Committee, in his *History of British Socialism* (1940 edn.), p. 384 derived – according to Mrs Middleton – from information supplied by her husband.

[5] B. Webb, *Diary*, remarks on some notable Labour women, written in May 1918 but inserted after the entry for 3 June 1917 (Passfield Papers).

[6] Report of Representative Conference, 5 August, 1914, with pencilled record of votes received. (W.E.W.N.C., 'Minutes etc.' box) W. J. Davis, John Stokes, Robert Williams, Fred Bramley and Richard Bell failed to secure election. Williams was subsequently co-opted and Bramley replaced Seddon in September 1915.

Guild) and Susan Lawrence, another close friend of the Webbs. Four trade unions, together with the National Union of Teachers, were accorded places on the Committee: the M.F.G.B., the N.U.R., the National Union of Transport Workers and the United Textile Factory Workers. Through this gate Herbert Smith and Robert Williams came on to the Committee. Applications for representation from local or regional trade-union organisations were refused, but exceptions were made in favour of the Scottish T.U.C. and the London Trades Council. Finally, the representation of the Labour Party and the socialist societies was enlarged. Ramsay MacDonald came on from the Labour Party, Fred Jowett and H. Dubery from the I.L.P., and Stephen Sanders from the Fabian Society. The personnel of the Committee changed over time. Occassionally this was a consequence of political differences and divisions. More usually it was the result of deaths or of elevation to government office.

The Worker's National Committee established numerous sub-committees, but it had beneath it no tiers of subordinate organisation. In February 1915 it did recommend Trades Councils and local Labour Parties to take the initiative in setting up local committees modelled on the national one. In a few towns, such as Norwich and Walsall, this call was answered.[7] In Norwich the local committee affiliated to the Trades Council, the Educational Committee of the Co-operative Society, the Women's Labour League, the I.L.P. and the B.S.P. But as Middleton pointed out, the National Committee, which received its supplies through grants from the T.U.C., the G.F.T.U. and the Labour Party, could not serve as a model so far as finance was concerned.[8] Nor were there local Labour Party organisers in the districts who could devote themselves to the work as Middleton could do centrally. (The Secretary of the Walsall Committee lost his job in consequence of his activities.) The National Committee communicated, for the most part, with trades councils, and local labour and co-operative organisations. Paradoxically, the re-

[7] There were attempts to establish local replicas of the National Committee in Manchester, Hutchesontown and Govanhill, Glasgow, Bolton, West Cumberland, Hull, Blackburn and Rochdale.

[8] J. S. Middleton to J. T. Abbott, Labour Agent of Whitehaven and District Labour Representation Committee, who had made a late inquiry about forming a local committee in his district, 28 February 1917 ('Executive–Food' box).

moteness of the National Committee from mass organisations in the country led it to enter into a uniquely direct and personal relationship with the individual workers, soldiers and working-class dependants with whom it carried on an extensive correspondence. However, its structure did arouse some criticism. Speaking in the spring of 1915, Fenner Brockway, for example while warmly praising the work of the Committee, complained about the manner in which it had been constituted. Self-appointment and co-option he said, had no place in the labour movement. He thought that there was a risk that this Committee might hold back the assembling of Labour Party Conferences and other duly constituted representative gatherings of workers.[9]

On the whole, Brockway's anxieties proved groundless. Far from preventing the summoning of the representative assemblies of the movement, the Committee was instrumental in ensuring that they were held.[10] On the other hand, the confusing mixture of principles governing the way in which it was constituted was bound to give rise to difficulties. Thus in 1916 the British Socialist Party repudiated Hyndman's pro-war leadership and sought to replace him by Tom Quelch. Since Hyndman had been elected at the inaugural conference, it was decided that he could not be removed by the B.S.P. At the same time Quelch was welcomed as an additional member.[11] The interesting questions about this extraordinary procedure are political rather than institutional. The important problem is not how the Committee's constitution allowed it to adopt such a solution, but how the pro-war and the anti-war leaders were able to arrive at such a compromise. From the beginning, the Committee resolved to concentrate exclusively upon the social consequences of the War and to preclude all debate about the merits of British participation in the struggle. It is easier to understand that such a resolve was possible on the second day of hostilities than it is to appreciate how it was consistently adhered to for four years.

[9] I.L.P. *Report of Annual Conference* (Norwich, April 1915), pp. 54–5.
[10] See below, pp. 244 ff.
[11] J. S. Middleton to H. M. Hyndman, 6 July 1916 ('Executive–Food' box).

II

How was any practical collaboration possible between, say, W. C. Anderson or Fred Jowett, on the one hand, and Henderson, Bowerman and Appleton on the other? Within a few days of the outbreak of hostilities, Anderson produced a draft manifesto for the I.L.P. It read: 'Out of the darkness and the depth we hail our working-class comrades of every land. Across the roar of the guns, we send sympathy and greeting to the German Socialists. They have laboured unceasingly to promote good relations with Britain, as we with Germany. They are no enemies of ours, but faithful friends.'[12] Shortly after this manifesto appeared, Henderson, Bowerman and others were appealing to workers to enter the munitions industry. They recommended that 'every man capable should become a War worker, a life saver' and explained that 'The workmen of Germany have been long the enemy of the British. They have been making munitions of war secretly, preparing to conquer you – to gain our trade – to take your work away.'[13]

If it were necessary to take at their face value the attitudes of the pro-war and anti-war groups as expressed in such sharp contrasts as this it would be difficult indeed to see how the work of the Committee could have been possible. It worked effectively because they cannot be so taken. There is a parallel in the history of Chartism, which we cannot understand if we draw some supposedly comprehensive division between the advocates of 'moral' and of 'physical' force. We can, in fact, broadly distinguish four different positions among the members of the Committee with respect to the War. The Committee's successful functioning depended upon the presence of all these tendencies and the preponderant weight of two of them.

There were, first of all, the Hun-hating Jingos and ultra-loyalists. They were in favour of 'eliminating Germany from civilisation' and wanted to commit Labour unreservedly to the national cause. They were easily persuaded that workers had no rights that ought not to be abandoned, no interests that ought not

[12] F. Brockway, *Inside the Left* (1942), p. 47.
[13] National Advisory Committee (Chairman A. Henderson), *To Skilled Workmen in Engineering and Kindred Trades*, one printed page (n.d.? early 1915) (Box 28, 'Rent–Seamen').

to be subordinated, to the task of securing a complete victory. They willingly submitted to the system of sticks and carrots by which Ministers drew them first into the Treasury Agreement and then into the Munitions of War Acts: first recruiting, then 'attestation', and finally conscription. They told their trade-union members:

> Mr Lloyd George is a Democrat of great repute. Those who are turning out implements of war are SAFE IN HIS HANDS, provided they RESPOND TO HIS APPEAL TO PRODUCE ALL HE REQUIRES. As the late Chancellor of the Exchequer he proved to the country what a DETER-MINED MAN HE IS. Parliament has given him the BROAD SEAL OF AUTHORITY, and expects him to use it should it be unfortunately needed. That he will do so, if forced to it, goes without saying.
>
> MEN AND WOMEN SPRING TO THE RESCUE. Give the man a chance who hates conscription and who asks you to help him without resort to any degree of force.
>
> Be of good cheer, and WORK, MORNING, NOON AND NIGHT to let shot and shell get to the danger zone where officers and men are fighting for right and the integrity of our great Empire.[14]

The most vociferous patriots of this type, like Havelock Wilson and W. J. Davis, failed to secure election on to the Committee. However, many of the trade-union M.P.s such as O'Grady and Bowerman, were closely identified with this stand-pont. Appleton thought that the British workers would do well to set all aside until the War be won. 'When it is over, then we will have something to say.'[15] While it was on, he was quite pre-pared to congratulate Havelock Wilson upon his intransigent attitudes. Ben Tillett's position was more complex and serves as a reminder that 'war attitudes' were not necessarily fixed once for all, but changed with the course of hostilities. At the beginning of the War he wanted to let the German people know that 'our quarrel has been imposed upon us by the German monarch and

[14] W. J. Davis to the National Society of Brassworkers and Metal Mechanics, headed *National Peril* (handbill, n.d. but 1915) (Box 28).
[15] W. A. Appleton, *The Workers' Resolve* (1917), p. 8.

the German Government'.[16] He told Lloyd George: 'there are six to ten millions of human beings in this Country, who could not be worse off, if the Germans or the most brutal savage was in Government and in ownership'.[17] Nevertheless he was 'quite prepared to stand with you on a platform, justifying this terrible War imposed upon us by the brutality of Germany's ruling and sordid class'.[18] By the summer of 1915 he was informing his comments on the struggle with a curious kind of class analysis. He called for the 'Conscription of Riches' as well as of men. 'The landed gentry had given their sons nobly and freely with the industrial classes, but the capitalist class were sitting at home in comfort and security behind the bodies of better men than themselves.' He added that anyone who could commit such murders and brutalities as the Germans must be 'eliminated from civilisation'.[19] With John Hodge, another member of the Committee, he appeared on the platforms of the Socialist National Defence Committee and denounced interruptors as 'Germans'. 'When the German democracy decided to throw their lot in with Junkerdom and Kaiserdom, he respected their right to love their Fatherland, but he claimed the same right as a Briton to love his King and Country'.[20] Far from the War having been imposed upon the German working class, he now discovered that the 'German trade unionists [had] openly boasted in their cafes of what they were going to do when the great War came. . . .'[21] He told the T.U.C. 'We are in this War for our own sake, and if we should lose in the struggle we should lose more than any other country. And, on the other hand, we shall gain more if we win. We shall gain trade and prestige, and we cannot allow the Germans to take from us the liberties we have so hardly won.'[22]

But although Tillett took an interest in the Committee, he was not a particularly regular attender. Hodge, who held that the men 'who talk about Peace today are traitors to their

---

[16] *The Times*, 12 August 1914.

[17] B. Tillett to D. Lloyd George, 2 September 1914 (P.R.O. T172/980/B).

[18] B. Tillett to D. Lloyd George, 9 September 1914 (P.R.O. T172/980/B). Tillett was one of the first to be alarmed at rumours of conscription. He told Middleton he hoped the Committee would resist it (10 January 1915) (Box 9).

[19] 'Mr. Ben Tillett's Warning', *The Times*, 26 July 1915.

[20] *Ibid.* 22 July 1915.

[21] *Ibid.*

[22] *Report of the 48th Trades Union Congress* (September 1915), p. 325.

country', hardly came at all.[23] W. A. Appleton, despite the fact that he was Treasurer, only managed to attend five times in four years. With the exception of H. M. Hyndman, the Committee's active members were not found among those who adhered to the 'super-patriot' tendency. And although Hyndman was unmatched in verbal ferocity against 'the Hun' and was quite prepared to denounce the I.L.P. as working in the pay of the Kaiser, he was not happy in the association of like-minded trade unionists. He thought that they were far too complacent about the capacity and good intentions of the government. He was not innocent enough to imagine that every sacrifice demanded of the working classes bore a positive relationship to victory. He wanted to force the government into the organisation of a total war as the best way of beating the Kaiser while knocking another nail into the coffin of capitalism.

Thus the influence of the super-patriots was diminished by their divisions, want of attention, and by the tendency for them to retire as they received government appointments. Henderson, for example, resigned upon entering the Cabinet in 1915. It is a pointer to the predominant mood of the Committee that he received a letter thanking him for the work he had done, while studiously avoiding any hint of congratulations upon the appointment he had received.[24]

This predominant mood was the product much more of the 'sane patriot' than of the 'super-patriot' tendency. The most influential trade unionist of this persuasion, apart from Tom Mann, who was not a member of the Committee,[25] was Bramley of the Railwaymen, who replaced Seddon as T.U.C. nominee at the same moment as Smillie became Chairman. The sane patriots did not repudiate their internationalist pasts. They accepted the justice and necessity of British participation in the

[23] *Ibid.* p. 328 (statements about attendances are based upon a complete examination of the minutes of the Committee from its foundation until December 1917).

[24] J. S. Middleton to A. Henderson, 21 June 1915 (Box 9). Henderson was, for a time, a super-patriot, less as a matter of temperament or conviction, perhaps, than by association.

[25] Mann's attitude towards the War is difficult to discover, but speaking on conscription to the Scottish T.U.C., he said that 'he would do everything possible to make ourselves and our allies more efficient in the conduct of the War, but no definite facts had been placed before the country to show that compulsion was necessary': *The Times*, 1 May 1916.

War while holding that there was a continuing need actively to defend working-class interests and 'to maintain the capacity of the Labour Movement for independent initiatives at home and abroad'.[26] Webb and his Fabian colleagues were the best representatives of this current. War was not exactly in Webb's line. Indeed, Beatrice noticed that they had not seen their old acquaintance Sir Edward Grey, since he had become Foreign Secretary, 'it being assumed that he and we were no longer interested in the same subjects'.[27] But once war had broken out Sidney had no qualms about the righteousness of the British cause. In 1914 he assured the Swedish Socialist Gustave Steffen that the entire country, including the Labour Party, was in favour of fighting out the War to the bitter end. The success of British recruiting was, he insisted, 'unprecedented in all the history of the world'. The entire Empire was unanimous. The Peace Movement had been swept away. War was the result of 'evil thoughts', of national pride and a belief in irresistible power. Thanks to insolence and blundering, England had put herself superficially in the wrong during the Boer War. This time she was 'scrupulously in the right'. She wished the prosperity of Germany. Unfortunately, the Germans regarded Britain as an effete, selfish, Imperialist power. They saw the British Empire as something which must be smashed because it stood in the way of their seizure of 'tropical and other colonies'.[28]

Shaw told the Webbs 'You don't understand this War a bit.'[29] Accordingly, he took it upon himself to improve their ethical sense. The Irishman himself accepted that the War had to be prosecuted vigorously, but he rejected any claim to moral superiority made by either of the main belligerents. Both England and Germany had declared themselves to be Imperial races, and they had prepared for the War through their alliances. Militarism, he considered, had to be fought at home as well as abroad. Beatrice was swiftly impressed by the many 'true and valuable things' which she found in this line of argument. With Sidney it took a little longer and, for a time, there was a distinct, if limited,

[26]*Report of the T.U.C. Conference* (September 1915) pp. 329–30, for F. Bramley's attitude.

[27] B. Webb, *Diary*, retrospective note dated August 1918, inserted in the entry for 5 August 1914.

[28] S. Webb to Gustav Steffen, 14 October 1914 (Passfield Papers).

[29] G. B. Shaw to B. Webb, 28 August 1914 (Passfield Papers).

difference of attitude within the 'Partnership'. Beatrice confessed to a friend: 'Even Sidney and I are not of one mind! He is a sane British patriot – governed by his ten years experience at the Colonial Office – regarding the British Empire as the germ of a world-state and intent on devising some scheme of a Federation of the Allies and the United States with compulsion upon Germany to come into an enforced world peace and a gradual development of international law. I have ceased [May 1915] to think about the war – I do not seem to have any foundation for thought – I only feel a quite immeasurable wretchedness about it.'[30] Yet Sidney remained 'the ideal companion for the self-tortured mind. "Let us do our own work," he says, "like the French peasant cultivates his fields close to the firing lines."' As the War continued and the 'butcher's bills' kept coming in and Beatrice became more and more painfully afflicted with 'war neurosis', Sidney came to see that 'War is clearly horrid – not in the least what we associate with Jesus of Nazareth, or even with Herbert Spencer.'

'The French peasant cultivating his fields close to the firing line' exactly expressed the predominant mood within the Workers' National Committee. Webb, the sane patriot, set its tone as much as its style of work: neither jingo-ruffianism nor the non-conforming fervour of those who fancied themselves to be the elect, neither thoroughgoing opposition to the government nor abject submission to it, but commitment to the national purpose without loss of a distinctive identity.

In imposing this style upon the Committee as a whole, Webb was assisted, not merely by the strength of his own Fabian and personal following,[31] but by the predominant tendency within the 'anti-war' grouping. Opposition to the War was usually a matter of renunciation, dissociation and withdrawal rather than of determined resistance. It was often imperfectly expressed and in an involved way, as with MacDonald;[32] or barely expressed at all,

[30] B. Webb to 'My Dear Friend' (?Betty Balfour), 30 May 1915 (Passfield Papers).

[31] Four out of the thirty or so members of the Committee might fairly confidently be placed in this category: Susan Lawrence, E. R. Pease, Marion Phillips and W. S. Sanders. The Secretary, J. S. Middleton, soon joined it.

[32] J. R. MacDonald first attended the Committee in September 1914. He managed thirty-nine attendances before the end of 1917, but he seems never to have asserted himself and he was at odds with a majority of the Committee on relief administration at the beginning of the War.

as with Middleton.[33] Among trade-union leaders, like Robert Williams or Bob Smillie, it took the form of holding fast by the old internationalist sentiments and stubbornly refusing to subordinate the class struggle, as they understood it, to the national one. Smillie certainly stood by his old socialist and humanist values and remained perhaps the most important trade-union opponent of the War. But aside from a moment of high romance at the Leeds Convention in 1917, it is difficult to find examples of Smillie talking out against the War or threatening to do anything to stop it. He was feared by the government.[34] Deranged patriots threatened him with an early death.[35] Lloyd George tried to charm him into submission. He showed courage, but it was the courage of a stubborn bargainer who was not going to allow himself to be deflected by chauvinistic appeals, rather than the courage of a strenuous and dedicated political fighter.

What gave Smillie his importance to the Committee and to the government was his leading position within the Miners' Federation of Great Britain. Thanks to the miners' astonishing response to 'the call to the Colours', combined with an unlimited demand for coal, the union was placed in an exceptionally strong bargaining position.[36] Even a miners' leader like Herbert Smith, who was with Smillie on the National Committee and who was 'patriotic to the core',[37] was not prepared to throw such an advantage away. The miners were dissatisfied with Labour's national leadership before the War, and during it they refused to be a party to the Treasury Agreement. The Committee gave them a 'national' platform. For their part, they gave the Committee backbone and contributed positively to its independence.

Of course, even if he had wanted to, Smillie could not have

[33] According to his widow, Mrs. Lucy Middleton, to whom I am indebted for this information.

[34] Professor E. V. Arnold, 'Labour in Revolt', a memorandum circulated to the War Cabinet at the request of Lord Milner (August 1917), referred to Smillie saying the workmen would 'compel' the governments to make peace: 'And the Miners' Federation, it may be remembered, is reputed to be one of the sanest trade unions.' P.R.O. CAB 24/24 G.T. 1849.

[35] R. Smillie, *My Life for Labour* (1924), p. 225.

[36] W.E.W.N.C., *Report on the Committee's Proposals on Military Pensions etc.* (n.d. but early 1915). Pp. 2–3 carry a list of trade unionist recruits to the army by union. From this it appears that 109,860 miners had joined up, a figure only slightly lower than that of all other trade unionists put together.

[37] J. Lawson, *The Man in the Cap* (1941), p. 128.

used the whole weight of the Miners' Federation against the prosecution of the War. The only working-class institution which, from first to last, declared itself in opposition to the War was the I.L.P. However, the I.L.P. decided to express its opposition by somewhat circuitous means. It emphasised demands which it imagined constituted an attack 'on the economic flank of the enemy'.[38] This meant taking up problems such as increases in rents and prices, invasions of trade-union rights and practices, maltreatment of old age pensioners and the dependants of soldiers and sailors. Even the ultra-loyalists and super-patriots could appreciate that too little attention to such working-class interests as these might be dangerous and damaging to the war effort. They must also have found it easier to reconcile themselves to the presence of the I.L.P. because one of its two representatives was Harry Dubery, a 'sane patriot' who belonged to the pro-war minority of the party[39].

Finally, there was a fourth tendency, but one which was barely represented on the Committee at all. This was the standpoint to which John Maclean in Scotland and James Connolly in Ireland approximated, the standpoint of 'revolutionary defeatism'. When Tom Quelch came on to the Committee in 1916 it might have been expected that the conventions upon which its unity depended would be called into question. This does not appear to have been the case. Within a few months Quelch was in the hands of the military. From the guard-room of Hounslow Barracks he wrote to Middleton: 'I feel that the Committee has been very helpful to me in broadening my understanding of the working-class movement. It has brought me in touch with men of wider experience who are naturally more cautious in their handling of problems, and has thus made me wary of apparently obvious solutions. I have always felt the Workers' Committee to be the best Committee of its kind we have had in this country....'[40] Quelch was succeeded by E. C. Fairchild, but the change was not much of an improvement by Leninist standards.[41]

[38] R. E. Dowse, *Left in the Centre* (1966), p. 24.
[39] *Ibid.* p. 21.
[40] T. Quelch to J. S. Middleton, 10 September 1917 ('Milk–Miscellaneous' Box).
[41] W. Kendall, *The Revolutionary Movement in Britain 1900–1921* (1969) p. 97.

III

The War Emergency Workers' National Committee was made possible by a general desire to maintain the unity of Labour. It was able to function because within it the sane patriots and the discreet opponents of the War were able to establish a harmonious working majority. In its first public pronouncement the Committee warned that the War was likely to be prolonged; that the State would be required to take energetic measures to promote social welfare and economic control; that such measures were not likely to be taken without a well-directed popular agitation. It announced that its task must be :

> to protect working class interests during the War ... arrest existing distress, and prevent as far as possible further distress, and unemployment in the future. The Nation is only at the beginning of a crisis which demands thorough and drastic action by the State and the municipalities. Any bold, far-reaching change, which will probably be resisted by existing bureaucracy, can only be made possible by the strong pressure of well organised, well directed popular agitation.[42]

When it came to suggesting what forms increased government provision and control might take, the Committee generally proved itself equal to the task. Over wide areas of social and economic policy it anticipated the type of decisions to which governments were driven in the end. As the I.L.P. pointed out, its programme proved to be 'strikingly prophetic'.[43] This does not, of course, imply that its choice of concerns and demands was invariably correct. Indeed, its first campaign was based upon the erroneous assumption that the outbreak of war would be accompanied by a sharp and stubbornly ineradicable increase in the number of unemployed. This opinion was widely shared, John Burns remarked, for instance, that 'we shall see the unemployed marching down Whitehall to destroy the House of Commons'.[44] Sidney Webb, who was no friend to apocalyptic forecasts, concurred in the expectation that unemployment

---

[42] W.E.W.N.C. *The Workers and the War* (n.d. but August 1914), p. 2.
[43] I.L.P., *Report of Annual Conference* (Leeds, April 1917), p. 17.
[44] B. Webb, *Diary*, retrospective note written in August 1918 and inserted in the entry for 8 August 1914 (Passfield Papers).

would be the main source of distress. Accordingly, he prepared a brief for the Labour representatives whom the Committee was seeking to enrol in the citizens' organisations which were being set up, on the direction of the Cabinet, in every borough and urban district which had a population of 20,000 or over. In *The War Emergency – Suggestions for Labour Members of Local Committees,* as well as in Fabian Tract No. 176, *The War and the Workers,* Webb argued that:

> the War upsets nearly all industries, and private employers are nearly everywhere discharging their 'hands', men or women, or putting them on short-time, whilst the courage or credit required for new business if often lacking. This is one of the drawbacks of private capitalism. The only effective remedy is for the public employer (that is, the National Government or the Local Authorities) to increase public enterprises and start additional public works of utility, so as to give employment in their own trades, at the standard Trade Union rate of wages, to as many as possible of the men and women who would otherwise be unemployed.[45]

In one of the first of the innumerable deputations which the Committee sent to wait upon Ministers, this issue was taken up with Lloyd George. The Chancellor of the Exchequer in an address to the Association of Municipal Corporations, far from encouraging them to enlarge their expenditure, had recommended stringent economy so as to supply 'silver bullets' for the prosecution of the War. Webb, on behalf of the Committee, told Lloyd George that his speech had been widely 'misunderstood' and that it had given encouragement to reactionary local authorities. While Webb argued that the government must adhere to its original commitment to maintain the volume of employment, the Chancellor confined himself to promising that it would prevent distress.[46] In fact, the Committee was on weak ground. Unemployment was confined to certain trades such as building, furniture making and cotton textiles. Webb himself was on an

[45] W.E.W.N.C., *The War Emergency–Suggestions for Labour Members of Local Committees* (September 1914), p. 3.

[46] Deputation by the War Emergency Committee to the Rt. Hon. David Lloyd George, M.P. (Chancellor of the Exchequer), the Treasury, 6 October 1914: shorthand notes (W.E.W.N.C. archives). Also P.R.O. T 172/142.

official 'intelligence committee' for London which soon established that there was no shortage of work in the metropolis. By the beginning of 1915 his wife acknowledged that 'there is less unemployment and higher wages [are being paid] than in times of normal good trade'.[47] The Committee's first effective public act had been to put a stop to the Queen's appeal for ladies to give their gratuitous services to the production of garments for servicemen. Within a few months Beatrice Webb herself was learning to knit – although it is difficult to believe that this promoted either the comfort or the fighting efficiency of the men on the western front.

The Committee's alarmist expectation concerning the level of employment was quite unrepresentative of its insight into the general character of the 'Emergency'. It rapidly brought itself back on to course by directing attention to the wrongful employment of women and children and to the distress which resulted from the maladministration of inadequate pensions and allowances. The demands which it made for controls over the supply of food were, indeed, 'strikingly prophetic'. At the outbreak of war it demanded that 'arrangements be made to press upon the Government and the municipal authorities measures for officially controlling (a) the purchase and storage of food (b) the fixing of maximum prices of food and trade necessities and (c) the distribution of food'.[48] By October 1914 it was calling for all stocks of grain in the country to be commandeered at the prices then ruling. It suggested that the farmers should be guaranteed a remunerative price for all wheat they might grow thenceforward, and that other steps should be taken by the Government to increase the home food supply. It demanded that large purchases of wheat should at once be made and shipped by the government from Canada, Australia and the Argentine. In order to keep down freight charges, it proposed that shipping should be taken over as a whole and placed, like the railways, under government control. The price of the quartern loaf and its equivalent in flour should be held at 6d., any loss to form a portion of war charges. Subsequently it offered still more elaborate suggestions for the control of sugar, milk, coal and other commodities. In February 1917 Middleton noted: 'We have made representa-

[47] B. Webb, *Diary*, Unpublished. Entry for 3 January 1915 (Passfield Papers).
[48] W.E.W.N.C., *Report, August 1914 to March 1916* (1916), p. 3.

tions to Government departments almost without end. Our proposals have generally been turned down to begin with, but have been adopted in very many important particulars after inordinate and simply damnable delays.'[49] After the end of the War at least one senior civil servant reluctantly acknowledged the substantial accuracy of Middleton's claim.[50]

Since the Committee could demonstrate that over a wide range of economic and social policy the government had followed where it had led, it showed an understandable tendency to attribute these official actions to the cogency of its own proposals. However, its claims to 'brilliant successes' have to be treated with critical reserve. First, the demands which it carried were not always peculiar to itself. For instance, it asked that relief should be given in cash, rather than in kind or in the shape of food tickets, and that unmarried mothers and illegitimate children should receive the same benefits as those in wedlock.[51] But by this time the leaders of the Charity Organisation Society saw that food tickets were 'in the worst spirit of obsolete district visiting. As a precaution it is futile, for it has always been found that tickets are saleable: it is likely to lead to the favouring of certain shops or stores over others; and it suggests very forcibly that the relief is expected to get into the hands of people who cannot be trusted.'[52] Although there were a number of resignations, the C.O.S. accepted the need to look after the mother who had 'gone wrong'.[53] The Committee certainly campaigned vigorously on these matters. The government reversed its policies, but it must have been impressed by the fact that these policies were no longer acceptable even to 'respectable society'. Again, in relation to inadequate separation allowances for the dependants of soldiers and sailors, the Committee campaigned for a higher scale and for administration through public agencies. In November 1914 it organised simultaneous district conferences on these matters all over the country.[54] Susan Lawrence,

[49] J. S. Middleton to J. T. Abbott, Labour Agent of Whitehaven and District Labour Representation Committee, 28 February 1917 (W.E.W.N.C.).
[50] F. H. Coller, *A State Trading Adventure* (Oxford, 1925), p. 14.
[51] W.E.W.N.C., *The Workers and the War*, p. 3.
[52] *The Charity Organisation Review*, September 1914, pp. 188–9.
[53] *Ibid.* April 1915, p. 10.
[54] W.E.W.N.C., *Report on the Committee's Proposals on Military Pensions etc.* (n.d. but 1914), p. 12.

reporting back to the Fabian Society, claimed that the Committee had been 'brilliantly successful'. Yet she was obliged to acknowledge that it had not been nearly as successful in improving the scale for civil relief. The mixed results of this campaign suggest that the government was moved by fear of the adverse effects which inadequate separation allowances might have on recruiting. Civil relief was another matter. As Miss Lawrence remarked, 'there is a feeling that there is something sordid and unpatriotic in concerted efforts to maintain the workers' standard of life'.[55] In other words, the pressures to which the government was most responsive were not necessarily organised at all.

Second, the Committee was the most representative body in the British labour movement and quite unique in its closeness to the problems of individual working people. Its Secretary dealt directly with reports of the hardships and injustices experienced by hundreds of citizens all over the country. Yet this familiarity with immediate, personal anxieties and sufferings did not ensure that the Committee always correctly sensed the mood of workers as a mass. In trying to apply pressure to government it occasionally reduced its effectiveness by getting out of step with popular feeling, either by running too far ahead or by allowing itself to be outpaced by the militants. Both these characteristics require illustration.

Middleton held that the most interesting aspect of his work lay in the services which he performed for individuals who wrote to the Committee in search of help and advice. The following are typical examples of cases dealt with by Middleton:

Mr Smillie: My dear Sir excuse me taking the liberty of addressing you on a very delicate matter. Well Sir it is concerning my son who is enlisted in the month of June and he is not 18 years of age till the 14th day of December his name is Thomas Weldon G.H.No 18412 B. Coy. 42nd T.R.B. attached 11th G.H.Tillicoultry and Sir I pray you to use your good influence and wise counsel to get him sent back home as he has been a coal miner and a member of the Union since he left school. Well Mr. Smillie the reason he wants home is because one of my other sons lost one half of his right hand at

---

[55] *Fabian News*, May 1915 (report by Susan Lawrence on the work of the Committee).

Ypres 2 years ago and my son in law was killed in France last year and his widow and three wee boys live with me and to make matters worse my other son James died from wound on the 27th of last month so now I am left without any of them praying Sir you will exert your influence. I beg to remain yours respectfully. Thomas Weldon Senr.[56]

The Censor of Literature for British prisoners in Germany returned a parcel containing Cicero's orations together with a selection of Fabian tracts. Since other prisoners had been allowed to receive Fabian tracts Middleton asked the War Office the grounds of its objection to Cicero's orations.[57]

Private Morgan of Walsall met two of his brothers in France. A few days later he heard that one had been taken prisoner and the other wounded and bitten by a horse. Pte Morgan then met another brother whom he had not seen for two years. This brother was killed two days later. Pte Morgan was billeted in an inn where 'he adopted the unfortunate way of consoling himself by getting beer'. He got drunk, lost an eye, and was then sentenced to twelve months' imprisonment. The War Office declined to interfere when Middleton took up the question of the sentence with them.[58]

Most of the correspondence was from workers:

Owing to the War I was dismissed from my employment as an Ironmoulder on 5th August [1914]. I got work as a casual labourer on 17th August and since then I have had an average weekly wage of 23/- I have a wife and seven children none of whom are working.... Now to the point for information. I got a registered letter from the House Owner terminating my occupancy of the house in which I live on 28th February [1915]. I am only behind with my rent from August 1914, that is six months up till February 1915. Please give me all possible information as I am only owing £5.12 for Rent and as this is the first case of the kind in the district it

[56] Enclosed with a letter from R. Smillie to J. S. Middleton, 21 September 1917 (Box 9).

[57] J. S. Middleton to the Censor of Literature for British Prisoners in Germany, 11 May 1916 ('War and War Office' box).

[58] J. Whiston, Secretary, Walsall local committee, to J. S. Middleton, 21 June 1915 ('War and War Office' box).

is as well to know how to proceed.... The War has been the cause of a decrease in weekly wages to me of 14/- and I have occupied the house since August, 1911, that is 3½ years. The House Owner has never had the slightest trouble before with me.

Further, when my wife went to the Convenor of the Relief Committee to solicit aid for the children she was told that she looked young enough to have many more children yet, but that he thought that she already had too many. Well I have no doubt that he might be speaking in a jocular manner but then another member of the Relief Committee handed to me shortly after copies of the Malthusian League, How to Limit Your Family. Taking these things in conjunction it does seem a bit of disgraceful treatment especially in these stirring times when the Nation in a year or two will be asking or forcing my youngsters to assist in defending the Country.[59]

As one would expect, some of the correspondence came, not from those directly involved but from local Labour organisers: 'A local landlord has given notice to his tenant for an increase in rent based on an expenditure for making of street, calculated at 6% of the outlay. The question is whether this can be termed under the Act "an improvement".'[60]

In September 1914 H. H. Slesser, a distinguished barrister, offered his services to the Committee.[61] His 'opinions' on a whole host of matters of this kind greatly improved the quality of the advice which Middleton was able to give. Of course, Sidney Webb was also 'learned in the law', but Slesser's presence released him for larger issues. Yet it was in relation to these larger issues and popular sentiment concerning them that the Committee diminished its usefulness by certain errors of judgement. For example, early in 1915 it mounted a series of simultaneous demonstrations in favour of food controls.[62] By November 1914

[59] R. Foulis of Galashiels to J. S. Middleton, 9 January 1915 (Box 27). On the other hand, the workers may have sensed that the Committee, in the words of G. D. H. Cole, had 'no economic power behind it': *op. cit.* p. 133.

[60] C. W. Hill of Wolverhampton Labour Party to J. S. Middleton, 20 September 1918.

[61] W.E.W.N.C. Minutes, 11 September 1914.

[62] W. Hannington, *Industrial History in Wartime* (1940), p. 26, refers to these conferences etc. but fails to acknowledge the leading role of the Committee.

food prices in small towns and villages were 12 per cent higher than they had been in July and the increase in the larger towns and cities was still greater.[63] Thus, while the family incomes of many workers who had joined the army and navy had been greatly reduced, the cost of the household budget sharply increased. This increase in the cost of living was due, in large part, to the fact that freight charges rose by between 25 and 50 per cent during the first six months of the War. This was not the result of the success of the German U-boats. The submarine offensive did not have a major impact until the enemy launched his second major U-boat offensive in the autumn of 1916. Dear food at the beginning of the War was a consequence, not of naval defeat, but of naval supremacy. As the *Journal of Commerce*, a periodical representing shipping interests, gleefully observed: 'The opportunities now open to British shipping are obvious. There are no more cut rates by subsidised German vessels. German ships being swept off the sea, we have now no serious competitors in the carrying trade of the world.'[64] In January and February 1915 the Committee held a number of conferences on food controls in all the main urban centres. They were successful, but rather less so than the ones that had been held two months earlier on military pensions and allowances. By the spring the Committee found that the wind had entirely gone out of its sails, and its spokesmen were soon expressing bitter disillusionment: 'the people were absolutely apathetic in regard to the question of prices. They showed no inclination whatever to look after their own affairs. They [the W.E.W.N.C.] diagnosed the situation in this way: Many of the people were working over-time and earning good money to cover the costs of commodities. It might also be the case that they could not attend meetings convened by the committee on account of working over-time. The Committee came to the conclusion that the people did not care a button about the work they were trying to do on their behalf, and they felt that all their efforts had been wasted.'[65]

While the Committee overestimated popular interest in food

---

[63] Board of Trade *Labour Gazette*, November 1914.

[64] *Journal of Commerce*, 27 November 1914.

[65] B. Williams, speech to the 47th Annual Co-operative Congress (Leicester, May 1915), *Report*, p. 6.

controls, it underestimated concern about rents. As early as October 1914 the Charity Organisation Society noticed that 'The payment of rent is becoming a serious problem, not so much because of inability to pay as because of a widespread belief that it is unnecessary to pay during the War. This must tell heavily on the small landlords, and will have its effects on the question of rates.'[66] By 1915 the Committee was awake to the fact that rents were rising in the munitions centres thanks to the pressure for house room. It urged the formation of Tenants' Defence Leagues. It issued a leaflet – *Why Pay More Rent?* – in which it called on tenants to resist fresh exactions, to demand that local authorities should build houses where there was scarcity and to require the government to establish Fair Rent Courts. However, the Secretary of the Scottish Labour Party warned Middleton that this would not do for Glasgow. He told him:

> It is true that the proposition of Fair Rent Courts is upon the Glasgow Labour Party's Municipal Programme ... but it is entirely abandoned and repudiated under existing circumstances. Notwithstanding some diversity of opinion upon minor questions there is a most emphatic and unanimous pronouncement against the application of Fair Rent Courts in Glasgow in this crisis. The only thing that is entertained by the Party is a demand that the Government shall by legislation fix the Bondholders Interest and the Landlords Rent at pre-war standards until a year after the War.[67]

This was written in the opening stages of the Glasgow rent strike. A month later the government rushed through the Rent and Mortgage Interest (Rent Restriction) Act of 1915, which prohibited any increase in the rent of small dwellings.

On food controls, then, the Committee anticipated what should be done, but it was not done until a recommendation arrived at the Ministry of Food from the Commissioners on Industrial Unrest.[68] On rents it failed to anticipate what could be done,

---

[66] *The Charity Organisation Review*, October 1914, p. 245.
[67] B. Shaw to J. S. Middleton, 10 November 1915 (Box 28).
[68] M. B. Hammond, *British Labour Conditions and Legislation During the War* (Oxford, 1919), p. 264.

given sufficient pressure from below. It was outpaced by the militants, and its services were confined to helping to ensure that the Act was not evaded and that thought was given to how the rent question could be settled after the War.

Such a failure by the Committee to bring itself into a consistently effective alignment with pressure from below was only partly due to its remoteness. What it could achieve was limited by its own purposes and structure. The predominant groups within it were committed both to victory and to the defence of the workers' standard of life. If it was to serve both these objectives, the pressure which it brought to bear upon government had to be finely adjusted. Independent working-class action to remove deeply felt grievances could contribute to national unity, but taken beyond a certain point it was felt that such action would imperil the war effort. Accordingly the Committee set out both to raise the waves and to calm them, to arouse the workers on dangers about which they were not yet fully conscious, to menace the government with reference to forces that the Committee itself did not control and with powers which it feared to exercise. At the beginning of the War Sidney Webb showed the Committee how to develop this political style in which pressure and permeation were subtly blended. He used the circulars of the Local Government Board as rallying points with which to mobilise pressure upon parsimonious local authorities[69] while simultaneously working privately to raise the standards set in the circulars. He was fully associated with the Committee's efforts to organise demonstrations concerning inadequate relief scales and miserly military pensions and separation allowances, while he was writing to Herbert Samuel in the following terms:

> My dear Samuel: For Heaven's sake hold up the proposal to fix the maximum scale of relief for persons in distress through the war *actually below* the Poor Law standard. I gather this will come before the Cabinet Committee this afternoon, and I think it will be useful to put some considerations before you at once.

He then demonstrated that the proposed scale was below that of the Charity Organisation Society, below that of the War Office

[69] As in Fabian Tract No. 176, *The War and the Workers* (1914).

Scale for soldiers' families, and – most glaring of all – actually less than the L.G.B. itself pressed on Boards of Guardians as the irreducible minimum of adequate relief.

How will things be if the Cabinet actually prescribes a scale which the L.G.B. declares to be inadequate for maintenance; and less than the Poor Law?

I wonder whether those who are pushing this *uneconomic* policy of an inadequate scale realise how serious this will be. It will, of course, be laid hold of by the hostile newspapers, *where it will come just in time to reinforce powerfully the movement which the I.L.P.* is fomenting against the Labour Party for supporting the War and the Government. I don't see how the Labour Members are to stand up against the outcry (I need not remind you how sore is already the feeling about the P. of W. fund[70] and its proceedings).

I cannot conceive what some of your colleagues are thinking of. It will, of course, seem that the whole idea of the P. of W. Fund *was a dodge of the rich to save their own pockets*! If there was no such Fund, all these people would have a legal right to poor relief, with a practical certainty of getting outdoor relief. In that case they would receive several shillings a week more than it is now proposed to give them; and the wealthy class would thus have had to pay many thousands of pounds more than they have actually subscribed to the Fund!

It would be useless to plead the provision of school meals: – over most of the country there was no school feeding at all and over the rest it was rarely adequate. It would not do to whisper that no stigma was attached to being reliefed from the Fund – how could this be a reason for giving people less than enough to live on? Finally – though I speak without consulting them – I really don't see how all the members representing Labour on your Committees can avoid dramatically

[70] This was a reference to the Prince of Wales Fund which was launched at the outbreak of war to relieve distress arising out of it. What this meant occasioned considerable controversy. It was frequently administered by charity-mongers who adopted a scale based upon total family income and who were sometimes not above instituting, in relation to able-bodied men of military age, their own local system of compulsory military service sanctioned by the threat of starvation.

resigning from them if anything less than the Poor Law Scale is prescribed by the Cabinet.[71]

This subtle tactic of simultaneously trying to improve the Local Government Board's regulations while using them as agitational points and of making use of independent popular forces while simultaneously taking the wind out of their sails by organising pressure of one's own, was hard to sustain. Webb and the Committee moved thereafter into a political no-man's-land. They came increasingly to deplore the way in which the 'patriotism' of many of the political and industrial leaders of labour led them to make concession after concession to the Government, and they anticipated a dangerous reaction against such men. But they would do nothing to encourage such a reaction. 'We dare not join in any agitation against the Government: the war is too serious.'[72] This being the case, they were obliged to wait for less 'responsible' elements to build up the head of steam required to carry their own proposals.

IV

The advent of Lloyd George in December 1916 meant a rapid expansion of the machinery of government and of government control over the economy. The prospect of carrying many of the Committee's demands therefore improved, but its members found it increasingly difficult to achieve the sort of relationship with Ministers which Webb had managed with Samuel in 1914. They were now to be offered Government appointments. If they accepted them, they were likely to be held responsible for policies of which they disapproved. If they rejected them, they could be reproached for irresponsibility by the men they were trying to influence. Thus in the summer of 1917 Lloyd George offered Smillie the post of Food Controller. In declining the offer Smillie explained that if he had been able to accept he would soon have been sacked. He would have demanded 'plenary powers to deal in my own way with the food profiteers.

[71] S. Webb to Herbert Samuel, 10 September 1914 (copy by courtesy of the International Institute of Social History, Amsterdam).

[72] B. Webb, *Diary*, 22 June 1915 (Passfield Papers).

Some I would be content to send to prison; others I should feel obliged to hang.'[73] H. J. May, a Co-operator, and another member of the Committee, was also sounded out about this appointment, but his attitude was much the same: he could not have taken the helm unless he was allowed to purge the Ministry of Food of all the private traders whom Devonport had brought into it.[74] Ministers and higher civil servants were extremely irritated by these refusals. They had a great appetite for the services of independent Labour leaders, an appetite which was necessarily insatiable since they had no sooner got one set of them into the administration's maw than they were in need of another. But while they complained bitterly about Smillie's refusal to be recruited,[75] they showed a patronising contempt for other members of the Committee, like H. M. Hyndman, who were induced to join the Consumers' Council. One of them remarked: 'it is always pleasant to gratify a child's desire to see the wheels go round; it is, moreover, a sound move for a conjurer to get representatives of the audience on the stage to assure their fellows, first that the trick is done properly, and secondly, that it is not as easy as it looks'.[76] Hyndman was soon writing apologetic letters to Middleton explaining why he had departed from the Committee's policy with respect to what farmers should be paid for their milk. It was 'blackmail', but it was necessary to yield to it.[77]

It would be incorrect to conclude that the Committee entirely failed no matter whether it guarded its independence or entered into a closer association with the government. Even on the Consumers' Council Hyndman and his associates could occasionally be formidable, thanks to the independent sources of

[73] Smillie, *op. cit.* p. 177.
[74] K. Middlemas (ed.), *Thomas Jones: Whitehall Diary*, vol. i: 1916–25 (1969), p. 36.
[75] Coller, *op. cit.*, p. 62.
[76] *Ibid.* p. 130.
[77] H. M. Hyndman to J. S. Middleton, 6 June 1918 (9/1/237 i–iii). Webb himself would not look at an appointment to the Consumers' Council. Robert Williams was prepared to consider it provided his Union Executive approved and that 'if and when the Department refuses to accept the advice offered for and on behalf of the working class the Committee shall resign en bloc'. His executive told him to refuse: 'Why should he pull the Government's chestnuts out of the fire?'

information supplied by the Committee and the Co-operative movement.[78] The point is simply that the Committee, even most of its 'anti-war' members, were determined not to imperil the safety of the Nation by encouraging an unrest which might pass out of control.

The Committee's structure, as well as its purposes, also limited its effectiveness. It had to take care not to arouse the jealousy of its parent organisations by turning its attention to matters which they regarded as falling within their own domains. This became apparent as the Committee developed its response to war profiteering, on the one hand, and to conscription on the other. These matters were related to each other through the Committee's demand for the 'Conscription of Riches', a demand which was to prove of great consequence for the further development of the labour movement.

V

Before the 'boys' went out to die on the wire, they were liable to be housed in barracks erected by sweated labour employed by contractors who were making six or seven times the normal rate of profit. While their mothers warned them to keep their feet dry, they were supplied with socks which had been sprinkled with water so as to bring them up to the weight required in War Office contracts. (Several of the 'drippers' employed by the hosiery industry gave evidence to the Committee's Special Government Contracts Commission and subsequently to the government.)[79] There were others who at the beginning of the War had been working for farmers below trade-union rates and who when war had started found that the low earnings of agricultural labourers were being advanced as a reason for not raising pensions and separation allowances for soldiers.[80] Far

[78] Coller, *op. cit.* p. 130.
[79] W.E.W.N.C., *Report, August 1914 to March 1916* (1916), p. 12.
[80] Letters by R. B. Walker, Secretary of the National Agricultural Labourers' and Rural Workers' Union, from 23 August to 6 October 1915 describing use of soldiers to break up union meetings and take harvests from the labourers ('War and War Office' box): 'It has been urged that a decent scale of Separation Allowances would be considerably in excess of the ordinary rates of wages paid in agricultural districts, and it would be injudicious, therefore, to assure a greater sum going into the home while the breadwinner is with the Colours than when he is engaged on the land at

from being exceptional, these examples of profiteering simply served to emphasise that many employers and speculators were getting rich out of the War.

So long as the Committee concentrated on exposing 'ramps' of this sort, it aroused no overt opposition from the other national Labour bodies. Yet these bodies quickly made it clear that the Committee existed on sufferance, suggested, as the War continued from month to month and from year to year, that its character as an 'Emergency' institution was more and more anomalous, and insisted, above all, that it had no business to make pronouncements in spheres reserved to senior organisations. The most influential and active members of the Committee were opposed to the Treasury Agreement and the Munitions Act, but they kept their opposition *sotto voce* out of deference to the acknowledged prerogatives of the T.U.C. However, towards the end of 1915, with the conscriptionist press in full cry, the Committee produced a pamphlet, *Compulsory Military Service and Industrial Conscription: What they mean to the workers*, which placed it well to the 'left' of the other national bodies. At a time when men like O'Grady were telling the workers how much the lads at the front rejoiced in the Munitions Act,[81] the Committee of which O'Grady himself was nominally a member, came out with an unequivocal and class-conscious statement of the objections to the so-called National Service Law. It was interpreted as a confession that the Munitions Act had failed.

The pamphlet began by asking: 'Do you understand what is meant by the 'National Service' which most of the militarists, perhaps half of the members of the two Houses of Parliament, and probably a majority of the property-owners are now trying to impose upon the nation by law?' It explained that its object was industrial, rather than military, conscription. It contended that it was shells, not soldiers, which the government was most interested in getting. Directly or indirectly the government aimed at placing the entire labour force under martial law. 'It is an attempt to make use of the present war to get Servile Labour.' By decreeing compulsory military service the govern-

home.' 'That Agricultural Labourer', being a section of W.E.W.N.C., *Report on the Committee's Proposals on Military Pensions, etc.*, p. 10.
[81] *The Times*, 23 August 1915: Interview with James O'Grady, M.P.

ment, it argued, was going to compel men under 40 to enter the munitions factories under whatever conditions the government chose to impose. If the worker was not 'docile' he would be told by the manager or foreman that he would be dismissed; with the hint that there would be a sergeant waiting for him outside the factory gate to take him instantly into military custody. How could the government pretend that this compulsory service was necessary when it was not 'seizing the wealth of the nation'; when it was only the lives, not the property of men, which the government was proposing to commandeer?

According to the pamphlet the supposed 'equality' of compulsory military service was a sham. It was not the workers, by and large, who would benefit from exemptions. The rich men's sons became officers while the young manual workers had to put up with whatever conditions their officers thought good enough for 'the lower classes'. The government, it stated, ought to live up to its principles and pay the market rate for its army instead of having to resort to this dodge for getting an army on the cheap. It ought to attract men to munitions work in 'controlled establishments' instead of devising a form of forced labour to enrich the capitalist owners of such 'controlled establishments'. Yet:

> the objection of the workers is not to Compulsory National Service in any real sense. The wage-earning class, indeed, always finds itself under compulsion to render service; and it would see nothing but justice in any such legal compulsion as would impose this obligation on the idlers.... And a great number of rich people, men as well as women, do no work of any kind. They render no National Service whatever. Is it proposed to compel these people to work for their living in the only effective way, namely, by depriving them of their present artificial power of levying tribute on the Labour of others – that is, by the Government taking in taxation for the purposes of the nation (with humane allowances for the aged and the helpless), all 'unearned' incomes; or, at any rate, raising the Supertax to Nineteen Shillings in the Pound on all such incomes in excess of, say, a thousand pounds a year? Is this the law of National Service which it is sought to impose on the country in this time of national peril?

Unfortunately, as we have shown, it is not.... The fatal blot in the present demand for a National Service Law is that it is not a demand that those who are at present idling away their lives ... on *our* incomes ... should be sternly called upon ... to work for their own living. What is being demanded is that those who are already working should be compelled to come under military law, in order that a great many of them may be arbitrarily sent to labour in the Munition Works under conditions of Servile Labour.

As usual, the Committee was putting itself in charge of unrest rather than arousing it. The leaders of the T.U.C. and the Labour Party were already vacillating as a result of the intense opposition which the prospect of conscription provoked. They dared neither oppose it nor encourage it, and they resented the activities of those who appeared to be capitalising upon it at their expense. The Committee made matters worse by taking the initiative in relation to *A Memorandum on Labour After the War*. This forced the hand of every other National Labour Committee: for none of them were prepared to concede a leading role to this *parvenu* organisation.

At the beginning of 1916 Middleton was writing to Smillie in gloomy terms: 'the position ... is somewhat serious and personally, I believe that the whole future of the Workers' National Committee is more or less at stake'.[82] In retrospect he concluded: 'Our line on the Munitions Act, more particularly certain references to its unpopularity in our Industrial pamphlet, as well as our confirmed opposition to the Military Service Acts, are the two chief instances where we have run counter to official policy. Our attempt to issue the *Memorandum on Labour Problems After the War* also upset some sections of the other committees largely because their representatives on the W.N.C. had not reported back to their own bodies on the subject.'[83] About the same time Beatrice Webb remarked: 'Sidney reports that the Trade Union M.P.s are doing their worst to prevent the War Emergency Committee getting to work ... largely from jealousy,

---

[82] J. S. Middleton to R. Smillie, 25 February 1916 ('Industrial Compulsion' box).
[83] J. S. Middleton to H. M. Hyndman, 6 July 1916 ('Executive–Food' box).

but also because they don't want to be compelled to think to the extent of accepting or refusing the proposals.' These men were 'mulish', as they had been in the days of the campaign for the Minority Report. As for the Labour Ministers, they did not contribute to 'independent thought' either.[84]

The Committee found itself drawn in turn into conflict or competition with every one of the senior national committees. The Parliamentary Committee of the T.U.C. began to play tit for tat with it over the Naval and Military War Pensions Act of 1915. This measure provided for central control by a Statutory Committee, under the Royal Patriotic Fund Corporation, with administration through special committees to be instituted by the local authorities. The Workers' National Committee had argued that the task of supplementing existing pensions to meet exceptional circumstances ought to have been under the control of the Local Government Board and that the local administrative work ought to have been conducted by the local old age pensions committees, augmented, if necessary, for this special purpose. It was most unsatisfactory that the scheme should have been dependent throughout on raising funds from charitable sources. However, the Committee was determined to make the most of the provision made in the Act for the inclusion of the representatives of women and of labour on the local bodies.[85] It informed and advised Labour activists all over the country, only to discover that the T.U.C. Parliamentary Committee had agreed, without any consultation, to take over the entire matter. The Statutory Committee, of which Beatrice Webb was a member, ignored the Committee because it was a quasi-political body and preferred to deal with the T.U.C. instead. The result was that local Labour councillors rather than directly chosen labour representatives were placed upon the local pension committees, which produced great dissatisfaction. Middleton received innumerable complaints, but could only report that 'the T.U.C. has taken this work directly out of our hands'.[86]

A more direct confrontation occurred at about the same time

[84] B. Webb, *Diary*, 4 April 1916 (Passfield Papers).

[85] W.E.W.N.C., 'Naval and Military War Pensions Act', a printed letter dated 24 December 1915 sent to all interested Labour organisations.

[86] J. S. Middleton to H. H. Hart, Secretary of Beeston and District Trades and Labour Council, 16 March 1916 ('Pensions–Postal' box). This is one of many such letters in this box.

between the Committee and the General Federation of Trade Unions over 'Labour After the War' problems. The G.F.T.U. felt that its position was being consistently undermined. It knew that the miners were still working against it, and it was no surprise when, on Smillie's proposal, the 1916 T.U.C. excluded it from the Joint Board.[87] The leaders of the G.F.T.U. took a very poor view of the Committee's first report, prepared in February 1916, on *Labour After the War*. W. A. Appleton held that this document was ill-written, stupid and, above all, unfair to the government; for he was wholly satisfied that Asquith and his colleagues were prepared to face the problems of peace and demobilisation.[88] Moreover, the G.F.T.U. had its own subcommittee working on these problems. In the midst of these difficulties with the T.U.C. and the G.F.T.U. Sidney Webb moved on to the Labour Party Executive. He did not leave the Committee, but Smillie feared that he was drifting away. Smillie told Middleton: 'I have a letter from Mr. Sydney [sic] Webb on the question of a joint meeting of representatives of all of the After the War Committees, and I wonder why he should allow himself to be appointed on to another committee on this question in view of the great work which he is doing on our own Sub and General Committee on this matter.'[89] Smillie feared that Middleton's position would be made uncomfortably difficult if the Labour Party insisted on developing its own independent position on this question.

In fact Webb had no intention of abandoning the Committee at this stage. So long as Henderson remained in the government he did not know where else to look for any independent representation of Labour at national level. Throughout 1916 he complained about the dull subservience of the great majority of Labour leaders. On 2 November of that year he wrote to Beatrice:

> The Trade Union Leaders are hopeless. Yesterday I spent two hours (on Labour After the War) struggling with their complacent stupidity and apathy, and with the cool desire of

[87] Roberts, *op. cit.* p. 283.

[88] W. A. Appleton to J. S. Middleton, 16 February 1916 (14/5/29 i and ii).

[89] R. Smillie to J. S. Middleton, 28 February 1916 ('Industrial Compulsion' box).

some of them to prevent anything being published that would 'arouse expectations', and lead to anything beyond what the Government is conceding. Bowerman does not believe there will be any serious labour difficulties or unemployment after the war; and has really no desire to get anything done. They fail altogether to realise the three quarters of the whole who are outside Trade Unionism, or the low paid labourers, or the incapacity and disorganisation of the Trade Unions themselves. (I did not get angry, and we are on the best of terms; but we have to adjourn and adjourn, and these leaders – who insist on being on the committee – can't come to meetings).

Webb had allowed Pease to persuade him to fill a vacancy on the National Executive of the Labour Party[90] partly, perhaps, because he sensed that the War Emergency Committee could not supply a permanent form of labour unity. He pressed Smillie to agree to a joint meeting of all the multitudinous 'After the War' Committees, not to obliterate its own work, but to ensure that it became the policy of the labour movement as a whole. Sidney was the perfect committee man and had no narrow organisational loyalties, being always prepared to multiply official positions if this would allow him to play into his own hand.

The joint meeting was held in the House of Commons on 9 March 1916 at which the Committee and its three parent bodies were represented. There was considerable discussion about the status and representative character of the W.E.W.N.C. Finally, on the proposal of Arthur Henderson, it was agreed by a majority of 6 votes to 5 that all four Committees should appoint members to a Joint Sub-Committee on Labour After the War.[91] However, on 23 March Webb was fully associated with a decision by the War Emergency Committee that the proposal of the Joint Conference of 9 March should not be

[90] E. R. Pease to Morgan Phillips, 26 October 1947 (Passfield Baron, Press Cuttings, Transport House): 'I consider my second best day that on which I persuaded Webb to join the Labour Executive. ... Webb had taken little interest in the L.P. but I decided he ought to be on their Executive. ... We went round to 41 Grosvenor Road and we persuaded him to allow me to propose him. My best day was when I invited the followers of Thomas Davidson to meet in my rooms, whence the Fabian Society.'

[91] W.E.W.N.C. Minutes, 9 March 1916.

accepted; that the other Committees be invited to appoint additional representatives to the Workers' National Committee; and that this Committee should assume the leading role in dealing with the government in relation to the problems of peace, problems which were expected to turn upon a calamitous level of unemployment.[92] This strong line reflected the very positive support which the Committee mobilised for itself from local Labour organisations throughout the country.[93]

When, in April 1916, the government proposed to extend the Military Service Act, the Committee felt strong enough not only to maintain its own independence but to call upon the T.U.C. to rise to its responsibilities and convene a special National Labour Conference. The T.U.C., the G.F.T.U. and the Labour Party all resisted this suggestion, holding that 'the Government's recruiting proposals were essential to the winning of the war'.[94] Nevertheless, the Committee persisted. Middleton told Bowerman that there had to be a national conference to consider the implications of the Military Service Bill, trade-union organisation and administration, the danger of industrial conscription, the ' Conscription of Riches', the position of boys of 18 years under the Act; food prices and the position of old age pensioners. 'I think it is only fair that you should be informed that it was reported to us yesterday that failing the Conference being convened by any representative National Organisation, several of the larger trade unions would consider

[92] *Ibid.* 23 March 1916 (Webb was on the sub-committee which submitted these proposals to the full meeting, where they were carried *nem. con.*). The Committee's privately printed report, *Labour After the War* (17 February 1916), was primarily concerned with the implications of demobilisation. Webb probably drafted it. J. S. Middleton wrote to R. Smillie, 22 December 1915: 'I think it is very important that we should have Webb at our first meeting [on After the War Problems]. Webb has been studying the whole problem, I understand, for several months and has got some definite ideas which it would be well to come through our Committee.' ('Labour After the War' box).

[93] See numerous resolutions of support from trade-union branches sent early in April 1916 ('Milk—Miscellaneous' box). The Committee's *Report, August 1914 to March 1916* was obviously issued at this point of time to check the campaign against it. Sections of the Labour Press came to its defence. Thus the *Yorkshire Factory Times*, 15 March 1916, wanted to know why Appleton had failed to attend many of the meetings of the Committee. It suggested that the Committee was 'even more valuable than the Labour Party, the T.U.C., or any of the sections that call themselves "national"'.

[94] Reported in W.E.W.N.C. Minutes, 11 May 1916.

taking action for themselves, with a view to focusing the opinion of the Movement as a whole on these various subjects.'[95]

Thus, those who had been hoping at the beginning of the year to cut the Committee down to size found that it was unrepentant, and presumptuous enough to teach its elders and betters their business. Bowerman's reply to Middleton was lofty, and yet uneasy. 'In communicating with the Parliamentary Committee upon the matter, it will be useful if you will give me the names of the "several larger unions in our Movement" (other than the Dock Workers' Union, as endorsed by the Miners' Federation) urging the convening of a National Conference.' He had heard this demand from trades councils, but it had been taken up by very few affiliated organisations.[96]

Middleton then warned him that the Postal Workers, many of the textile unions, and the Railwaymen wanted action. There was a 'great danger' of certain sections acting independently.[97] On 25 May the representatives of the T.U.C. on the National Committee, who were frequently absent, attended in force. A few days later Bowerman informed Middleton that the Parliamentary Committee had decided to convene a Special Congress for 30 June in the Memorial Hall.[98] The agenda for this Congress corresponded in almost every particular with the topics set down in Middleton's original letter to Bowerman. In the event, the Congress passed resolutions recommending the setting up of a special government department to regulate food and fuel prices, with power to commandeer commodities and to arrange distribution through municipal channels; to own and control merchant shipping so as to secure the fixing of freightage rates; to commandeer the home-grown crops at a fair price; to secure control of the necessary foreign and colonial supplies, and to amend the Coal Price Limitation Act by fixing standard prices in various areas. It further demanded that old age pensions, which had been kept at the pre-war rate of 5s. per week, should be increased by 50 per cent and that far heavier taxation should

[95] J. S. Middleton to C. W. Bowerman, 26 May 1916 ('Ships–T.U.C.' box).
[96] C. W. Bowerman to J. S. Middleton, 26 May 1916, *ibid*.
[97] J. S. Middleton to C. W. Bowerman, 29 May 1916, *ibid*.
[98] C. W. Bowerman to J. S. Middleton, 8 June 1916, *ibid*., Roberts, *op. cit.*, fails to mention this Special Congress. For a critical discussion of Professor Roberts's volume, see my 'Practical, Capable Men', *New Reasoner*, No. 6 (Autumn 1958), pp. 105–19.

be imposed upon the wealthy. Will Thorne had carried a resolution which suggested that 'the Government ought to have brought in a Bill for the conscription of riches as a natural corollary to the conscription of men, and calls upon the Government to take immediate steps in this direction'.

Having pressed the T.U.C. into convening the Special Congress, the Committee itself assumed responsibility for publicising its decisions, It published a special leaflet in which it subjected the reply of the Prime Minister to the deputation which had waited upon him after the Special Congress to a cruel and mocking analysis.

> A little more daring upon the part of some of the leaders of public thought, and we shall find ourselves considering the desirability of leasing the Navy to a private company, with a percentage profit on war results! ... The Contrast between the tenderness of the Government for the wealthy and their contempt for the aged poor is one of the most illuminating aspects of modern politics.... A man with an income of £5,000 per year can live at the comfortable rate of £20 per week, thus spending roughly £1,000; the Exchequer will take about £1,500 as income tax; and the balance in War Loan will bring in *30/- per week for life* – which has been held to be too excessive an amount to give as a pension to the disabled Tommy who is making the investment safe.[99]

Now that the 'Conscription of Riches' had become a demand of the movement as a whole, the Committee redoubled its efforts to popularise it. Great play was made with the confession of *The Economist* that the terms offered to investors in War Loan were so favourable that had such a proposal been put to the country twenty years earlier it would have seemed 'an impossibly beautiful dream'.[100]

Yet even after its victory in the summer of 1916 the Committee was not free from threats and reprisals from its

[99] W.E.T.U.C., *Labour and Social Conditions Caused by the War: Some Notes on the Speech of the Prime Minister in Replying to the Trades Union Congress Deputation on July 19th 1916* (n.d. but 1916).

[100] W.E.W.N.C., *The Conscription of Riches: War Taxes and War Loans*. There were several variants of this leaflet, all issued in 1916 or early 1917, but undated.

constituent bodies when it dared to trespass upon what they regarded as their own special territory.[101] Thus following the Special Congress there was a joint meeting of the leading national committees at which W. J. Davis, an ardent supporter of the War and the government, made a savage attack on the Committee for daring to override others and for trying to set itself up as the supreme directing body for the whole movement. 'I was by no means pleased,' wrote Hyndman, 'with Mr. Davis' charge against the National Workers' War Emergency Committee ... and I regret that Mr. Sidney Webb interfered with my challenge. I do not put up with that sort of imputation myself – *ever* : and I do not see why the Committee should. It was a direct attack upon all who have done the work. I think it would be well that I, not being a Trade Unionist or a member of the Labour Party but only a revolutionary Social-Democrat, should move a resolution at the next meeting of the W.N.C. regretting that such a charge should have been made and entirely repudiating any over-riding, or attempt to over-ride, the Trade Union and Labour Committees.'[102] Middleton managed to calm him down and he decided to absent himself from the next meeting of the Committee. 'If I were present I should be unable to refrain from commenting on Mr. Davis' uncalled for remarks and the indifference with which they were received. As others, who were much more directly attacked than myself, take no offence – I shall simply keep away this time.'[103]

Sidney Webb's industry, inventiveness and intellectual ascendancy over the Committee was a standing provocation to Hyndman. But what exasperated him beyond all endurance was Webb's humility, and the apparent absence of any personal pride or pique. Hyndman tried to satisfy his own pride by

[101] The Co-operative representatives withdrew from the Committee – much against their own personal wishes–between September 1917 and January 1918. The Co-operators favoured a ninepenny loaf when the Committee was advocating a sixpenny loaf. The Co-operators disagreed with the Committee's demand for a government subsidy to stop prices rising, preferring to advocate the fixing of maximum prices by the government. ('Co-operative Representation–Enlistments' box.) At about the same time the Labour Party was hesitating to renew its financial assistance to the Committee.

[102] H. M. Hyndman to J. S. Middleton, n.d. but early July 1916 ('Executive–Food' box).

[103] H. M. Hyndman to J. S. Middleton, 18 July 1916 ('Executive–Food' box).

observing: 'Happily Mr. Sidney Webb and I understand each other perfectly. It is, I agree, therefore, far better in every way – as neither he nor I have any personal object whatever to subserve – that a resolution drawn by Mr. Webb should be carried by the Committee unanimously, than that a similar resolution written by me should be defeated.'[104] Webb, for his part, went out of his way to seek Hyndman's 'corrections' for several draft memoranda and resolutions while quietly avoiding what he termed 'Hyndman's impossibilisms'.[105] The relationship between these two men became critically important in relation to the one great task which was left to the Committee after 1916. It had got the 'Conscription of Riches' placed at the forefront of the Labour programme; it remained to determine what that slogan meant.

In the summer of 1917 Hyndman submitted a memorandum to the Committee according to which the 'Conscription of Riches' was to be understood as the placing at the disposal of the community of all home and foreign bonds, all shares and debentures in public or private companies with all interest earned and payable thereon: 'thus giving the Community entire control for the purposes mentioned over all Mines, Factories, Workshops, Railways, Shipping, Tramways, Waterways, etc.' Furthermore, the community was to acquire complete control of all banks and insurance companies, and all land in town and country with all the buildings thereon being held as public property. The whole adult population was to be liable to conscription for productive and distributive labours, 'as may be decreed by a constituent Assembly elected under proportional representation, all adults having the right to vote'.[106]

[104] H. M. Hyndman to J. S. Middleton, 2 September 1914. Hyndman told his wife: 'When anything important comes up *I* bring out a root-and-ground revolutionary proposal, and set it well before them. That puts them in a fright; and then Webb comes in with *his* proposal, only a few degrees milder than mine; and they are so relieved that they pass Webb's motion unanimously.' R. T. Hyndman, *The Last Years of H. M. Hyndman* (1924), p. 87.

[105] e.g. Sidney Webb to J. S. Middleton, n.d. but probably 1918, ('Conferences (Food)–Consumers' Council' box).

[106] H. M. Hyndman to J. S. Middleton, 22 July 1917, enclosing duplicated sheet headed 'The Conscription of Riches: The means for creating and distributing wealth' ('Conferences (Food)–Consumers' Council' box). Despite references to the Committee's printed minutes, C. Tsuzuki, *H. M. Hyndman and British Socialism* (Oxford, 1961), p. 223, fails to identify Hyndman's

Webb was very much preoccupied with other matters. Throughout the War he kept up weekly consultation with the Director of the L.S.E., wrote a large part of the *New Statesmen,* and kept an eye on G. D. H. Cole. In 1917 he was also helping Beatrice with her work for the Machinery of Government Committee. (It was, in fact, Sidney who formulated the one and only large principle in the history of British administrative law: that the shape and number of government departments should be determined by the character of the services they supplied rather than by the class of people with whom they dealt.)[107] He had long been pondering, with Leonard Woolf, on Labour's proposals for a new international order after the War. Once Arthur Henderson – in the words of a senior government agent – became ready to parade 'a certain door mat as an altar-cloth',[108] Sidney become more and more committed to the future of the Labour Party, and he began working on its *Memorandum on War Aims* and its new constitution. Nevertheless, he hastened to prepare a printed set of notes on Hyndman's memorandum on the 'Conscription of Riches'. Webb insisted that it was necessary and customary to distinguish between the acquisition of wealth by the State and the acquisition by the State of controlling powers over the use to which economic resources were put. What Lloyd George was doing – without conscripting wealth – was taking over the administration of one industry after another: railways, shipping, mines, food importing, all 'war trades'. 'It does not seem desirable to urge that the present

---

position, or to recognize the distinction between a tax on capital and a tax on income.

[107] S. Webb, 'Notes of the Conspectus' (n.d. but 1917), Reconstruction Papers, ii, pp. 388–93 (Passfield Papers). W. J. M. Mackenzie, *The Structure of Central Administration in British Government Since 1918* (1950), describes this as 'a great principle – the first principle even enunciated on the subject in England' (p. 58).

[108] E. McGegan, 'Private Report on the Labour Party Conference, January 23–25' (Nottingham, 1918), circulated to the Cabinet by G. H. Roberts (P.R.O. CAB 24/42 G.T. 3609). The report was dated 13 February 1918. After stressing the very real dangers represented by the pacifist and revolutionary sections, McGegan went on to explain that much depended on Henderson, who was rebuilding the movement from the personal aspect: 'a certain doormat, for example, is now being very effectively used as an altar-cloth'. Henderson was determined to restrain the revolutionary sections and was determined to see a Labour Cabinet, probably with himself as Prime Minister.

Ministry should take over, in addition, the administration of all the 300,000 farms, or to press the existing Town and District Councils to take over the management of the half-a-million retail shops.'

Webb argued that the Committee should press for the 'Conscription of Riches' irrespective of nationalisation or municipalisation. It could do this in one or all of three ways: (*a*) by doubling the yield from income tax and super tax so as to confiscate an additional £150,000,000 from the 70,000 family incomes in excess of £1000; (*b*) by imposing a capital tax on the lines of existing death duties; (*c*) by following the proposals of W. C. Anderson, M.P. for the sequestration, until further notice, of all unearned incomes. The Committee might perfectly well think it advisable to recommend all three plans.[109]

Hyndman replied that mere taxation of incomes and capital was not 'Conscription of Riches'.

> Taxation of incomes and capital does not give us State or National or Communal Ownership and Control. Neither does it tend to improve general production and administration for the common benefit.... It is better to run the risk of increased opposition, by combining complete conscription of riches with the organisation of co-operative production and distribution of wealth for the common good, than to run the much greater risk of confusing the real issue for the whole of the wage-earning and disinherited classes by separating the two mutually-dependent measures.[110]

As usual, Webb carried the day. In November 1917 the Committee, in the company of the T.U.C., the Labour Party Executive and the Miners' Federation of Great Britain, waited upon the Chancellor of the Exchequer, Bonar Law, to press for the 'Conscription of Wealth, etc.' Webb was the opening spokesman. 'We wish to urge upon you that as men have been conscripted, we suggest, in common fairness, that should be accompanied by

[109] S. W. [Sidney Webb], *Notes Submitted to the Sub-Committee on the Conscription of Riches* (printed, n.d. but August 1917) ('Conferences (Food) –Consumers' Council' box).

[110] H. M. Hyndman, 'The Conscription of Riches: Observation on Notes by "S.W."' (undated duplicated sheets, but certainly written in August or September 1917) ('Conferences (Food)–Consumers' Council' box).

the conscription of wealth. I need not go into details, but we suggest that a suitable measure would be the immediate imposition, in lieu of any further loans, of a graduated levy on all capital wealth on the basis of the existing death duties.' Bonar Law promised to buy Webb's book on *How to Pay for the War,* but he entered into no other undertakings. He admitted that he had not thought enough about a capital levy, but was sure it was impracticable in war-time. 'It is,' he said, 'my real belief that you cannot have a capital levy in the middle of a war, which would certainly dislocate all financial arrangements and frighten people – because people with money are the most timid I have ever come across.'[111] Hyndman was not present. Characteristically, he refused to 'wait upon' such a rascal as Bonar Law. Had he been there he would doubtless have enjoyed teasing the Chancellor about the risk of 'frightening' the rich in war-time. He would also have been able to use this exchange to illustrate the argument that public ownership and control were, indeed 'mutually dependent'.

Webb, in drawing attention to the fact that public ownership and public control had been promoted separately, was not committing himself to the proposition that this should be done or that it could be done indefinitely. On the contrary, he was insisting that it was the expropriation of capitalist wealth and income which was lagging behind. He certainly wanted to improve the efficiency of public control, but he saw this in terms of detailed proposals for the reorganisation of the machinery of government rather than making it a matter of extending controls under the auspices of a Constituent Assembly. Whereas Hyndman was, in his own words, 'an old man in a hurry', Webb was reconciled to the existence of a 'mixed economy' for a long time to come. He offered the Labour Party Executive two statements of party objects. The first read simply: 'To secure for the producers by hand or by brain the full fruits of their industry by the common ownership of all monopolies and essential raw materials.'[112]

---

[111] 'Conscription of Wealth, etc.': deputation from the T.U.C. Parliamentary Committee, the W.E.W.N.C., the Executive Committee of the Labour Party and the Executive of the M.F.G.B. to the Chancellor of the Exchequer, House of Commons, 14 November 1917, transcript of shorthand notes (P.R.O. T172/503). Webb spoke on behalf of both the Committee and the Labour Party.

[112] Following the Minutes of the National Executive of the Labour Party

VI

The War Emergency Workers' National Committee lingered on until 1920,[113] but once the Labour Party re-emerged as an independent force in British politics it ceased to play any significant role. This essay has merely outlined the history of the Committee on the basis of an incomplete examination of its immense and miscellaneous records. Nevertheless, it should be clear that no history of labour in war-time nor any social history of Britain between 1914 and 1918 can be adequate if it ignores its activities. In particular, it should be impossible henceforth, to consider the extension of government controls during the War as something which the working class merely witnessed and which it did nothing to encourage or influence.[114]

However, the importance of the Committee lay far less in what it may have directly accomplished in its immediate relations with government than in what it portended for the future of Labour. When Pease invited Beatrice Webb to comment on the draft of his *History of the Fabian Society* she remarked:

> In your last chapter you mention socialist unity and you say it has been deferred until after the War. But ought not you to mention the War Emergency Workers' National Committee which is none the less significant because it has been a quite unconscious manifestation of Socialist Unity? It is certainly remarkable that all sections of the Labour and Socialist Movement, including three Socialist societies and also the Co-oper-

---

for 18 July 1917 there is a draft of the new constitution which contains the alternative statements of 'party objects'. It is not certain that Webb drafted them both or that he did so on his own behalf.

[113] *Report of Co-operative Congress* (1920), pp. 178–9. (It was reported that in the previous year there had been only one meeting of the Committee, when it was summoned to hear an account of the work of Carmichael, Cramp and Hyndman on the Consumers' Council.)

[114] Thus Arthur Marwick, *The Deluge* (Pelican edn. 1967), has no references to the War Emergency Committee in his index, although two references occur in the text. In his own words, Mr. Marwick attempted to bring out from the shadows of historical inevitability some of the individuals who participated in the challenge to *laissez-faire* which is one of the salient and enduring features . . . of the first World War' (p. 163). His attempt is full of interest, but his highly schematic account of 'influences' (pp. 164–8), and his undeveloped references to 'agitation' (pp. 183–4) take us but a short way from the shadows of which he complains.

ative Movement, are here combined with a larger number of Trade Unions than are represented by the Trade Union Congress. I think it quite possible that this Committee will become the germ of a United Socialist Party. Anyhow it ought to be mentioned in connection with Socialist Unity even if you dismiss it as a mere ad hoc and temporary body.[115]

The Webbs had always thought of the labour movement in tripartite, institutional terms. The unions, the Co-operative Societies and the party were to provide for the distinct, but related, interests of the worker as producer, consumer and citizen. The Committee certainly advanced labour unity conceived in this way. It developed the habit of concerted action among the leaders of all the principal working-class institutions. It is less obvious that the basis of that unity was 'socialist'. Yet it would be a great mistake to overlook the contribution which the 'Conscription of Riches' campaign made to what the Webbs would have termed 'the theoretic progress' of the working people.

The 'Conscription of Riches' slogan was a demand for the public ownership and control of all the most vital sectors of the economy. Despite Webb's differences with Hyndman, it was a demand for control because the Committee had, from the very beginning of the War, insisted that what had been brought into the public sector must not be returned to private hands.[116] As the Committee won support for this slogan, so it transformed what had hitherto been the academic shibboleth of a minority into an immediate issue, and into a 'practical' demand of the organised workers as a whole. In place of resolutions carried in sometimes badly divided conferences in favour of the nationalisation of this or that industry or service, there was now a global demand. What it amounted to, on the face of it, was the 'expropriation of the expropriators'. Their wealth, their incomes, their capacities were no longer to be treated as their own, but confiscated and conscripted in the interests of the community as a whole. Before the War this had seemed a distant prospect; it was the War that made it appear possible and even logical, a serious agitational point. The Labour Party was made over into an

---

[115] B. Webb to E. R. Pease, 20 October 1915 (Academic Centre Library, University of Texas).
[116] W.E.W.N.C., *The Workers and the War*.

avowedly socialist party not merely by the passive observation of how the government managed the economy, but by the active experience of demanding that it *should* manage the economy, and that it should manage it upon equalitarian lines.[117]

However, it was highly characteristic of the British labour movement that when, thanks to the leadership of the Committee, it began to make socialist slogans its own, it did so with great initial reluctance and as a defensive response to developments which it did not pretend to control. It would be an over-simplification to see the demand for the 'Conscription of Riches' as the occasion upon which socialist attitudes and popular working-class consciousness were, at last, brought into correspondence. Of course, clause 4 needs to be placed in the context of this demand, but this only serves to bring into relief the way in which that celebrated objective itself should be historically understood. In the first instance, the 'Conscription of Riches' was introduced as a bargaining counter in relation to the Munitions Act and the Military Service Acts, and as such it could be regarded as an evasion of a direct confrontation with authority over conscription. Subsequently it was seen in terms of 'fair play' and 'equality of sacrifice' between classes, and after the summer of 1916 it was increasingly treated as a prescription for the effective prosecution of the War or as an indispensable means of paying for it.

In none of these uses did it place its advocates in direct opposition to the interests or purposes of the State. Churchill himself is alleged to have said: 'Our whole nation must be organised – must be organised and mobilised – MUST BE SOCIALISED.'

[117] A failure to take account of the Committee and of the 'Conscription of Riches' campaign makes it difficult to give an adequate explanation of how the Labour Party came to adopt clause 4. For instance Ralph Miliband, in his admirable *Parliamentary Socialism* (1961) accepts, quite uncritically, Ramsay MacDonald's assertion that organised labour during the War became 'a mere echo' of the old governing classes' opinion (p. 39). After the briefest of references to the Committee (p. 43) he goes on to refer to 'Official Labour's total involvement in the first World War ...' (p. 47). Ignoring the 'Conscription of Riches' campaign, he expresses some bewilderment that the Labour leaders did not demand that the workers' sacrifices 'should be more nearly matched by employers' (p. 51). He recognises that the principles and programme which the Labour Party adopted at the end of the War were 'a considerable step forward' (p. 62), but he has hardly prepared his readers for an understanding of how such a step was possible. E. Eldon Barry, *Nationalisation in British Politics* (1965) is open to much the same sort of objections.

... There must be asserted, in some form or other by the Government, a reserve power to give the necessary control and organising authority, and to make sure that everyone, of every rank and condition, men and women, shall do their fair share. Democratic principles enjoin it; social justice requires it; national safety demands it.'[118] The 'Family' of senior civil servants were delighted when articles appeared in the press making out that the War would have to be paid for by the conscription of wealth. Their pleasure was in no way diminished when they saw in such articles 'traces of Sidney Webb'.[119]

In short, the 'Conscription of Riches' demand led on to clause 4. But the 'Conscription of Riches' was a slogan advanced by a committee which had renounced all intention of considering the major issue confronting the labour movement and the country. It maintained its unity by concentrating exclusively on relatively humdrum second-order questions. The peasants cultivated their fields directly behind the firing line. Even in relation to these relatively modest concerns, the Committee's unity had a complex and somewhat spurious character. Every faction excused its participation by reference to the use that it imagined it was making of every other. While the representatives of the I.L.P. fancied that they were turning 'the economic flank of the enemy', the patriots supposed that they were emasculating the I.L.P. Yet all this political cleverness was, perhaps, only hypocrisy: only so many rationalisations of a common concern to keep at a safe distance from the world crisis.

On the first day of 1917 Bernard Shaw wrote: 'We must keep the old flag waving. Of course, it may turn out that under the test of war we have discovered, as Clifford Sharp did, that we do not belong to the old flag at all, and are neither socialists nor republicans nor anything else out of the beaten Garden Suburb cinder path. If so let us find ourselves out and have done with it.'[120] The War found men out, but such self-discovery as there was lacked the searching character which Shaw required. The

[118] Cited in the manifesto of the Socialist National Defence Committee: *The Nation in Danger! A call for National Industrial Mobilisation, Control and Administration* (n.d. ?1916).

[119] Middlemas (ed.), *Thomas Jones: Whitehall Diary* vol. i: 1916–25, p. 37.

[120] G. B. Shaw to E. R. Pease, 1 January 1917 (Box 6, Fabian Archive, Nuffield College, Oxford).

British labour movement was not finished with the politics of nods and winks. Clause 4 did not remove confusions and ambiguities; it merely raised them to higher levels of complexity. Beatrice Webb was closer to the mark than she could have known when she detected in the War Emergency Workers' National Committee a great precursor. If it foreshadowed a united socialist party, it was a party in which socialism was fated to be a subordinate question.

VII

This essay makes no more pretence to offer a definitive account of how the Labour Party came to adopt clause 4 than it does to supply a complete history of Labour in wartime. It has served its purpose if it has persuaded the reader to reconsider such questions as: What did socialism mean to the Labour Party in 1918? Why did that party commit itself to the socialist goal?

It may be objected that these questions have already been dealt with by others in a satisfactory and convincing manner. For example, S. H. Beer confronts them quite explicitly in the fifth chapter of his *Modern British Politics* (1965). Like Ralph Miliband in *Parliamentary Socialism*, Beer recognises that socialism is of secondary or subordinate importance in the history and politics of the Labour Party. Yet much depends upon how this subordination is understood and explained. Beer sees the adoption of clause 4 not as the result of changes in the party's sources of power but in terms of the structure of power and the struggle for power between parties. He makes light – far too light – of changes in mass attitudes. He neglects the impact of the Russian Revolution. Ignoring the active demand made by organised Labour for an extension of public ownership and control to global dimensions, he insists on the distance that separated greater State control from the 'comprehensive ideology of socialism'. He fails to notice that this is a distinction which many Labour leaders, including Webb and Henderson, were reluctant to draw except intermittently, and then with some embarrassment. But it was such Fabian, and Fabian inspired, thinkers rather than the I.L.P. men who were most immediately influential when Labour was casting its new constitution. Beer gives a brilliant, but profoundly restricted and misleading, account of the 'comprehensive ideology of socialism' in which that ideology appears exclusively in terms of a higher sentimentality joined to a *penchant* for 'system thinking'. He seems to imagine that the meaning of socialism to the Labour Party is exhausted in Edward Carpenter and *Seed Time* arriving, *post festum,* in the shape of Ramsay MacDonald or Bruce Glasier holding forth on altruism and fraternity. If the meaning of Labour's socialism really reduced itself without remainder to these forms of piety it would, indeed, be difficult to imagine that it was the commitment to socialism which explained the re-structuring and re-energising of the party. Beer's argument is, of course, that it worked the other way round. Without suggesting that socialism was a mere 'efflux' or 'echo' of the need to create an independent party capable of making a play for ascendancy, he does contend that the adoption of this ideology was functional to the choice of political independence. He sees Labour introducing clause 4 into its new constitution so as to set the seal on that independence. Given the immense war-time increase in trade-union and Labour Party membership, along with the divisions within the Liberal Party, such a 'thrust for power' became virtually inevitable.[121]

It is not clear that questions about the primacy of socialism or the thrust to power are meaningful or helpful. Why should they not be seen as mutually reinforcing each other? Major political developments can rarely be understood in terms of simple relations of cause and effect. Beer is certainly correct to point to the new opportunities which were opened up for the Labour Party by increased membership and the simultaneous break-up of a still class-bound Liberalism. But these developments occurred within the forcing house of the war economy and can hardly be understood apart from it. The problem of State management and control was, to say the least of it, involved in the conflict between Asquith and Lloyd George. The triumph of the latter meant that individualism and free trade, the central tenets of

---

[121] Beer ignores the fact that the commitment to socialism had some negative consequences for the 'thrust to power' (i.e. office). For example, Webb tried to explain it away when he was attempting to get J. M. Keynes to stand as a Labour candidate: 'The Labour Party wishes to run a candidate for each university election just to emphasise that it is not a workman's party ... With the alternative vote or proportional representation it can do the Liberal Party no harm. ... No Labour candidate need commit himself to anything in particular.' Sydney Webb to J. M. Keynes, 14 January 1918 (Keynes Papers, King's College, Cambridge).

classic Liberalism, were redundant. There was, accordingly, a vacancy to be occupied in British politics. The position of 'the Party of Principles', moral and economic principles, required to be filled. However, the Labour Party would hardly have secured this appointment had there not been an already established body of socialist opinion and had the War and the Russian Revolution not called into question the permanence of the existing order. War and revolution also increased the likelihood of competition to the Labour Party from the left and made it essential for it to establish its socialist credentials.

Thus, despite its important insights, Beer's interpretation of the origins of the commitment to socialism may cause more confusion than it dispels. We do not require his hypothesis in order to explain the subordinate character of Labour's socialism. His account both of the socialist ideology and of the calculations of the managers of the Labour Party is too limited, for the meaning of political slogans and the statement of political principles are rarely fully disclosed by explicit accounts made on formal occasions. As with the 'Conscription of Riches', so with the 'Common Ownership of the Means of Production': the meaning of the demand has to be discovered by observing how the slogan was used. If this procedure is followed it becomes apparent that clause 4 did not indicate – any more than the 'Conscription of Riches' – the presence of a coherent ideology. It is better regarded as a rallying point around which the adherents of different ideologies and the representatives of different interests assembled.

Because he rejects this view Beer is obliged to exaggerate the discontinuity between the pre-1914 Labour Party and the party of the 1918 constitution.[122] The adoption of clause 4 did not imply that the whole membership came to have a common objective, but rather that an objective had been proclaimed which both accommodated and concealed a large diversity of particular concerns.

---

[122] 'This change in purpose made the Labour Party a different kind of political formation – a radically different kind of "whole" – from a mere coalition. As a coalition the various groups in the party were joined by the logic of log-rolling fortified by wide similarities among their particular interests. The commitment to Socialism, however, meant that now all groups had the same object, the Socialist Commonwealth.' *Modern British Politics* (1965), p. 127.

10

MARGARET COLE

GUILD SOCIALISM AND THE LABOUR
RESEARCH DEPARTMENT

THE title of this chapter describes its purpose: it is to chronicle, and to some extent to evaluate, two diminutive movements which during part of the first quarter of the present century exercised an influence out of all proportion to the number of their direct adherents. The amount of this influence may seem the more surprising because there was so much duplication in membership. The staff, paid and unpaid, of the Labour Research Department, at least until 1921, were Guild Socialists almost to a man, as were most of the general secretaries of the trade unions, trades and labour councils, and trade-union branches which sustained the L.R.D. with modest affiliation fees. Not all of them, by any means, were enrolled in the tiny paid-up membership (never reaching a thousand) of the National Guilds League; but it was assumed that any N.G.L. member would support the work of the L.R.D., and if he or she lived in London, would join actively in it. For some years, in fact, the two movements were in effect two sides of the same coin – that coin which the war correspondent Henry Nevinson, using a different metaphor, characterised once and for all as *The Stage Army of the Good* – the Guild movement providing the theory and the propaganda, while the L.R.D. worked at getting out the facts which were to be the sinews of the propagandists' war.

This double-sided phenomenon, the constituents of which, in London above all, lived and worked so much in one another's pockets that they compendiously referred to themselves as 'the Movement', is what I shall be trying to describe – as one who in youth was 100 per cent part of it; and I shall be trying to recreate it as a living thing. This means concentrating less on the details of the creed which it preached – which could not be done within the compass of a single essay, and which has been the subject of more than one study – but rather upon the soil in which it sprang up, the conditions in which it grew, what it was like in its prime, and why it so quickly came to an end: its life-history, rather than its anatomy. And before I deal even with its origins, there are two or three characteristics of the movement as a whole on which I want to say something, because they differentiate it to an important extent from any other I have known.

Its principal leaders, and a large number of its rank and file, were young – for the most part in their early twenties; they were middle-class and highly intellectualised. They aimed at being realistic, and believed they were; but they were in fact romantic. The youthfulness is a matter of fact – even though it was not true of either of the first leading protagonists, S. G. Hobson and A. R. Orage; the intellectualism – indeed, the *cultured* intellectualism – was considerable, not only in the case of the middle-class leaders but also of those working-class adherents who played any considerable part in discussion and the formulation of policy. Romanticism, indeed, may be regarded by present-day historians as an essential element in the make-up of any group of radical or revolutionary thinkers from the Levellers onwards; but the romanticism of the Guild Socialists had two more or less distinguishing features. One, particular to itself, was that it tended to centre upon trade unions and trade-union structure – odd though this may sound today, when trade unions seem the institutions least likely to inspire romantic affection in either economists or sociologists; the other was a kind of pristine, almost schoolboyish innocence which Guild Socialists in common with many others owed to the long shelter of the late-Victorian age in England.

There come to my mind, frequently, two lines from a good-natured lampoon of G. K. Chesterton's on the remarkably unremarkable Tory politician Walter Long, who had delivered himself of some ineptitude or other upon not having had personal experience of revolutions.

> *From his first hour, in his expensive cot,*
> *He never saw the tiniest viscount shot*

wrote Chesterton, thinking of the French Revolution. It was the governing class that he was holding up to gentle ridicule; but the charge was only slightly less applicable to the whole country, steeped as it was in a tradition of non-violent law-abidingness in which the remark most typical of the working classes was supposed to be 'All right: I'll come quietly'. The working classes were oppressed, no doubt; but it was a general oppression, showing itself in low wages and the cold mercilessness of the Poor Laws rather than in jackboots, whips and guns. The British worker had not had to fight the real physical battles which his American cousin had endured at Lawrence, at Homestead, at Paterson, and in the Pullman strike; the worst place-name he looked back on was 'Tonypandy' – where as a matter of fact nobody at all was killed. It made it quite easy to think of violent physical revolution as a relief from the tensions of industrial capitalist society, a kind of beneficent blood-letting in which a few tiny viscounts and other parasites would perish and everyone would live happily ever afterwards. Chesterton himself, for all his scorn of Walter Long, was not immune from this kind of thinking: in the dedication to Belloc which prefaces that pleasant fantasy on local self-government, *The Napoleon of Notting Hill*, he wrote

> *Likelier the barricades shall blaze*
> *Slaughter below and smoke above,*
> *And death and hate and hell declare*
> *That men have found a thing to love.*

And it is astonishing to recall that William Morris's *News from Nowhere*, a romantic utopian vision if ever there was one, was sometimes quoted as realistic because in it Morris spoke of civil war as preceding the establishment of his socialistic society – rather than the peaceful intellectual conversion envisaged by Robert Owen, for example.[1] This attitude, this insular innocence, is also quite apparent in the minor literature of the period, in the files of *Punch* for instance, in that curious phenomenon the 'public-school story', and in such one-time best-selling novels as the adventures of *Raffles*, the gentleman burglar, and E. F.

[1] Marxists, of course, looked also to a revolutionary convulsion of sorts to be produced by the final 'crisis of capitalism'. But they were not particularly precise; Hyndman, indeed, and some others of the Social Democratic Federation in its early days, were romantic enough to suggest 1889 – the centenary of the taking of the Bastille – as a likely date for it.

Benson's *The Babe, B.A.*; even the problems of the early Forsytes seem mild compared with what was to come. The impatience with this kind of cushioned existence can be partly seen in verse like that of Henry Newbolt demanding 'a cause on earth for which we might have died', and Rupert Brooke, a little later, welcoming the outbreak of real war 'as swimmers into cleanness leaping'. It was in this atmosphere of uneasy calm that Guild Socialism was born; and it grew to maturity in an atmosphere just as transient – that of near-total war.

The principal *immediate* cause of the 'social unrest' of the years before 1914, of which the Guild movement was only a part, was undoubtedly the failure of the Liberal government, after the staggering electoral landslide of 1906, to come up to the expectations of its supporters and produce a new heaven and a new earth. The expectations can be read in the cool pages of R. C. K. Ensor's *England, 1870–1914*, and their disappointment is found most vividly in George Dangerfield's *The Strange Death of Liberal England*, which, though completed some years after the events, remains the most penetrating study of the great disillusion – which might be described as the popular realisation, for the first though certainly not for the last time, that a reforming government, however handsome the electoral majority which put it in power, could neither control the economic tides nor fulfil the more sweeping of the expectations which it had aroused. Dangerfield begins his survey only about 1910, the year in which the overwhelming Liberal majority fell heavily in the two successive general elections; but it was long before then, as early as July 1907, that Victor Grayson ran away with the Colne Valley by-election on the issue of failure to deal with continuing unemployment, and not much later that 'unrest' was rising on the railways and in the Cambrian coalfield. The Poor Law Commission was still sitting, and the Fabian campaign for the prevention of destitution by Beatrice Webb's scheme for social security was yet to be born.

Arthur Penty's little book, *The Restoration of the Gild System*, which appeared in May 1906, is generally taken as the start of the Guild movement; but this is only true in the strictly historical sense. The proposals of that shaggy stammering architect – he once bellowed to me, over the noise of a crowded Tube train, that 'the only way to f-fight the views of K-K-K-Karl

263

Marx was J-J-J-Jesus C-Christ!' and when he rose to speak at a meeting he was always liable to shake anyone sitting in front of him out of his chair – were altogether too medievalist and backward-looking for his contemporaries. A devotee of William Morris – though a member of the Fabian Society at the time his book came out – he was an uncompromising advocate of the skilled craftsman and a hater of modern industrial production, and called for a general return to what he believed to be the essentials for the good life – control of production, standards and conditions of work by the real producers, the Just Price, local self-government like that of the chartered towns, the whole medieval bag of tricks. He deplored the dead hand of official bureaucracy and hinted, a trifle vaguely, at the trade-union movement as a possible basis for a modern Guild system; but in the first flush of radical triumph his book was premature and it is doubtful whether anything more would have come of it than had of Ruskin's writings and his Guild of St. George, for example,[2] had he not succeeded in selling the general idea to A. R. Orage (another Fabian) and the remarkable team which Orage collected around the *New Age*. For a little while Orage and Penty, with the help of the journalist Holbrook Jackson, had tried to get an anti-collectivist, pro-trade-union movement going in the Fabian Arts Group (founded in 1907 in the rush of new entrants into the Fabian Society which followed the election and the emergence of H. G. Wells as a leading Fabian propagandist); but they were even less successful than Wells at denting the firm and skilful opposition presented by Shaw and the Webbs, and they quickly abandoned the Arts Group in favour of work on the journal which they had just bought – ironically enough, partly out of funds provided by Shaw from the profits of *The Doctor's Dilemma* at the Royal Court Theatre.

A good deal has been written in recent years about Orage, the ex-elementary schoolteacher from Leeds, and the *New Age* under his editorship – Jackson removed himself after a year to better-paid fields – and little more need be said here about the most brilliant editor, in weekly journalism, of his day, who relied

---

[2] Ruskin was a strong general influence on the *thought* of many working-class leaders of that time, as is shown by frequent references in their autobiographies, but it remains difficult to pick out particular influences exerted by him.

scarcely at all upon advertising to pay for his paper or on fees to attract contributors, or on anyone's judgement but his own on what was proper or exciting to put in it. Any man who could induce the business-minded Arnold Bennett to produce week after week a literary column for no remuneration at all, or, conversely, to print *twenty-four* successive articles on the contents of railway-station bookstalls, written by Ezra Pound[3] at a time in the poet's fortunes when he badly needed the scanty guineas which were all the paper could afford at best, could hardly be accused of subservience to the market; and the number of important new developments, from Bergsonian philosophy onwards, which were discussed by *New Age* writers makes a formidable list. By the time of the outbreak of war, the *New Age* had become really compulsive reading for everyone who was anyone in left-wing radical circles, however much they might individually detest any particular contributor or his contribution; and there is no question that the *New Age*, with its high intellectual content, played a great part in ensuring that Guild Socialism had a considerable philosophic content informing its revolt against poverty, insecurity and bureaucracy, or that the platform it provided for the movement in its early years was essential to its growth.

This espousal did not come at once. In its first issue the *New Age* went no further than the rather vague 'indication of intent' which read: 'Socialism as a means to the intensification of man is even more necessary than socialism as a means to the abolition of economic poverty'; and it was not until April 1912 – after the passing of Lloyd George's Insurance Act had not merely 'dished the Webbs' and their anti-Poor Law campaign but had also aroused the rage of all those who (like Belloc in *The Servile State*) were fiercely critical of the bureaucratic State and the parliamentary system – that it began publication of the series of articles, unsigned but written by S. G. Hobson, which first systematically proposed Guild Socialism as a system for society. The proposal, as everyone knows, was put forward, in the first instance, as a means of ending the present system of 'wage-slavery' (Hobson's coinage) by a marriage of democratically self-

[3] One of the last of these contained a lively scathing attack on a Church family journal calling itself the *Quiver*; it had a fairly wide circulation, but not, one feels, among the usual *New Age* public.

governing Guilds of workers with the political organisation of the State, the State providing the capital, i.e. land and capital goods. These the Guilds – of which Hobson suggested there might be about twenty-two needed – would rent under 'charter', themselves providing the goods and services required by the public, maintaining their own members whether working or not working, and being responsible for both the conditions and the standards of work. This marriage proposal was, of course, intended to make the most of what was right and attractive in what was variously called syndicalism or industrial unionism without throwing away what was sound in the traditional, democratic collectivism as preached by the I.L.P. and the Fabian Society and by the Labour Party in Parliament – in so far as its members preached socialism at all.

In 1912, however, it was syndicalism, or industrial unionism, that held the attention of press and public, rather than anything appearing in the *New Age*. In 1910 Tom Mann of the A.S.E., once known as one of the leaders in the great London Dock Strike and in the nineties as the author, under Sidney Webb's part-guidance, of the minority report of the Royal Commission on Labour, came home from Australia bubbling with excitement; and immediately started spreading his subversive doctrine in the fertile fields of mining and transport labour. The difference between syndicalism proper and industrial unionism was not always, it seemed, very clear to Mann himself; and the strikes of 1910 to 1913 still await their historian in detail. What I can here testify to is the public alarm created in August of 1911, when the city of Liverpool was part-paralysed by a miniature general strike lasting a few days. The public employees (scavengers and tramwaymen) joined the railway and dock workers; trucks of vegetables rotted in record summer heat outside Edge Hill station; wealthy American tourists from the White Star's *Baltic* sat unhappily on their Saratoga trunks at Pier Head; the destroyer *Antrim* lay, a grey guard, in the Mersey; the evening papers brought out smudged pink and green editions every hour or so, as though war had broken out – and very few of the scandalised readers had much idea of what it was all about. Scarcely a single one of them read or knew of the *Daily Herald*, the Miracle of Fleet Street, which had started life that year as a strike sheet.

It was industrial unionism, I should say – the idea of the One Big Union and the story of the Industrial Workers of the World, the chant of 'Solidarity for Ever', and the Wobbly battle songs, 'Casey Jones', 'Pie in the Sky', 'Hallelujah, I'm a Bum' and the rest of them – which chiefly roused the enthusiasm of the young socialists.[4] Their 'straight' revolutionism was more suited to the shape of British industry, even before the War, than the extreme localism and guerrilla methods on which the much more intellectual concepts of French syndicalism were based – though it was perhaps Larkin, the Irishman, who made the most use of I.W.W. example; and notwithstanding the admiration which British Socialists like Keir Hardie felt for French Socialists like Jaurès, it is doubtful whether more than a handful even of the most learned young socialists knew much about Sorel, Pelloutier, Griffuelhes or the C.G.T. in its great militant days, until G. D. H. Cole's first book, *The World of Labour*, ordered them to study foreign trade union movements and the tactics of revolutionary trade unionism.

The World of Labour came out in 1913, a year after Hobson's *New Age* articles, and shortly after its author had been elected a Fellow of that unrevolutionary institution, Magdalen College at Oxford. Cole did not, in the first edition, declare himself a Guild Socialist, though he made sympathetic references to the proposals now being advanced in the *New Age*; but the whole book was in effect an eloquent plea for the sort of industrial society which they envisaged. If one were to go by title only, *The World of Labour* might be supposed to be the successor to the Webbs' monumental *History of Trade Unionism* of nearly twenty years earlier, and their *Industrial Democracy*; in fact, the difference could hardly have been greater. The books by the Webbs were a sober factual analysis of a hitherto neglected part of the British social system; Cole's was a detailed and excited description of what might be a force for changing the system, not in Britain only but throughout what we now call the Western world. It is a far cry from the concept of 'a continuing association of wage-earners for the purpose of improving the conditions of their working lives' to that of an army whose prime business was to fight their employers, as far as possible, all the time; and it is not

---

[4] *Not* 'Internationale', of which the English translation was, and is, practically unsingable. The American version is just slightly better.

surprising that Raymond Postgate, for example, then a school-boy of just 17 found that *The World of Labour* 'opened a completely new world to me. The education which I, and every other middle-class boy, had received, had not referred to one single thing mentioned in the book.'

The World of Labour repudiated the extremes of syndicalist theory: it did not demand that the organisations of producers should rule the world unaided, and it accepted the continuance of civil government, assumed to be socialist, i.e. non-profit-making, in character. It was therefore tailor-made to fit in with Hobson's proposals; and two other streams of current thought contributed to help build up the single idea of National Guilds into a coherent system of social philosophy. The first of these was what is generally called 'Distributivism', associated with the names of Belloc and Chesterton. The 'Chesterbelloc' idea of a wide redistribution of property and a return to small landowning was itself as medievalist as Penty's and commanded little support; what appealed in the work of these two fascinating journalist-poet-novelists was their satire and the continuing scorn which they poured on the world of finance, the 'culture of cities' (to use a later phrase), and the sham of parliamentary democracy, the accent being on the adjective. It was the age of the muckrakers in the United States: Sinclair's *The Jungle* came out in 1909. Belloc and Chesterton had nothing so spectacular as Chicago to offer, but they had the Marconi scandal, of which they made the most, and the more fatuous observations of Liberal (and Labour) politicians to play with. It was at this time that Will Dyson, the cartoonist from Australia, whose drawings brought into British politics a savagery hardly known since Gillray, produced for the young and impudent *Daily Herald* his stereotype of the Fat Man as representative of the capitalist system and poured contempt on the Labour leaders making their obeisances to the emblem of the Top Hat. It was no accident that, as the 'Movement' got going, it ritually ended its meetings by singing the songs from Chesterton's *Flying Inn* adapted to traditional tunes, several from *Hymns Ancient and Modern*.

Chesterton may be felt to be 'light reading' – though his importance in the atmosphere of the time should not be underestimated and has recently been reappraised. A more weighty contribution came from the political pluralists, who from the time of

F. W. Maitland's attack upon the Austinian theory of sovereignty had been concerned to repudiate the idea of the omnicompetent State and to assert the contrary right of 'groups' created for various purposes not merely to exist but to have individualities of their own and to claim comparable allegiance from their members. This theory was eagerly taken up by the Guild Socialists under the name of 'functional democracy'. Philosophically, it can be found most succintly expressed in a paper, 'Conflicting Social Obligations', read by Cole to the Aristotelian Society in 1915; it later took larger and more formidable shape in the book by the Spaniard Ramiro de Maeztu called *Liberty, Authority and Function in the Modern State.*[5] But it underlies a good deal of Guild Socialist writing, e.g. by Maurice Reckitt, R. H. Tawney and Bertrand Russell, and accounts for some of the support which the movement received from Churchmen – the Church being of course one of the most obvious bodies claiming rights of independence of the State and of allegiance from its membership. The respectable William Temple, who was to become Archbishop of Canterbury, was sympathetic; Conrad Noël, the Red Vicar of Thaxted, sat on the first Executive Committee of the National Guilds League. This, then, was the social and theoretical setting for Guild Socialism. The force which turned the *New Age* articles into a 'movement' was already in the making before the first of the articles appeared; it had its roots in the Fabian Society – more particularly, in the university members of that body, mostly those of undergraduate status.

I have already mentioned what Pease, the official historian of the Fabian Society, called 'The Episode of Mr. Wells', and his defeat. Wells's defeat, however, as he himself candidly acknowledged in his autobiography, was due almost entirely to himself, to his own tactical incompetence and lack of any positive programme other than that the Society should cease to be 'petty minded' and should become great and glorious – and spend a great deal of money. The Fabian Old Gang had only to sit back and let their vehement squeaky-voiced antagonist fall over his

[5] De Maetzu later became a Fascist, as did one or two other Guild Socialists in countries overseas. This part of Guild Socialist theory did lend itself to adaptation by supporters of the 'corporative State' – but in a much later phase of development.

own feet. But this did not mean that there was not a great deal of emotional support among the 1906–7 recruits, as Shaw pointed out to Mrs. Webb after the battle, for the mood and intention of the author of *A Modern Utopia* and *New Worlds for Old*. There was a corresponding impatience with the drab and discouraging appearance of the parliamentary Labour Party and its leaders,[6] particularly after the 1910 elections had tied the party firmly to the tail of the Liberals, who alone were likely to release it from the effects of the Osborne judgement. For a brief while immediately after the appearance in 1909 of the *Minority Report* of the Poor Law Commission, this unrest was canalised into Beatrice Webb's mass (for those days) campaign in support of the report which eventually came to bear the name of National Committee for the Prevention of Destitution. But Lloyd George with his 'ninepence for fourpence' effectively outflanked the N.C.P.D.; and the assumptions and methods of the leaders of the campaign – Beatrice, with manifest satisfaction, enjoying to the full powers of organisation, not to say exploitation, which she had presumably inherited from her father but had not hitherto had a real chance of using – incidentally produced a strong anti-Webb attitude in the minds of some of the most active of the campaigners. These included Cole and William Mellor, both of the Oxford University Fabian Society, and it was their criticisms, combined with the fierce lampoon on the Webb ménage drawn by the wounded Wells in *The New Machiavelli*, which was, I believe, chiefly responsible for the image of the Webbs as unscrupulous social spiders, anxious to lure the coming generation into their net, to set them to work at tasks and for objects dictated by themselves and to appropriate the results of others' labour – the last a wholly unwarranted accusation – which has been so persistently revived from time to time; in this generation, by some young Marxist historians and Mr. Malcolm Muggeridge.

By 1912 the N.C.P.D. had manifestly failed of its purpose, and the syndicalists and the other anti-parliamentarians were riding high. The Webbs, returning from a world tour, recognised the fact, sensed the new currents in the air, and with character-

[6] Even Beatrice Webb, when the Partnership decided to abandon the effort to 'permeate' the two old political parties, could find nothing more attractive to call the alternative than 'a poor thing, but our own'.

istic resilience sought to make use of them and of the energy and ability of the young Socialist recruits by the establishment, under the aegis of the Fabian Society, of a large organisation for research and education, of which the only part which concerns us here is a committee called the Control of Industry Committee – and only a part of that. At the beginning of 1913 this Committee, with a membership of over eighty Fabians and sixty-odd outside 'consultants', was already calling itself the 'Fabian Research Committee', with a small office and a subscription of its own. Sidney Webb proceeded to draft for it an immense and detailed scheme of work, instructing it to examine and report on four possible forms for the future control of industry – by Associations of Consumers, i.e. Co-operative Societies, by Associations of Producers, by extension of Public Services, and by Associations of Wage-Earners. The fourth section of the inquiry was designed to finish off, by cool and patient study of facts, the dangerous nonsense about syndicalism and industrial unionism now taking hold of too many of the 'manual working wage-earners' (Webb), and of those who should have known better.

The outcome of all this flurry was not all what he intended, for the new recruits, reinforcing the rebels within the Fabian Society, neatly turned the tables on the Webbs. They manned the Research Committee, packed the sessions of the Fabian Summer School which were supposed to discuss its possible findings, and within the next couple of years came to within an ace (once within a single vote) of capturing the Fabian Society itself for the new doctrines. There is no space, or need, in this chapter to reproduce in detail the struggle inside the Fabian Society, which I have described in considerable detail in chapters of my *Story of Fabian Socialism* and in *Growing Up Into Revolution*: the only point that needs to be made is that the opposition, almost up to the final defeat in June 1915, which resulted in Cole's resignation from the Society as well as from its Executive Committee, was still almost entirely a middle-class and on the whole a highly intellectual grouping. Beatrice Webb's *Diary*, in its pained and rather comic comments on the behaviour of the Guild Socialists at Summer Schools and elsewhere, seems really to be charging them with not behaving like 'gentlemen'. She cannot understand why they should be so ill-mannered and take such pleasure in breaking rules, drinking beer, banging the tables and annoying (though not, be it noted, morally scandalising) everyone else. She admitted their 'cleverness', but was certain that they would never condescend to work at the job as Sidney and Shaw and the other early Fabians had done; in which she could scarcely have been more mistaken.

The 1915 defeat was no real set-back, for the Guild Socialists retreated, in effect, to prepared positions. They already had firm hold of the Research Committee, which in 1914 turned itself into the Fabian Research Department, with independent membership and with R. Page Arnot, the future historian of mining trade unionism, as its paid secretary, and with the first recruits to an army of volunteers preparing to establish it as a general inquiry bureau. This was to be the fact-finding organisation; the body to make use of the facts, the propagandist wing of the movement, was the National Guilds League, founded in London in April 1915 by a meeting of about forty persons, with Mellor as its Secretary, and Cole, with a dozen others, on its Executive Committee. At that date the N.G.L. enrolled neither Orage nor Hobson. Orage disliked the idea of any organisation at all, preferring to confine discussion to his own journal; Hobson was out of England at the time, and was unenthusiastic when he returned. But by then the League was in full being, and pushing energetically a programme based on a statement of principle and policy which had been worked out in a week of prolonged and ardent discussion by a group meeting at the end of the previous December; it was known thereafter as the 'Storrington Document'.

The Storrington Document had never been printed until its appearance in the present volume; but its dozen folio pages of close typing were in fact the agreed basis for all the Guild propaganda which followed, though it was of course amplified and modified to a considerable extent in pamphlets, conference discussions and resolutions, articles and lectures by leading N.G.L. members. It should perhaps be emphasised, at this point, that N.G.L. propaganda was very definitely a collaborative effort: the voluminous literary output of G. D. H. Cole, in the years from 1917 onwards, has caused some historians to write as though he was the dominating if not the only formulator, but that is not correct. At most he was *primus inter pares*; others, such as Hobson when he returned to England, Reckitt, W. N.

Ewer, later the *doyen* of foreign editors, Arnot, and above all William Mellor, his close collaborator in their Oxford days and afterwards for a time editor of the *Daily Herald* under the Odhams Press régime, were perfectly capable of standing up to him and quite often of winning the argument. The Mellor-and-Cole Board, as the two of them were termed when they wrote their column of 'Industrial Notes' for the *Herald*, was a real partnership which had a considerable influence among active trade unionists.

The Storrington Document does not now require to be summarised here in any detail. What may be noted is that it opens with a recognition of the need for the State, regarded as 'a grouping of people on a geographical basis', but severely limited in function; on questions of foreign policy and of taxation, for example, the State should act only in consultation with other organisations, of which the National Guilds are naturally the most important. These Guilds (whose number is no longer specified) are to be industry-based, all-inclusive, completely democratic and autonomous (with allowance for necessary consultations); and they will be completely responsible for the finance of their own industries, including all payments to their membership; distribution of their products to the public will be undertaken, generally speaking, by a Distributive Guild which will supersede existing shops -- and the Co-operative Movement. This fairly simple scheme of society was very much developed by Cole in his two books *Self-Government in Industry* (1917) and *Guild Socialism Restated* (1920), of which the latter in particular recognises a status for the Co-operative movement itself, and also envisages a number of other representative institutions such as a Council of Public Utilities and a Cultural Council, all coming together in the commune, local or national. But refinements of this nature did not really affect the basic pattern.

The Document also laid down objectives for the time of transition, viz. securing a 'majority of expropriators' in Parliament and on local governing bodies, reorganising the trade-union movement on industrial, all-inclusive lines, and insisting on full 'workers' control' being established if and when any industry or service was nationalised. (The newly born National Union of Railwaymen had already made this demand.) In the case of industries still in private hands, the unions should proceed by means of regular 'interference'; by developing existing machinery of negotiation so that their voice should be heard on matters at present deemed the exclusive concern of the management; by securing the election of foremen, under-managers and eventually of top management; and finally, by taking the control of wages and salaries into their own hands, negotiating with the employers a lump sum payment which they would then distribute to the workers on principles which they themselves would determine. These measures, under the names of 'Encroaching Control' and 'Collective Contract', became an important part of Guild propaganda for industries not 'ripe' for nationalisation.

One or two comments may perhaps be made. Besides being pretty utopian and also set out in considerable detail – which was due partly, at any rate, to the determination of the policy-framers to show their audiences that they really meant business, that they wanted to describe a possible working society and not a vague vision – the society which they did describe seemed to lay a great stress on *voting. Guild Socialism Restated,* in particular, appeared to envisage such a host of elections, to all manner of bodies, that the interest of the ordinary man would lapse altogether, and the final result would be the not very exciting spectacle of a small handful of busybodies manning all the 'functional' committees. To this the Guild Socialists generally replied that the apparatus sketched out was no more complicated, in fact, than the web of institutions actually existing in modern society. This defence is a fair one (and far truer today than it was then) but I suspect that a more honest answer would have been that even if the accusation were correct they would not greatly care. They were not concerned with voting for voting's sake, if people were not sufficiently concerned to play their part in a functional democracy provided for them, they did not deserve to have it – a dangerous doctrine, perhaps.

A more serious reflection is that the Guild proposals, especially for the 'transitional' period, implied an effective control of labour power by the unions which could only exist when there was a real scarcity of labour. In Edwardian England this would seem a large assumption, yet within a very few months it was to be more nearly realised than it had ever been before, or would be again for many years to come. It was, of course, the War, and the labour famine created by it, which produced a hot-house blooming for the Guild Socialists, which made socialisation of industry seem a possible goal, and 'encroaching control' a not impossible tactic. Moreover, as the War continued, their audiences could see with their own eyes live, actual trade-union leaders being taken into consultation at hitherto undreamt-of levels;[7] while at the same time, owing partly to the complexity of the adjustments which had to be made and partly to the prohibition of strikes in the war industries – which of course did not mean that strikes did not occur, only that they could not be officially sanctioned – the organisation and deployment of 'labour power' locally devolved more and more upon locally based and locally chosen leaders – which was exactly what the Guild Socialists had said ought to happen.

I do not suggest that shop stewards in general were converted to Guild Socialism – far from it. But shop stewards and shop committees were fertile ground for the propagandists, and their task was made much easier by the contacts which some of the leaders, notably Cole, Mellor and Arnot, had already made with left-wing and even not-so-left trade-union men. Besides the notes in the *Herald* already mentioned – and a good deal of other journalism as well as speaking and lecturing – the most important influence was probably Cole's appointment, early in 1915, as unpaid Adviser to the Amalgamated Society of Engineers, a development unprecedented in the trade-union world of that date; it was due largely to his friendship with F. S. Button, a member of the A.S.E. executive and shortly to become the T.U.C. representative on the three-man Committee on Production. This appointment, incidentally, by making Cole a trade-union officer, gave him protection from call-up under the Military Service Acts – which in due course removed Mellor, Arnot and Ewer, as conscientious objectors, from the immediate scene.[8] More important, it kept him in regular contact with what

[7] On the Committee on Production, for example, on the Cotton Control Board, and even in the War Cabinet itself.

[8] A word should perhaps be added about the Guild Socialists and the War. The N.G.L. took no official attitude; its membership included serving soldiers as well as C.O.'s and exempted persons who all worked alongside in complete amity. The War with Germany was a fact of life, but it was not the War with which the League was concerned. As time went on and opposition grew, there developed something of a give-and-take between, for example, N.G.L. members and I.L.P. agitation – 'You back my Workers' Con-

was going on in the industrial world and the world of governmental control. Once, for example, he obtained some information very valuable in a current dispute by accidentally tapping a telephone conversation of Sir Robert Horne, then Minister of Labour. Conversely, it brought trade unionists, local and national, to visit the office in Tothill Street, Westminster, where, sandwiched between the Fabian office, the Fabian Bookshop and Fabian Hall below and the residuum of the N.C.P.D. above, the workers in the Research Department were in the jubilant process of establishing themselves as a general inquiry and information bureau for trade unions, their branches and their branch secretaries, and kindred organisations. 'Being clerks to Labour', the Webbs had described the job in the nineties, when they had thought of doing it themselves, but they had then transferred their attention to the L.C.C., the London School of Economics, public education, and their many other ploys. Now the young opposition had taken over the idea, and brought to its carrying-out a fervid devotion which the Webbs themselves would never have felt. The present generation can scarcely conceive of itself, I imagine, as deriving excitement from having learnt by heart the extraordinary sets of initials which identified some of the pre-war trade unions,[9] from discovering that washery workers in colliery districts were not to be classified with laundresses, or that flannel workers formed a branch in the Tinplate Division of the Dockers' Union. The Webbs were not so excited, but it is worth remarking that they and others of the older Fabians retained interest and on the whole remarkably benevolent co-operation with those who abused them up and down dale – even when, at the beginning of 1918, the ebullient Guildsmen repudiated the word 'Fabian' altogether, and called themselves the *Labour* Research Department. It is not, however, always sufficiently realised that there was not, until the Communists appeared, anything like hard-and-fast barriers between different political sections within the labour movement as might be inferred from their periodic exchanges of insults. It is a fact

---

trol Resolution and I'll back yours for Peace by Negotiation'. But neither group were spies or 'traitors'.

[9] e.g. N.A.U.S.A.W.C. = National Amalgamated Union of Shop Assistants, Warehousemen and Clerks. There were even more impressive sets in the building trades.

that both Tom Mann and George Lansbury, to take only two examples, joined the I.L.P., the S.D.F. and the Fabian Society – and Lansbury the N.G.L., though I cannot be sure about Mann. And members of the British Socialist Party, the left-wing organisation formed in 1911 which a decade later provided the bulk of the foundation membership of the Communist Party of Great Britain, were frequently to be found walking about the L.R.D. offices.

The stage thus set – or the heating apparatus installed in the hot-house – the two bodies began to grow, and grew rapidly as the labour market tightened as a result of the appalling losses on the Somme, which also reduced enthusiasm for the War. As I said earlier, the active membership of both was often the same; workers in the L.R.D. joined the N.G.L. as a matter of course, and Guildsmen in the provinces tended to subscribe to the L.R.D. and to induce their own branches or trades councils to affiliate. Yet the two were clearly separate and their activities distinguishable.

The L.R.D. was the research and inquiry body. In the summer of 1917 it produced a duplicated document of information called the *Monthly Circular*, the demand for which turned out to be so large that it soon had to be printed to the number of several thousands, bought for distribution by Labour organisations; it was a kind of socialist *Labour Gazette*, full of dry facts about wages, negotiations, the cost of living, strikes, Government Orders and circulars and, as time went on, about profits and employers' combines, and about labour organisation and struggle in other countries. Informatory pamphlets (called *Labour White Papers*), study circle syllabuses and a few books, of which the earliest example was Arnot and Cole's *Labour and Capital on the Railways*, were also produced. In addition to a regular stream of day-to-day inquiries on a great variety of subjects which the staff had to try to answer, sometimes 'off the cuff' or by inspired guesses, when a large important trade-union secretary appeared in person in the office, factual briefings were provided for some trade unions presenting wage claims. The most spectacular effort of the Department in this direction (and one in which the greatest fun was had by all) came after the end of the War, when Sir Auckland Geddes on behalf of the government (which still controlled the railways) threatened a very unfavourable wage settlement. In September 1919 the railwaymen came out on strike, which the government tried to break; Arnot persuaded the N.U.R. to buy advertising space in the newspapers, which the L.R.D. filled so effectively as to swing public opinion and force a much milder settlement. This effort, which was thoroughly organised in detail, with a special committee (including Sidney Webb and Bernard Shaw) meeting every day to decide upon action, was only the highlight of the Department's activities in the new class war which followed the armistice; it all made for confidence in the Guild Socialists.

The L.R.D. had a nucleus of paid workers, and an office. The N.G.L. had none except for a brief while in 1919 and 1920, but it too poured out a stream of pamphlets expounding its ideas both in general and as applicable to industries like coal mining and the railways, and in different situations; one of the most characteristic of these appeared after the once-famous Whitley Report of 1917 for joint consultation in industry. The League drew up its own facsimile publication, telling all the 'reconstructionists' who might be disposed to welcome it that the Whitley proposals were totally inadequate. On the Clyde there was a strong branch, which at the end of 1916 began publication of the *Guildsman*, a monthly under the editorship of John Paton, an able working engineer, who unfortunately died young.[10] Meantime the members of the League held vehement discussions over the exact formulation of its programmes and policies, 'joyfully splitting ideological hairs', as Hobson remarked with a certain cynicism; others said it reminded them of the controversies in the Church of Athanasius.

Nevertheless, membership, and influence, increased. In the hopeful days of the Ministry of Reconstruction (most of whose proposals, it will be remembered, went promptly down the drain as soon as the post-war coalition had got firmly in control) the ideas of Guild Socialism 'infected' a wide band of thought; there was even talk of G. D. H. Cole as a coming leader of Labour – he had drawn close to Arthur Henderson, was Secretary to the collection of advisory committees newly set up by

---

[10] After Paton's death the journal was moved to London, where it was edited by G. D. H. and M. Cole, changing its name to the *Guild Socialist*.

the reconstituted party, and was collaborating in the discussions which led to the reorganisation of the T.U.C. and the creation of its General Council. No doubt the Guildsmen tended to exaggerate the importance of the trend. They were too busy working night and day at their own job, manning what they really felt to be the Thin Red Line of coming change, to stop and consider what all the ferment meant and what was really going to come of it. Not that they would have been much wiser if they had. Their enthusiasm received an enormous fillip from the two Russian revolutions, the Month of Revolution in Europe (November 1918) and the strikes and demonstrations which followed upon the end of the War. They barely noticed the emergence of the 1918 Labour Party – equipped by Sidney Webb with a milk-of-the-word collectivist programme! As to the coupon election, they took it in their stride, having expected nothing better from the parliamentary system; they noted rather the numbers of national trade unions which, rather late in the day, began to follow the example of the N.U.R. in putting 'workers' control' into the tale of their objectives.

Late in the day it was. For even before the catastrophic break in prices which began at the end of 1920 and so soon led to the ending of Labour's monopoly position, cracks had begun to appear in the movement itself. Ironically enough, the instrument of the cracking was the October revolution in Russia.

The first reaction of the majority in the N.G.L. to the Bolsheviks was one of unqualified joy. But there was, even at the beginning, a group, mainly Christian adherents, who were filled with apprehension at the violence of the Revolution, which clearly went beyond shooting tiny viscounts, and of the 'dictatorship of the proletariat'. This group, led by Reckitt, strongly opposed a resolution moved at the League's 1918 Conference congratulating the Bolsheviks; and their views were reinforced by the *New Age*. Orage, who also disliked the Bolsheviks, swung over to vehement advocacy of a scheme of 'Social Credit' devised by Major C. H. Douglas. This scheme was only one of the perennial suggestions for bringing about a major change in society, without inconveniencing anyone, by juggling with the monetary system, but the prestige of the *New Age* helped to make it a temporary rallying ground of what came to be a 'right wing' of those who did not like revolutions when they saw them in being.[11]

At first, the surprised majority thought that the difference was no more serious than earlier quarrels over phraseology, and certainly no more than differences about the War and about Germany, which had never resulted in splitting the movement. But gradually it became clear that the difference was only the first manifestation of a much deeper cleavage concerning 'workers' control' itself. As G. D. H. Cole wrote, nearly forty years afterwards:

It did not appear clearly until later how much the different advocates of 'workers' control' were at cross-purposes. To some of the Industrial Unionists, and subsequently to the Communists, it meant control by the workers *as a class*, to be exercised through the dictatorship of the proletariat as a whole, and was thus quite consistent with centralisation and imposed discipline provided that the discipline was imposed by representatives of the class. The Guild Socialists, on the other hand, were strongly anti-authoritarian: the 'workers' control' they stood for was, above all else, control by the actual working group over the management of its own affairs within the framework of a wider control of policy formulated and executed as democratically as possible, and with the largest diffusion of responsibility and power.[12]

These differences were not fully apparent at the time – before the Bolsheviks had clamped down firmly on the chaotic experience of 'workers' control' in factories which immediately followed the Revolution – and no one then wanted to press the dispute to extremes or to break up the N.G.L. For some two years, accordingly, attempts at compromise proceeded, under the guidance particularly of Cole, whose ardent sympathy with the Russians made him very unwilling to side with those who attacked them; but the gulf proved in the end unbridgeable, and towards the end of 1920 some of the extreme right resigned from the League, just after others of the leaders, including

[11] Including, at this date, Beatrice and Sidney Webb.
[12] *History of Socialist Thought*, iii (1956), p. 246.

Arnot and Mellor, had taken part in the foundation of the Communist Party. These latter retained League membership; but troubles were to come.

Meantime, what may be termed the 'middle' membership had been embarrassed by what was intended to be a 'practical' demonstration of Guild principles. In 1919 the Addison Housing Act offered to the local authorities a subsidy for working-class house-building amounting to all costs in excess of the product of a penny rate. This seemed to Hobson a marvellous opportunity to apply the Guild idea to the building trades, where the union membership had already shown considerable interest. Virtually the same idea had come to Malcolm Sparkes, a Quaker company director in London; and eventually the National Federation of Building Trades Operatives helped to set up a single body, the National Building Guild, to consolidate the movement in these and other centres.[13] The Building Guild was registered as a limited company; and it was clear from the start that it was not a Guild in the full sense of the term. It had to borrow its working capital from the banks, although this was covered by the payments as they came in from the State via the local authorities. But the Guilds did embody many of the principles of the League; they were formed by the unions; they were democratically organised; and they operated a 'collective contract' on a non-profit basis, and made themselves responsible for 'continuous pay' to all their members. In fact, they were a cross between Co-operative Societies and Guilds as they would have been in an ideal system; but they were near enough to the latter to make it impossible for the N.G.L. not to support them and their occasional imitators in other industries such as furnishing, whatever private doubts they might feel about the experiment. Much good work seems to have been accomplished and considerable enthusiasm aroused, but there were flaws and errors – some not unconnected with the irregularities, financial and other, of Hobson as the Guild's General Secretary; and the whole venture collapsed when early in the slump the government repealed the Addison Act, and so removed both the financial prop and a good part of the market. 'Continuous pay' became an impossible drain; the wage system

[13] [See the essay in this volume, pp. 284–331.]

was not so easily disposed of.[14] Of the leading Guild Socialists, only Hobson had been directly involved; but the League and its journal had cheered the builders on and found their own left wing as well as outsiders crying, 'We told you so.'

It was the slump, of course, which administered the *coup de grâce* to the building guilds and only a little later to the N.G.L. itself. The successive decline in the power of the trade unions – most startlingly shown in the disaster of Black Friday (April 1921) and in the engineering lock-out of the following year – put paid to all dreams of 'encroaching control', though the ideas themselves continued to attract backing for two or three years after the slump began. (As late as 1923 the I.L.P.'s Annual Conference registered a not very useful conversion.) But the steam went out of it as the labour movement as a whole turned to politics. When politics, as represented by the 1924 Labour government, proved a disappointment and the return to the gold standard laid a heavy hand on wages, there was in 1926, a final kick. The General Strike proved the existence of plenty of local spirit, leadership and organisational ability among trade unionists, but there were no 'expropriators' to complete the picture. 'Workers' control' even as a phrase vanished for many years.

The N.G.L. and the National Building Guild both came to an end in 1923. The situation in the L.R.D. was less immediately affected. Working-class organisations needed its services no less in defeat, and the non-Communist workers could go on answering inquiries and disseminating information, though with a certain sense of uneasiness. At the end of 1921 a storm was raised with the proposal to accept a fair-sized annual subsidy from the Soviet Trade Delegation. The old Fabians, Bernard Shaw and Mrs. Webb's niece Barbara Drake, resigned in horror at the possibility of domination by Russian gold. Cole's influence, however, persuaded the executive to accept, and I should say that, comparatively large as the subsidy was, it had remarkably little direct effect upon what the Department did, save in one important respect – in influencing the composition of personnel. On personnel the effect became manifest after the third congress of the Comintern had dictated a strict programme of 'bolshevisation' for its member parties, including the ousting of

[14] For a fuller account by G. D. H. Cole, see his *A Century of Co-operation* (1946), pp. 284–92.

non-Communists from key positions in any organisation where this could be done. Within the L.R.D. the party cell set about working in concert against 'centre' elements, and the basis for collaboration disappeared.[15] Cole resigned the honorary secretaryship early in 1924 and the last remnants of Guild Socialism were eliminated within a twelvemonth. The L.R.D. continued; and the trade unions found so much use for it that it survived all attempts by the central direction of the labour movement to outlaw it as Communist-tainted. But it had no further concern with workers' control.

[15] See the Appendix to Raymond Postgate's *How to Make a Revolution* (1934).

11

FRANK MATTHEWS

THE BUILDING GUILDS

NEATLY encapsulated in the years between the outbreak of war in 1914 and the General Strike of 1926, the Guild Movement has now taken on some of the gilt, and the unreality, of period charm. It seems, perhaps, a homespun and utopian creation, idealistic in the worst sense of the word. Mrs. Cole has emphasised that many of its intellectual guides were 'romantic', despite their own denials;[1] but at the time the movement seemed less a romantic than an eminently practical method of guiding the trade unions out of the morass of pre-war industrial conflict into a more secure haven of regionally organised and worker-controlled groupings by union. Much of the political and industrial thought of the pre-war period had pointed this way, and the National Guilds League was, in effect, the culmination of an international movement which had begun before the turn of the century in France as 'syndicalism', which had migrated and been transmuted into 'industrial syndicalism' in America and which was subsequently popularised among the unions in Britain largely through the efforts of Tom Mann.

Many of the trade unionists who subsequently joined the National Guilds League had already fallen under Mann's influence; either directly, via the *Industrial Syndicalist*[2] and its prompted publication *The Miners' Next Step*[3], or through propaganda of a syndicalist type which pervaded labour writing of the period. Such writing appeared, for example, in the *Daily*

[1] See above, Ch. 10.

[2] T. Mann (ed.), *The Industrial Syndicalist* (1911), a series of twelve pamphlets published in the course of 1911.

[3] *The Miners' Next Step* (1912), published by the South Wales Miners' Federation. Mrs. Cole (above p. 267) has emphasised that British 'syndicalism' was often in fact industrial unionism, but 'syndicalism' was the word used. See also R. Page Arnot, *South Wales Miners 1898–1914* (1967), p. 327.

Herald from the early part of 1912.[4] The *New Age* was initially fairly hostile to syndicalism, but began publishing the articles by S. G. Hobson[5] (which eventually became the book *National Guilds: An Enquiry into the Wage System and the Way Out*) in the years 1912 and 1913. In 1914 G. D. H. Cole, along with his friend and colleague William Mellor,[6] began the publication of a series of articles in the *Daily Herald*[7] with the hope that these would popularise the Guild idea among the working classes. In the next year the National Guilds League was formed.[8]

This is necessarily only an outline of a development which was much more complex, but it is safe to say that what the National Guilds League did was to offer an operational centre for the more organised dissemination of ideas which had been current in various guises in the labour movement for six or seven years before the formation of the League. And as the personality who already had considerable experience with the trade unions and the working classes, G. D. H. Cole was the essential link-man of the group. It is perhaps correct to refer to him, as Mrs.

---

[4] These articles began in April 1912 when Ben Tillett commented that the *Daily Herald* was to express 'an entirely revolutionary phase of British Labour' (*Daily Herald*, 22 April 1912). By the end of the year the *Daily Herald* was supporting the idea of One Big Union and in 1913 came the first mention of Guild Socialism, when the paper printed, at some length, the letter advocating a Guild system and sent by the *New Age* to the T.U.C. (*Daily Herald*, 1 September 1913). In 1914, when the paper ran into financial troubles because of the War, one of those given notice was A. J. Penty, who had obviously had some sort of retainer. Rowland Kenney, William Mellor and G. D. H. Cole were retained to write only 'special articles'. (See MS. '*Daily Herald*: Analysis, compiled by R. W. Postgate and others in Nuffield College, MSS. CZ 1529.)

[5] See above, pp. 264 ff.

[6] William Mellor (1888–1942) was, for a time, Cole's closest associate in the Guild movement and in the L.R.D. He was educated in Cheshire and at Oxford; became Secretary of the Fabian Research Department in 1913 and joined the staff of the *Daily Herald* in the same year. He continued with the paper throughout the War as its Industrial Correspondent (with Cole) and was its editor from 1926 to 1931. See above, p. 273.

[7] Cole and Mellor were given an industrial page on 13 January 1914 specifically to advocate 'The Greater Unionism'. This was also the title of the one joint pamphlet which they issued on the subject in 1913. It was published by the National Labour Press under the general title *Pamphlets of the Greater Unionism*.

[8] The National Guilds League was formed at a meeting gathered at the Steel Smelters' Hall, 70–78 Swinton Street, Gray's Inn Road, London on 20 and 21 April 1915. Invitations had been issued to trade unions and other interested bodies.

Cole does, as *primus inter pares*,[9] but this remains true only of his role within the League, since his influence with the A.S.E. and, incidentally, through his writings and speaking, on the whole area of trade-union thought was more extensive than it is possible to assess. Certainly almost every trade unionist and former Guildsman ever consulted by the present writer has acknowledged some measure of intellectual debt to Cole. His influence through the *Daily Herald* alone must have been enormous, but consider, too, the effect of the *World of Labour*, first published in 1913 and not, then, confessedly Guild Socialist in outlook. By 1917 the book had been revised once and reprinted three times, war-time industrial conditions ensuring a receptive audience for its theories which suggested the formation of a society based on devolution both in government and industry. Add to this the favourable economic and industrial conditions created by the War, and it becomes more possible to understand the mood of ebullient optimism which encouraged the period of experiment with Guilds in being which was initiated after the War. The first of these in point of time was the Building Guild which was set up in Manchester in January 1920, but its predecessor in conception and plan was the Guild of Builders (London) Ltd., the creation of the virtually unknown London employer Malcolm Sparkes.[10]

I

The nature of Sparkes's idealism makes him an unfashionable figure at the present time. A practising Quaker, he was totally unable to divorce any part of his life from a fundamental, informing belief in human perfectibility. Although because of this he was often exploited, this is not to imply that he was necessarily inefficient or a fool. Faced with subterfuge or deceit, he could clearly see signs of danger and take steps to avoid it.

---

[9] See above, pp. 272–3.

[10] Malcolm Sparkes's widow, Mrs. Elizabeth (Leila) Sparkes, compiled a MS. biography of her husband entitled 'Malcolm Sparkes – Constructive Pacifist'. Details on Sparkes, unless otherwise indicated, are taken from this biography, the original of which is still in the possession of Mrs. Sparkes. A copy of this MS. (hereafter referred to as the 'Life') is on microfilm in the Library of the University of Hull, where there are also other items of Mrs. Sparkes's record (hereafter referred to as Sparkes MSS. H.U.L.).

In the midst of the Building Guild experiment he risked, and lost, a considerable amount of popularity by suggesting that S. G. Hobson was precipitating the Guild towards collapse. He was right, but it was psychologically the wrong moment to have chosen. He was not, therefore, in any sense devoid of moral courage. No man could have been who suffered as much as he did in the form of financial and personal loss.

Malcolm Sparkes was born in Rochdale in 1881. He did not play a prominent part in the National Guilds League since his interests lay more directly in industry, and in this field he had a significant, though characteristically muted, influence. Born into a Quaker family, Sparkes was not the first of his line to display powers of imaginative thought. His grandfather, William Pollard, had been 'an original thinker on theological matters and a great advocate for peace'[11] at a time when the Society of Friends was passing through one of its more conservative phases. Sparkes seems to have inherited this taste for inquiry, and he combined with it a very strong practical ability. Educated at the Friends' schools at Ackworth and at Bootham, York, he was apprenticed by his own choice to the London firm of architectural woodworkers H. C. Cleaver Ltd. He remained with this firm until the First World War, resigning when it began to produce war materials. Until this time his progress was unexceptional, though rapid, and he became a junior partner soon after completing his apprenticeship.

In 1910 he married and took a house at Gerrard's Cross, where he organised a reading circle which reflected the range of his interests. The subjects debated included Tolstoy, Norman Angell's *Great Illusion* and Plato's *Republic*, but greater emphasis was laid on more urgent problems of the time, including women's suffrage, plans for a more equitable organisation of industry and the qualities of a true pacifist. Thus Sparkes was already probing the difficulties of industry and the problems of labour when industrial unrest was beginning to cause general concern, but before the publication either of the *New Age* articles or of Cole's *World of Labour*.

Even earlier than this Sparkes had given evidence of a real

[11] William Pollard (1828–93) was one of the three authors of *A Reasonable Faith* (1884), a book which 'altered the whole trend of Quaker theology and philosophy': E. Sparkes, 'Life'.

concern for industrial welfare when he instituted at Park Royal[12] a Premium Bonus Scheme of profit-sharing for the employees. The year was 1906, the year in which A. J. Penty published *The Restoration of the Guild System*. G. D. H. Cole was still at St. Paul's School and Orage was not yet editor of the *New Age*. At this point, however, Sparkes was no more than a model employer who allowed his Christian principles to inform his practice in business. Although he was constantly concerned with his employees' welfare, it was the disruption caused by the 1914 lock-out in the building trade which finally set him on the chain of ideas which culminated in the formation of the Building Guild.

The lock-out in the London building trade began ostensibly as a measure by the Master Builders to enforce their prerogative to employ non-union men at will, and as a condemnation of un- official strikes. Feeling in the building trade unions was already militant because of the general unrest over the fall in real wages and because of the stiffening attitudes of the employers, begin- ning with the Liverpool lock-out early in 1913. When the London Master Builders' Association (L.M.B.A.) required union executives to condemn unofficial strikes which 'infringed' the Working to Rule Agreement, the Bricklayers' representa- tives attending the joint meeting of employers and unions re- fused to give guarantees and were ordered to withdraw.[13] The employers countered this refusal with an ultimatum which the unionists considered 'completely insulting to the mentality of the entire trade-union leadership'.[14] Of more significance was the fact that this 'Memorandum' amounted to another mani- festation of the 'Document' which had dogged the history of the building trade since 1834.[15] Excuse for the presentation of the Memorandum was found in a dispute in which two electricians working on the site of the new Pearl Assurance Company offices in Holborn refused to join the union at the demand of others on the same site. The operatives at once downed tools, whereupon

[12] The address in Willesden of H. C. Cleaver Ltd.

[13] W. S. Hilton, *Foes to Tyranny* (1963), p. 200.

[14] *Ibid.* p. 201. This gives the text of the ultimatum issued to union executives.

[15] R. W. Postgate, *The Builders' History* (1923), p. 416 gives the 'Docu- ment' as presented to individual building-trade workers.

the members of the L.M.B.A. presented the Document.[16] After its automatic rejection a general lock-out followed from 24 January 1914. Subsequent details are of concern here only as they affected the thinking of Malcolm Sparkes.

For the first month or two of the strike, Sparkes's factory remained uninvolved since he had refused to proffer the L.M.B.A.'s five-point Memorandum. To Sparkes, the masters' demands undermined the whole principle of trade-union negotiation:

> A firm believer in the future of the Trade Union Movement and in the principle of collective bargaining by working under agreement, he resolutely declined to take any part in any attempt to undermine it.[17]

Just before Easter 1914, however, the unions issued a demand that all employers still staffed should immediately give up their membership of the Employers' Association or face a strike in the workshops.[18] Sparkes felt himself forced to resist this ultimatum since he regarded it as equivalent to a demand to employees to resign union membership, a demand which he had never made. In the resulting strike Sparkes contrived to keep the works going with a makeshift staff of foremen, apprentices, labourers, clerks and draughtsmen. But this was a threatening situation as the company was small and did not have large resources. Sparkes had every sympathy with the trade unionists, but he remained an employer and was forced to attempt the completion of his business orders. Since this involved the hiring of blackleg labour, the end result was union demands on Sparkes which proved

[16] The employers would probably have preferred to wait until slightly later in the winter when the weather might have been at its worst (Hilton, *op. cit.* p. 201). The original demand had required a reply by 5 January 1914 and when this was not forthcoming the L.M.B.A. announced, on 7 January 1914, that the Working to Rule Agreements were no longer in force. After this they sought only the excuse to precipitate the conflict.

[17] E. Sparkes, 'Life'. Mrs. Sparkes was primarily concerned with her husband's stand as a conscientious objector in the First World War, but the 'Life' also deals fairly comprehensively with her husband's connection with the Building Guild movement.

[18] This was probably in response to a continued demand by the employers that all matters under dispute should come before Conciliation Boards. (Hilton, *op. cit.* p. 205).

even more restrictive than those with which they were presenting other employers. There followed the episode which turned him definitely towards the search for a new industrial order.

The conditions had been presented by a delegation of the unions which left his office late after a long discussion. Leaving shortly afterwards himself, Sparkes was joined by one of his men who was reluctantly on strike. He went with this man to the station, where they boarded the train together, only to be faced by the whole of the union delegation, which immediately drew the false conclusion that Sparkes and the workman had been 'collaborating'. This resulted in a report to the union which accused the employee of having 'secret' meetings with Sparkes, causing the man extreme distress since he feared expulsion from the union and exclusion from work as a blackleg.

Sparkes was a man of such transparent integrity that it is easy to understand his bewilderment at this development. He sent a letter to the union disclaiming any arranged meetings and exonerating the workman from any 'guilt',[19] but further than this, he seems to have realised that in this particular instance the unions were so entrenched in the class war that there was no hope for the exercise of reason. He therefore offered twelve months' guaranteed employment to the man concerned and to any others who would return to work. Fruitless negotiations with the union were followed by the return of all the machine-shop men. Despite double picketing, the strike was broken; but only at the expense of expulsion for those workmen who had defied the union. Meanwhile, the general London stoppage continued and the National Federation of Building Trades Employers (N.F.B.T.E.) announced a national lock-out to begin on 15 August 1914. The outbreak of war on 4 August 1914 suspended the other, and, as it seemed at the time hardly less bitter, conflict.[20]

It has been necessary to set out some of the details of the London stoppage in order to clarify the image of Sparkes the

[19] M. Sparkes to F. P. Woodcock, 13 July 1914 (Sparkes MSS. H.U.L.).

[20] Hilton *op. cit.* p. 209. The tenacity of the building workers is not surprising in view of the threat to their livelihood and conditions in the previous years. With so much in the balance, the integrity of employers such as Sparkes was largely ignored and probably misunderstood. It was precisely this atmosphere of distrust which Sparkes found so depressing and so debilitating to any real progress.

man. Certainly by orthodox trade-union standards Sparkes had been at fault, but he was, emotionally, entirely on the side of the workers and the bitterness and hostility aroused at Park Royal and throughout the entire building trade had thoroughly depressed him. The depression had positive results, however, for the whole episode served to reinforce him in his growing belief that some other structure of relationships must be created not only for his own but for the whole of industry.[21] In this demand he was not very far removed from the 'romantic' image of the Guild Socialists, whose work he was soon to be studying keenly. But they differed entirely in the fact that Sparkes refused to accept the idea of the class war. To him this was a degrading and distorting theory which destroyed more than it made clear. Only real human relationships could matter. Men have 'a higher side to their natures which will respond to influences that have nothing to do with its so-called Laws'.[22]

Seeking to find the key to this 'higher side', Sparkes suggested, as early as 1914, the creation of a Federal Parliament of Industry to be elected by National Parliaments of Industry which in turn would be drawn from all trades:

> Their purpose would be re-organisation of the whole social structure for the service of humanity. Of course, there would be honest divergence of opinion, but there would be no class divisions.[23]

There are Guild analogies in these ideas, although Sparkes was still approaching the problem from the employers' standpoint.[24] But this was a fairly radical position for an employer. Not only did Sparkes wish to see complete co-operation rather than joint consultation. He wished also to abolish unemployment, to establish an international code of minimum conditions, to introduce a minimum wage, and to secure the seven-hour day, national

[21] Sparkes commented on 1914: 'The terrible futility of that struggle followed immediately by the still more terrible European war, have given me food for some of the hardest thinking I have ever done.' Hilton, *op. cit.* p. 216.

[22] E. Sparkes, 'Life'.

[23] *Ibid.*

[24] It is not suggested that Sparkes was entirely original in his ideas, although the idea for a 'Parliament', as such, was his own. Certainly he read the *New Age* assiduously.

standards for housing, child care and education and a number of other assorted social measures. Reforms of this type would be ratified by the Industrial Parliaments and by the government, and these minima once established, the industrial situation would then allow the development of more liberal ideas.[25] Although there was apparently no hope of spreading his ideas in the middle of a war which Sparkes as a Quaker opposed root and branch, he continued to extend and to develop them, and in 1916 an unexpected development in the industry encouraged an attempt at their dissemination.

In the February 1916 edition of the *Builder*[26] forewarning was given that the building trade unions intended to issue three months' notice of termination of working agreements with the Master Builders. Fearing a repetition of 1914, Sparkes saw this as an opportunity to put forward his scheme. But it was obvious that hostility to himself as an employer would vitiate any objective consideration of the proposals if he were to make them himself. He therefore contacted S. Stennet of the London District Management of the Amalgamated Society of Carpenters and Joiners. To Stennet he proposed that the unions should consider the scheme and, if it were acceptable, should themselves propose its adoption to the employers.[27] Despite the prevailing pessimism it was accepted. Within a week the London Committee of the A.S.C. & J. acceded, to be followed within the month by the N.F.B.T.E.,[28] the scheme having been presented by the Building Trades Council[29] and signed by representatives of most of the larger unions.

[25] The lecture from which this information is taken was given only to the local reading circle at Gerrard's Cross, in July 1914, but it illustrates the way in which Sparkes's thought was developing and indicates that he had already evolved his ideas fairly fully. This was long before he was given the chance to publicise a scheme which, in all probability, was the real origin of Whitley Councils.

[26] E. Sparkes, 'Life'.

[27] *Ibid.* Sparkes had written to Stennet on 9 March 1916 after first showing his draft to the foreman and some of the men at his factory. Neither he nor they had been hopeful of the outcome.

[28] Despite Sparkes's small hopes, the employers were enthusiastic, and Sparkes's proposals ran into four editions because of the N.F.B.T.E. demand alone.

[29] The National Associated Building Trades Council was a body inaugurated on 25 February 1915 primarily as a collection of building trade-union executives uniting to resist the implied opposition of the Building Workers' Industrial Union, a breakaway body formed just before the out-

The idea was to have even wider repercussions. In the December 1916 issue of the *Venturer*[30] Sparkes published an article on his 'Industrial Parliaments' which was later reissued as a pamphlet. J. H. Whitley saw this article and asked Sparkes for more details.[31] Since Whitley was Chairman of the newly formed Governmental Committee on Industrial Reconstruction, Sparkes was greatly interested and began the production of another memorandum. He was now employed by the Garton Foundation[32] after his resignation from H. C. Cleaver Ltd.[33] Because of his pacifist views he was living constantly under the threat of arrest – he had refused to register under the Military Service Act – yet he nevertheless continued with the preparation of the scheme. On 28 January 1917 he approved the final proofs of the special *Whitley Memorandum*.[34] The next day he was arrested as an absentee. He was to spend just over two years in Wandsworth and other prisons.

break of war in 1914 (Hilton, *op. cit.* p. 211). Ironically, the N.A.B.T.C. eventually developed into a body consciously seeking to foster the amalgamation tendency which had inspired the B.W.I.U. Its success was manifest in the formation of the National Federation of Building Trades Operatives (N.F.B.T.O.) on 5 February 1918. The N.F.B.T.O. plays a large part in the saga of the Building Guilds (*ibid.* ch. 20).

[30] The *Venturer*, 'A Monthly Journal of Christian Thought and Doctrine'. ran from October 1915 to September 1921.

[31] The exact sequence was that Whitley saw the article and questioned Arthur Greenwood, who wrote to Sparkes asking for details. Sparkes used this Government contact to explain his position apropos of the military and had the promise of help although nothing was finally achieved. Arthur Henderson refused to intervene on the grounds that the army needed men, reflecting the official Labour attitude towards the C.O. (A. Greenwood to M. Sparkes, 12 December 1916 (Sparkes MSS. H.U.L.). Whitley had first written on 9 December 1916; Sparkes to Greenwood, 12 December 1916).

[32] J. Hilton to M. Sparkes, 16 August 1916 (Sparkes MSS. H.U.L.). The Garton Foundation was set up in 1912 with the backing of Sir Richard Garton, to propagate the ideas which Norman Angell had publicised in *The Great Illusion*. It was primarily intended as a centre for the unbiased study of international relations. John Hilton (1880–1941) was the Foundation's first Acting Secretary (E. Nixon, *John Hilton* (1946), pp. 52 ff.; and see N. Angell, *After All* (1951), pp. 162 ff.).

[33] This was in July 1916 when the firm became 'controlled'. Sparkes ceased to have any contact with the firm from October 1916.

[34] The full text of the Whitley Memorandum can be seen in the Reckitt MSS. H.U.L. Its full title is 'A Memorandum on Industrial Self-Government (1917, 28 pp.). Reckitt MSS. is the title given to the microfilm of material made available to the writer by Maurice Reckitt. It is now in the Library of the University of Hull.

Sparkes utilised his period in prison to the fullest possible extent. Rather like an early Christian martyr, he looked on imprisonment as a form of testimony which could be turned to all sorts of positive advantage,[35] and he immediately began to plan the scheme which was to develop into the Building Guild after the War. In this he was perhaps prompted by the fact that he was associated in Wandsworth with a number of building workers who were also conscientious objectors. The idea was planned on scraps of paper which were passed at some risk from hand to hand. These were 'read and discussed under conditions of almost incredible difficulty. Slowly but surely it was hammered into shape and when the end of the War at last brought freedom, it was ready and waiting its opportunity.'[36] Wandsworth gave Sparkes time to think and to get through an astonishing amount of reading, despite official opposition. This is evident from letters to his wife,[37] with whom he discussed, among many other topics, the Industrial Parliaments scheme[38] and his slowly coagulating ideas on the formation of Building Guilds.[39]

It is clear from the correspondence that both Malcolm Sparkes and his wife had been considering Guild schemes before his imprisonment, and Sparkes saw his Industrial Parliaments as only a staging post on the way to the Guilds proper. Mrs. Sparkes played an important role in the discussion, and he constantly referred to the idea of 'constructive goodwill', a favourite phrase, as 'our' scheme. So in a letter of 31 May 1917 he discussed with his wife a scheme for a National Guild of Builders, Managers and Educationalists, which she had originally proposed. By the beginning of 1918 he was declaring, not for the first time:

[35] Evidence of E. Sparkes and Maurice Reckitt. They both comment that Sparkes's friends were amazed at the manner in which he took his imprisonment as a positive joy. For Sparkes, imprisonment was an essential nuisance, disturbing only in so far as it brought both emotional and economic distress to his wife and children.

[36] E. Sparkes, 'Life'.

[37] The prison letters which are appended to Mrs. Sparkes's 'Life' form an outstanding record of prevailing conditions, as well as of Sparkes's reactions (Sparkes MSS. H.U.L.: hereafter referred to as 'Letters').

[38] 'Letters', 17 May and 28 November 1917; 29 November 1918.

[39] *Ibid.* 31 May and 28 December 1917; 22 February 1918.

I am a keen National Guildsman. I am not, emphatically NOT, a state socialist or collectivist. I believe that the Industrial Parliament is going to be a short cut to the National Guild and that in the principles of constructive goodwill and voluntaryism we are going to discover the true road of Industrial Advance.[40]

By the next month a full plan for a Guild of Builders had been outlined. This ante-dates Hobson's scheme by a considerable time and although there is no proof of plagiarism, it is difficult not to imagine Hobson deriving many of his own ideas from Sparkes. Certainly it has been suggested that both Cole and Hobson 'picked Sparkes's brain on this',[41] and Cole had certainly visited Sparkes in prison on more than one occasion, doubtful though he was about the merits of the whole scheme.[42] Undeterred by this, Sparkes set about attempting to convert the Garton Foundation to a declaration for the Guild system. After writing to the Foundation's Secretary, John Hilton, he commented to his wife:

I've asked him [Hilton] to declare definitely for the Guildisation of Industry and for the Industrial Parliament Scheme as the road thereto. If he sends a copy ... will thou tell me what he thinks of it.... Hast thou joined the Labour Party? I am thinking that it might be right for us to join.[43]

[40] *Ibid.* 22 February 1918.
[41] Evidence of Sir Richard Coppock: interview, 11 April 1964.
[42] Sparkes had first seen Cole some time in May 1917, and there were subsequent visits. On two visits in 1918 ('Letters', 6 September and 1 November 1918) Cole had been dubious about the Building Guilds. Sparkes quotes him as saying 'I simply do not believe that you'll get people to do it.' Cole having claimed on another occasion that he lacked Sparkes's faith, Sparkes replied by letter: '... it really is no good you saying you suppose you lack my faith! No-one who had read *Self-Government in Industry* could ever admit that. The book simply abounds in Faith – it leaps out at one from a score of pages.' (Sparkes to Cole, Nuffield College, Cole Collection, N.G.L. Various Papers.) It should be emphasised that this essay is not accusing either Cole or Hobson of conscious plagiarism. Cole was never much in contact with the practical development of the Guilds, but he may well have discussed possibilities in theory with Hobson, in the light of his conversation with Sparkes.
[43] 'Letters', 15 November 1918.

The last statement shows how averse Sparkes was to doctrinaire ways of thinking about politics. National Guildsmen were not inclined to sympathy towards the Labour Party, which seemed too massively meliorist and collectivist. Sparkes himself was more concerned with aims than methods, and his lack of real political interest may have handicapped him in his relations with the National Guilds League. His primary concern was for industrial betterment and the establishment of fully functioning guilds.

But after his discharge from Wandsworth,[44] Sparkes was faced with the task of practical rather than theoretical organisation, and he concerned himself with creating conditions under which the whole scheme might be brought into existence. While maturing his plans he worked for six months for a publisher, producing in this time an anonymous pamphlet on the Industrial Parliament scheme for the Garton Foundation.[45] He was supported in the view that extensive basic planning was necessary by Thomas Foster,[46] with whom he had corresponded while still in prison. At this time Foster did not consider the scheme to be viable, especially since he could not see that the Builders' Industrial Parliament was either 'imaginative or sympathetic enough to consider it as practical politics'.[47] Foster's own *Report*[48] had recommended the conversion of the building industry into a self-governing body, and this gave added encouragement to Sparkes, who, in the autumn of 1919, put his scheme for a Building Guild before the London District Council of the N.F.B.T.O. Officials of this body were studying the plan with no great sense of urgency when the whole pace of events was accelerated by the formation of a Building Guild in Manchester.

[44] On 11 February 1919 (E. Sparkes, 'Life').

[45] Garton Foundation, *The Industrial Council for the Building Industry etc.* (1919, 153 pp.).

[46] Thomas Foster was an employer and President of the North Western Association of Master Builders. He had persuaded the Scottish trade unions to agree to the Industrial Parliament Scheme ('Letters', 29 November 1918).

[47] Sparkes to Cole, 26 September 1918 (Nuffield, Cole Collection, N.G.L. Various Papers).

[48] The Foster Report was addressed to the Industrial Council for the Building Industry. Its full title is *Organised Public Service in the Building Industry etc.* (1919, 12 pp.).

I I

As in London, the Manchester Guild was not formed without a considerable amount of preparation. S. G. Hobson has described how he began to consider the formation of a Guild when he was working in Manchester as a demobilisation officer.[49] Here, his general reflections on the social results of neglect and confusion in the field of housing enabled him to develop a constructive plan based on Guild theory. But he had little real influence either in business or in trade-union circles, and it was a largely fortuitous meeting with Richard Coppock[50] which brought him into contact with a power which might add reality to a vision as yet utopian.

It is necessary at this point to explain how and why Hobson became involved in this question. Both he and Sparkes had the bond of Quaker forebears in common, though they were at one in nothing else. The older man, Hobson, was born in 1870 in the village of Bessbrook, near Newry in County Down.[51] His parents were strict Quakers, the family having had a long and close association with the Society of Friends almost from its inception.[52] William Hobson, his father, became a plain Quaker in his teens, but in the early 1880s the family adopted modern dress and manners and their tone of life seems to have lightened when they migrated to England. The change may have been encouraged by Hobson's mother, a woman whose youthful lapses had included an addiction to the crinoline and who seems somewhat to have meliorated the austerity which came, by nature and inheritance, to his father.[53] In January 1880 Hobson was sent to the Friends' school at Saffron Walden and in 1883 he went on to Sidcot, in Somerset. Neither of these schools had a marked academic bias, and it seems that Hobson, who was frail as a

---

[49] S. G. Hobson, *Pilgrim to the Left* (1938), p. 212. Hobson had also been influenced by the Garden City movement and was involved in the establishment of Letchworth: see W. H. G. Armytage, *Heavens Below. Utopian Experiments in England* (1961), pp. 370 ff.

[50] Richard, later Sir Richard Coppock (b. 1885). Famous for his long tenure of the secretaryship of the N.F.B.T.O. In 1919 he was working in Manchester as Regional Organiser for the Operative Bricklayers' Society.

[51] Hobson, *op. cit.* p. 9. Bessbrook, like Jordans, near Beaconsfield, was founded as a Quaker village.

[52] *Ibid.* p. 16.

[53] *Ibid.* pp. 17–20.

child, was deliberately sent to schools with a less burdensome curriculum. At Sidcot he associated with Alfred Thorne, who later founded the Socialist Quaker Society, a body which was influenced by Guild Socialist ideas.[54] Also at Sidcot he came under the influence of the science master, Basil Megahy, an unavowed but suspected socialist. It was reading *The Origin of Species* from Megahy's library which set Hobson on the way to unbelief.[55]

Just missing a university scholarship which would have sent him into a medical career, Hobson went instead to an unspecified industrial job in Cardiff. With others of his generation he was strongly influenced by *Fabian Essays*, and in 1891 he joined the Fabian Society; he was a member of the Fabian Executive from 1900 to 1910.[56] He was also a foundation member of the I.L.P., retaining membership until 1905 and for a time serving as Hardie's secretary.[57] Indeed, in common with many other left-wingers of this time, Hobson remained a member of a multitude of socialist groups even after his own predilections became 'Marxist'. Publishing and speaking for the I.L.P. only drove him farther along the road which led from 'meliorism' to 'an attack on the wage system itself'. He was influenced in this by personal contact with Morris and Hyndman, but also by his own considered reactions to the Labour leaders of the period, in most of whom he discovered only power-seeking and self-interest.

The end result of this process was his association with the *New Age* and the contribution of his own gifts to Guild Socialist theory; a contribution which was probably the largest single influential factor on the younger generation, who attempted to develop it into a practical political force.

There was, however, something in Hobson which kept him

[54] *Ibid.* p. 22.

[55] *Ibid.* p. 23. Hobson was 'disassociated' by the Society some time in the early years of the twentieth century (*ibid.* p. 21).

[56] Hobson was increasingly concerned by the failure of socialism and the spread of gradualism within the Labour Party. His final breach with the Fabians came after the rejection of a motion put by him urging the Society to disaffiliate from the Labour Party in order to create an 'avowed Socialist party' (*ibid.* pp. 116 ff.).

[57] *Ibid.* pp. 45–54. Hobson mentions 'helping' Keir Hardie. It is his obituary which makes him Keir Hardie's secretary: *The Times*, 6 January 1940.

short of major political stature and influence. In part this was his habit of debunking without setting about the slow practical grind which might have produced a constructive improvement in politics. He himself analysed his main character fault as a failure to make a choice between idealism and opportunism. There is truth in this, but in common with his other confessions, it hints at exposure while revealing nothing. In practice, his life veered wildly between the two; and the later part of it discloses a succession of rather dubious financial deals.[58] Both his personal and his political life lie outside the scope of this essay, but it is relevant to mention that his common nickname was 'Soapy Sam'. It is apposite: his biography is full of bubbles, and he slips out of every situation which might provoke censure simply by rarely printing anything which could be called a fact. It is almost impossible, for instance, to trace his ways of making a living at any period of his life. What is certain is that these changed frequently and took him to many parts of the world.

But Hobson did have one asset which Sparkes did not possess – the advantage of a long and varied political apprenticeship which brought him into close association with rank-and-file trade unionists. Like Cole, he had an enviable flair, not common among the middle classes, for making contact with working men. Cole, however, has been described as a cool and intellectual platform speaker while Hobson was never this; and his euphoric optimism struck the note of the time when he began to propagandise the Building Guilds proper.

Hobson met Coppock when the latter called on Hobson officially to press for the demobilisation of building operatives.[59] Coppock was already noted for his energy,[60] and Hobson immediately saw in him the practical organiser through whom he might realise his schemes. He put the idea of a Guild to Coppock, who was at first extremely dubious.[61] As a young trade

[58] Information from the Reverend Arthur Peacock: interview, 6 July 1965.

[59] There was almost as acute a shortage of building workers as of houses, which raised the cry for 'dilution' in the building industry as it had been raised elsewhere during the War. The N.F.B.T.O. fought against this as it was later to fight, unsuccessfully, against wage cuts.

[60] Hilton, *op. cit*. p. 214.

[61] Coppock himself produced a memorandum on the negotiations preceding the formation of the Guild which forms the principal and possibly the most objective account (Hobson, *op. cit*. pp. 216–21). When Sir Richard Coppock was interviewed, early in 1964, he had little to add to it.

unionist, he was not convinced that Guild methods stood any chance against competition from organised business. But he was willing to listen, and to sound out his colleagues; and he soon became a keen supporter of the scheme until its imminent collapse threatened the finances of the N.F.B.T.O.

After propaganda among the trade unions, a meeting of the Manchester branch of the N.F.B.T.O., of which Coppock was Chairman, was called and here Hobson outlined the position; explained the principles of Guild organisation; and reassured the unions against doubts of the financial stability of the project. Concurrently Richard Coppock, as a member of the Housing Committee of Manchester City Council, began to consider that a Guild might be the solution to its massive housing problem. Further discussions prompted a conference of building trade unions in Manchester which set up a committee to consider the matter, and there followed a period of active propaganda by Hobson and Coppock throughout the north-western areas where smaller committees were instituted.

This activity culminated in a large-scale conference in January 1920, when representatives of most building trade unions in the Manchester area, together with men from all parts of the country, met in the Milton Hall, Deansgate. There, under the chairmanship of Richard Coppock, they gave unanimous approval to this resolution:

> That this meeting of Management, District and Branch Committees representing all the organised building workers of Manchester and District heartily approves of the Building Guild Committee and hereby pledges its support and agrees to nominate and elect a direct representative of each trade union on the Building Guild Committee.[62]

Nine days later the Provisional Committee met in the rooms of the trade council in Manchester and elected officers. Amid a general atmosphere of optimism and goodwill plans were made

[62] Manchester Building Guild, *Housing: A Way Out* (1920). This pamphlet covers the formation of the Building Guild Committee and was reprinted from articles which first appeared in the *Manchester Guardian*. It is undated, but a *Manchester Guardian* article bearing the same title was published on 14 January 1920. It makes it clear that negotiations were proceeding for some time before January 1920 (Reckitt MSS. H.U.L.).

to submit tenders to local authorities. The press, though guarded, was in the main favourable, the *Manchester Guardian* especially giving the Guild balanced coverage. Its leader of 14 January 1920 emphasised the importance of the scheme should it succeed:

> Much ... depends on the outcome of this single experiment. We trust that neither the government nor the Corporation will let either the novelty of the idea or the difficulty of adapting the administrative machine to its execution, put any unnecessary barriers in the way.

It was a well-voiced hope, for the Guild began with no advantages other than the Government Housing Act, and at the moment of foundation there was no guarantee that the Ministry of Health, then responsible for housing, would accept any proposition put forward by the Guild.[63] But press support was useful, and both the *Manchester Guardian* and the *Herald* continued enthusiastic.

It is clear from the press reports why there should have been such massive support for the Guild, the housing shortage was acute throughout the country, and there seemed little hope of a swift solution. Building workers, therefore, clutched at the Guild both as a possible immediate solution of the crisis and as the long-term answer to submerged creative impulses. Utopia once more reared its ambiguous head when an operative exclaimed:

> By an organisation such as this we again become master craftsmen. We are the oldest organised craft in the country, and if these proposals can be carried through, we shall lay more bricks than private enterprise dreams of.[64]

While the operatives waited in hope, Hobson was pressing Coppock to take over as General Manager of the Guild. Al-

[63] The Housing and Town Planning, etc. Act, 31 July 1919. The Act included clauses which eventually enabled the Guilds to take advantage of the financial aid offered.

[64] *Manchester Guardian*, 14 January 1920. This remark by an operative seems to support Malcolm Sparkes's remark in the 'Life' that rank-and-file trade unionists knew little of Guild theory but that they were quick to react to the practical idea when it was put forward.

though tempted, Coppock already had a demanding position as Regional Secretary for the N.F.B.T.O., and following the advice of trade-union friends – as well as his own conviction – he declined the offer. It was a decision which robbed the Guild of a much-needed professional, who had experience at every level from site work upwards and whose complete practicality would have more than counter-balanced Hobson's genial optimism in negotiation and administration. Coppock might, in the long term, have made the Guild economically viable if only by restricting the spread of its activities, since localisation represented basically the only possible way of carrying on Guild enterprises. However, he adhered to his decision, continuing as unpaid 'general consultant', with Hobson as the 'financial advisor' and Secretary of the Guild.[65]

Hobson was unable to work immediate miracles, and although the various trade unions subscribed £280[66] for foundation expenses, it was obvious that the Guild must either conquer swiftly or dissolve at once. He therefore submitted a tender for the Manchester Corporation Housing Scheme, a tender for 100 houses at £101,000. The Guild did not yet have so much as a permanent office,[67] and the consent of the Housing Committee was, in itself worthless until the Ministry of Health should agree to some form of legal contract for the Guild. Initially the proposition was put to Sir Thomas Robinson, described as acting in Lancashire as a 'sort of Super Housing Commissioner'.[68] His reaction was helpful, and members of the Guild Committee had two lengthy meetings with him, after which he agreed that the Guild should be able to tender on the same terms as other contractors, if the necessary legal entity could be ensured.[69] In consequence, the whole Guild idea was laid before the Minister

[65] Hobson, *op. cit.* p. 220.
[66] *Ibid.* p. 222.
[67] Hobson wrote '... we had neither ladder nor scaffolding: no manager, no foreman, no staff, no operatives; nor a penny of credit. And yet we sent in our tender like any old-established firm of contractors. Clearly we could go no further unless we had a contract, yet how to get a contract unless we were a going concern? My cousin [Harold Hobson] addressed the Housing Committee with the air of a millionaire. As indeed he was; for he had the labour of many millions behind him.' Hobson, *op. cit.* p. 222.
[68] *Manchester Guardian*, 14 January 1920. The Housing Act had divided Britain into regions each supervised by a Housing Commissioner.
[69] *Ibid.*

of Health. Negotiations on a form of contract were begun before
the end of January 1920 and were not concluded until July of
the same year.[70]

At the Ministry the Guild had the advantage of the favourable opinion of Raymond Unwin,[71] then Chief Architect to the
Ministry and already famous as one of the designers of Letchworth and of Hampstead Garden Suburb. Unwin was a convert
to Guild Socialism,[72] and both he and Dr. Addison[73] were sympathetic towards the Guild scheme. This did not noticeably
expedite negotiations, which were protracted until a memorandum, detailing the terms of contract allowed, was issued
by the Ministry in July.[74] Armed with this contract, the Guild
was able to offer solid assurances to the Co-operative Wholesale
Society, which till then had been reluctant to give unconditional
support to a body as yet untried and whose principles were
mostly at variance with those of the Society.[75] However, agreement was reached on 6 August 1920,[76] when a model contract,
based on the memorandum, was drawn up between the Ministry
of Health, the Building Guild Ltd. and the Co-operative Insurance Society.[77]

At this point the Building Guild may be said to have come
fully into existence as a factor in the government scheme, although local Guilds had been in existence and working for some
longer time. On 28 May 1920 work had started at Halifax, for

[70] *The Building Guild. It's Principles, Objects and Structure* (1921, 24 pp.).
[71] Sir Raymond Unwin (1863–1940).
[72] Hobson, *op. cit.* p. 223.
[73] Christopher Addison (1869–1951). Addison had a medical training and
was an academic before becoming a politician. He was the principal mover
behind the 1919 Housing Act and was concerned with it in his position as
Minister of Health from June 1919 until April 1921 when political expediency
prompted Lloyd George to oust him from the post.
[74] A copy of this memorandum is in the T.U.C. Library (Pamphlets, HD
9715).
[75] The C.W.S., as a consumers' association, could hardly fail to irritate
Hobson, who laid solid emphasis on the importance of the producer (*Building Guildsman*, No. 3 (February 1922), p. 35). The C.W.S. Bank had
refused to accommodate the Building Guild until it had assumed full legal
entity.
[76] The date appears in *The Building Guild. Its Principles ...* (1921).
[77] The Co-operative Insurance Society (C.I.S.) was used to insure the
Guild against possible losses on contracts. Negotiations had been preceded
by some fears on the part of the C.I.S. Committee, and details of their part
in the scheme were given in a memorandum issued on 20 July 1920.

example, where the local Building Guild took up an incomplete direct labour scheme which had been abandoned because of a labour shortage.[78] But the Guilds could not tolerate direct labour as a solution of the class problem. That implied only a change of master, not of principles; and the solution of the problem, seen as the only hope for the future, was the extension of the Building Guilds.

III

By now the London Guild had been formed. The appearance of the Manchester Guild encouraged the N.F.B.T.O. London officials to believe in the feasibility of a similar body being developed and organised by the workers themselves in the London region. Yet already they had a wider vision, and in February 1920 the Emergency Committee of the N.F.B.T.O. met to consider the formation of a Building Guild which it conceived as something which would eventually work on a national scale.[79] Further deliberation upon these ideas was abruptly shortened when the operatives sprang the initiative, as they had done in other parts of the country. In Walthamstow and Greenwich local branches of the N.F.B.T.O. organised their own Guild Committees and tendered for housing schemes to their respective councils. The councils were not unco-operative, but could offer no definite acceptances until the Guilds had somehow obtained legal recognition. It was this initial rank-and-file activity which provided the real impetus, as it had done at Manchester.[80] In consequence, resolutions were immediately placed before the London District Council of the N.F.B.T.O. by a number of trade-union branches in the London area.[81] A meeting of building trade workers was called for 28 April 1920, when a unanimous vote was given for the organisation of the London Guild of Builders under the management of Malcolm Sparkes.[82] Sparkes at once set about the preparation of a pros-

[78] *The Building Guild. Its Principles* ...

[79] *Manchester Guardian*, 17 February 1920.

[80] The earliest Guild Committees in the north had been organised after Hobson and Coppock had toured the north-western area groups of the N.F.B.T.O. (Hobson, *op. cit.* p. 218).

[81] Prospectus of the London Building Guild, *An Industry Cleared for Action* (May 1920, 6 pp.).

[82] *Ibid.*

pectus, which was issued in May 1920 with an accompanying leaflet signed by John Murrey, Secretary of the N.F.B.T.O., and a standard letter signed by Sparkes welcoming recruits to the Building Guild. The prospectus aroused immense enthusiasm and 20,000 copies were sold, the interest extending to many foreign countries.[83] Sparkes continued to stress the 'constructive' nature of the Guild; and the differing ideologies of London and Manchester – perhaps more correctly, of Sparkes and Manchester – were already prominent:

> Up in Manchester they are still talking about the class struggle and the abolition of the wage system; in London we talk of democratic control of a public service. We have psychology on our side, but as yet no history.[84]

From this time until the agreement between Manchester and the Ministry of Health in August 1920, there was an understandable lack of activity in the Guild movement. In May 1920 the C.W.S. made an offer of credit and an arrangement for buying materials which greatly strengthened the Guilds in negotiation with the Ministry.[85] Also in May the newly formed Architects' and Surveyors' Professional Union held its first Conference at Sheffield, where Arthur Penty was elected Chairman.[86] As an architect and first protagonist of a revived Guild system, Penty was extremely interested in this new demonstration of workers' control, but he could not see it promising a real breakthrough to industrial supremacy. Nor could its example be imitated by other industries:

> ... it [the Building Guild solution] obviously could not be applied to other, larger industries where immense fixed capital is required and where the market is not so easily localised.[87]

[83] E. Sparkes, 'Life', p. 239. The countries included the U.S.A., Germany, Holland, France, Norway, Sweden, Russia, Finland, Italy, Austria, Canada, New Zealand and Australia. South Africa alone took 1000 copies.

[84] *Ibid.*

[85] M. B. Reckitt and C. E. Bechhofer, *The Meaning of National Guilds* (2nd edn. 1920), p. 284.

[86] *Building News*, 4 June 1920. Arthur Penty (1875–1937) published *The Restoration of the Guild System* in 1906 and had a great, if unacknowledged, influence on A. R. Orage. He was the recognised leader of the 'medievalists' in the National Guilds League, but his influence was never extensive since he was largely non-political.

[87] A. J. Penty, *Guilds, Trade and Agriculture* (1921), p. 67.

In 1920, however, there was a dominant mood of optimism, and in London Sparkes was busily organising funds, initially from friends and acquaintances.

There was, however, a growing pressure for the amalgamation already suggested by the N.F.B.T.O. On 4 September 1920 a Conference of Building Guild Committees was held in Manchester, where the need for further centralisation was discussed. The result was a meeting on 9 October in Manchester where Harry Frankland, Chairman of the Manchester Guild, presided over 95 delegates, 48 representing Guild Committees, the remainder from local branches of the N.F.B.T.O. The conference expressed dissatisfaction over the tardy progress made with tenders and blamed this on the Ministry of Health because of its tendency to over-centralise the whole housing scheme. The natural solution, in Guild terms, was devolution, and the Conference passed a motion calling for the establishment of Regional Housing Councils which should have a more local membership, including representatives of the 'functional bodies concerned with building'.[88] Of greater importance was the recommendation of the assembly that there should be a national body to control materials; and a committee was formed to consider and report on a constitution for a National Guild. At this time contracts amounting to £66,000 had been signed, and further tenders for £3,000,000 accepted but not ratified.[89] There were murmurs of troubles with local authorities,[90] but largely the mood was still one of hope. Once everything was agreed with the Ministry of Health, the way lay clear for the acceptance of contracts. An initial twenty had been approved, the agreement stating that more might be allowed once the Guilds had proved the quality of their workmanship and their ability to complete on time.[91] The earliest contract signed was at Walthamstow on 20 October 1920. George Hicks[92] came down to cut the first

[88] 'Memorandum on Housing and the Building Guilds'. This was prepared by S. G. Hobson and presented to the Labour Party some time shortly after 9 October 1920 (Nuffield College, Cole Collection, Pamphlets 9).

[89] *Daily Herald,* 11 October 1920.

[90] 'Memorandum on Housing and the Building Guilds'. The memorandum also contains some of the first hints of opposition from the Master Builders.

[91] Transcript of meeting with the Minister of Health, 20 January 1921, where the promise was repeated (Sparkes MSS. H.U.L.).

[92] George Hicks (1879–1954), President of the N.F.B.T.O. 1920–40.

turf on 7 November, and on 18 June of the following year the first houses were formally opened.

IV

On 7 and 8 November 1920 a Reconstruction Committee of the Building Guild met in Manchester to discuss the amalgamation of the London and Manchester Guilds.[93] Negotiations were not rapid. The London Guild already had its first – and very large – contract and Sparkes could not unreservedly support amalgamation. Credit was good, and Sparkes had always envisaged a number of semi-autonomous units as the ideal Guild form in preference to one centralised unit. Nor was this the only reason for holding back. It is not clear when Sparkes first met Hobson, but it was probably some time late in 1919.[94] The important aspect of the relationship is that Sparkes did not care for Hobson and could not trust him; and in subsequent meetings Sparkes may well have shown this distrust, since he was quite incapable of dissembling. While Hobson had rejected his Quaker beliefs, Sparkes was a lifelong member of the Society of Friends and he maintained a tolerance and a faith in human nature which the other had rejected. In some respects it made him naïve where Hobson was realistic to the point of cynicism. Hobson constantly preached the class war while Sparkes just as firmly adhered to a belief in the reasonableness of man, and the two concepts brought them into opposite camps. But instinct apart, Hobson's lack of experience in the building trade may also have made Sparkes wary of a close legal association.

For the time, however, Sparkes put aside his doubts and co-operated, though his was probably the main influence which caused a revision of the provisional constitution to give greater recognition to the London Guild. In the re-draft, London became a Federation area with the Guild as the Regional Council. The revision came out of a conference between the Boards of

[93] 'First Draft Report of the Reconstruction Committee' (Nuffield College, Cole Collection, Pamphlets 9, File 2).

[94] Evidence of Mrs. Sparkes. She thinks it impossible that the two men would have met before the War since her husband only came into contact with Guildsmen after the beginning of his own interest in the Guild solution to industrial problems. This was during the War, and especially when he was imprisoned.

the Building Guild Ltd. and the Guild of Builders (London) Ltd. held in London on 16 February 1921. At this meeting both Sparkes and Hobson put forward amalgamation motions. Sparkes's motion was defeated, but both he and Hobson agreed on centralised credit arrangements. Hobson's own motion for amalgamation, carried after discussion, gave greater power to Central than to Regional Councils.[95]

By June 1921 plans for the amalgamation were well advanced, although the Building Guilds were by this time working under increasing difficulties. On 10 June a meeting of the representatives of the Building Guild Ltd. and the Guild of Builders (London) Ltd. was held at Guild House, Manchester. The meeting resolved to recommend the acceptance of the Maximum Sum Contract and the principles of the Guild Labour Contract, concluding with the resolution that both groups should raise a Guild Loan.[96] This underlined the increasing financial troubles which had accumulated with the ending of the first phase of the government scheme. Hopes that the building trade workers themselves would subscribe to the loan were quite unfulfilled, and difficulties increased after the end of July when the government summarily curtailed the Housing Scheme as it then existed because of its unanticipated expense.[97] This did not prevent the continuation of the amalgamation scheme, and a conference of all Guild Committees met in Manchester on 23 July 1921. Present were the Board of Directors of the Building Guild Ltd., the Reconstruction Committee and eighty delegates from all Area Committees. From a welter of resolutions, two were outstanding – the amalgamation motion, and a motion deploring the government's action in repudiating its pledge to provide adequate housing for the working classes. Amalgamation came with the simple declaration:

[95] Arrangements for the amalgamation were made by a Joint Reconstruction Committee set up at the November meeting: *Building Guildsman*, No. 1 (December 1921). Copies of this are at Nuffield College, Cole Collection, Pamphlets 9, File 1.

[96] Minutes of meeting (Nuffield College, Cole Collection, Pamphlets 9, File 3).

[97] The scheme was curtailed in July 1921 after the issue of the *Report of the Departmental Committee on the High Cost of Building Working Class Dwellings* (Cmd. 1447, 1921), pp. 32–3. For details of the 1919 Housing Act in practice, see M. Bowley, *Housing and the State* (1947), pp. 23–35.

That the Building Guild Ltd. and the Guild of Builders (London) Ltd., be herewith amalgamated.[98]

With this resolution the 'first National Building Guild in the history of the world came into being'.[99] Hobson had successfully engineered centralisation for the whole system, and complete workers' control may have seemed within the grasp of the entire building trade.

IV

The amalgamation marks the apogee of the Guild movement, but the success of Hobson's ambition came when the Guilds were already threatened from several quarters. By the end of 1920 the Master Builders had openly declared themselves against the Guilds. Earlier in the year property owners had protested against the Building Guild's demand for a pegged rent of ten shillings a week for working-class houses.[100] Private builders, too, feared the very real challenge offered by the Guilds, which, they felt, had obtained an unfair advantage in a contract which included the provision of £40 per house for continuous pay, one of the main tenets of Guild beliefs. This, it was argued, seriously endangered the solvency of builders, and it led directly to the resignation of Stephen Easten, O.B.E., from the post of Director of Production in Housing in the Ministry of Health.[101] Since he was also the President of the National Federation of Building Trade Employers, his resignation underlined a growing hostility. Easten argued that the Ministry was persistently ignoring expert advice and that the aid given to the Guilds was prodigal and unfair. Speaking at the 43rd Annual Conference of the Building Employers he attempted to prove, in a rather muddled argument, that the Guilds received unfairly varying

[98] *Building Guildsman*, No. 1, p. 10. This also contains the minutes of the conference.

[99] *Ibid.* But see this account for the meaning of 'amalgamation'.

[100] *Manchester Guardian*, 28 January 1920. The objection was raised by the Manchester, Salford and Counties Property Owners' Association, which also rejected the Building Guild demand for a continuation of the Rent Act of 1915.

[101] *Manchester Guardian*, 30 December 1920. Easten resigned on 29 December 1920.

profits on the saving which they might make on any house, neglecting to indicate that any saving made was to be shared between the Guild and the local authority. Private employers were forbidden to offer any inducements other than the standard rate, although the nature of the ban was not specified. The result was that workers 'naturally stampede from the ordinary contractor to the Guilds and their wasteful system'.[102] Easten concluded with a polemic against the building trade unions and a defence of the Master Builders, who had 'pledged themselves to do all in their power to forward housing production'.[103] The employers would unite in the fight for a livelihood. George Hicks replied for the operatives:

> Let me say for the Building Trade Operatives of this country that if the Municipalities will entrust their Housing to us and the Building Guilds, we will save them millions of money by a superior article and prove the fitness of labour for constructive government.[104]

Goodwill alone, however, could not counter growing pressures on the movement. On 13 January 1921 the Ministry of Health placed an embargo on further Guild contracts.[105] Under the first arrangement with the Ministry a maximum of twenty contracts had been agreed, four for London and sixteen for the remainder of the country. But by now even the first twenty had not been sanctioned. London had two and the rest of the country 'at the most a dozen'.[106] The embargo seemed a direct consequence of Easten's resignation,[107] and by removing the £40 and 6 per cent per house it placed the Guilds in a most difficult position. The Guild countered accusations of extravagance by pointing out that continuous pay accounted for less than 1 per cent of wages

---

[102] *43rd Annual Report of the National Federation of Building Trades Employers* (31 December 1920).

[103] *Manchester Guardian*, 30 December 1920.

[104] 'The Building Guild in London', pp. 13–14 (Sparkes MSS. H.U.L.).

[105] This was only on local authority building under the government scheme. Private contracts were a matter between buyer and Guild only.

[106] *Manchester Guardian*, 13 January 1921.

[107] *Ibid.* The *Manchester Guardian* certainly saw the embargo as part of a conscious attempt to curtail or stifle the Guild movement and saw it, too, as only the onset of a serious struggle in which employers would attempt a total defeat of the Guilds.

paid, and more detailed statements were published in the *Quarterly Report of the Manchester Building Guild*. The Guild obviously expected a fight with the employers, who, it was claimed, were 'forcing a press campaign against the Guild Movement'.[108]

On 20 January 1921 a deputation representing the London and Manchester Guilds met Addison to discuss the situation.[109] Hobson complained of a breach of faith over the number of contracts and Addison agreed that the number of twenty should stand. He hinted at the possibility of further contracts, emphasising that a 'satisfactory form of contract' would be needed. Guild representatives stressed the fact that they were not seeking to shelter under an artificial protection by asking Addison to devise a new form of contract which would not be open to the criticisms directed at the £40 agreement. And although the nature of the ban on employers offering continuous pay was not made clear, it is obvious that this charge, too, had hurt. Sparkes was seeking some resolution which might placate both employers and Guilds.[110]

Relations with the Ministry in no way improved. It seems probable that Addison had been influenced by the arguments of the Master Builders and that he considered the Guild contracts unfair. Certainly he could not then argue a need for economy in view of rising prices since he himself stated that prices in this period were falling.[111] Here he was misled, since although the tender prices of houses were falling, wholesale prices of building materials had yet to reach their peak.[112]

But contracts were still delayed, and complaints continued throughout the year.[113] In London Sparkes considered that the

---

[108] See also *Manchester Guardian*, 15 January 1921.

[109] The deputation was at the request of Sparkes, who wished to put forward the Guild reply to accusations made by the N.F.B.T.E. (Nuffield College, Cole Collection, Pamphlets 9, File 3).

[110] *Ibid.* Sparkes appended to the transcript of the meeting an amendment to clause 3 of the original contract which covered continuous pay. He hoped this amendment might be inserted in employers' contracts so that the Ministry might make it public that the bar of which the employers complained had now been dropped.

[111] C. Addison, *The Betrayal of the Slums* (1922), pp. 25–6.

[112] Bowley, *op. cit.* Appendix 11, Tables 4b and 4c.

[113] A tender accepted by Enfield Council for 100 houses with a possible extension to 232 was held up for lack of Ministry approval. At Greenwich, where the Guild had tendered for its fourth Council contract, the Mayor

best counter to the Ministry's excuses was to make every effort to prove the superiority of Guild houses, and he therefore pressed on with attempts to complete the Walthamstow and Greenwich contracts so that the real costs could be published. Cole apparently agreed with these ideas, which he had discussed with Sparkes.[114] But difficulties still continued and the Ministry embargo on a Guild contract at Heywood brought the matter into question in the House of Commons, where Sir Alfred Mond[115] replied that the contract had been rejected because, although the lowest, it was yet too high.[116] Sparks saw a double attack in this: firstly on the generally high level of prices and then, incidentally, on the Guilds. In a letter to Cole he commented:

> The real meaning of all this is that the Ministry has decided definitely to stop all housing contracts until the cost of building has fallen considerably below its present level.
>
> In so far as this would bring down the prices charged by the rings of building material suppliers it is a policy for which something might be said, but when its effects must be to restrict employment still further it begins to look as if it were part of a definite attack on wages.[117]

Despite protests from Sparkes the official blockade continued, while the Ministry pressed the Guild to accept a Lump Sum Contract which would cover cost, profit and the risk of loss. The principle of continuous pay would thus be dependent on the Lump Sum profit, which, because of see-sawing building costs, could not be reliable. A more vital objection lay in the fact that this form of contract would turn the Guild into a

---

thought that the Ministry was attempting to prevent work from being carried through. (Sparkes to Cole, 4 March 1921, Nuffield College, Cole Collection, Pamphlets 9, File 3).

[114] *Ibid.*

[115] Sir Alfred Mond, later Lord Melchett (1868–1930). He replaced Addison as Minister of Health on 1 April 1921.

[116] *Manchester Guardian*, 13 April 1921.

[117] Sparkes to Cole, 6 April 1921 (Nuffield College, Cole Collection, Pamphlets 9, File 3). Sparkes informed Cole that a tender for Enfield Council had been rejected even though it was the lowest submitted. The Council had been informed that no tender, even if lower than the Guild's would have been sanctioned.

'capitalistic institution'. It would cease to be a 'Labour organisation'.[118]

The Lump Sum Contract was rejected at a joint meeting of the two main Guilds held in Manchester on 9 and 10 June 1921. An alternative Maximum Sum Contract was agreed on, and a contingency fund established to cover any losses. One per cent of all contracts was to be paid into this fund and 5 per cent was to be saved from all or any savings on Maximum Sums. Half of the total was to go to the central fund, half to local funds.[119] Other technical matters were agreed, but the most significant and ominous inclusion was the decision to raise a Guild Loan. The sum decided on was £150,000, which was imperative for further expansion since, as the minutes point out, the Guilds were now to face stiffer competition for private contracts:

> The future of industrial control depends largely on us. If we succeed, an industrial revolution may be speedily achieved.[120]

The comment is apposite. Guild theorists tended to play down the part taken by the Building Guilds in the fight for industrial control. But the Guilds had had a huge success with the workers, more so than the intellectual National Guilds League, which suffered from the suspicion which had dogged the Fabian Society – that of being too middle-class for the ordinary trade unionist. This was not a feeling which members of the N.G.L. desired, and Cole in particular had always hoped that the League would, in part at any rate, contact those very people whom the Fabians would never attract. He was rewarded by the membership of a number of trade-union officials and working-class intellectuals, but the rank and file never came to the League in large numbers. The Building Guilds attracted both through their practical idealism and because they offered unusual conditions of employment not found elsewhere. The example of the Guilds had been taken up by other trades,

[118] *Future Forms of Guild Contract* (Manchester, 1921 8 pp.), p. 5. This pamphlet was issued by the Building Guild Ltd. on 27 June 1921. (Nuffield College, Bedford Collection, Box 2, File 11).
[119] Meeting at Guild House, Manchester, Minutes (Nuffield College, Cole Collection, Pamphlets 9, File 2).
[120] *Ibid.*

notably by engineering and furnishing workers, and it was obvious that any outstanding success might well snowball, especially when the militancy of the First World War was a very fresh inspiration. The current of industrial unionism was still present in the building industry,[121] and the bitterness of working-class antagonism was increasing as the country slipped towards the conditions of slump which in the end were to break this particular phase of the movement for workers' control.

Sensible of the dangers, both Sparkes and Hobson were eager to accumulate a sufficient sum of money to meet the problems of a period when they might need to fight it out with the private builders. It was not unnatural, therefore, that they should have turned to the N.F.B.T.O. The Federation was very much involved in the amalgamation movement and represented considerable wealth in its federated unions; and there was the natural expectation that building trade workers would be more susceptible to the appeal than those in any other industry.

On 16 August 1921 a meeting of the Emergency Committee of the N.F.B.T.O., then at Perth where the delegates were assembled for their Annual Conference, agreed to allow statements on behalf of the Guilds. In his presidential address George Hicks, himself a Guild Socialist, declared that the Guilds had evolved successfully despite attempts to impose an 'economic checkmate'. As a trade unionist, he emphasised that the Guilds recognised the principle of the 'full week'. Both Hobson and Sparkes then addressed the Conference, and a resolution was put calling for a conference of the General and Executive Councils of the affiliated unions to consider the matter of a loan.[122] This was not carried unquestioningly, since Hicks among others had already felt some unease at a meeting with the Guild representatives that morning, where, he claimed, he had felt himself to be at a directors' meeting. Hobson disclaimed any

[121] N.F.B.T.O., Minutes of Emergency Committee, 10 and 11 May 1921. At this meeting a letter was read from the Amalgamated Union of Building Trades Workers explaining a motion from the Plymouth branch which called on the Council of the A.U.B.T.W. to 'approach all executives of the building industry with a view to setting up a national propaganda campaign whose object shall be one union and one card for the whole of the building industry recognising the emancipation of the workers from wage-slavery'. The A.U.B.T.W. endorsed these sentiments and passed them on to the N.F.B.T.O. See also N.F.B.T.O., *Minute Books* (1921–2), p. 61.
[122] N.F.B.T.O. Minutes.

'capitalistic' tendencies, emphasising his devotion to Guild ideas. The motion for a loan was then put to the meeting and carried unanimously. From now until late in 1922 negotiations were continued with the N.F.B.T.O., and on these Hobson in particular began to pin greater hopes than either the statements or the actions of the N.F.B.T.O. justified.

Official relations with the Federation had been first initiated on 27 January 1921. It was at this meeting of the Guild Committees and the N.F.B.T.O. Executive that the idea of amalgamation was originally discussed. There followed a meeting presided over by George Hicks at which he stressed that a Guild was not, in itself, a total solution to the problems of the working class. The real need was for a radically new social order:

> We cannot get our political freedom until we get our industrial freedom: it is impossible to get one without the other.[123]

No appeal for money was made at this meeting, but by June 1921 Sparkes was writing with a request for £500–£1000 towards the new Guild joinery works which were being built at Paddington. After some opposition the motion for a loan was carried,[124] and on 16 August, immediately before the Perth meeting, Sparkes reported on the progress of the new works.[125] After the request for a loan for the National Guild, protracted negotiations ensued at a meeting between the Executive and General Councils of the N.F.B.T.O. and the Guild in Manchester.[126] Hobson claimed that the Guild was in a healthy financial position, but that it was facing financial difficulties through the intransigent attitude of the C.W.S. Bank, which refused to extend credits. Both Sparkes and Hobson emphasised the possibilities of the Guild and even Hicks referred to the Guild idea as 'revolutionary'. The motion was considered on 14 September but, although passed, it remained conditional. By 15 November

---

[123] 'Transcript of Negotiations with the National Building Guild Ltd.' N.F.B.T.O., *Circular Letters* (1923), ii, pp. 58 ff. The Transcript covers the whole period of association between the two bodies.
[124] N.F.B.T.O. Minutes, 1 and 2 June 1921.
[125] *Ibid.*
[126] N.F.B.T.O. Minutes, 25 and 26 October 1921.

1921, the date of the executive meeting held to consider details of the loan,[127] various unions had denied aid to the Guild.[128]

At this November executive meeting the idea of a Penny Levy to be added to the standard trade-union contribution was put forward to the assembled members. The subsequent development of misunderstanding between the N.F.B.T.O. and the Guilds was more than anything else concerned with this levy. Possibly as a result of a misconception on the part of the Guild leaders, the idea was fostered that the levy was to help only the Guild. It is not known how much of the discussion in the executive meeting was disclosed to the directors of the Guild, but it is clearly stated in the minutes that the levy was to accumulate a fund not only to aid the Guild but also to consolidate the N.F.B.T.O. into a more effective fighting force. Unemployment in general was rising and a warning of a further decline in employment had already come with the cessation of the government housing scheme. The Federation naturally saw its first responsibility as being towards its own members; Hobson and Sparkes took the longer view that their own scheme offered a real hope for complete industrial control. The caution of the Federation eventually triumphed over its avowed leanings towards industrial democracy, but meanwhile the meeting, after considerable argument hinging on the possible confusion arising from the bracketing of Federation affairs with specifically Guild affairs, passed a motion which allowed an extra penny to be added to members' contributions, 'half of the total extra sum to go to the Building Guild Ltd'.[129] Proceeds were to be deposited with the C.W.S. and administered as a trust fund.[130]

---

[127] *Ibid.* The motion makes it clear that some part of the intentions of the N.F.T.B.O. had been to act as guarantor of the Guild. It reads: '*That* we welcome the introduction of a National Building Guild, and pledge ourselves as units of the N.F.B.T.O. to advise our respective unions, within certain limits, to stand as financial guarantors of the National Building Guild. The details and extent of such a guarantee to be worked out by the Emergency Committee of our Federation, and the same to be submitted to a further meeting of the Joint General and Executive Councils to be called at an early date.'

[128] N.F.B.T.O. Minutes, 8, 9 and 15 November 1921.

[129] *Ibid.* 15 November 1921.

[130] *Ibid.* There are parallel trends of Guild Socialism and industrial unionism involved here. The meeting made it clear that it was the wish of the members of the N.F.B.T.O. that the Federation should be co-ordinated into an effective fighting force in order to initiate a special strike which would

The Executive of the N.F.B.T.O. then appointed a deputation which met the Manager of the C.W.S. Bank in Manchester, having previously seen the directors of the Building Guild. The Manager, Goodwin, could offer no optimistic news since the Guild was running a large overdraft. Nevertheless, it was argued that the affiliated unions of the N.F.B.T.O. should act as guarantors, should this become necessary, while the Guild agreed to accept representatives of the Federation as trustees. Since the industrial situation was continuing to worsen and an attack on hours was imminent, it may have been that the N.F.B.T.O. chose to ignore the overdraft in the hope that the Guild might attain sufficient strength to support the Federation in an eventual confrontation with the employers. It agreed, therefore, in January 1922, to guarantee the Manchester Guild up to £5000, and a circular letter was issued on 2 February suggesting the amounts needed from each union and giving a detailed breakdown of costs. In return for this support, the Guild was to supply weekly accounts to the N.F.B.T.O. giving accurate data on the current financial position.[132] The next day a meeting of the Special Purposes Committee of the Executive Council investigated the possibility of the Guild offering aid in a current threat against the 44-hour week.[133] It was decided:

> That a sub-committee be elected to at once enter into conversations with the Building Guild to see how far its machinery and industrial capacity are capable of rendering assistance to the Building Trade Operatives to defend the principle of the 44 hour week.[134]

The resolution indicates that the Building Guild was still regarded as an organisation with considerable potential, a belief that was soon to be shattered.

---

help to increase the striking power of the Federation. Accordingly, the levy was also to help in this plan.

[131] 'Transcript of Negotiations . . .' *loc. cit.*

[132] There is no evidence that this was ever done.

[133] The N.F.B.T.O. had successfully negotiated a country-wide 44-hour week from 1 May 1920. By 1921 this agreement was under attack and in May only long argument between Hicks and the Wages and Conditions Council prevented any attrition of the position already gained. Longer hours were eventually reimposed in August 1924. (Hilton, *op. cit.* pp. 225–31).

[134] N.F.B.T.O. Minutes, 3 February 1921.

The earliest intimation of trouble came with a request from Hobson that the N.F.B.T.O. appoint trustees for the plant and assets of the Building Guild Ltd. Assent was given and trustees elected,[135] since this was in accord with the earlier agreement; but evidence was later to be given that the trustees were devoid of power. It was later made clear that the £5000 already voted to the Guild had been used only to cover expenses. The Guild was 'in a very serious position in consequence' and the C.W.S. was, in effect, demanding repayment.[136] This did not yet ring serious alarms since the Federation was expecting an affirmation of support for the levy from the affiliated unions. When the figures were published in March 1922 this hope seemed massively vindicated, with a majority in favour of 27,341 out of a total vote of 82,463;[137] a decision which proved little more than a paper victory since the levy never came in at the anticipated rate. Even had it done so, it could hardly have saved the Guild, which was now in a desperate financial position. Seeking to save it, Hobson seems to have seen the completion of amalgamation as a hopeful measure which might improve credit.

Although consent for amalgamation had been given at the July 1921 meeting of the Joint Reconstruction Committee, the ostensible merger did not take place until some time later.[138] The first National Board of the Guild met on 28 November 1921, when officers were elected and certain decisions taken concerning the Guild loan.[139] Malcolm Sparkes was not elected, although he was given the position of a trustee of the loan. The omission may have been due to the influence of Hobson, who was always antagonistic to Sparkes. But Sparkes was not always trusted even in his own sphere, the doubt almost certainly arising because of his former position in the industrial world. And since Hobson was the more popular man with the rank and file, it is probable that members of the London Committee were conscious of Sparkes's mistrust of him and resented it. Added to

---

[135] N.F.B.T.O. Minutes, 16 and 17 February 1921.

[136] *Circular Letters*, 20 February 1922. Coppock, writing to all General Secretaries of affiliated unions, made it clear that the C.W.S. Bank was becoming impatient with the situation.

[137] *Ibid.* 55,902 For; 26,561 Against.

[138] See below, p. 319.

[139] *Building Guildesman*, No. 1 (December 1921). This gives details of the membership of the Board.

this was a more recent grievance, since Sparkes had moved that London should withdraw from the amalgamation consequent on the National Guild appealing for funds to the N.F.B.T.O. He saw this as a threat to the whole movement and sought to save London from the imminent débâcle by reassuming autonomous status. The move failed, and he was forced to preside over the final negotiations for amalgamation which at last took place as from 1 April 1922.[140]

All Fools' Day seems a suitable choice for so hopeless a merger. The position of the amalgamated Guild was worsening almost daily although, in the first issue of the *Building Guildsman*,[141] Hobson had used much space to publicise the Guild Loan and to detail the numbers of Guild Committees. Although on paper the number of Committees, at 120 looked impressive, many of these existed in name only. By June 1922 their number had risen to 140. The reasons for the growth are probably those which are associated with the decline of the whole movement. This, as we have seen, was a period of shrinking employment, and in such conditions co-operative enterprise is not uncommon, if rarely successful.[142] It is not surprising to find many Guild Committees moribund through lack of work, and in May 1922 only 70 were actually working, with contracts totalling nearly £3,000,000.[143]

Living in daily contact with these developments, Sparkes and Barham took fright. In an attempt to salvage London, they prepared and issued a plan which proved to be the final provocation which decided Hobson to get rid of Sparkes.[144] The plan, a 'Scheme for the Re-Organisation of the National Building

---

[140] *Ibid.* No. 4, p. 64.

[141] Issued December 1921.

[142] See, for example, the earlier co-operative building experiments detailed in S. Higenbottom, *Our Society's History* (1939), pp. 148–56.

[143] *Building Guildsman*, No. 5 (May 1922). It is doubtful if the figure of £3,000,000 can be relied on since even Guildsmen knew the figures from area offices were quite unreliable.

[144] Sparkes and Barham seem finally to have decided on their move after a meeting, on 18 May 1922, of the Council of the National Building Guild Ltd. where Hobson stated that the N.F.B.T.O. had already loaned £2000 and that he hoped for more. Sparkes later learnt that the actual sum borrowed was £10,000, reinforcing his suspicion that Hobson's financial dealings were unreliable. He seems to have been convinced, too, at this special meeting of the Council, of Hobson's hostility towards him.

Guild Ltd.', was issued in May 1922.[145] In itself this would have been enough to provoke Hobson, but the matter was made worse when he discovered its existence only in a roundabout way. This was not in fact intended, but the damage was done, although Sparkes at one point thought of the incident as 'closed'.[146] He was quite wrong, since Hobson countered Sparkes's scheme for further devolution with a plan which was obviously aimed at ousting Sparkes from the movement. Hobson suggested the re-organisation of the London Region by setting up ten offices in place of the existing one.[147] Sparkes knew this offered no real economy and saw the whole scheme as a move to eliminate himself and Barham. Both were threatened with a 50 per cent reduction in salary or dismissal on refusal. No other officials were offered the same terms and, refusing, they were dismissed.[148] Since the London Guild went on to produce its own scheme for an independent conference in the London area at which proposals remarkably similar to those of Sparkes were put forward, it seems possible that members of the London Committee were as eager as Hobson to see Sparkes go. The new plans included the resumption of separate legal entity for London. This was assumed on 15 July 1922, the date of the conference.[149] It had never really lapsed since the deed of transfer had not been signed, but now it again became a matter of working fact.[150]

The subsequent squabbles about the blame for what had hap-

[145] The 'Scheme' was issued on 26 May 1922 (Friends' House Library, Sparkes MSS. cxlvi, File 1). A covering letter for the scheme can be found in the Reckitt MSS. H.U.L.

[146] Sparkes to Cole, 9 June 1922 (Nuffield College, Cole Collection, Pamphlets 9, File 3). Hobson discovered the scheme through the Solicitor of the N.F.B.T.O., who had given a copy to Coppock. He, in turn, referred to it in public before a copy had reached Hobson.

[147] The evidence for most of the following section is from the 'Verbatim Report of a Conference Between the Emergency Committee of the National Federation of Building Trade Operatives and the Representatives of the National Building Guild' (2 and 3 November 1922). Hereafter referred to as the 'Verbatim Report' (Nuffield College, Cole Collection, Pamphlets 9, File 8; there is also a copy at the headquarters of the N.F.B.T.O. in Cedars Road, Clapham).

[148] On 21 July 1922 (Friends' House Library, Sparkes MSS. cxlvi, File 1).

[149] H. Barham and M. Sparkes, 'The Case for Enquiry' (after 17 July 1922) (Reckitt MSS. H.U.L.).

[150] *Ibid*. The conference also passed resolutions in favour of Sparkes's proposals for reorganisation; a reasonable proof that these had not been capricious.

pened can only have done the dying movement harm. Although Sparkes had reached a point where he felt he must clarify his motives,[151] something for which he felt an acute distaste, yet he seems not to have benefited by his subsequent vindication. It was, in fact, his pamphlet which provoked the final chaos. A meeting of the Committee of the National Guilds Council[152] passed a resolution calling for a full and impartial inquiry into the circumstances of the dismissals and of the Guilds' decline.[153] In September the N.F.B.T.O. decided that an inquiry was justified and put in hand the arrangements for a conference to be held in Manchester on 2 and 3 November. The background to this conference, however, involves not only the relationship of Sparkes with the N.F.B.T.O. but also that of the National Guild and the Federation.

Doubts on the viability of the Guilds had inevitably been growing for some time. An N.F.B.T.O. circular of 20 April made it clear that some form of crisis had come upon the National Guild,[154] and on 2 May a letter – 'strictly private and confidential' – went out to the members of the Emergency Committee of the N.F.B.T.O. This discussed the action to be taken, still suggesting that support might be given the Guild if this seemed suitable. The Manager of the C.W.S. Bank had already discussed the position of the Guild at length and emphasised that the Bank could do little more for it unless some form of collateral security were offered.[155] This the Federation could not do, and further discussions made it clear that the Manager was passing on the decisions of his Directors. The conditions they laid down for any transactions were that each associated society

[151] *Ibid.* The pamphlet details the decline of relations between the Guilds and the events which led up to the dismissal of Barham and Sparkes.

[152] The National Guilds Council came fully into being, under the aegis of the National Guilds League, in April 1922. It had first been mooted in February of the same year, and its purpose was to promote active contact with the trade unions. Its initial inspiration had been individual Guild Committees set up by the building workers. (Nuffield College, Bedford Collection, Box 1, File 6.)

[153] N.G.C. Minutes, 1 August 1922 (Nuffield College, Bedford Collection).

[154] N.F.B.T.O., *Circular Letters*, 20 April 1922. The crisis is mentioned here and a meeting to consider it was called for 26 April 1922. Minutes of this meeting of the Emergency Committee of the N.F.B.T.O. have disappeared.

[155] *Ibid.* 27 April 1922, report of deputation to the Manager of the C.W.S. Bank.

of the N.F.B.T.O. should put down a cash security in anticipation of the levy. Not only was this impossible but it was now made clear that the Guild was in an even worse plight than the representatives had anticipated. Guarantees amounting to £9000 had been given by the Guild to the Bank, but withdrawals were in excess of this by £1000. In addition, the Guild was demanding £3800 to meet only that week's expenses. The Emergency Committee was obviously concerned and emphasised that it was unable to continue support for the Guild while it remained in so dubious a condition.[156] In effect, all progress was suspended until production of an auditor's report on 16 May 1922.

The report vindicated only to condemn.[157] While the accountant could discover no real abuses, he revealed a great deal of neglect. Returns from Area Committees were quite incomplete and none of the figures were based on audited accounts. There was a possibility that existing plant and machinery could be utilised to keep things ticking over, but the existing figures did not present a strong enough case for obtaining any sort of aid from bankers. Representations of this sort would have to await complete accounts due in June, but there were doubts of any hope with these.

It was a long and detailed report, which discussed various possibilities at some length. It led to a conference on 25 May 1922 at the Y.M.C.A. in London between the Emergency Committee and Guild representatives. Here it was made clear that the total amount of money which the associated unions were willing to pledge was very far short of the £150,000 for which Hobson had hoped. Furthermore, the N.F.B.T.O. had already gone beyond the limits of its authority in paying sums of money to the Guild, then amounting to £8000.[158] Faced with this, Hobson could still utter an appeal for £3750 in addition to the £1000 to meet the current wage bill. Coppock refused, but he requested the Federation's solicitor, W. H. Thompson,[159] to

[156] *Ibid.* 2 May 1922.

[157] 'Report of Mr. T. W. Collins, Chartered Accountant, to the National Federation of Building Trade Operatives on the Financial Affairs of the National Building Guild Ltd., as at 30 April 1922', *ibid.* (1922).

[158] *Ibid.* 23 May 1922.

[159] W. H. Thompson was also a Guild Socialist and later the husband of Joan Beauchamp, for many years Secretary of the National Guilds League.

draw up debentures for £8000, although Thompson regarded this as a dangerous procedure because of the serious position the Guild was in with the Bank.

A situation was developing in which loyalty to the N.F.B.T.O. demanded a demonstration of financial stability which the Guild was unable to make. And at this point in time there occurred the friction between the two main Guilds which precipitated the dismissal of Barham and Sparkes. Ostensibly these economies were effected because Hobson believed that London persistently allowed too high a percentage for overhead charges, but the campaign only resulted in bad publicity for the whole Guild idea. Through all this the N.F.B.T.O. remained loyal, even providing another opportunity for explanation before the Annual Conference of August 1922. Hobson here emphasised that the dismissals were 'incidental' and that the Guilds had as their focus the relationship with the Federation. He ended with a calculated appeal:

> He concluded by earnestly asking for the goodwill of the Federation with a view of ultimate industrial control, as he felt sure it would strengthen the hands of the Trade Unions in the struggle in which they are at present engaged.[160]

The Federation, however now showed itself seriously alarmed and ignored the appeal. The meeting with Hobson resulted in a decision to set up a Committee of Inquiry to consider the position, this body to be the full Emergency Committee.[161] In the meantime, the C.W.S. Bank was approached with a request for the redemption of the Federation's guarantees to the Guild. Later arrangements were put in hand for the November Conference, the results of which were to be considered at a meeting of the Executive Council of the Federation on 8 November 1922.[162]

[160] N.F.B.T.O. Minutes, 1922; meeting of the Emergency Committee at Bangor, 15 August 1922.
[161] *Ibid.* 12 and 13 September 1922.
[162] N.F.B.T.O., *Circular Letters* (1922). i, p. 177.

V

The November Conference confirmed the suspicions of the N.F.B.T.O. Executive and revealed the complete disintegration of the National Guild. The long 'Verbatim Report'[163] provided detail which can only be briefly summarised here; and it underlined the fact that there had been a history of evasion by Hobson in all his relations with the N.F.B.T.O. Special emphasis was laid on the dispute which led to the dismissal of Barham and Sparkes and the effect which this had on the standing of the Guild in London and on the movement in general. The chief importance of the report lay in its discussion of the expected and actual amount of support given by the N.F.B.T.O. to the Guild. It became quite clear that Hobson had not only allowed himself to see the Federation as a perpetual guarantor, but had deliberately persuaded other members of the staff that this was the Federation's explicit wish.

It is difficult to understand why Hobson should have done this. He was, obviously, tremendously keen on the Guild idea and, though their motives differed, no less enthusiastic than Sparkes. Naturally, as an early advocate of Guild Socialism he was eager to see the fruition of his ideas; but he was also of a type which demands unnaturally rapid results. With the Guild as his life, he defeated achievement by over-reaching himslf. In so far as he alone was involved personally, this was regrettable, but where it involved others, as of course it did, his irresponsibility was considerable, since his influence was far-reaching. Evidence given at the Conference made it clear that one of the basic faults of the movement was a mushroom growth which overwhelmed organisation. Accounts, kept by inexperienced men, had been haphazard, and until the formation of a National Committee both the central and local Guilds were allowed to negotiate their own overdrafts. Considerable financial confusion had therefore already developed prior to the organisation of the National Guild. Mounting difficulties were ascribed to lack of capital, even though the total amount which had been loaned to the Guild came to £100,000; this was money which had come in piecemeal, whose effect was diminished by the fact that £25,000 had been paid out in retention money. Lack of

[163] See p. 320, n. 147.

capital inhibited expansion, and the Guild Building Society[164] had been set up in an attempt to deal with the problem. So far the explanations were plausible, but Hobson's rationale of events began to break down over the question of the Sparkes–Barham dismissal. Despite the fact that it would seem that Sparkes's own optimism over the Federation Levy had helped to lose him the support of the London Guild, it is obvious that N.F.B.T.O. sympathies remained largely with him. When the London Guild claimed that it had been damaged by the Sparkes–Barham letter, Coppock commented;

> You had better be careful. You see, if a communication of this character signed by Mr. Barham and Mr. Sparkes has ruined you, or has affected you seriously, then the whole of your clients must rest upon the abilities or otherwise, of Mr. Sparkes.[165]

The point of the Federation's position once raised, both Coppock and Hicks made it plain that they and their Committee were extremely sympathetic towards the Guild idea and had become more so when Barham had convinced them that the Guild could be solvent.[166] But they had made no real offer to stand as guarantors to the London Guild:

> We said we were prepared to take part in any movement which would bring about the solidarity of the Guild. It is probably upon that that our optimistic friend Mr. Sparkes would seize and magnify.[167]

It was then made clear that the Federation had never offered the large amount of funds which both Hobson and Sparkes seem to have expected. Hobson, too, had been warned early in 1922 that the Federation Levy could not bring in the anticipated amount, but despite this he had gone ahead with projects or had continued to imply that money would be supplied by the N.F.B.T.O. By the time of the Conference the National Guild

---

[164] 'Verbatim Report', p. 9. The client was to provide one-third of the required amount in cash.
[165] *Ibid.* p. 85.
[166] *Ibid.* p. 88.
[167] Coppock, *ibid.* p. 89.

was at least £30,000 in debt,[168] and Harold Hobson[169] stressed its obligation to the many small investors who had entrusted vital sums of £50 to £200 because of their faith in the Guild. He therefore sought further N.F.B.T.O. help, without which he could only see collapse.

The Federation, weary of S. G. Hobson's tactics, made it plain that the extent of the Guild's embarrassment was the new discovery of the Conference. Even now, however, S. G. Hobson could not or would not realise that the scheme was ending. He insisted that it was almost the duty of the Federation to back the Guild. When Hicks explained that Hobson misunderstood the uses of the N.F.B.T.O., Hobson replied that it was their business to find business. Hicks countered with a classic definition of the trade-union function, emphasising that the Federation had got near to the point of exceeding its legal rights in aiding the Guild.[170] Added to this, he remarked, the Federation's finances were in a poor state. The growing hostility of members and the failure of the Guilds would lead to demands for retrenchment, but this did not imply that the ideals had become distasteful. When he was accused of hostility to the Guilds, Hicks replied sharply:

I have preached the Guild. Do not preach that to me. It is a question of a desperate struggle as far as finance is concerned, not ideology. I have been trying to get some understanding about the economic side of the question with our chaps. They tell me I have got cold feet. I could see and everybody could see, we were bound to get this difficulty at some time or another.[171]

The conclusion he drew was that the National Guild had fostered a deliberate attempt to make the Federation responsible for 'its failure or success'. When Hobson denied that any attempt had been made to compromise the N.F.B.T.O. Hicks accepted the explanation, but the acceptance was delivered in

[168] *Ibid.* p. 94.
[169] Harold Hobson was S. G. Hobson's cousin and a qualified Quantity Surveyor. He worked in this capacity for the Building Guild. See S. G. Hobson, *op. cit.* p. 221.
[170] 'Verbatim Report', p. 100.
[171] *Ibid.* p. 102.

such formal terms that suspicion remained.[172] Arrangements were made for Hobson to be present at an executive meeting to consider the position in detail, and the conference closed. It was known by now that the C.W.S. Bank was threatening to put in a Receiver.[173]

On 8 November 1922 the Executive Council met at Federal House to consider the report. After discussion Hobson and other members of the Guild spoke to the meeting. Only a Resolution and a Statement survive. The Resolution moved, surprisingly, for some further support for the Guild if suitable assurances could be given. But this decision was at once suspended while the Committee withdrew to 'consider the position in the light of information which had come to hand in the course of the day'.[174] The new information supplied could only have revealed further chaos, since the long Statement refused further support and called for an independent inquiry into the position of the National Guild. It also completely vindicated Sparkes and Barham, details of the affair subsequently being published in a letter issued to the National Union of Clerks and the Amalgamated Society of Woodworkers, respectively the unions of the two men. This endorsed their Report and corroborated their accusations of hostility from Manchester. It also claimed that the Sparkes–Barham scheme might have salvaged the London Guild. It concluded:

That the statements made by Barham and Sparkes to the Committee concerning the financial mismanagement of the National Building Guild Ltd. and the circumstances leading up to their dismissal were correct at every point and were not even contradicted by the Guild representatives.[175]

Even at this moment, Hobson was not able to grasp that the affair was at an end, at least in relation to the N.F.B.T.O. Some time later in November he asked the Federation for £50,000.[176]

[172] *Ibid.* p. 103. Hicks replied to Hobson's justification: 'I am pleased to have that assurance.'

[173] 'Transcript of Negotiations . . .', *loc. cit.*

[174] N.F.B.T.O. Minutes, 8 November 1922.

[175] The origin of this letter lay in a request from Sparkes for some form of vindication: N.F.B.T.O., *Circular Letters* (1922), pp. 223 ff.

[176] 'Transcript of Negotiations . . .', *loc. cit.* Coppock comments on this immediately after giving details of the November Inquiry. It is apparent that

This was refused, and the Federation continued its attempt to sort out affairs with the C.W.S. Bank. Before serious negotiations could begin a Receiver was appointed to wind up the affairs of the National Building Guild. In the interim, the guarantees of the affiliated societies had been redeemed from the Bank and the Federation continued to consider the 'Verbatim Report' and to make arrangements for its printing.[177] From this point the Federation acted as Executor, dealing with further inquiries from Guilds, the C.W.S. Bank and societies querying the position of some of their members who had been left in financial difficulties by the collapse of the Guilds. These closing activities extended well into 1923 and included fruitless negotiations with the new Guild Housing Ltd. and with the National Guilds Council.[178] Eventually the Federation remained as a centre of appeal for debts left by the Guild, a position which Hicks greatly resented.[179] The C.W.S. Bank continued to press for repayments,[180] and there were also pathetic appeals from Guilds attempting to survive alone. An independent Guild in Manchester asked for advances, and in March 1923 the North Hertfordshire Guild of Builders requested £200 which was 'not available'.[181]

VI

It is hardly possible that the Guild experiment could have succeeded given the number of factors militating against it: the degenerating industrial situation, a lack of capital, too rapid a growth without adequate organisation. That Hobson had taken on more than he could cope with is apparent from the Report

---

this was before the meeting of 22 November 1922 and the request was possibly made after or at the 8 November meeting.

[177] N.F.B.T.O. Minutes, Quarterly Executive Meeting, 23 and 24 November 1922.

[178] Guild Housing Ltd. was set up by Sparkes after his dismissal from the Guild of Builders (London) Ltd. The National Guild Council contacted the N.F.B.T.O. with a request that it should send representatives (N.F.B.T.O. Minutes, 24 and 25 January 1923) but the idea was rejected at several meetings of the Federation's executive and finally dismissed at a quarterly meeting of the Executive Council on 20 and 21 May 1924: Minutes, 1924.

[179] 'Verbatim Report', p. 97, and evidence of Sir Richard Coppock.

[180] N.F.B.T.O. Minutes, 21 February 1923. The C.W.S. Bank was demanding £4604 14s. 9d., but the sum seems never to have been paid.

[181] *Ibid.* 8 March 1923.

of the November Conference. But more culpable than this was his dual folly in attempting to implicate the N.F.B.T.O., and in informing his associates that the Federation was willing to be fully implicated, in the financial bases of the Guild. While this lost for him the support of the Federation, it did immensely greater harm to others. At the November Conference a member of the Plymouth Guild made a rending but fruitless appeal which clearly illustrates how much the idealism of the Guilds had demanded of their adherents:

> Do you realise there are many working men who have given their last halfpenny into this movement? I, myself, have given every halfpenny. I have not a halfpenny in the world on purpose to pay wages, simply because finance is tight.... I have had no wages myself for six weeks. I am absolutely destitute. I had a matter of £200 saved up. Every halfpenny has gone into the Guild – everything – to keep the thing going. I realise the possibilities of this movement.[182]

Many working men went down with the Guilds, which makes it harder to understand Hobson's irresponsibility when he suggested in March 1923 that the whole wage arrears of the National Building Guild might soon be paid.[183] The N.F.B.T.O. circularised the associated unions, but in the course of inquiries it was discovered that there was simply no money to pay out.[184] It may have been conscience or one last fling at influence – nothing in the original letter explains why Hobson should have inflicted this final blow – but it is the last seen of him in connection with the Guilds. His later career was much less affected than that of Sparkes, and he continued to associate with fringe movements affecting trade unionists almost until his death in 1940.[185]

[182] 'Verbatim Report', p. 95.
[183] Hobson to Coppock, N.F.B.T.O., *Circular Letters*, 26 March 1923.
[184] N.F.B.T.O., *Circular Letters*, 24 April 1923: 'It was stated that the Receiver had been written to and a reply had been received by the A.U.B.T.W. that he had not the money in hand to make the necessary payments of arrears due to men who had been working for the Building Guild.'
[185] Hobson continued to re-work his ideas on Guilds, putting forward a scheme, more politically orientated, for a House of Industry in 1930 (*Daily Herald*, 22 July 1930). In 1932 he came into contact with the New Europe Group, then under the influence of Dmitri Mitrinovic, and together they

The subsequent career of Malcolm Sparkes was shorter and more orthodox. Grieved at the failure of the National Guild, he attempted to salvage the idea by organising Guild Housing Ltd.[186] The Guild of Builders (London) Ltd. continued as a separate organisation, but ran into increasing difficulties, and a winding-up order was submitted to the Official Receiver on 24 November, 1924 by the Secretary of the Guild, Richard Thomas Holness. Guild Housing Ltd. fared no better. It was a hopeless proposition from the start since Sparkes was suffering from the effects of a bad press, however unjustified. In addition, the economic situation was unfavourable and it is obvious that Sparkes again attempted too swift a development. By the end of 1924 this Guild also was in trouble. Sparkes, who had founded the subsidiary firm of Drytone Ltd.[187] to bring additional work to the Guild joinery works at Acton Vale, London, was again ousted from the Board of Directors of the Guild, although this time he was allowed to resign.[188] At a subsequent inquiry he was not fully exonerated; it was clearly shown that he had again planned on an ambitious scale and that office expenses had been too high. His own accusations against malingering workers were found to be only partially justified.[189] The Guild, under a new manager, did not survive.

Sparkes continued to run Drytone Ltd. until his comparatively early death, from heart failure, in 1933. Even here he had trouble which, according to one of the Directors, was caused mainly through his too good nature.[190] It is obvious that he expected of others the standards he set himself, but that he was not a man to enforce them. Sparkes's practical abilities, which

---

began to form a new Guild-type organisation calling itself the House of Industry League, with Hobson as its first President. In turn, this set up a Council for Workers' Control which attempted to influence trade unionists. Hobson continued to work along these lines until his death in 1940.

[186] Sparkes to Cole, 10 August 1922 (Nuffield College, Cole Collection, Pamphlets 9, File 3).

[187] Sparkes to Reckitt, 6 July 1923 (Reckitt Collection, H.U.L.).

[188] In June 1924, when he resigned as Managing Director. He left the Board entirely in September 1924. (H. Barham to Loan Stock Holders, 10 October 1924, Reckitt Collection. H.U.L.)

[189] W. H. Close, 'Enquiry into the Affairs of Guild Housing Ltd.' (24 November 1924) (Reckitt Collection, H.U.L.).

[190] Evidence of Mrs. Dorothy Thurtle. Mrs. Thurtle was a working Director of Drytone Ltd., in which both she and her husband had shares.

might have balanced his idealism, were, in effect, overruled by the enthusiasm of others. Like many idealists before him, he contributed one more failure to the sequence of intermittent attempts to establish a new system of economic and social relationships within an on-going competitive society.

12

GUILD SOCIALISM:
THE STORRINGTON DOCUMENT

The following pages embody the results of a series of discussions held by a small group of Guild Socialists at the end of December 1914. The discussions extended over a week which the members of the group spent together at Storrington in Sussex. From this fact the report came to be known among certain National Guildsmen as the 'Storrington Document'. The method adopted was that, at each meeting, a particular aspect of the Guild problem was discussed. When the fullest possible interchange of views had taken place, an effort was made to reach an agreement on all points of difference, and, after long and heated arguments, this was accomplished at all but one of the meetings. At the end of meeting the points agreed upon were written down.

The report, as it now appears, was slightly revised at an adjourned meeting of the group held in Oxford early in 1915. The published version which follows was taken from an MS. in the possession of Mrs. Margaret Cole. Other known copies in existence are in the Cole collection, Nuffield College, Oxford and in the library of the University of Hull (the latter being a xeroxed copy of an MS. in the possession of Mrs. J. Henry Lloyd).

GUILD Socialist profess themselves democrats in both industry and politics. They admit that political democracy, in so far as it has been tried, has hitherto failed; but capitalism, which necessarily reduces the workers to an inferior economic status, renders political democracy impossible of achievement. For, if the economic conditions are servile, the political system will be servile; the basis of freedom is economic, and unless the workers have industrial freedom they cannot be politically free. A ruling class in industry implies a ruling class in politics. But, if political democracy without industrial democracy is illusory, industrial democracy without political democracy is essentially incomplete.

THE NATION

The members of a nation form a community with a common purpose. The political organs of that community exist to deal with those questions which affect all the citizens equally and in the same way. While all that concerns the public life of the community must ultimately affect all the citizens in a greater or less degree, there exist many tasks and problems which demand the special attention of those immediately concerned, and these will in many cases be the sphere of special associations composed of those persons who are directly concerned.

THE STATE

1. There are things outside industry, for which bodies elected on a geographical basis are required:

  i. Law and justice, including questions of social conduct.
  ii. The attitude of the community to organised religion.
  iii. Questions of general policy relating to general education.
  iv. Public amenities, both local and national.
  v. The relations between locality and locality.

2. The State should not be a highly centralised and universally sovereign authority, regulating from above the life of its citizens, but should be the grouping of people on a geographical basis, whether the area for such grouping be that of the nation, the county, town or rural district. In each of these areas there should be representative bodies elected on a geographical basis, and powers and functions should be so distributed among them that the national State may be the expression of the common social purpose of the nation; the municipal or urban authority of the common purpose of the dwellers within its area, and the intermediate (or county) authority of the purpose common to the various districts included in its area. These divisions would probably coincide with similar divisions in the industrial organisation.

3. For the conduct of foreign affairs a body representing the geographical State and the industrial Guilds will be necessary, since it is impossible to separate economic from national problems in foreign relations, and since the connection between them will become even more intimate in a democratic system.

4. There are also industrial questions with which the State, as an organisation of consumers on a geographical basis, must concern itself:

1. Under a Guild system the revenue of the State will be raised not by means of taxation upon individuals – direct or indirect – but, in the main, by a tax on the Guilds. Obviously it will be a function of the State to decide what revenue is needed for communal purposes, and the State must have a voice in the assessment of the necessary taxation among the Guilds.

2. The organised consumers are interested in the determining of the price at which commodities are to be sold. This 'social' price need not correspond to the economic cost of production of the commodity concerned, and is a matter for the organised consumers alone. The determination of the cost of production, the economic price, is from the point of view of Guildsmen more important, for upon it depends the apportionment of taxation. Taxation, therefore, and the estimated cost of production on which it depends, should be determined by some authority upon which both producers and consumers are represented.

3. The State's total requirements having been ascertained, the tax levied on each Guild should be in proportion to its net income, and should be assessed on such a basis as to allow each Guild, after setting aside the necessary amounts for depreciation and normal development, to retain a sum approximately in ratio to its membership.

4. Taxation should be apportioned at regular intervals, and the bodies responsible for this apportionment should be:

i. As a court of first instance, a Joint Committee representing in equal proportions the organised consumers, i.e. the *State*, the organised producers, i.e. the *Guild Congress*, and *the particular Guild concerned*. This Joint

Committee should endeavour to arrive at a decision concerning the amount of taxation that should be apportioned to the particular Guild concerned – the fixed selling price being taken into account. Such Committees should deliberate in the case of each Guild separately.

ii. As a final appeal court, before which these decisions may be brought for ratification, a Joint Committee consisting half of representatives appointed by the *Guild Congress* for this purpose (on which each Guild would be represented) and half of the Industrial Committee of *Parliament*. This joint session should constitute a final court.

Guild Organisation

1. The governing principle of the Guild is Industrial Democracy. It follows therefore that (*a*) the ultimate authority must rest with the Guild members; (*b*) Guild officials must emerge from the Guild itself, and that no person who is not a member of the Guild shall have a voice in the election of any official. The electorate will vary according to the function of the person to be elected, and eligibility to all offices, though not necessarily to all committees, shall depend upon the attainment of a standard ascertained by qualifying examination.

2. The first step towards a change in the running of industry is the introduction of democracy and the transference of control to the workers themselves. The establishment of National Guilds will enable the workers to place machine production on its trial, and there will be then a far better chance of securing a settlement of this problem satisfactory to producers and consumers alike.

3. The system of National Guilds does not involve a highly centralised and universally sovereign national authority, and it is essential to avoid either stagnation in the methods of production or excessive standardisation of the product. The local branches of each Guild will therefore be free to adopt and apply new inventions, to specialise in certain products, and in general to adopt production to its own ideas and local needs. This freedom will however be subject to the observance of the regula-

tions laid down by the National Guild authority and to the national fixation of general conditions, e.g. hours and factory amenities, etc.

The amount of local autonomy in the Guild will vary according to the type of industry concerned, e.g. the transport and railway system will be far more highly centralised than the building industry, which produces for a local market. Though orders will to a great extent continue to be placed with and payment to be made to the local Guild authorities, these authorities will act solely as receivers for the National Guild, to which all monies will belong. Competition of quality will thus continue between the various branches of the Guild, but the incentive to better workmanship will not be financial.

Pay and Property

The labour of man is not a commodity and cannot be appraised at a market value. The basis upon which payment will be made should be neither what a man's labour will fetch nor what a man is supposed to need nor what a man's service is estimated to be worth to the State, but the fact that he is a member of a Guild. As such, he will be entitled to full pay both when he is working and when he is unemployed, and to a pension when he ceases to produce.

The democratic principle which is the basis of the Guild system does ultimately involve equality of income for every *individual adult producer*. But the equality must come spontaneously from the Guilds, and must not be the result of dictation from without. This equality of income does not preclude the possibility of the differentiation of hours and conditions according to the character of the occupation.

Individual property will persist in the Guild system only in its true form of personal effects. The individual will be free to save or bank such portion of his earnings as he may choose, but no interest will be paid upon such savings. The present method of individual saving will be no longer necessary to the reproduction of capital, since this reproduction will be arranged for by the Guilds themselves; and, in the event of large sums of new capital being necessary for the development of any particular industry, such sums will be provided either by a remission of the tax due from the Guild in question to the State, or, in the event of that sum being insufficient, by the grant of a sum from the State revenue to the Guild concerned. The normal stimulus to the expansion of productive enterprises will come from demand: and the Joint Committee which fixes the taxation due from the various Guilds will see to it that each Guild makes adequate provision for normal development, as well as for depreciation.

Foreign Trade and Investments

International barter will be a function of the Guilds, and this part of foreign trading can be carried on by the Guilds far more efficiently than it is by the rings and combines of today. That part of our overseas trade which now represents, not the direct exchange of commodities or services, but the investment of a portion of the national wealth, will be carried on while it continues by the State, but, with the increase in home consumption and as the economically more backward nations develop their own industries, such overseas investment of surplus capital will tend continually to decrease. The Socialist is not opposed to international trade as barter, for this only means that each country is producing the things it is most fitted to produce. Foreign investment, on the other hand, involves the exploitation of one nation by another, and this is ultimately no less objectionable than the exploitation of individual by individual.

Inter-Guild Relations.

1. The Principle of Guild organisation must be industrial or vertical and not occupational or horizontal. That is to say, it must follow the lines of what men are making and not of what they are doing; for the control of industry can only be assumed by single bodies covering completely all classes of workers engaged in each industry.

This principle affords general guidance; but it is not easy to say what precisely constitutes an industry. There are vertical groupings of varying extent: thus among industrial groups, there are the smaller group of ship-building workers and the larger group including all the kindred metal industries.

It is impossible to lay down absolutely the extent of Guild grouping, but generally the number of Guilds should be as small as is consistent with the need for autonomy of the distinct and self-contained industrial groups. The principle of grouping must be throughout industrial, but the number of groups and their extent is a matter not of principle, but of detail and convenience.

2. In some cases the Guilds covering a closely connected group of industries will need to form Federations for the settlement of questions common to them all.

3. As one Guild will in many cases consume in its own production the products of another, and as many problems connected with demarcation, transference of membership, and the dovetailing of seasonal industries will arise, it will be necessary that there should be some machinery for the discussion of such questions. For this purpose the Guilds will probably set up Joint Sub-Committees, local or national, temporary or permanent, responsible to the executives of the two or more Guilds concerned.

Relation to State and Municipality as Buyers

1. As the Guilds will stand in the relation of sellers not only to other Guilds, but also to the State, to municipalities and to other organised bodies, Joint Sub-Committees will be necessary in these cases, in order that buyer and seller may have an opportunity for discussion.

2. Any association, whether Guild, State, municipality or other organised body, which stands in the relation of a frequent buyer to a Guild, will find it necessary to retain an expert, or experts, who understand the work of that Guild. Such experts will in most cases be chosen from the selling Guild; but they will not be entitled to hold any official position in it when they pass into the service of the buyer.

The Guild Congress

1. All the Guilds will be linked up in a Guild Congress, on which each Guild will have representation. The Congress will be always in being, and will hold a regular Annual Meeting, and in addition such Special Meetings as may be necessary. Each Annual Meet-

ing will elect a permanent Executive Committee, on which each Guild will have representation. The Executive Committee will be under the control of the Guild Congress.

2. The Guild Congress will be the ultimately sovereign authority in all matters affecting the Guilds as a whole, and will decide such differences as may arise in the relations of Guild to Guild.

3. The Executive Committee, or such persons as the Congress or Executive may appoint, will sit upon the Joint Committee with the State, and upon the Joint Sub-Committees concerned with fixing the taxation to which each Guild is liable.

4. In each locality there will be Guild Councils, on which all the local Guild branches will be represented, and before these bodies local Guild questions will come for settlement.

5. Cases of disagreement between a selling Guild and the State or the municipality as buyer will be referred to a Joint Sub-Committee equally representing, in the case of local disputes, the seller, the buyer and the Trades Council; or in national disputes, in the first instance the selling Guild, the Guild Congress and the State; in the event of any of the three parties represented demanding an appeal, the Guild Congress and the State.

Entrance to the Guilds

1. Entrance to the industrial Guild will not presuppose any qualifying examination. Each man will be free to choose his Guild, and actual entrance will depend on the demand for labour. In fact, the principle will be that of first come, first served. In the event of there being no vacancy, it will be open for the applicant either to apply for entrance to another Guild or during his period of waiting to take up some occupation of a temporary character. He will then secure the option of entering the Guild of his choice when a vacancy occurs.

2. To the occupations requiring technical knowledge, there will be a double system of entry. One way will be by apprenticeship in the Technical Colleges followed by qualifying examination for entrance to the craft, but it will also be open for any working member of the Guild who passes the qualifying examination to enter any craft without apprenticeship, and so, whatever his method of entry to the Guild, to rise to any position in it.

3. Labour in 'dirty industries' (scavenging, etc.) will probably be in the main of a temporary character, and will be undertaken by those who are, for the time, unable to obtain an entry elsewhere. Workers in unpleasant or exhausting occupations should be compensated by shorter hours, longer holidays, etc., but not by differences in pay. One of the functions of a democratic industrial system will be to invent machines not merely to cheapen production but to eliminate dirty work.

4. Individual producers, whether craftsmen, authors, journalists, or artists of any kind, or associations of such producers, will be free to remain outside Guild organisation, and to live, individually or collectively, by the sale of their products. Such individuals or associations will be subject to taxation on the same basis as the industrial Guilds.

Distribution

1. Retail trade will be partly in the hands of the producing Guilds, and partly in the hands of the Distributive Guild.

Where the maker of the goods is, from the nature of the commodity, also naturally the retailer, as in the case of clothing, the producing Guild should organise distribution through its own shops.

Where the retailer is naturally divided from the maker, retailing should be controlled by a distributive Guild, with shops in every locality. (This Guild will succeed to the functions of the private tradesman and the Co-operative Store in the Society of today.)

The Distributive Guild will be non-productive, that is, it will sell its products at the prices at which it buys them from the producing Guilds or from foreign producers. This applies except where, in the case of imported products, a different selling price is fixed by the Joint Committee of consumers and producers, and accordingly taken into account in fixing the sum due from the State to the Distributive Guild. There will thus not be two standards of price, the one wholesale and the other non-productive, and Guilds will receive from the State a sum calculated according to the number of persons whom it employs.

2. Both the producing Guilds and the Distributive Guild will have wholesale warehouses. (In this aspect, the Distributive

Guild will succeed to the distributive functions of the Co-operative Wholesale Society.)

3. Foreign products which compete with the products of the producing Guilds will be imported through the Distributive Guild, subject to the right of the Guild Congress to exclude any product made under unfair conditions by the foreign producers.

Such articles as form either the raw material, or the instruments of production, of a productive Guild will be imported by the Guild concerned.

4. In order that the individual consumer may have an opportunity of making his demand effective, there will be Associations of Consumers among the buyers connected with the local branches of the Distributive Guild.

5. All passenger and freight charges should be abolished for home traffic, so that there would be no variation in the selling price of commodities according to the varying cost of transport to the districts in which products are to be consumed.

6. Charges would necessarily remain for the carrying of goods on vessels plying either to a foreign country or between two foreign countries. In the case of such goods, the freight charge would enter into the price at which commodities are sold to the foreign buyer. Passenger charges would probably be also retained in such cases.

Women

1. The question of sex is not relevant to the democratic principle.

2. In a democratic system, there must be complete equality of rights between men and women. The community is the organisation of individual wills, and every adult person within the community, as a possessor of will, should have an equal voice and vote in the affairs of the country, both political and industrial.

3. This involves that every person, man and woman alike, must have the rights of entry to any occupation, subject to the attainment of the Guild standard for such occupation, or to a definite exclusion from a particular occupation by the community as a whole, including both men and women.

4. Democracy involves the economic independence of every adult person in the community, whether man or woman. Such

independence will be secured either by the producing of some commodity or by the rendering of some service. Women as wives or housekeepers are rendering a service, for which they should receive direct remuneration from the State, or through associations, which would be in the position of an unproductive Guild, and would as such receive from the State a sum calculated on the basis of their membership, the division of which would, as in the case of the Guilds, be in the transitional stage decided by themselves. The basis of such division would be the number of children below the age at which they could become self-supporting.

Education

1. In general, the 'consumers' should decide the type of education to be provided, the chief subjects to be taught and the minimum standard to be attained. The Educational Guild, on the other hand, should determine the method of producing the results desired by the 'consumer'. This division corresponds in effect to that laid down in the case of industrial Guilds, where, roughly speaking, the consumer will determine the demand and the producer the methods of meeting it. There is indeed throughout a fairly exact parallel between the relation of an Educational Guild to the 'consumers' of education, and that of an industrial Guild to the consumers of its commodities.

2. All education should be free, and entrance to the higher branches should be determined by fitness and not by the ability or willingness of the parent to pay.

3. The whole teaching profession, apart from technical education, should form a single Guild; its Executive should consist of an equal number of representatives of School Teachers and University Arts Teachers; the former selected probably on a district basis, the latter on the basis of 'faculties'. The two sections should meet together for discussion of problems affecting both, and apart for problems special to either.

4. Technical education will form an integral part of the educational system, and the Technical Colleges will have their share, equally with the Arts' Colleges, in the government of the Universities. Such Technical Colleges will be controlled by the Guilds or Craft Associations which their students intend to enter.

5. Some faculties in each University will thus be outside the Teaching Guild. The University as a whole will however form a federal unit for the settlement of the relations between the Faculties and Colleges, both Arts and Technical.

6. Technical Teachers will be members of the Guild controlling the subjects which they teach, but will have an association of their own federated with the Teachers' Guild.

7. School education will form a unified system, through which every child will pass. This national education policy involves a broad standardisation of subjects, but not of method.

8. School education will continue up to 18 or 19, but in the later years a certain amount of technical or special education will be given.

9. The Teachers' Guild will have travelling inspectors who will see that the national standards are observed in the various localities.

10. There will be a Central State Education Department, and local *ad hoc* School Boards. The Local Boards will appoint inspectors who will report both to them and to the Central Education Department. They will be liable to dismissal by the Local Boards, but will have the right of appeal to the Central Department.

11. Technical and arts university education will be as a rule alternatives and will be open to everybody subject to the attainment of the standard required.

12. University students will be in the main of two kinds – whole-time and extension students. Whole-time students will fall into three classes:

a. Students in Arts Faculties.
b. Technical students intending to enter professional occupations.
c. Students entering upon manual crafts, who will at the same time be serving their apprenticeship in a Guild.

Extension students fall into two classes:

a. Students engaged in the less skilled occupations, who will be released for part of their time if they desire further education.
b. Older students who continue to attend classes in their leisure.

13. An important function of the Universities will be the endowment of Research both in Science and in Arts. The more practical branches of Technical Research will be carried on by the various Guilds, both locally and nationally, in connection with their productive work.

Transition

1. Guild Socialism involves not only the placing of industrial control in the hands of the workers but also the placing of surplus value in the hands of the community.

2. It is impossible for the expropriation of the capitalists to take place in such a way as to place surplus value in the hands of the community, except by securing a majority of expropriators in Parliament and on local authorities.

3. A revolutionary change in the ownership of capital will never be effected without the existence of a strong, revolutionary Trade Union movement. The primary function of such a movement will be industrial; but out of it, though independently of it, will come a revolutionary Socialist movement in politics.

4. Guild Socialism, as involving communal ownership and producers' control, will only be realised by the joint action of these two movements.

5. Industrial Unionism is essential to lead up to the industrial Guilds; it is also essential for fighting the capitalist and securing control of industry. Industrial Unionism means not only a vertical form of organisation within each industry, but also a complete solidarity of the whole army of labour. It will come by the amalgamation of existing Unions and by the complete organisation of those who are now unorganised.

6. It is essential, both for the maintenance of Trade Union rates and standards and for the control of industry by the producers, that men and women who work in the same industry should be organised, without regard to sex, in the same industrial Unions or Guilds.

7. It is essential that Trade Unions in each industry should be recognised by the employers, and that recognition should include the right to interfere in questions of discipline and management.

8. To make recognition effective, the Trade Unions must secure machinery for the exercise of such continuous interference. Such machinery will in many cases develop out of the existing machinery of negotiation. Conciliation and Arbitration Boards, which have so far served to tie down the workers and to impose upon them the final verdict of a supposedly 'impartial' authority, must be changed into Negotiation Boards, free from all restrictive time agreements and recourse to external authority. The object of this negotiaition will be not merely to deal with questions of wages, conditions and discipline, but also to assume an ever-increasing control of management.

9. At the same time, the workers in every industry and in every workshop should demand the right to elect first the foreman, deputies, etc., under whose direction they work, and then in turn under-managers and finally head managers and high officials.

10. By these means the Trade Unions will secure co-management with the employers, but they should in no case assume co-partnership in the business of profiteering. The Unions should demand that their members shall no longer be paid wages on an individual basis, but that the Union itself shall receive from the employers a lump sum which it will then divide among the members. This lump sum should, however, never depend either upon the price at which the product is sold, or upon the profits secured by the capitalist, but should be a collective standard rate, developed out of the individual standard rates of today.

11. The winning of control involves that the Unions of manual workers should, at the earliest possible moment, bring into their ranks the existing organisations of clerks, foremen, deputies, under-managers, etc. When this has been done, and as the workers assume a greater share in control, it will become possible to induce high officials and managers, who are largely recruited from the grades below them, to join an organisation by which they will, if they refuse to join it, run a serious risk of being ousted from their positions. An Industrial Union or a National Guild must, in fact, include everybody connected with the industry.

12. It is necessary further that the Unions should organise the professionals and experts connected with the various industries. These brain-workers, who are now organised in professional

'Institutes', are in the main of two classes, whole-time experts employed by a single firm or group of firms, and independent consultants called in by the employers on specific occasions. As the Unions attract or force into their ranks the upper managerial grades, it will become possible for them to adopt the same policy in the case of the whole-time expert. At the same time, the Unions, as they interfere to an increasing extent in management, will employ their own experts, who will be members both of the Union which employs them, and of their professional Institute. In this way, the professionals will be leavened by the Guild principle, and a gradual process of conversion, not unaffected by self-interest, will take place.

13. While it is not necessary that any particular industry should pass through the stage of national or municipal management, it is probable that those industries in which the workers first secure a large measure of control will be either industries already under such management, or will, before complete control has been secured, pass into such management. Whenever such a transference is suggested, the Trade Union concerned should demand that it shall be accompanied by the grant of a greater share in the control of the industry. The Trade Union Movement as a whole must adopt this attitude towards all proposals to nationalities or municipalities, and must put out all its strength in support of the Union directly concerned.

14. Whenever an industry is nationalised, the share-holders should receive in exchange for their holdings government stock bearing interest at a fixed rate either indefinitely or for a stated period; and the interest on this stock should be a charge on the total revenue of the State, and not on the nationalised industry or service.

15. Profiteering co-partnership with the State is no less objectionable than such co-partnership with the private employer.

16. Nationalisation or municipalisation alone does nothing to reduce the burden of rent, interest and profits upon the workers, except in so far as it communises future unearned increment; it is therefore necessary that every measure should be accompanied by a corresponding measure directly expropriating the capitalist class. This can be begun by a heavy increase in taxation, graduated against large incomes, and by a system of heavy and heavily graduated death and estates duties, or by a system of terminable

annuities coupled with such taxation.

17. The complete transference of the ownership of land and industrial capital will not take place until the workers are strong enough industrially and politically to dispossess the capitalists as a whole by a general measure of expropriation, backed if necessary by the strike and by force replying to force.

18. Where the starting of a new private capitalist enterprise involves government and municipal sanction, as in the case of tramways, railways, etc., the concession should be on lease only, and at the end of a fixed period the enterprise should become automatically and without compensation the property of the community. The system whereby private enterprises require government sanction should be gradually extended over the whole of industry.

The following is a Minority Report on the position of Women prepared by a number of members who dissented from the paragraphs dealing with the question in the main Report. Except in this instance, the Report was unanimous.

Women in a Guild Socialistic State

1. The position of women in any society depends mainly upon the manner in which the twin institutions of marriage and of family are regarded by that Society. If that idea of the family be adopted which regards it as a social contrivance of a temporary or purely utilitarian character, the home ceases to make its demands upon the special service and devotion of women, who are therefore released to engage in identical occupations with men. If on the other hand, the family be regarded as an essential and permanent element in Society, comparable to the special associations of Guild and Church within the State, it follows that the home, though not necessarily 'the sphere' of all women, will continue to be the chief pre-occupation of the majority.

While not attempting to deny the possibility of change and modification in many respects, Guild Socialists (who value the principle of association) may accept the latter view of the family as in the main a true one.

2. The family should in normal cases be considered as a homogeneous unit, and the 'economic independence' of its female members should be rather an ultimate possibility than a compul-

sory, and perhaps unwelcome, condition. The Guildsman should thus receive his pay calculated upon a basis which takes into consideration the number of women in his house.

In the case of *the wife*, her share should be obtainable by her directly from the Guild should she desire, and specifically claim, that it should be so paid; but normally the amount would not be so divided. In the event of her husband's death, payment would be made direct to her from the Guild and with regard to the same basis.

Children would be similarly provided for in the amount paid to the family until their entrance to some Guild or association.

Daughters electing to remain at home without engaging in any work outside, should not necessarily be regarded as 'social parasites'. Apart from their discharge of domestic duties, women in the home may be performing services which, though not immediately obvious, are not therefore unreal. Normally they should be provided for through the pay allotted to the Guildsman's family. To avoid any ureasonable charge being thrown upon the community, payment in the case of more than (say) three women in a single house, might be made on a reduced scale.

3. Provision having been made for the maintenance of women in the home should they desire to remain there, it is necessary in a free society to provide for women being able to leave their parents' home should they desire to do so. It is necessary to remember that, with artificial economic restrictions withdrawn, the commonest obstacle to marriage disappears. But many women will doubtless desire to concentrate their attention upon other spheres, and no limit should be set to the activities of women in any direction if they do not run contrary to the maintenance of the family and the interests of society as a whole.

In general it may be said that the services of women would be valuable ánd desirable in the case of

a. Associations of professionals.
b. The Distributive Guild.
c. Certain small or subsidiary industries.

In these cases the services of women being equally valuable with those of men would be carried on under similar conditions and for equal pay.

4. There is good reason to believe that women as a whole do

not now, and will not in a Guild Socialist State, desire to enter industry, more especially when it becomes apparent that their entrance into it would be prejudicial to the best interests of the community. Their exclusion from industry may therefore be assumed, and is not likely to give rise to any constant friction.

5. The entrance of women into industry is undesirable because :

i. The wear and tear of modern industrialism is liable to impair the services of women to the race as the bearers of children.

ii. By demanding a continuous absence from the home, it deprives the mother of opportunities of training and influence over her children, and prevents the due care necessary to the maintenance of the household.

iii. It involves the lowering of the standard of Guild workmanship to meet the peculiar disabilities of women. But the fixing of this standard is the concern, not of any individual Guild, but for joint conference between the Guild Congress and the State. And it should be impossible for this joint conference of the organised producers and consumers to tolerate the lowering of the Guild standard to satisfy the demands of a small body of women, whose entry into industry would thus clearly be contrary to the interests both of the Guild and of society as a whole.

6. The relation of women to the State is not an essential part of Guild Socialist doctrine in the strict sense.

But the State has, beyond its political function, its relation to industry as the means of safeguarding the interests of the consumer. Women being in the majority of cases essentially consumers, it would be in every way unreasonable to exclude them from any organisation intended to represent the consumers' point of view.

To what extent the assimilation of women to the position of men in the political government of the State is natural and desirable should remain a question for individual decision, since the special interpretation to be placed upon the idea of political democracy is not essentially involved in the principle of Guild Socialism.

INDEX

Index

as a culmination of syndicalism, 284–5; effects of slump on, 282; and the Labour Research Department, 277; publications of, 278; and the Russian Revolution, 279, 280; breaks up, 282

National Industrial Conference (1919), 106

Naval and Military War Pensions Act (1915), 242

Nelson Weavers' Association, 66

Neue Zeit, 53

Nevinson, H., 260

New Age, 264, 265, 269, 279, 285, 287, 288, 298

New Leader, 148

New Statesman, 250

Noël, C., 269

North British Daily Mail, 40–1

Norwich, Local Committee of War Emergency Workers' National Committee, 215

O'Brien, B., 53, 54, 56

Orage, A. R., 261, 264, 265, 272, 279, 288

Osborne decision, 135, 270

Owen, R., 262

Oxford University Fabian Society, 270

Paton, J., 278

Patterson, A., 20

Paviors, 75; strike (1913), 74

Pearson, G. H., 79, 81

Pease, E. R., 244, 269

Penty, A., 264, 305, 205 n. 86; *The Restoration of the Guild System*, 263–4, 288

Petroff, P., 169, 169 n. 70

Phillips, Dr Marion, 214

Pickfords, 96

Plebs League, 66

Plymouth, Co-operative Society, 192, 198, 200, 202

Police strike (1919), 109

Pollard, W., 287, 287 n. 11

Ponsonby, A., 140

Poor Law Commission, Minority Report (1909), 270

Port of London Authority, 96

Postal Workers, 246

Pound, Ezra, 265

Punch, 262

Quelch, H., 53, 65

Quelch, T., 216, 224

Railway Clerks' Association, 106, 124

Railway Executive Committee, 106

Railway Review, 116

Railway Servants, Amalgamated Society of, 98, 99

Railway strike (1919), 105, 110, 208, 277–8

Railwaymen, 97, 98, 99, 109, 112, 114, 115, 116, 121, 122, 123, 127, 128, 246

Railwaymen, National Union of, 67, 97, 100, 102, 103, 106, 107, 108, 109, 110, 112, 113, 116, 120, 121, 124, 125, 126, 127, 273, 278

Reckitt, M., 269, 272

'Red Friday', 126

Rent and Mortgage Interest (Rent Restriction) Act (1915), 233

Rents, 232–3

Rey, C., 154, 154 n. 9, 184

Rhondda, Lord, 197, 208

Robertson, R. C., 38

Robinson, Sir T., 302

Robinson, W. C., 192, 192 n. 12

Robson, J., 118

Rochester, A. E., 125

Rothstein, T., 51, 62, 67

Royal Patriotic Fund Corp, 242

Ruskin, J., 264, 264 n. 2

Ruskin College, 66

Russell, Bertrand, 269

Russian Revolution, the, 144, 257, 259, 279

Rymer, Sir J., 73

Sadler, Dr M. E., Vice-Chancellor of Leeds University, 73, 88, 89, 90–2

Sailors and Firemen, National Union of, 126

Salford: unemployment, 121; Co-operative Society, 192

Samuel, H., 234

Sanders, S., 215

Scheu, A., 35

Scottish Anti-Royalty and Labour League, 36, 37

Scottish Home Rule Association, 130

Scottish Land and Labour League, 35

Scottish Land Restoration League, 34, 36, 37

Scottish Liberal Party, 46

Scottish Miners' National Federation, 38, 39, 40, 42, 44

Seamen's Union, 144

Seddon, J. A., 212, 213, 220

Shaw, G. B., 63, 256, 264, 270, 282; attitude to war, 221–2; *The Doctor's Dilemma*, 264

Shaw, Lord, 114

Sheffield, 99, 116

Shipbuilders, 126, 156

Shipping Federation, 96